MMC: DEVELOPING COMMUNICATIVE COMPETENCE
IN ENGLISH AS A FOREIGN LANGUAGE

By Mary Newton Bruder

UNIVERSITY OF PITTSBURGH PRESS
and the
ENGLISH LANGUAGE INSTITUTE
of the
UNIVERSITY OF PITTSBURGH

PITT SERIES IN ENGLISH AS A SECOND LANGUAGE—3
Distributed by the University of Pittsburgh Press, 127 N. Bellefield Ave.,
   Pittsburgh, Pa. 15260
Formerly distributed by the University Center for International Studies,
   University of Pittsburgh

Copyright © 1974, University of Pittsburgh Press and the English Language
   Institute, University of Pittsburgh
Manufactured in the United States of America

ISBN 0-8229-8203-X

10   9   8   7   6

CONTENTS

Contents

Contents   Page

Contents

Contents

Contents

Contents

Contents

Contents   Page

PREFACE

For the past ten years, I have been involved with teaching foreign or second languages. Whether I used mim-mem pattern practice techniques or free-wheeling conversations around a constructed theme, I was always disappointed with the ultimate product—the language performance of the students. Mim-mem texts resulted in performance which was letter-perfect in the controlled frame of the drills, but which could not help the student in the simplest of every day situations. The "conversation technique" resulted in students who could have marvelous discussions in class but who were hopelessly incomprehensible to native speakers of the language.

It became increasingly clear that students needed controlled as well as free exercises in developing the necessary competence to be able to function in a communicative situation.

In 1970, Christina Bratt Paulston began work on the problem of classifying the types of exercises essential in learning the structural patterns of a second language. The ensuing article, "The Sequencing of Structural Pattern Drills"[1] provides the theoretical framework and the impetus for this text.

To summarize the Paulston classification, a set of materials purporting to teach the structural patterns of a language ought to contain three classes of drills: mechanical drills to train the student's tongue and ear to the forms of the language, meaningful drills which allow the students some freedom to choose answers of their own in using the prescribed structures, and lastly communicative drills which allow the student maximum freedom to communicate and add new information to the common body of knowledge of the speech community. (The speech community is here defined as the members of a class in English as a second or foreign language.) The major difference between the types of drills is the decreasing control by the teacher of the response by the student. Meaningful and communicative drills are by definition individual response types and require more class time than mechanical ones.

The major objective of the text is to provide maximum opportunity for communication *by the students*, which means that the majority of class time should be spent in "student talk". The teacher must react to and encourage reaction to what the students say, and the teacher's role in directing the class activities should diminish as the students' proficiency increases.

Paulston's warning that communicative drills are still *drills* needs to be emphasized. Just because the students can answer questions fluently and grammatically in the classroom is no guarantee that they will be able to do so in "the real world." To help the students bridge the gap, I have included a series of interaction activities modeled on the discussion by Wilga Rivers in "Talking off the Tops of Their Heads."[2] The exercises consist of solving problems in situations in which the students are likely to find themselves; e.g., ordering a telephone, opening a bank account. The majority of these exercises have been included in the Instructor's Manual.

The text is intended for use with adults in beginning classes in English as a second language (0-65 Michigan Test of Written Proficiency in English—Form B).[3] It should be completed in one term by advanced beginning students (50-65, Michigan Test) in an intensive program of fifteen weeks.

---

1. Christina Bratt Paulston, "The Sequencing of Structural Pattern Drills," TESOL Quarterly, Vol. 5, no. 3; September 1971, 197-208.
2. Wilga M. Rivers, "Talking off the Tops of Their Heads," TESOL Quarterly, Vol. 6, no. 1; March 1972, 71-81.
3. English Language Institute, University of Michigan, 1965.

The structures in this text are not significantly different from other beginning texts, but the sequencing may seem different. In order to communicate, the students need control of the question forms of each structure, so that each new pattern also includes practice of the question forms associated with it. We have found that students in intensive courses need to work most on the tenses of verbs used in oral communication. The text, therefore, contains the verb tenses which are most common in speech in the first fifteen lessons. In the remaining lessons, other items are introduced using the verb patterns that the students have already learned.

The following features of *MMC* reflect the theoretical framework of the text as well as my own bias toward the nature of language teaching and learning:

1. The structures are presented first in context.

2. The sequence of patterns provides for maximum contrast between old and new structures, but is strictly controlled so as to eliminate presentation of more than one pattern at a time.

3. The vocabulary is limited, not by frequency lists, but by contexts. The lexical items which seemed useful and interesting for each situation were chosen with the hope that the students would be able to use them in the United States.

4. The practice of the patterns progresses from mechanical through communicative use of each item.

5. The drills are constructed so as to provide a maximum of "student talk" and a minimum of "teacher talk."

6. There are exercises to acquaint the students with the features of language styles other than the formal classroom style.

Furthermore, since a major part of competence in a second language involves knowledge of its culture, the situations for the dialogues and the interaction activities have come for the most part from the experiences of our students trying to become accustomed to life in Pittsburgh. I hope that the dialogues will provide useful information to the students as well as providing a point of departure for class discussions.

ACKNOWLEDGEMENTS

My heartfelt thanks go to all the students in the English Language Institute who have been the source for many of the ideas contained in the text and who have patiently suffered the delays and changes of the past two years.

I owe a special debt to Christina Bratt Paulston whose classification and constant support have been instrumental in the development of the text, and to Charles E. Bruder who contributed information for many of the dialogues and without whose continued encouragement, the text never would have been completed.

I am also grateful to William E. Norris who reviewed many of the lessons, contributed valuable suggestions, and helped eliminate many of the pitfalls in the preliminary version; also to the instructors, especially Lois I. Wilson and Dorothea Gottlieb-Akhand, who tested the materials and offered helpful ideas and advice, and to Edward M. Anthony, during whose course in Thai this all began. Whatever inadequacies remain are entirely my own.

—MNB   June 1973

DIRECTIONS FOR USING THE TEXT

The text consists of 22 lessons introduced by a dialogue which presents in context the syntactical patterns and lexical items contained in each lesson. The dialogues are followed by an outline of the patterns presented in each lesson, a set of comprehension questions about the dialogues and a vocabulary list. The major part of the lesson is the presentation and drilling of the patterns, and each lesson ends with a short summary dialogue and a summary chart of the patterns in the lesson. Suggested procedures for using the text follow.

I. Dialogues

The Introductory dialogues are meant to be read aloud but not memorized.

A. Read the Introduction aloud as the students read along silently. (I do not have the students read the dialogues aloud because it is wasteful of class time, and it provides an imperfect model for the other students. The students profit more by practicing the dialogues individually in the laboratory.)

B. Ask for and answer student questions about vocabulary items. (Questions concerning new grammatical structures should be deferred to E.)

C. Read the dialogue again and ask about items which the students may have missed. (The questions are essential, especially with students who are just beginning to study English, because they will not be proficient enough to ask questions about things they don't understand.)

D. Ask the students the comprehension questions. (For beginning groups, the questions should be used as feedback on comprehension. The questions not marked with (*) can be answered directly from the text of the Introduction. Questions marked with an asterisk (*) require a higher productive competence in that the students must infer or synthesize information. Most lessons also include opinion or discussion questions which are the most difficult. Choose the question types according to the ability of the individual class.)

E. Ask the students to discover other examples of the patterns to be studied in the upcoming presentation of grammatical points. (Each new pattern is italicized in the dialogue at its first occurrence.) Put the example on the board or point it out in the text and ask the students to find the other examples in the dialogue. The lines of the dialogue are numbered for easy location. This procedure helps the students see the exact nature of the structures, and if the students identify sentences with the wrong structure, it helps the teacher know what kinds of things are going to cause difficulties.

II. Vocabulary Lists

The lists are for the students' use at home. I ask the students to look up the words in advance so that little class time need be spent on vocabulary, and also so that the students can do the grammar drills with vocabulary that they know. (I do not believe that students should practice patterns of which they do not know the meaning.) In Lessons 1-6 there is a list with each section of grammatical presentation; in the remaining lessons, there is only one list at the beginning of the lesson.

III.   Presentation of Structures and Drills

I put the Model sentence (usually from the dialogue) on the board and briefly point out the important features before beginning the drills which are always done with books closed.

Mechanical Drills (M1). The term "mechanical" refers to the automaticity of the oral response by the student. I do not believe (and Paulston does not intend) that the drills be devoid of meaning in a lexical sense. Even in a mechanical drill, the students must know what they are saying; this is the reason for assigning the vocabulary for study prior to any of the drills.

These drills are usually repetition or simple substitution exercises, practiced for the purpose of learning the form of the new pattern. They should always be done chorally and at a very rapid pace— no more than a minute or a minute and a half per drill. As soon as the students can do the M1 drills with ease, I erase the model from the board and proceed to the next set of drills.

Mechanical-testing Drills (M1T). The purpose of these drills is to contrast the new pattern with ones learned previously and to ensure that the students can manipulate the distinctions. These drills also should be done chorally (except for ones which have two possible arrangements of the answers) and very rapidly in order to keep the pace brisk and to arrive as quickly as possible to the last sets of drills which are much more interesting for the students. The answers are given for the M1 and M1T drills so that the students can practice them at home.

Meaningful (M2) and Communicative (C) Drills. These drills are completely individual and the students are allowed to answer with any grammatically correct response which is appropriate to the speech situation. I usually insist that the students provide long, full-sentence answers in the M2 drills, and short, conversationally appropriate answers in the C drills. It is very easy to fall into the trap of allowing the students to use long answers in the C drills (and, besides, it is very impressive to any visitors who might come around), but since the objective is communicative competence, the students need to practice what is appropriate in conversations.

Some of the drills are preceded by the notation *Picture Cue.* Pictures are very helpful to students of low English proficiency, but text-provided pictures are usually not applicable to particular classroom situations; therefore, the teacher is encouraged to develop his own set of illustrations for the materials.

No explicit directions are given for most of the drills. The teacher should model the first two or three items, giving his cue and the expected response as examples, and then have the class begin the drill, starting with the items modeled by the teacher. The students do not need an explanation of what to do; the examples are usually sufficient. Parentheses should be filled by names of the students or their countries or items pertaining to the particular class. Sometimes the class should be divided into groups for responses and this is indicated by *G1* and *G2*. For the sake of conserving space, the abbreviations *Rep* (Repeat) and *Sub* (Substitute) have been used. Drills marked (***) are explained further in the Instructor's Manual.

IV.   Generalizations

The grammatical generalizations should be reserved until after the class has done the mechanical drills. At this point, the students themselves are usually able to make the analysis of the "rule" and should be encouraged to do so. There is a minimum amount of linguistic information for the simple reason that it doesn't seem to be necessary for the students' performance. As often as possible, the structures and transformations are presented visually for the students' use at home. Sometimes the generalizations ask questions which the student should be able to answer, e.g., p. 28. The correct answers are given in double parentheses (( )) following the question.

Not all of the occurrences of each pattern are presented in the text. For example, the students are told that *already* is used with affirmative sentences; *yet* with negative and interrogative sentences. Obviously, this does not account for such items as: Has he already come?, but at this level of proficiency, such subtleties might cause confusion and are best left to intermediate and advanced texts.

V. Summary Dialogue

There is a short dialogue at the end of each lesson which can serve as a reinforcement for the most important patterns of the lesson. The teacher may want to ask the students to memorize this dialogue.

VI. Summary of Patterns

The summary is for the use of the students at home and for the teacher to know in advance what will be covered in the lesson. As a rule, only the verb tenses have been summarized.

VII. Cumulative Exercises

In the Instructor's Manual there are rejoinder and problem-solving exercises which may be done immediately following each lesson or delayed as review exercises depending on the class and the time available. Most of the rejoinders are taken from the Introduction and Summary Dialogues. The problems concern such things as ordering a telephone and are intended to help the students gain confidence in using English outside the classroom.

VIII. Styles of Language

Following Lessons 7 and 14 there are short dialogues in contrasting styles. The informal style dialogues should be practiced as listening comprehension exercises, but not practiced orally, because until the students become quite proficient, they will mix the styles, causing great confusion and further complicating their attempts to communicate.

The teacher should help the students analyze the variables involved in each situation (age, sex, familiarity) and translate some of the striking differences between the styles. It is not intended that a great deal of time be spent on the dialogues; one class hour on each set of variations serves to give students the comprehension skill necessary to their feeling at ease outside of the classroom situation. (Further discussion of the individual dialogues is included in the Instructor's Manual.)

IX. Appendices

Appendix I is a list of common given names and their nicknames for the benefit of students from non-Western cultures. Some classes like to adopt American names for use in class. Appendix II is a list of very common abbreviations and acronyms. Neither list is meant to be exhaustive. Appendix III is a list of the symbols used in the text to represent sounds.

X. Tailoring the Text for Individual Classes

Most of the patterns in Lessons 1-4 are meant for students who have never studied English, and should be done very briefly as review with classes of higher proficiency. The teacher of advanced-beginning classes should pick items such as the WH Questions, the Tag Questions, and the Indefinite Pronouns, which even quite proficient students will have trouble with, and skip the rest or have the students practice in the laboratory.

XI. The Instructor's Manual

The Instructor's Manual contains many drills not included here, plus extra linguistic information not necessary to the student. It also has tips on pitfalls we've encountered and hints on how to tailor the text to your class. You should write for it and use it at least the first time you use this text.

LESSON ONE

INTRODUCTION   First day of class

Carlos and Chen are students at a large American university. It is in a large city. They are foreign students; Carlos is from Latin America and Chen is from Asia. The campus is confusing and the boys are lost. The buildings are all gray.

Carlos: *Is the class here?*

5   Chen: No, it isn't. It's in room 232.

Carlos (to a young man in the hall): Excuse me . . . Where is room 232?

Bill: It's three doors down, on the left. Are you in Biology 110?

Carlos: Thank you. Yes, we are.

Bill: Good. I'm Bill Jackson. I'm in the class too.

10   Chen and Carlos (shaking hands as they introduce themselves): How do you do? I'm
        Chen. I'm Carlos.

Bill: *Where are you from?*

Chen: I'm from Asia.

Carlos: I'm from Latin America.

15   Chen: *Who's the professor?*

Bill: Dr. Brown.

Chen: Who are the people in the front of the room?

Bill: The tall girl is the Assistant Instructor. She's a biology student.

Carlos: *Is she a graduate student or an undergraduate student?*

20   Bill: Graduate. Are you undergraduate students?

Chen: Yes, we are. We're freshmen.

Bill (to other students): I'd like you to meet Chen and Carlos. This is Nancy and Ali. (They
        shake hands.)

OUTLINE OF PATTERNS   Example

COMPREHENSION QUESTIONS

1. Is the university big?

2. Where is the university?

3. Who are Chen and Carlos?

*4. Why are they lost?

5. Where is Chen from? Carlos?

6. Where is room 232?

7. What class are the boys in?

8. Where is Bill from?

9. Who is the professor?

10. Who is the tall girl?

11. Are Carlos and Chen graduate students?

NOTES

Line 5:   Room numbers are pronounced in groups of two if possible. Example: Room 232 (two, thirty-two); Room 1025 (ten, twenty-five).

                 In room numbers, the first digit (the first two in a four-digit number) indicates the floor of the building. Room 232 is on the second floor; room 1025 is on the tenth floor.

Line 22:   The phrase *This is* is used before names no matter how many people are introduced: "This is Carlos." "This is Carlos and Chen."

Line 22:   In the United States, men shake hands with other men when they are introduced. With women the custom varies; ask your teacher.

SECTION ONE

BE — STATEMENTS AND QUESTIONS

Part A.   *Third Singular + BE + Adjective*

```
Vocabulary

Nouns                                    Adjectives

answer          girl          beautiful          graduate
apartment       house         big                gray
boy             instructor    biology            green
brother         lady          cheap              handsome
building        name          clean              intelligent
campus          pencil        confused           large
capital         professor     confusing          long
car             room          difficult          lost
church          sister        dirty              polite
class           student       economical         pretty
country (nation) university   expensive          short
exercise        weather       fat                small
friend         *woman/women   foreign            tall
                                                 thin
                                                 white

               *irregular plural
```

Model: The campus is confusing.

1. M1   Rep: The campus is confusing.
                   The boy is handsome.
                   The girl is beautiful.
                   The house is white.
                   The car is small.
                   The pencil is long.
                   The girl is confused.

2. M1   Rep: The campus is big.
         Sub: small   S: The campus is small.
                   beautiful   The campus is beautiful.
                   confusing   The campus is confusing.
                   large   The campus is large.
                   dirty   The campus is dirty.
                   big   The campus is big.

3. M1 Rep: The boy is tall.
        Sub: girl   S: The girl is tall.
                building   The building is tall.
                church   The church is tall.
                student   The student is tall.
                instructor   The instructor is tall.
                professor   The professor is tall.

***4. M1 (Picture Cue)
         T: confusing   S: The campus is confusing.
                handsome   The boy is handsome.
                beautiful   The girl is beautiful.
                white   The house is white.
                small   The car is small.
                long   The pencil is long.

GENERALIZATION

The sentences in drills 1-4 represent a basic English sentence pattern:

	SUBJECT	+	VERB	+	COMPLETER
Lesson 1 A	Noun	+	BE	+	Adjective
	The campus		is		confusing.

Most of the sentences in this book will have the same basic structure; the elements in each part of the sentence will change.

***5. M2 (Picture Cue)
         T: Describe the campus.   S: The campus is (confusing).
                Describe the boy.   The boy is (handsome).
                Describe the girl.   The girl is (beautiful).
                Describe the house.
                Describe the car.
                Describe the pencil.
                Describe the building.
                Describe the professor.

□ SUBSTITUTE WORDS (Pronouns)

Model: The campus is confusing. It is large.
        Chen is a foreign student. He is from Asia.
        The tall girl is an instructor. She is a biology student.

6. M1 Rep: The boy is handsome. He's handsome.
            The boy is lost. He's lost.
            The boy is from Asia. He's from Asia.
            The boy is from Latin America. He's from Latin America.
            The boy is tall. He's tall.
            The boy is confused. He's confused.

7. M1 Rep: The girl is beautiful. She's beautiful.
            The girl is thin. She's thin.
            The girl is tall. She's tall.
            The girl is intelligent. She's intelligent.
            The girl is from Latin America. She's from Latin America.
            The girl is from Paris. She's from Paris.

8. M1 Rep: The car is small. It's small.
            The car is economical. It's economical.
            The car is cheap. It's cheap.
            The car is green. It's green.
            The car is big. It's big.

GENERALIZATION

Use *he* to substitute for masculine subjects, *she* for feminine subjects, and *it* for non-human subjects.

Note the difference between the written and spoken forms. Contractions are most often used in speech with a pronoun (substitute word) subject.

Written	Spoken
Carlos is from Latin America.	He's from Latin America.
The book is cheap.	It's cheap.
The woman is beautiful.	She's beautiful.

---

9. M1T T: The car is small.   S: It's small.
            The girl is beautiful.   She's beautiful.
            The professor is tall.   He's tall.
            The house is big.   It's big.
            The boy is from Asia.   He's from Asia.
            The campus is confusing.   It's confusing.
            The girl is intelligent.   She's intelligent.
            The woman is pretty.   She's pretty.
            The building is gray.   It's gray.
            The car is economical.   It's economical.

***10. M2   (Picture Cue)

T:	Describe the house.	S:	It's (white).
	Describe the girl.		She's (pretty).
	Describe the car.		It's ( ).
	Describe the boy.		
	Describe the professor.		
	Describe the campus.		
	Describe the woman.		

11. C   T: Describe your country.   S: It's (beautiful).
             Describe your room.
             Describe your sister.
             Describe your friend.
             Describe the capital of your country.
             Describe your brother.
             Describe your house.
             Describe your professor.
             Describe your apartment.
             Describe your class.

□ QUESTIONS AND AFFIRMATIVE SHORT ANSWERS

Model: Is the class here? Yes, it is.

12. M1 Rep: Is the campus confusing?
              Is it confusing?
              Is the girl beautiful?
              Is she beautiful?
              Is the boy handsome?
              Is he handsome?

GENERALIZATION

Statement: The campus is confusing.

Question: Is   the campus   confusing?   Answer: Yes, it is.

---

13. M1T T: The girl is intelligent.   S: Is the girl intelligent?
              The boy is tall.   Is the boy tall?
              The building is confusing.   Is the building confusing?
              He's handsome.   Is he handsome?
              She's lost.   Is she lost?
              It's economical.   Is it economical?
              The professor is confused.   Is the professor confused?

14. M1 Rep: Is the girl beautiful?   Yes, she is.
                  Is the girl tall?   Yes, she is.
                  Is the girl fat?   Yes, she is.
                  Is the boy handsome?   Yes, he is.
                  Is the boy from Asia?   Yes, he is.
                  Is the car small?   Yes, it is.
                  Is the building tall?   Yes, it is.
                  Is the campus confusing?   Yes, it is.

***15. M1T (Picture Cue)
        T: beautiful   G1: Is (the girl) beautiful?   G2: Yes, she is.
              handsome   Is (the boy) handsome?   Yes, he is.
              economical   Is (the car) economical?   Yes, it is.
              fat
              tall
              thin
              small
              cheap

***16. M2 (Picture Cue)
        T: Ask a question about the girl.
        S1:   Is the girl (fat)?   S2:   Yes, she is.
        T: Ask a question about the car.
        S1:   Is the car (small)?   S2:   Yes, it is.
        T: Ask a question about the house.
               Ask a question about the campus.
               Ask a question about the girl.
               Ask a question about the professor.
               Ask a question about the instructor.
               Ask a question about the car.
               Ask a question about the lady.
               Ask a question about the boy.

□ NEGATIVE AND SHORT ANSWERS

Model: Chen isn't from the United States.
         Is the class here? No, it isn't.

17. M1 Rep: The girl isn't beautiful.
                 The boy isn't tall.
                 The car isn't cheap.
                 The house isn't white.
                 The car isn't economical.
                 The car isn't big.
                 The girl isn't thin.

***18. M1T Listen.   If you hear an affirmative statement, raise one hand; if a negative statement,
                         raise two hands.

T:	The girl isn't beautiful.	S:	(2)
	It's confusing.		(1)
	He isn't a graduate student.		(2)
	It isn't cheap.		(2)
	She's intelligent.		(1)
	The professor isn't from Asia.		(2)
	The campus is confusing.		(1)
	The boy is intelligent.		(1)
	The campus isn't confusing.		(2)
	The house is gray.		(1)

19. M1 T:	The campus is confusing.	S:	The campus isn't confusing.
	The class is difficult.		The class isn't difficult.
	The boy is intelligent.		The boy isn't intelligent.
	The student is handsome.		The student isn't handsome.
	The name is long.		The name isn't long.
	The lady is beautiful.		The lady isn't beautiful.
	The girl is polite.		The girl isn't polite.
	The car is expensive.		The car isn't expensive.
	The house is cheap.		The house Isn't cheap.

20. M1 T:	Is the girl beautiful?	S:	No, she isn't beautiful.
	Is the boy tall?		No, he isn't tall.
	Is the car cheap?		No, it isn't cheap.
	Is the house white?		No, it isn't white.
	Is the car economical?		No, it isn't economical.
	Is the pencil long?		No, it isn't long.
	Is the girl thin?		No, she isn't thin.

***21. M1T (Picture Cue)

T:	fat	G1:	Is the (girl) fat?	G2:	No, she isn't fat.
	thin		Is the (boy) thin?		No, he isn't thin.
	cheap		Is the (car) cheap?		No, it isn't cheap.
	tall				
	economical				
	expensive				
	beautiful				
	handsome				
	long				
	big				
	short				
	fat				

22. M1 Rep: Is the girl fat?   No, she isn't.
                 Is the car cheap?   No, it isn't.
                 Is the man handsome?   No, he isn't.
                 Is the campus confusing?   No, it isn't.
                 Is the house cheap?   No, it isn't.

23. M1 T: Is the woman beautiful?   S: No, she isn't.
                 Is the man tall?   No, he isn't.
                 Is the pencil long?   No, it isn't.
                 Is the car economical?   No, it isn't.
                 Is the house white?   No, it isn't.
                 Is the campus confusing?   No, it isn't.
                 Is the woman thin?   No, she isn't.
                 Is the boy short?   No, he isn't.

***24. M2 (Picture Cue)
        T: Make up a question about this picture.
        S1:   Is the house (white)?   S2: No, it isn't.
        S2:   Is the boy (tall)?   S3: Yes, he is.
                 etc.

***25. C   T: Is the capital of your country big?   S: (Yes, it is.)
                                                             (No, it isn't.)

                 Is (Pittsburgh) clean?
                 Is the weather in your country warm?
                 Is the university confusing?
                 Is the English class hard?
                 Is your friend intelligent?
                 Is your room big?
                 Is the answer difficult?
                 Is the exercise easy?
                 Is the capital of your country big?
                 Is (Pittsburgh) beautiful?
                 Is the professor tall?
                 Is your car economical?

Part B.   *Third Plural + BE + Adjective*

Vocabulary

	Nouns		Adjectives
book	*man/men		busy
*child/children	paper		rich
city	picture		
lesson	tree		

*irregular plural

Model: The boys are lost.

1. M1 Rep: The boys are lost.

    Sub: girls   S: The girls are lost.

       ladies   The ladies are lost.

       students   The students are lost.

       cars   The cars are lost.

       papers   The papers are lost.

       pencils   The pencils are lost.

       pictures   The pictures are lost.

       men   The men are lost.

       women   The women are lost.

       children   The children are lost.

2. M1 Rep: The boys are lost.

    Sub: intelligent   S: The boys are intelligent.

       thin   The boys are thin.

       handsome   The boys are handsome.

       short   The boys are short.

       big   The boys are big.

       from Latin America   The boys are from Latin America.

       confused   The boys are confused.

GENERALIZATION

Singular	(Part A)	The boy	is	lost.
Plural	(Part B)	The boys	are	lost.

Note: Adjective (*lost*) remains the same.

Note: Irregular plural of the nouns and the verb BE:

The man	is	lost.	The men	are	lost.
The woman	is	lost.	The women	are	lost.
The child	is	lost.	The children	are	lost.

---

3. M1T Listen. If you hear a singular statement, raise one hand; if you hear a plural statement, raise both hands.

    T: The girl is tall.   S: (1)

      The girls are tall.   (2)

      The boys are lost.   (2)

      The boy is short.   (1)

      The car is expensive.   (1)

      The houses are expensive.   (2)

      The pencils are short.   (2)

      The woman is beautiful.   (1)

      The men are handsome.   (2)

      The cars are big.   (2)

4. M1   T: The boy is lost.   S: The boys are lost.
                 The girl is intelligent.   The girls are intelligent.
                 The boy is handsome.   The boys are handsome.
                 The girl is beautiful.   The girls are beautiful.
                 The house is white.   The houses are white.
                 The tree is green.   The trees are green.
                 The man is tall.   The men are tall.
                 The woman is rich.   The women are rich.
                 The car is cheap.   The cars are cheap.

***5. M2 (Picture Cue)
         T: Tell something about the boys.   S: The boys are (tall).
                 Tell something about the cars.   The cars are (cheap).
                 etc.

□ SUBSTITUTE WORDS (Pronouns)

Model: The boys are lost.   They're lost.

6. M1   Rep: The boys are lost.   They're lost.
                 The boys are intelligent.   They're intelligent.
                 The girls are beautiful.   They're beautiful.
                 The girls are fat.   They're fat.
                 The buildings are tall.   They're tall.
                 The cars are cheap.   They're cheap.

GENERALIZATION

The boys	are tall.
The girls	are tall.
The buildings	are tall.
They	are tall.

They is the substitute word for all plural subjects. Note the difference between usual spoken and written forms:

Written	Spoken
They are tall.	They're tall.

---

7. M1   T: The buildings are tall.   S: They're tall.
                 The women are beautiful.   They're beautiful.
                 The cars are economical.   They're economical.
                 The boys are short.   They're short.
                 The girls are fat.   They're fat.
                 The students are confused.   They're confused.
                 The books are expensive.   They're expensive.
                 The pencils are long.   They're long.

***8. M2 (Picture Cue)

T:	Describe the boys.	S:	They're (handsome).
	Describe the boy.		He's (tall).
	Describe the girl.		
	Describe the cars.		
	Describe the houses.		
	Describe the cars.		
	Describe the girls.		
	Describe the campus.		
	Describe the buildings.		
	Describe the man.		
	Describe the woman.		
	Describe the student.		

9. C T: Describe the capital of your country.
       S: It's (beautiful) (big).
       T: Describe the cities in your country.
       S: They're (small and friendly).
       T: Describe the weather in your country.
            Describe the people in your class.
            Describe the buildings in the capital of your country.
            Describe the houses in your country.
            Describe your city.
            Describe the capital of this country.
            Describe the capital of your country.
            In your opinion, describe the weather here.
            Describe this city. Give your opinion.
            Describe your classes. Give your opinion.
            Describe your best friend.

☐ QUESTIONS AND AFFIRMATIVE SHORT ANSWERS

Model: Are the boys lost? Yes, they are.

10. M1 Rep: Are the boys lost?
               Are the girls tall?
               Are the girls intelligent?
               Are the cars expensive?
               Are the cars cheap?
               Are they confused?

GENERALIZATION

Part A   Statement: The boy is lost.
         Question: Is the boy   lost?   Answer: Yes, he is.

Part B   Statement: The boys   are lost.
         Question: Are the boys   lost?   Answer: Yes, they are.

---

11. M1 T: The boys are intelligent.   S: Are the boys intelligent?

The boys are intelligent.	S: Are the boys intelligent?
The girls are short.	Are the girls short?
The cars are cheap.	Are the cars cheap?
They're long.	Are they long?
They're green.	Are they green?
The houses are expensive.	Are the houses expensive?
The names are difficult.	Are the names difficult?
The professors are busy.	Are the professors busy?

12. M1T   Listen. If you hear a singular subject, raise one hand; if plural, raise two hands.

T:	S:
Are the boys tall?	(2)
Is the boy tall?	(1)
The girls are fat.	(2)
Are the students confused?	(2)
The campus is dirty.	(1)
Are the boys lost?	(2)
Is the building tall?	(1)
The books are big.	(2)
Is the lady intelligent?	(1)

13. M1T T:

The boy is tall.	S: Is the boy tall?
The boys are tall.	Are the boys tall?
They're tall.	Are they tall?
The cars are expensive.	Are the cars expensive?
It's expensive.	Is it expensive?
The girl is thin.	Is the girl thin?
The girls are thin.	Are the girls thin?
She's thin.	Is she thin?
It's white.	Is it white?
The girl is fat.	Is the girl fat?
The boys are tall.	Are the boys tall?
The car is expensive.	Is the car expensive?
The houses are cheap.	Are the houses cheap?

14. M1 T:

Are the houses expensive?	S: Yes, they are.
Are the cars cheap?	Yes, they are.
Are the boys tall?	Yes, they are.
Are the men handsome?	Yes, they are.
Are the women beautiful?	Yes, they are.
Are the instructors intelligent?	Yes, they are.

15. M1T T:

Is the car expensive?	S: Yes, it is.
Are the cars expensive?	Yes, they are.
Is the campus confusing?	Yes, it is.
Is the house white?	Yes, it is.
Are the boys confused?	Yes, they are.
Is Nancy from the United States?	Yes, she is.
Are the girls thin?	Yes, they are.
Is Carlos from Latin America?	Yes, he is.
Are the houses cheap?	Yes, they are.
Is the boy intelligent?	Yes, he is.

□ NEGATIVE AND SHORT ANSWERS

Model: The girls aren't confused.
         Are the girls confused? No, they aren't.

16. M1 Rep: The girls aren't confused.
              The cars aren't cheap.
              The boys aren't confused.
              The houses aren't expensive.
              The classes aren't difficult.
              The buildings aren't tall.

Note the difference between written and spoken forms:

Written	Spoken
The boy is not tall.	The boy isn't tall.
The buildings are not tall.	The buildings aren't tall.

Contractions are not usually used in formal written style.

---

17. M1 Listen.   Affirmative, raise one hand; negative, raise two hands.
    T: They're lost.   S: (1)
         They aren't lost.   (2)
         The boys are lost.   (1)
         The boys aren't lost.   (2)
         The girls aren't thin.   (2)
         The women are thin.   (1)
         The cars aren't cheap.   (2)
         The houses are cheap.   (1)
         The boys are intelligent.   (1)
         They aren't long.   (2)

18. M1 T: The girls are fat.   S: The girls aren't fat.
            The boys are lost.   The boys aren't lost.
            The cars are cheap.   The cars aren't cheap.
            The houses are white.   The houses aren't white.
            The cars are expensive.   The cars aren't expensive.
            The lessons are difficult.   The lessons aren't difficult.
            The boys are confused.   The boys aren't confused.

19. M1 Rep: Are the girls fat?   No, they aren't.
              Are the buildings tall?   No, they aren't.
              Are the boys lost?   No, they aren't.
              Are the houses cheap?   No, they aren't.
              Are the women beautiful?   No, they aren't.

20. M1T T: girls—fat   G1:   Are the girls fat?   G2:   No, they aren't.
               girl—fat   Is the girl fat?   No, she isn't.
               boy—handsome   Is the boy handsome?   No, he isn't.
               boys—tall   Are the boys tall?   No, they aren't.
               building—tall   Is the building tall?   No, it isn't.
               woman—thin   Is the woman thin?   No, she isn't.
               cars—expensive   Are the cars expensive?   No, they aren't.
               house—white   Is the house white?   No, it isn't.
               men—rich   Are the men rich?   No, they aren't.
               professors—busy   Are the professors busy?   No, they aren't.

21. C   T: Ask if (student) is from Iran.
        S1:   Is ( ) from Iran?
        S2:   (Yes, she is.)
        T: Ask if ( ) is from Taiwan.
        S1:   Is ( ) from Taiwan?
        S2:   (No, he isn't. He's from Hong Kong.)
        T: Ask if ( ) is from Mexico.
              Ask if ( ) is from Colombia.
              Ask if the teacher is from the United States.
              Ask if ( ) and ( ) are from Iran.
              Ask if ( ) and ( ) are from the United States.
              Ask if the campus is confusing.
              Ask if the books are expensive.
              Ask if the houses in (country) are expensive.
              Ask if the cars in ( ) are expensive.
              Ask if VWs are expensive.
              Ask if Rolls-Royces are expensive.

Part C.   *Statements and Questions — X + BE + Noun Phrase*

Vocabulary

Nouns   Adjectives

actor   nurse   bad   slow
actress   operator   business   terrible
artist   secretary   easy
dentist   spy   engineering
doctor   stewardess   excellent
employee   teacher   fine
engineer   waiter   good
immigrant   waitress   history
lawyer   poor (not good)

□ SINGULAR

Model: The girl is a student.

16

1. M1 Rep: The girl is a student.
       Sub: waitress   S: The girl is a waitress.
              spy   The girl is a spy.
              stewardess   The girl is a stewardess.
              hairdresser   The girl is a hairdresser.
              teacher   The girl is a teacher.
              student   The girl is a student.

2. M1 Rep: The girl is an actress.
       Sub: artist   S: The girl is an artist.
              immigrant   The girl is an immigrant.
              operator   The girl is an operator.
              employee   The girl is an employee.
              actress   The girl is an actress.

GENERALIZATION

Part A & B:	The girl is	beautiful.	(Adjective)
	The girl is	a student.	(Noun)
Part C:	The girl is	an actress.	(Noun)

Use *a* before a noun beginning with a consonant sound; use *an* before a noun beginning with a vowel sound.

---

3. M1T Rep: The girl is a student.
        Sub: teacher   S: The girl is a teacher.
               artist   The girl is an artist.
               actress   The girl is an actress.
               spy   The girl is a spy.
               operator   The girl is an operator.
               stewardess   The girl is a stewardess.
               immigrant   The girl is an immigrant.
               hairdresser   The girl is a hairdresser.

4. M1T Rep: The man is a professor.
        Sub: tall   S: The man is tall.
               artist   The man is an artist.
               handsome   The man is handsome.
               immigrant   The man is an immigrant.
               doctor   The man is a doctor.
               fat   The man is fat.
               lawyer   The man is a lawyer.
               confused   The man is confused.
               spy   The man is a spy.

5. M2 (Picture Cue)
       T: Tell about the man—tall/short.   S: He's·(tall).
             Tell about the man—artist/lawyer.   He's (an artist).

(exercise continued on next page)

Tell about the woman—actress/secretary.
Tell about the girl—student/actress.
Tell about the man—doctor/spy.
Tell about the campus—big/small.
Tell about the lady—artist/actress.
Tell about the man—lawyer/artist.
Tell about the girl—tall/short.

□ PLURAL

Model: The boys are students.

6. M1   Listen: The boy is a student.   Repeat: The boys are students.
                  The girl is an actress.   The girls are actresses.
                  The woman is a secretary.   The women are secretaries.
                  The man is a professor.   The men are professors.
                  The building is a church.   The buildings are churches.

***GENERALIZATION

Singular: The boy   *is a*   student.
Plural: The boys   *are*   students.

---

7. M1   T: The boy is a student.   S: The boys are students.
             The girl is a nurse.   The girls are nurses.
             The building is a church.   The buildings are churches.
             The girl is an actress.   The girls are actresses.
             The doctor is a teacher.   The doctors are teachers.
             The lady is a spy.   The ladies are spies.
             The lawyer is an artist.   The lawyers are artists.
             The doctor is an immigrant.   The doctors are immigrants.

8. M1   T: The lawyers are artists.   S: The lawyer is an artist.
             The ladies are spies.   The lady is a spy.
             The doctors are teachers.   The doctor is a teacher.
             The girls are actresses.   The girl is an actress.
             The buildings are churches.   The building is a church.
             The girls are nurses.   The girl is a nurse.
             The boys are students.   The boy is a student.
             The doctors are immigrants.   The doctor is an immigrant.

9. M1T T: The boy is a student.   S: The boys are students.
             The girls are nurses.   The girl is a nurse.
             The women are actresses.   The woman is an actress.
             The man is a doctor.   The men are doctors.
             The lawyers are artists.   The lawyer is an artist.
             The building is a church.   The buildings are churches.
             The woman is a doctor.   The women are doctors.
             The men are doctors.   The man is a doctor.

18

10. M2 T: boy—student
    S1:   Is the boy a student?
    S2:   (Yes, he is.) (No, he isn't. He's a waiter.)
    T: boys—professors
    S1:   Are the boys professors?
    S2:   (No, they aren't. They're students.)
    T: girls—nurses
           child—spy
           man—lawyer
           boys—engineers
           ladies—spies
           women—teachers
           doctors—waiters
           lawyer—immigrant

11. C   T: Ask if ( ) is an engineer.
    S1:   Is ( ) an engineer?
    S2:   (Yes, he is.) (No, he isn't. He's a student.)
    T: Ask if ( ) and ( ) are secretaries.
    S1:   Are ( ) and ( ) secretaries?
    S2:   (No, they aren't. They're students.)
    T: Ask if ( ) is an actor.
           Ask if ( ) is a nurse.
           Ask if ( ) and ( ) are doctors.
           Ask if ( ) is a professor.
           Ask if ( ) is a teacher.
           Ask if ( ) and ( ) are doctors.
           Ask if ( ) is an actress.
           Ask if ( ) and ( ) are instructors.
           Ask if ( ) is a dentist.
           Ask if ( ) is a spy.
           Ask if ( ) and ( ) are lawyers.

□ ADJECTIVE + NOUN

Model: The tall girl is a good student.
        The tall girls are good students.

12. M1 Rep: The tall girl is a student.
    Sub: fat   S: The fat girl is a student.
           thin   The thin girl is a student.
           pretty   The pretty girl is a student.
           intelligent   The intelligent girl is a student.
           beautiful   The beautiful girl is a student.
           short   The short girl is a student.

19

13. M1 Rep: The tall girl is a good student.
    Sub: bad   S: The tall girl is a bad student.
            slow   The tall girl is a slow student.
            graduate   The tall girl is a graduate student.
            biology   The tall girl is a biology student.
            history   The tall girl is a history student.

> Note: *a* doctor/*an* excellent doctor
>   *an* actress/*a* good actress

14. M1 Rep: The fat boy is a history student.
    Sub: excellent   S: The fat boy is an excellent student.
            graduate   The fat boy is a graduate student.
            undergraduate   The fat boy is an undergraudate student.
            engineering   The fat boy is an engineering student.
            business   The fat boy is a business student.
            English   The fat boy is an English student.

GENERALIZATION

The patterns in Parts A & B are combined with Part C.

Part A: The boy is tall.   (Noun + BE + Adjective)
Part B: The men are good.
Part C: The boy is a student.   (Noun + BE + Noun)
           The men are engineers.
A & C: The tall boy is a student.   (Adjective + Noun + BE + Noun)
B & C: The men are good engineers.   (Noun + BE + Adjective + Noun)

The pattern may also have an adjective before both nouns: "The tall men are business students."

---

15. M1T   Rep: The tall boy is a history student.
          Sub: engineering   S: The tall boy is an engineering student.
                girl   The tall girl is an engineering student.
                thin   The thin girl is an engineering student.
                man   The thin man is an engineering student.
                fat   The fat man is an engineering student.
                woman   The fat woman is an engineering student.
                biology   The fat woman is a biology student.
                tall   The tall woman is a biology student.
                boy   The tall boy is a biology student.
                history   The tall boy is a history student.

16. M1 Listen: The tall girl is a graduate student.
         Repeat: The tall girls are graduate students.
         Listen: The thin lady is a good spy.
         Repeat: The thin ladies are good spies.
         Listen: The tall man is a fine doctor.
         Repeat: The tall men are fine doctors.
         Listen: The little child is a terrible student.
         Repeat: The little children are terrible students.

> Note: The adjective does not change in the plural statements.

---

17. M1 T: The little child is a terrible student.
        S: The little children are terrible students.
        T: The fat man is a good lawyer.
        S: The fat men are good lawyers.
        T: The thin boy is a slow student.
        S: The thin boys are slow students.
        T: The tall man is a graduate student.
        S: The tall men are graduate students.
        T: The happy man is a good doctor.
        S: The happy men are good doctors.
        T: The pretty girl is a fine nurse.
        S: The pretty girls are fine nurses.

***18. M2 T: man/lawyer   S: The (big) man is a (bad) lawyer.
             women/students   The (thin) women are (good) students.
             lady/actress
             men/hairdressers
             girl/spy
             child/student
             woman/secretary
             ladies/teachers
             girls/waitresses
             woman/lawyer
             boys/actors
             children/actors

***19. M2 T: lawyer   S1: Is (the young man a good) lawyer?
                                           S2: No, he isn't. He's a (terrible) lawyer.
             actresses   S1: Are (the beautiful girls fine) actresses?
                                         S2: No, they aren't. They're (bad) actresses.
             spy
             waitresses
             professor
             doctors
             teachers
             student
             teacher
             lawyers
             spies

(exercise continued on next page)

actor
waiter
waitress

20. C   T: Describe the capital of your country.   S: It's (a beautiful city).
                Describe the people of your country.   They're (friendly people).
                Describe your university in your country.
                Describe the leader of your country.
                Describe the houses in your country.
                Describe the weather in your country.
                Describe your family home.
                Describe TV actors in your country.
                Describe movie actresses in your country.
                Describe the English classes.
                Describe your apartment.
                Describe your room.

Part D.   *Second Person*

□ STATEMENT

Model: You're from Latin America.

1. M1   Rep: You're from (Venezuela).
                You're from (Iran).
                You're tall.
                You're undergraduate students.
                You're an undergraduate student.
                You're from Asia.
                You're from Latin America.

Note: Use the contraction *you're* in speech, but *you are* in writing.

□ QUESTION

Model: Are you in the class?

2. M1   T: You're lost.   S: Are you lost?
                You're from the U.S.   Are you from the U.S.?
                You're from Venezuela.   Are you from Venezuela?
                You're confused.   Are you confused?
                You're an undergraduate student.   Are you an undergraduate student?
                You're teachers.   Are you teachers?
                You're a student.   Are you a student?

3. M1T   T: You're lost.   S: Are you lost?
                He's a good student.   Is he a good student?
                She's lost.   Is she lost?
                It's lost.   Is it lost?
                They're good instructors.   Are they good instructors?
                You're confused.   Are you confused?
                He's from Colombia.   Is he from Colombia?

☐ NEGATIVE

Model: You aren't lost.

4. M1   Rep: You aren't lost.
         Sub: confused   S: You aren't confused.
                 a doctor   You aren't a doctor.
                 a student   You aren't a student.
                 from Cuba   You aren't from Cuba.
                 lawyers   You aren't lawyers.
                 graduate students   You aren't graduate students.

5. M1   T: You're lost.   S: You aren't lost.
               You're in the class.   You aren't in the class.
               You're an undergraduate.   You aren't an undergraduate.
               You're students.   You aren't students.
               You're a spy.   You aren't a spy.
               You're from Asia.   You aren't from Asia.
               You're graduate students.   You aren't graduate students.
               You're from South America.   You aren't from South America.

6. M1T   T: You're from Asia.   S: You aren't from Asia.
                He's a good student.   He isn't a good student.
                The girls are tall.   The girls aren't tall.
                She's a stewardess.   She isn't a stewardess.
                You're confused.   You aren't confused.
                He's handsome.   He isn't handsome.
                They're lost.   They aren't lost.

Part E.   *First Person*

Model: I'm Bill Jackson.
         We're freshmen.

1. M1   Rep: I'm a student.
         Sub: lawyer   S: I'm a lawyer.
                 nurse   I'm a nurse.
                 confused   I'm confused.
                 lost   I'm lost.
                 from Mexico   I'm from Mexico.
                 professor   I'm a professor.
                 from Iran   I'm from Iran.

23

2. M2   T: Are you a graduate student or an undergraduate student?
        S: I'm (a graduate student).
        T: Are you from ( ) or ( )?
             Are you a student or a professor?
             etc.

3. M1   Listen: Miss Wilson and I are from the United States.
                  We're from the United States.
                  We're instructors.
        Repeat: We're in the English class.
                  We're foreign students.
                  We're from Latin America.
                  We're from Iran and Venezuela.
                  We're confused.

GENERALIZATION

X + I = *we.*   You and I are instructors. We're instructors.

Question: Are you in the class?

Short Answers: Yes, I am.   No, I'm not.
                 Yes, we are.   No, we aren't.

***4. M2   T: Are you students or teachers?   S: We're (students).
                Are you from the U.S. or ( )?
                Are you from ( ) or ( )?
                Are you and ( ) from ( ) or ( )?
                Am I from ( ) or the U.S.?
                Is ( ) from ( ) or ( )?
                Are ( ) and ( ) from ( ) or ( )?
                etc.

***5. M2   T: Are you students?   S: Yes, we are.
                Are you professors?   No, we aren't. We're students.
                Are you graduate students?
                Are you from Taiwan?
                Is ( ) from ( )?
                Is ( ) an undergraduate student?

***6. M2   Listen: Are you a student?   Yes, I am.
                    Are you a professor?   No, I'm not.
           T: Are you an undergraduate student?   S: Yes, I am.
                Are you from ( )?   Yes, I am.
                Are you a foreign student?   Yes, I am.
                Are you in the English class?   Yes, I am.
                etc.

24

T: Are you from ( )?   S: No, I'm not, I'm from ( ).
        Are you a professor?   No, I'm not. I'm a student.
        Are you an American student?
        Are you a lawyer?
        etc.

Note: When mentioning someone else and yourself, the other person's name is first.
        Example: *John and I . . .*

---

7. C   T: Ask ( ) if he is from (Iran).
        S1:   Are you from Iran?
        S2:   (Yes, I am.) (No, I'm not. I'm from ( ).)
        T: Ask ( ) if he and ( ) are from ( ).
        S1:   Are you and ( ) from ( )?
        S2:   (Yes, we are.) (No, we aren't. I'm from ( ). He's from ( ).)
        T: Ask ( ) if he is from Taiwan.
                Ask ( ) if he's a professor.
                Ask ( ) if she's a graduate student.
                Ask ( ) if he and ( ) are from the U.S.
                Ask if ( ) is from ( ).
                Ask ( ) if she and ( ) are from ( ).
                Ask ( ) if ( ) and ( ) are graduate students.

SECTION TWO

ALTERNATIVE QUESTIONS

Vocabulary: ugly (adjective)

Model: Is she a graduate student or an undergraduate student?

1. M1   Rep: Is the girl tall or short?   She's short.
                Is the professor fat or thin?   He's fat.
                Is the boy a graduate student or an
                   undergraduate student?   He's an undergraduate student.
                Is the man a good lawyer or a bad lawyer?   He's a bad lawyer.
                Are the women tall or short?   They're tall.
                Are they secretaries or nurses?   They're nurses.

2. M1   Rep: Is the lady tall or short?
        Sub: fat or thin   S: Is the lady fat or thin?
                a nurse or a secretary   Is the lady a nurse or a secretary?
                a biology student or an English student   Is the lady a biology student or an
                                                                English student?

                boys   Are the boys biology students or
                                                                English students?

                good students or bad students   Are the boys good students or
                                                                bad students?

(exercise continued on next page)

Sub:	men	Are the men good students or bad students?
	doctors or lawyers	Are the men doctors or lawyers?
	ugly or handsome	Are the men ugly or handsome?
	tall or short	Are the men tall or short?

GENERALIZATION

The word *or* is a conjunction. It indicates a choice.

	Answer
Is the professor tall or short?	Tall.
Is Chen from Hong Kong or Taiwan?	Taiwan.

---

3. M2 T: Ask about the lady.   tall/short
    S1:   Is the lady tall or short?   S2: She's (tall).
    T: Ask about the girls.   beautiful/ugly
         Ask about the house.   white/green
         Ask about the woman.   lawyer/professor
         Ask about the cars.   cheap/expensive
         Ask about the lawyers.   good/bad
         Ask about the man.   doctor/lawyer
         Ask about the women.   actresses/stewardesses
         Ask about the students.   from Colombia/Venezuela
         Ask about the man.   engineer/professor
         Ask about the car.   Rolls-Royce/Cadillac

4. C T: Ask about the weather in (Chen's) country.
    S1:   Is the weather (hot or cold) in (Taiwan)?   S2: It's (hot).
    T: Ask about the size of buildings in ( )'s country.
    S1:   Are the buildings in ( ) big or small?   S2: They're (small).
    T: Ask about the size of ( )'s capital.
         Ask about the country ( ) is from.
         Ask about the price of cars in ( )'s country.
         Ask about the price of a haircut in ( ).
         Ask about ( )'s status as a student. (graduate/undergraduate)
         Ask about the size of cars in ( ).
         Ask about the size of ( )'s apartment/room.
         Ask about the condition of ( )'s room/apartment.

5. C T: I think (Pablo) is from (Mexico).
    S1:   Is Pablo from Mexico?
    S2:   (Yes, he is.) (No, he isn't. (Carlos) is from Mexico. Pablo is from Ecuador.)
    T: I think (New York) is the capital of (the U.S.).
    S1:   Is New York the capital of the United States?
    S2:   No, it isn't. Washington, D.C. is the capital of the U.S.
    T: I think ( ) and ( ) are from ( ).
         I think ( ) is a (doctor).

(exercise continued on next page)

I think ( ) and ( ) are engineering students.
I think ( ) is a graduate student.
I think ( ) and ( ) are undergraduates.
I think ( ) is the capital of ( ).
I think ( ) and ( ) are from ( ).
I think ( ) is from (city).
I think ( ) and ( ) are nurses.
I think (city) is beautiful.
I think ( ) are interesting.
I think ( ) is the capital of ( ).

SECTION THREE

WH QUESTIONS

Part A.   *Who/What? (In Subject Position)*

```
Vocabulary

            Nouns                          Adjectives

        advisor                        broken
        sport                          married
        waste basket                   popular
                                       sad
                                       single (not married)
```

Model: Who is from Latin America?   Carlos is.
         What is confusing?   The campus is.

1. M1   Rep: Who is from Latin America?   ( ) is.
               Who is from Asia?   ( ) is.
               Who is beautiful?   The girl is.
               Who is handsome?   The man is.

               What is confusing?   The campus is.
               What is tall?   ( ) is.
               What is expensive?   The car is.
               What is difficult?   The class is.

GENERALIZATION

The questions in Sections 1 and 2 are answered by *yes* or *no*. The questions in this section are introduced by a word beginning with *wh* and are answered differently.

Statement: | Carlos | is from Latin America.

Wh Question: | Who | is from Latin America?   Answer: Carlos.

Statement: | The campus | is confusing.

Wh Question: | What | is confusing?   Answer: The campus.

Which question asks about people?   ((*who?*))
About things?   ((*what?*))

---

2. M1   T: Someone is sad.   S: Who is sad?
               Someone is fat.   Who is fat?
               Someone is handsome.   Who is handsome?
               Someone is intelligent.   Who is intelligent?

        T: Something is confusing.   S: What is confusing?
               Something is expensive.   What is expensive?
               Something is economical.   What is economical?
               Something is tall.   What is tall?

3. M1T   T: Someone is tall.   S: Who is tall?
               Something is tall.   What is tall?
               Someone is lost.   Who is lost?
               Someone is a lawyer.   Who is a lawyer?
               Something is confusing.   What is confusing?
               Something is cheap.   What is cheap?
               Someone is from the U.S.   Who is from the U.S.?
               Something is expensive.   What is expensive.

4. M2   T: Someone is from ( ).   S1:   Who is from ( )?
                                                    S2:   ( ) is.
        T: Something is on the floor.   S1:   What is on the floor?
                                                    S2:   (The book) is.
        T: Someone is married.
               Something is on the chair.
               Someone is single.
               Someone is from Latin America.
               Something is in the waste basket.
               Someone is from Asia.
               Something is broken.
               Someone is from the United States.

28

5. C   T: Ask ( ) about the capital of his country.
        S1:   What is the capital of (Venezuela)?
        S2:   (Caracas) is.
        T: Ask ( ) about the leader of his country.
        S1:   Who is the leader of ( )?
        S2:   ( ) is the (king/president, etc.).
        T: Ask ( ) about his advisor.
                Ask ( ) about a large city in his country.
                Ask ( ) about something expensive in his country.
                Ask ( ) about something cheap in his country.
                Ask ( ) about a popular movie actor/actress.
                Ask ( ) about the reading teacher.
                Ask ( ) about a good TV program.
                Ask ( ) about a good book in English.
                Ask ( ) about a popular sport in this country.
                Ask ( ) about the leader of his country.
                Ask ( ) about a beautiful city in his country.

Part B.   *Question — Where are you from?*

Note:	Are you from Iran?	No, I'm not.
	Where are you from?	Turkey.

1. M1   Rep: Where are you from?
                Where is he from?
                Where is she from?
                Where are they from?
                Where is it from?

2. M1T   Rep: Where are you from?
        Sub: they   S: Where are they from?
                he   Where is he from?
                she   Where is she from?
                it   Where is it from?
                they   Where are they from?
                you   Where are you from?

3. C   T: Ask ( ) where he's from.   S1:   Where are you from?
                                        S2:   I'm from ( ).
        T: Ask ( ) where ( ) and ( ) are from.   S1:   Where are ( ) and ( ) from?
                                        S2:   ( ) is from ( ); ( ) is from ( ).
        T: Ask ( ) where she's from.
                Ask ( ) where the teacher is from.
                Ask ( ) where ( ) is from.
                etc.

SECTION FOUR

***ALTERNATE NEGATIVE FORMS

Model: He isn't tall. He's not tall.

1.   Listen: I'm not tall.
                  He's not tall. . . . . He isn't tall.
                  She's not tall. . . . . She isn't tall.
                  They're not tall. . . . . They aren't tall.
                  We're not tall. . . . . We aren't tall.
                  You're not tall. . . . . You aren't tall.

2. M1   Rep: I'm not a student.
   Sub: We   S: We're not students.
           He   He's not a student.
           She   She's not a student.
           They   They're not students.
           You (1)   You're not a student.
           You (Pl)   You're not students.
           I   I'm not a student.

GENERALIZATION

Except for *I*, there are two forms for the negative contraction in speech.

        He is not   =   He isn't.
                        He's not.

Both forms are very common; you should practice the form which is easiest for you to pronounce.

---

3. M1T   T: He isn't tall.   S: He's not tall.
               She isn't a nurse.   She's not a nurse.
               We aren't professors.   We're not professors.
               They aren't spies.   They're not spies.
               You aren't from North America.   You're not from North America.
               She isn't beautiful.   She's not beautiful.
               He isn't handsome.   He's not handsome.

4. M1T   Rep: Is he a professor?   S: No, he's not.
                Are they from Iran?   No, they're not.
                Are we in New York?   No, we're not.
                Is she a teacher?   No, she's not.
                Are we students?   No, we're not.

5. M1T   T: Am I a student?   S: No, you're not.
                Are we in California?   No, we're not.
                Is she from South America?   No, she's not.
                Are you professors?   No, we're not.
                Is he a spy?   No, he's not.
                Are they from Iran?   No, they're not.
                Am I from Central America?   No, I'm not.
                Is he from Canada?   No, he's not.
                Are they secretaries?   No, they're not.
                Are we nurses?   No, we're not.

SUMMARY DIALOGUE

SITUATION: Two students meet before class.

S1:   Hello. Are you in the English class?

S2:   Hi, Yes, I am. I'm Carlos.

S1:   I'm Michael.

S2:   Are you from the United States?

S1:   No, I'm not, I'm from Greece. Where are you from?

S2:   I'm from Colombia.

LESSON ONE – SUMMARY OF PATTERNS

	Subject	Verb (BE)	Completer	Short Answers
Statement	The boy	is	(not) a (good) student.	
	He	is	tall.	
	The coffee	is	from Colombia.	
	It	is	delicious.	
	The girl	is	beautiful.	
	She	is	from Iran.	
	The boys	are	history students.	
	They	are	intelligent.	
	We	are	graduate students.	
	I	am	an undergraduate student.	
Question (Who/What)	Who	is	from Iran?	Ali.
	What	is	confusing?	The campus.

	BE			
Question (yes/no)	Are	you	a student?	Yes, I am. No, I'm not.
	Is	she	a (good) secretary?	Yes, she is. No, she isn't.
Question (alternative)	Are	you	a student or a professor?	A student.
	Is	the boy	a graduate or an undergraduate?	An undergraduate.
Question (where)	Where are	the girls	from?	Latin America.

LESSON TWO

INTRODUCTION   The student union

Bill is talking with Chen and Carlos after the class.

Chen: Mr. Brown is a good lecturer, *isn't he?*

Bill: Yes, he is. *Where are you going now?*

Carlos: The next class isn't until 11:00. Where are you going?

5   Bill: I'm having coffee in the Student Union cafeteria. *Who's coming with me?*

Carlos: We are. Come on, Chen.

(At the cafeteria.)

Chen: It isn't very crowded, is it?

Bill: No, it isn't. Everyone is starting classes today. Are you both taking the same classes?

10   Carlos: No. Only biology. I'm studying English and history. Chen is taking engineering
          courses.

Chen: You're taking engineering too, aren't you, Bill?

Bill: Yes, I am. It's pretty interesting.

Carlos: What are those people doing?

15   Bill: They're playing bridge. It's a tradition in the Union. The big table is the "bridge
          table." Are you living in the dorms?

Carlos: Chen is. I'm not. I'm staying with a family.

Bill: That's great! It's a good way to learn English.

Carlos: I'm not learning English. The family is improving their Spanish.

OUTLINE OF PATTERNS   Example

Section One	Present Continuous	
Part A	Statements	Bill is talking to Carlos and Chen.
Part B	Questions and Short Answers	Are you taking the same class? No, we aren't.
Part C	Negative Statements	I'm not living in the dorm.
Section Two	Wh Questions	
Part A	*Who?*	Who is coming with me?
Part B	*What?*	What are those people doing?
Part C	*Where?*	Where are you going?
Section Three	BE—Tag Questions	
Part A	Type I	It isn't crowded, is it?
Part B	Type II	You're taking engineering, aren't you?

COMPREHENSION QUESTIONS

1. Who is Bill talking with?

2. When is the next class?

3. Where are the boys going? (Why?)

4. Is the cafeteria crowded? (Why?)

5. Are Carlos and Chen taking the same classes?

6. What is Carlos studying? (Chen? Bill?)

7. What are the people doing?

8. Which table is the "bridge table"?

9. Where is Chen living? (Carlos?)

10. Is Carlos learning English? (Why?)

NOTE

Line 13:   "pretty interesting." *pretty* + adjective means "quite" in informal speech.

SECTION ONE

PRESENT CONTINUOUS

Part A.   *Statements*

```
Vocabulary

Nouns                                    Verbs                      Adverbs

    bridge (game)    language lab        do      stay               today
    computer science lunch               drive   study
    dinner           movie               go      take (a course)
    dorm             restaurant          live    talk
    downtown         school              play    teach
    grammar          spelling            have    walk
    home             supper
```

Model: Bill is talking with Carlos and Chen.
         They're playing bridge.

1. M1   Listen: The man is teaching the class.
                   The woman is walking downtown.
                   The girl is teaching English.
                   We're studying English.
                   I'm staying with a family.
                   They're living in the dorms.
                   You're studying engineering.

2. M1   Repeat: The man is teaching the biology class.
                   The girl is teaching the English class.
                   The man is taking the history class.
                   The girls are taking the history class.
                   The men are teaching the history class.
                   We are taking the English class.
                   I am teaching the English class.
                   You are taking the English class.

GENERALIZATION

This verb tense (BE + verb -*ing*) is called Present Continuous. It indicates that the action is happening right now, or will happen in the near future. Note that the BE forms are the same as in Lesson One:

Lesson One: The girl is   downtown.   (BE—Simple Present)

Lesson Two: The girl is walking   downtown.   (Present Continuous)

---

3. M1   Rep: The man is teaching biology now.
        Sub: taking   S: The man is taking biology now.
               learning   The man is learning biology now.
               studying   The man is studying biology now.
               teaching   The man is teaching biology now.
               learning   The man is learning biology now.

4. M1   Rep: The girls are walking downtown now.
        Sub: working   S: The girls are working downtown now.
               going   The girls are going downtown now.
               driving   The girls are driving downtown now.
               staying   The girls are staying downtown now.
               living   The girls are living downtown now.
               walking   The girls are walking downtown now.

Note: Place Expressions —

The girls are going	to the	movies.
	to the	restaurant.
	to	school.
	to	class.
	to	church.
		home.
		downtown.

Some place expressions are preceded by *to*; some by *to the*; others by no preposition. The expressions should be learned in sentences.

---

5. M1   Rep: The girls are walking downtown.
        Sub: to school   S: The girls are walking to school.
               to church   The girls are walking to church.
               home   The girls are walking home.
               to class   The girls are walking to class.
               to the movies   The girls are walking to the movies.
               to the restaurant   The girls are walking to the restaurant.
               downtown   The girls are walking downtown.

6. M1   Rep: I'm having lunch at the cafeteria today.
        Sub: breakfast   S: I'm having breakfast at the cafeteria
                                                    today.
               dinner   I'm having dinner at the cafeteria today.
               supper   I'm having supper at the cafeteria today.
               coffee   I'm having coffee at the cafeteria today.

7. M1T Rep: The man is teaching the English class.
        Sub: girl   S: The girl is teaching the English class.
               boy   The boy is teaching the English class.
               men   The men are teaching the English class.
               women   The women are teaching the English class.

(exercise continued on next page)

students	The students are teaching the English class.
I	I am teaching the English class.
we	We are teaching the English class.
you	You are teaching the English class.

8. M1T Rep: The girl is walking downtown now.

Sub:		S:	
home			The girl is walking home now.
driving			The girl is driving home now.
girls			The girls are driving home now.
to school			The girls are driving to school now.
going			The girls are going to school now.
I			I am going to school now.
to class			I am going to class now.
walking			I am walking to class now.

9. M2 T: Are you studying English or German now?
    S: I'm studying English now.
    T: Are you living in the dorm or with a family now?
        Are you having lunch at the cafeteria or a restaurant?
        Are you going home or to the restaurant?
        Are you going to the language lab or to reading class?
        Are we studying English grammar or English spelling?
        Am I teaching English or Spanish?
        Is ( ) studying English or engineering?
        Is ( ) studying computer science or English?
        Are you going downtown or to class?
        Are you going to the laboratory or to class?
        Are you going to the cafeteria or to a restaurant?
        Are you having a snack or dinner at the cafeteria?

10. C T: What are you studying?   S: I'm studying (English literature).
        Where are you living?
        Where are you studying?
        Who is teaching the 9:00 class?
        What is ( ) studying?
        What are ( ) and ( ) doing?
        Where are you going at 3:00?
        What are ( ) and ( ) studying?
        Where are ( ) and ( ) living?
        What is ( ) doing at 2:00?
        What are ( ) and ( ) studying at 9:00?
        Where is ( ) having dinner?

Part B.   *Question and Short Answer*

```
┌─ ─── ── ─── ── ── ── ─── ── ── ── ── ──┐
│   Vocabulary                                               │
│                                                            │
│   Nouns                  Verbs      Adjectives    Adverbs  │
│   basketball    poker    buy        young    next week     │
│   bus           shirt    learn               this afternoon│
│   karate        soccer   meet                this weekend  │
│   library       tennis   speak               tonight       │
│   office        yard     wear                              │
│   party                  work                              │
└── ── ── ── ─── ── ── ── ── ─── ── ── ── ──┘
```

Model: Are you taking the same classes? Yes, we are.

1. M1   Rep: Is the girl driving home?
                 Is the lady studying English?
                 Is the man walking to class?
                 Are we having coffee?
                 Are the boys studying engineering?
                 Are the women walking to church?

```
┌──────────────────────────────────────────────────────────┐
│   GENERALIZATION                                           │
│                                                            │
│   Lesson One:        The man is a professor.              │
│                      Is the man    a professor?    Answer: Yes, he is.  No, he isn't. │
│                                                            │
│   Lesson Two:        The man is teaching the class.       │
│                      Is the man    teaching the class?  Answer: Yes, he is.  No, he isn't. │
│                                                            │
│   Note:  Usually the Present Continuous refers to the present, but: │
│                                                            │
│        "Are you playing bridge tonight?"                  │
│                                                            │
│   By using the "time word" tonight, the question asks about the future. │
└──────────────────────────────────────────────────────────┘
```

2. M1   T: The girl is walking downtown.   S: Is the girl walking downtown?
               The man is driving to work.   Is the man driving to work?
               The student is taking the bus.   Is the student taking the bus?
               The professor is teaching the class.   Is the professor teaching the class?
               The child is playing in the yard.   Is the child playing in the yard?
               The instructor is teaching English.   Is the instructor teaching English?
               The waitress is working today.   Is the waitress working today?
               The woman is studying biology.   Is the woman studying biology?

3. M1   T: The young ladies are studying chemistry.
        S: Are the young ladies studying chemistry?
        T: We're going downtown this afternoon.
        S: Are we going downtown this afternoon?

(exercise continued on next page)

T: You're playing bridge tonight.
S: Are you playing bridge tonight?
T: The professors are meeting in the office.
S: Are the professors meeting in the office?
T: The men are buying new cars next week.
S: Are the men buying new cars next week?
T: They're playing bridge or poker.
S: Are they playing bridge or poker?
T: The children are playing basketball.
S: Are the children playing basketball?

4. M1T T: The ladies are walking to church.
        S: Are the ladies walking to church?
        T: You're going to the cafeteria.
        S: Are you going to the cafeteria?
        T: The man is walking to class.
        S: Is the man walking to class?
        T: The girl is driving home.
        S: Is the girl driving home?
        T: The boys are studying engineering.
        S: Are the boys studying engineering?
        T: We're having coffee after class.
        S: Are we having coffee after class?
        T: The lady is studying English.
        S: Is the lady studying English?

5. M1   Listen: Is the student taking English?   Yes, he is.
             Is the student teaching the class?   No, he isn't.
             Are the boys going home?   Yes, they are.
             Are they going downtown?   No, they aren't.

GENERALIZATION

The short answers are the same as Lesson One.

---

6. M2   T: Is (teacher) teaching the class?   S: Yes, ( ) is.
           Is (teacher) taking the class?   No, ( ) isn't.
           Is ( ) studying computer science?
           Is ( ) living in the dorm?
           Is ( ) studying karate?
           Are you and ( ) living in the dorm?
           Is ( ) living with her family?
           Are ( ) and ( ) learning Spanish?
           Is ( ) working in the library?
           Is ( ) wearing a green shirt?
           Am I speaking Russian?
           Is ( ) studying ( )?
           Is ( ) going to Iran this weekend?
           Are you and ( ) going to New York next weekend?

7. C T: Ask ( ) if he's living in the dorm.   S1: Are you living in the dorm?
                                                          S2: (Yes, I am.) (No, I'm not.)
      T: Ask ( ) if he and ( ) are studying English. S1: Are you studying English?
                                                          S2: (Yes, we are.) (No, we aren't.)
      T: Ask ( ) if he's studying English.
             Ask ( ) if she's having dinner at home tonight.
             Ask ( ) if he's going to the party Saturday night.
             Ask ( ) if he's coming to class tomorrow.
             Ask ( ) if ( ) and ( ) are going downtown today.
             Ask ( ) if he and ( ) are coming to class tomorrow.
             Ask ( ) if ( ) and I are studying Thai.
             Ask ( ) if he's walking downtown after class.
             Ask ( ) if he's playing bridge tomorrow.
             Ask ( ) if he and ( ) are driving home at 3:00.
             Ask ( ) if he's studying Arabic.
             Ask ( ) if ( ) and ( ) are playing soccer this weekend.

Part C.   *Negative*

```
Vocabulary

Nouns              Verbs
chemistry          attend
concert            read
magazine           write
```

Model: I'm not learning English.

1. M1 Rep: I'm not learning English.
             He isn't learning French.
             You aren't teaching the class.
             The girl isn't living with an American family.
             I'm not studying Arabic.
             We aren't going downtown.
             The men aren't going to class.
             She isn't staying in the dorm.

2. M1T T: I'm having lunch in the cafeteria.   S: I'm not having lunch in the cafeteria.

             The girl is learning English   The girl isn't learning English.
             The girl is walking downtown.   The girl isn't walking downtown.
             The women are working at the office.   The women aren't working at the office.
             The men are studying business.   The men aren't studying business.
             We're attending the concert.   We aren't attending the concert.
             He's studying computer science.   He isn't studying computer science.
             She's living with her family.   She isn't living with her family.
             They're having lunch in the cafeteria.   They aren't having lunch in the cafeteria.

40

***3. M1   T: He isn't studying engineering.   S: He's not studying engineering.
            We aren't watching the movie.   We're not watching the movie.
            They aren't working at home.   They're not working at home.
            She isn't going to class.   She's not going to class.
            You aren't studying business.   You're not studying business.
            The boy isn't talking with his friend.   The boy's not talking with his friend.

***4. M2   T: live in the dorm   S1:   ( ) is living in the dorm.
                                           S2:   I'm not living in the dorm. (I'm living
                                                 with a family.)

       T: study chemistry   S1:   ( ) is studying chemistry.
                                         S2:   I'm not studying chemistry. (I'm studying
                                               biology.)

       T: learn Korean
            have lunch at the cafeteria
            speak Spanish
            walk downtown
            work at the library
            teach English
            play bridge
            drive home
            go to the movies
            study Arabic
            read a magazine

5. C   T: Tell something you're doing now.
       S: (I'm studying English now.)
       T: Tell something you're not doing now.
       S: (I'm not studying Math.)
       T: Tell something ( ) is doing now.
            Tell something ( ) and ( ) are not doing.
            Tell something ( ) is not doing.
            Tell something ( ) and ( ) are doing.
            etc.

SECTION TWO

WH QUESTIONS

Part A.   *Who?*

Vocabulary		
Nouns	**Verbs**	
cards	come	sing
piano	cook	watch
TV	eat	write

41

Model: Who is studying?   The boy is.
        Who is playing bridge?   The students are.

1. M1   T: Someone is studying.   S: Who is studying?
                Someone is playing cards.   Who is playing cards?
                Someone is driving home.   Who is driving home?
                Someone is learning Spanish.   Who is learning Spanish?
                Someone is having dinner.   Who is having dinner?
                Someone is having a party.   Who is having a party?
                Someone is watching TV.   Who is watching TV?

2. M1   T: Some people are studying.   S: Who is studying?
                Some people are playing cards.   Who is playing cards?
                Some people are driving home.   Who is driving home?
                Some people are learning Spanish.   Who is learning Spanish?
                Some people are having dinner.   Who is having dinner?
                Some people are having a party.   Who is having a party?
                Some people are watching TV.   Who is watching TV?

GENERALIZATION

| Someone | is studying.

| Who | is studying?   Answer: Chen.
                                        Chen and Carlos.

The question *Who* used with the Present Continuous is almost always followed by
is. (The person who asks the question cannot know whether the answer will be
singular or plural.)

---

3. M1T   T: Someone is singing.   S: Who is singing?
                Some people are coming.   Who is coming?
                Someone is having a party.   Who is having a party?
                Some people are going downtown.   Who is going downtown?
                Someone is speaking Arabic.   Who is speaking Arabic?
                Some people are having coffee.   Who is having coffee?
                Someone is watching TV.   Who is watching TV?

4. M2   T: Someone is studying.   S1:   Who is studying?
                                                  S2:   ( ) is.
         T: Some people are watching TV.   S1:   Who is watching TV?
                                                  S2:   ( ) and ( ) are.
         T: Someone is walking downtown.
                Some people are playing bridge.
                Someone is playing the piano.
                Some people are learning English.
                Someone is having coffee.
                Someone is staying home.
                Some people are cooking dinner.

(exercise continued on next page)

Some people are going to a party.
Someone is studying in the library.
Someone is going to a movie.

5. M2   T: Ask ( ) if she's studying biology.   S1:   Are you studying biology?
                                                                 S2:   No, I'm not.
                                                                 S1:   Who is studying biology?
                                                                 S2:   ( ) and ( ) are.

         T: Ask ( ) if she's watching TV tonight.
                   Ask ( ) if he's having coffee after class.
                   Ask ( ) if he's going home at 2:00.
                   Ask ( ) if he's playing the piano this afternoon.
                   Ask ( ) if he's studying Korean.
                   Ask ( ) if he's walking downtown this afternoon.
                   Ask ( ) and ( ) if they're walking home after class.
                   Ask ( ) and ( ) if they're driving to the language lab.
                   Ask ( ) if he's studying the English book.
                   Ask ( ) if he's speaking Spanish.
                   Ask ( ) if he's going to the movies tonight.

Part B   *What?*

Model: What are those people doing? Having coffee.

1. M1   Rep: What is John studying?
         Sub: reading   S: What is John reading?
                  learning   What is John learning?
                  doing   What is John doing?
                  studying   What is John studying?
                  eating   What is John eating?
                  buying   What is John buying?
                  teaching   What is John teaching?

2. M1   Rep: What are Carlos and Chen doing?
         Sub: reading   S: What are Carlos and Chen reading?
                  the boys   What are the boys reading?
                  Sally   What is Sally reading?
                  eating   What is Sally eating?
                  cooking   What is Sally cooking?
                  Sally and Jane   What are Sally and Jane cooking?
                  the lady   What is the lady cooking?

GENERALIZATION

Question *Yes/No:*   Is John studying something?

Question *Wh:*   What is John studying?   Answer: Engineering.

---

3. M1   T: Is John studying something?   S: What is John studying?
                Is Chen eating something?   What is Chen eating?
                Is Carlos doing something?   What is Carlos doing?
                Are the girls cooking something?   What are the girls cooking?
                Are the boys studying something?   What are the boys studying?
                Is Bill buying something?   What is Bill buying?
                Is Sally studying something?   What is Sally studying?
                Are the men learning something?   What are the men learning?

4. M1   T: Carlos is studying.   S: What is Carlos studying?
                Bill is eating.   What is Bill eating?
                The boys are playing.   What are the boys playing?
                The women are cooking.   What are the women cooking?
                The man is teaching.   What is the man teaching?
                The girl is reading.   What is the girl reading?
                The students are learning.   What are the students learning?

5. M1T T: Someone is eating.   S: Who is eating?
                She's eating something.   What is she eating?
                They're buying something.   What are they buying?
                Some people are coming.   Who is coming?
                They are studying something.   What are they studying?
                Someone is cooking.   Who is cooking?
                She's cooking something.   What is she cooking?
                He's reading something.   What is he reading?

6. M2   T: Someone is eating.   S1:   Who is eating?
                                                       S2:   ( ) is.
                                                       S1:   What is ( ) eating?
                                                       S2:   (An apple.)
        T: Some people are studying.   S1:   Who is studying?
                                                       S2:   ( ) and ( ) are.
                                                       S1:   What are they studying?
                                                       S2:   (American politics.)
        T: Someone is teaching.
                Some people are cooking.
                Someone is playing.
                Someone is studying.
                Someone is learning.
                Some people are eating.
                Someone is reading.
                Some people are playing.
                Some people are reading.
                Someone is speaking.

Note: In normal conversation, the answer to a _Wh_ question usually omits most of the
        words in the question.

        A: What are you doing?
        B: Eating an apple.

        A: What are you eating?
        B: An apple.

***7. C   T: Ask ( ) what he's doing.   S1:   What are you doing?
                                                            S2:   (Studying English.)
            T: Ask ( ) what he's reading.   S1:   What are you reading?
                                                            S2:   (A novel.)
            T: Ask ( ) what he's learning.
                      Ask ( ) what he's studying.
                      Ask ( ) what he's doing.
                      etc.

Part C.   *Where?*

Model: Where are you going now? Downtown.

1. M1   Rep: Where are you going now?
         Sub: John   S: Where is John going now?
                 the men   Where are the men going now?
                 Carlos and Chen   Where are Carlos and Chen going now?
                 we   Where are we going now?
                 Sally   Where is Sally going now?
                 the student   Where is the student going now?
                 you   Where are you going now?

GENERALIZATION

Question *Yes/No:*   Are you going   somewhere?

Question *Wh:*   Where   are you going?

---

2. M1T   T: Is the man going somewhere?
         S: Where is he going?
         T: Are the men doing something?
         S: What are they doing?
         T: Is the girl walking somewhere?
         S: Where is she walking?
         T: Are the women cooking something?
         S: What are they cooking?
         T: Are the students driving somewhere?
         S: Where are they driving?
         T: Is the boy going somewhere?
         S: Where is he going?
         T: Is the woman reading something?
         S: What is she reading?
         T: Are Sally and Jim going somewhere?
         S: Where are they going?

3. M2 T: The man is walking.   S1: Where is he walking?

                                                                    S2: (Downtown.) (To the store.)

          T: The lady is working.
The boys are studying.
The men are eating.
The boys are attending the concert.
The girls are learning English.
The girl is driving.
We're studying tonight.
The students are playing cards.
The lady is cooking dinner.
The girls are having lunch.

4. M2 T: Someone is teaching.   S1: Who is teaching?

                                                                     S2: ( ) is.

                                                                    S1: What is (s)he teaching?

                                                                    S2: (English.)

                                                                   S1: Where is (s)he teaching?

                                                                     S2: (At Pitt.)

                 T: Some people are eating.   S1: Who is eating?

                                                                       S2: (The boys are.)

                                                                     S1: What are they eating?

                                                                      S2: (Lunch.)

                                                                        S1: Where are they eating lunch?

                                                                            S2: (At the cafeteria.)

          T: Someone is driving.
Some people are studying.
Someone is singing.
Some people are reading.
Someone is writing.
Someone is cooking.
Some people are playing.
Some people are writing.
Someone is studying.
Some people are singing.
Someone is eating.

5. C   T: Are you studying?   S: (Yes, I am.) (No, I'm not.)

                 What are you studying?   (English.) (Computer science.)

                 Where are you studying?
Are ( ) and ( ) reading?
What are they reading?
Where are they reading?
Where are you going after class?
Where is ( ) going after class?
Where are you going tomorrow?
Are you having coffee after class?
Who is studying Math?
What are you doing after class?
Who is going downtown this week?

***SECTION THREE

TAG QUESTIONS

Part A.   *Type I*

Model: It isn't crowded, is it? No, it isn't.

1. M1   Rep: It isn't crowded, is it?
                  She isn't studying, is she?
                  The boy isn't working, is he?
                  The lesson isn't difficult, is it?
                  The men aren't tall, are they?
                  The girls aren't working, are they?
                  The lessons aren't long, are they?
                  You aren't studying engineering, are you?
                  You aren't from the U.S., are you?

2. M1T   T: It isn't crowded.   S: It isn't crowded, is it?
                 She isn't studying.   She isn't studying, is she?
                 The boy isn't working.   The boy isn't working, is he?
                 The lesson isn't difficult.   The lesson isn't difficult, is it?
                 The men aren't tall.   The men aren't tall, are they?
                 The lessons aren't long.   The lessons aren't long, are they?
                 You aren't studying engineering.   You aren't studying engineering, are you?
                 You aren't from the U.S.   You aren't from the U.S., are you?

3. M1   Rep: It isn't crowded, is it?   No, it isn't.
                 The boy isn't studying, is he?   No, he isn't.
                 The men aren't working, are they?   No, they aren't.
                 We aren't going, are we?   No, we aren't.

GENERALIZATION

   The question at the end of a statement is a Tag Question. It is a conversational device to encourage agreement with the statement. The intonation is the same as a statement. The response to a tag question usually (but not always) is the same as the main verb. The tag questions are the same for Present Continuous as for sentences which have only the verb BE.

Statement (Negative)	Tag (Affirmative)	Response (Negative)
It isn't crowded,	is it?	No, it isn't.
He isn't teaching,	is he?	No, he isn't.
—	+	—

4. M1T   T: It isn't crowded.   G1:   It isn't crowded, is it?
                                                       G2:   No, it isn't.

          T: The lesson isn't difficult.   G1:   The lesson isn't difficult, is it?
                                                       G2:   No, it isn't.

          T: The man isn't tall.   G1:   The man isn't tall, is he?
                                                       G2:   No, he isn't.

          T: The ladies aren't spies.   G1:   The ladies aren't spies, are they?
                                                       G2:   No, they aren't.

          T: The lessons aren't long.   G1:   The lessons aren't long, are they?
                                                       G2:   No, they aren't.

          T: The boys aren't working.   G1:   The boys aren't working, are they?
                                                       G2:   No, they aren't.

          T: You aren't studying engineering.   G1:   You aren't studying engineering, are you?
                                                       G2:   No, I'm not.

          T: He isn't from Iran.   G1:   He isn't from Iran, is he?
                                                       G2:   No, he's not.

          T: They aren't from South America.   G1:   They aren't from South America, are they?
                                                       G2:   No, they're not.

          T: You aren't from the U.S.   G1:   You aren't from the U.S., are you?
                                                       G2:   No, I'm not.

5. M1T   T: Make an observation about the food.
                  —good   S1:   The food isn't good, is it?
                                                       S2:   No, it isn't.

          T: about the weather. —hot   S1:   The weather isn't hot, is it?
                                                       S2:   No, it isn't.

          T: about cars. —cheap   S1:   Cars aren't cheap, are they?
                                                       S2:   No, they aren't.

          T: about ( ). —studying Korean   S1:   ( ) isn't studying Korean, is he?
                                                       S2:   No, he isn't.

          T: about ( ) and ( ). —living in a hotel S1: ( ) and ( ) aren't living in a hotel, are they?
                                                       S2:   No, they aren't.

          T: about clothes. —cheap   S1:   Clothes aren't cheap, are they?
                                                       S2:   No, they aren't.

          T: about the teacher. —from Mexico   S1:   ( ) isn't from Mexico, is he?
                                                       S2:   No, he isn't.

          T: about the students. —from Canada   S1:   The students aren't from Canada, are they?
                                                       S2:   No, they aren't.

6. M2   T: Make an observation: about someone—
                  from Iran   S1:   (The boys) aren't from Iran, are they?
                                                       S2:   No, they aren't.

          T: about something—crowded   S1:   (The cafeteria) isn't crowded, is it?
                                                       S2:   No, it isn't.

          T: about something—big
                  about something—cheap
                  about something—cheap
                  about something—expensive
                  about someone—fat
                  about someone—thin
                  about something—pretty
                  about someone—a professor

(exercise continued on next page)

about someone—from England
about something—good
about something—cheap
about something—cheap

Part B.   *Type II*

Model: You're studying engineering, aren't you?

1. M1   Rep: You're studying engineering, aren't you?
                    You're studying English, aren't you?

                    He's going home, isn't he?
                    She's beautiful, isn't she?
                    The room is big, isn't it?

                    The boys are studying at home, aren't they?
                    The girls are working downtown, aren't they?

2. M1   T: You're studying engineering.   S: You're studying engineering, aren't you?
                    You're studying English.   You're studying English, aren't you?
                    He's going home.   He's going home, isn't he?
                    She's beautiful.   She's beautiful, isn't she?
                    The room is big.   The room is big, isn't it?
                    The boys are studying at home.   The boys are studying at home, aren't they?
                    The girls are working downtown.   The girls are working downtown, aren't
                                                               they?

GENERALIZATION

A: It isn't crowded, is it? No, it isn't.
        —   +   —

B: You're from Iran, aren't you? Yes, I am.
            +   —   +

---

3. M2   T: Is ( ) from Iran?   S1: (to another student): ( ) is from
                                                          Iran, isn't he?
                                                     S2: Yes, he is.

        T: Is ( ) living in the dorm?
                  Is ( ) studying ( )?
                  Are ( ) and ( ) from ( )?
                  etc.

4. M2 T: taking computer science classes   S1: You're taking computer science classes,
                                                              aren't you?
                                                        S2: Yes, I am.
       T: learning Thai   S1: You aren't learning Thai, are you?
                                                        S2: No, I'm not.

       T: living in the dorm
                 going to the party
                 buying a car
                 teaching English
                 taking Spanish
                 learning Turkish
                 learning English
                 having lunch at the cafeteria
                 going home after class
                 studying engineering
                 going on a vacation
                 learning about American culture

5. C   Situation: You're at a party with many people you don't know, but your friend told you
                   about some of the people. Using the tag questions start a conversation with the
                   people near you.

SUMMARY DIALOGUE

Bill: Where are you going now, Chen?

Chen: I'm playing bridge in the Union until the next class.

Bill: It's a good way to improve your English.

Chen: I'm not learning English; I'm learning bridge. You're going to the party Friday,
         aren't you?

Bill: Of course, I am. That beautiful girl in our biology class is going with me.

Chen: Great. See you later, Bill.

Bill: So long. Good luck in the game.

Chen: Thanks.

LESSON TWO — SUMMARY OF PATTERNS

Statement

Subject	BE	Verb -ing	Object	Place	Short Answer
I	am	studying	English	at the university.	
The girl	is	walking		downtown.	
We	are	taking	biology.		

Question (Who)

Subject	BE	Verb -ing	Object	Place	Short Answer
Who	is	playing	the piano?		The men are.
Who	is	living		in the dorm?	Mona is.

(NOTE: With this pattern it is always "Who *is?*")

Question (Yes/No)

BE	Subject	Verb -ing	Object	Place	Short Answer
Are	you	living		with a family?	Yes, I am./No.
Is	the man	having	coffee	in the cafeteria?	Yes, he is./No.

Question (What, Where)

QW	BE	Subject	Verb -ing	Object	Place	Short Answer
What	are	you	doing?			Playing bridge.
Where	are	you	going?			Downtown.
Where	is	the boy	having	lunch?		At the cafeteria.

Tag Questions

Subject	BE	Predicate	Tag	Short Answer
The cafeteria	is	crowded,	isn't it?	Yes, it is.
He	is	studying English,	isn't he?	Yes, he is.
You	are	taking biology,	aren't you?	Yes, I am.
The boys	are	living in the dorm,	aren't they?	Yes, they are.
The girls	aren't	staying with a family,	are they?	No, they aren't.
You	aren't	having coffee,	are you?	No, I'm not.
She	isn't	cooking dinner,	is she?	No, she's not.

NOTES

LESSON THREE

INTRODUCTION   Taking the bus

   Bill, Nancy, Chen and Carlos are going downtown on Saturday. They are waiting on the corner for the bus.

Chen: Are you *going to buy* a new camera?

Carlos: I'm going to look, but they're very expensive. What are you going to buy, Bill?

5   Bill: I'm not buying anything today. I'm broke.

(A bus is coming down the street.)

Chen: *Is this our bus?*

Nancy: No, it isn't. *Ours is number 73 or 75.*

Carlos: What's the fare?

10   Bill: Forty cents . . . exact change.

Carlos and Chen: Exact change?!

Bill: It's a quarter, a dime, and a nickel, or any combination of coins. It's faster and easier for the driver.

Nancy: It's safer, too. People aren't going to rob the driver if he isn't carrying change.

15   Bill: This bus is ours. Come on. It's pay-enter; put your money in now.

(A few minutes later.)

Carlos: *Which stop?*

Bill: Smithfield and Fifth . . . near the large department stores. It's the next stop. *Whose camera is this?*

20   Chen: It's mine. Thanks. I'm always losing my things . . . an "absent-minded professor."

Carlos: Which store are we going to?

Nancy: My favorite is Gimbel's.

OUTLINE OF PATTERNS   Example

Section One	"going to"	Future	

Part A	Statement		I'm going to look.
Part B	Question		Are you going to buy a camera?
	Negative Statement		I'm not going to buy anything.
Part C	*Wh* Questions		What are you going to buy?

Section Two   Possessive Adjectives and Pronouns

Part A	Adjectives	Where are my gloves?
Part B	Pronouns	Are these yours?
Part C	*Whose*	Whose gloves are on the seat?
Part D	*Who's/Whose*	

Section Three   Demonstrative Adjectives and Pronouns

Part A	Adjectives and Pronouns	my gloves/mine
Part B	*Which*	Which store . . .

COMPREHENSION QUESTIONS

1. What day is it?

2. Where are the students going?

*3. Is Carlos going to buy a camera?

4. What is Bill going to buy? (Why?)

5. What number is their bus?

6. What is the fare?

7. What is the exact change for 40 cents?

*8. Why do the buses require "exact change"? (Three reasons.)

9. When do they pay? (*Discuss.)

10. Where do they get off?

11. Who's the "absent-minded professor"? (Why?)

12. Which store are they going to? (Why?)

NOTES:

Line 5:   "broke" — informal expression — "no money"

Line 10:   Exact change. Many metropolitan areas have the "exact change" system. Ask
            your teacher about your area.

Line 15:   "pay-enter": Depending on the bus route, the fare is paid when you enter or
            when you leave the bus. There are usually signs in the front window, or ask
            the bus driver.

SECTION ONE

"GOING TO" — FUTURE

Part A.   *Statement*

Vocabulary

Nouns		Verbs
airplane	radio	fly
bus	sale	get (obtain)
cab	street car	graduate
camera	suit	look for
coat	taxi	practice
department store	term	see
dress	trip	sell
jacket	typewriter	travel
motorcycle		visit
pen		wait

Model: I'm going to buy a camera.

1. M1   Listen: I'm studying English now.
                   I'm going to study engineering next year.
                   I'm living in the dorm now.
                   I'm going to live with a family next year.

         Rep: I'm going to buy a camera.
                   I'm going to study engineering.
                   The girl is going to take a bus.
                   The men are going to study business.
                   You are going to learn English.
                   We are going to take a bus downtown.
                   Carlos is going to wait for the bus.

GENERALIZATION

This pattern *always* indicates a future time. The Lesson Two (Present Continuous) pattern requires a time word in order to indicate the future.

Lesson Two: The man is   walking downtown (now) (tomorrow).

Lesson Three: The man is going to walk   downtown.

Note that the Present Continuous is BE + verb *-ing*. The "going to" Future is BE + *going to* + the simple form of the verb.

---

2. M1   Rep: I'm going to buy a new camera.
       Sub: coat   S: I'm going to buy a new coat.
               pen   I'm going to buy a new pen.
               house   I'm going to buy a new house.
               car   I'm going to buy a new car.
               radio   I'm going to buy a new radio.
               TV   I'm going to buy a new TV.
               suit   I'm going to buy a new suit.
               dress   I'm going to buy a new dress.

3. M1   Rep: He's going to walk downtown.
       Sub: drive   S: He's going to drive downtown.
               home   He's going to drive home.
               take a bus   He's going to take a bus home.
               to school   He's going to take a bus to school.
               walk   He's going to walk to school.
               to church   He's going to walk to church.
               take a taxi   He's going to take a taxi to church.

4. M1T Rep: I'm going to buy a new typewriter.
       Sub: he   S: He's going to buy a new typewriter.
               she   She's going to buy a new typewriter.
               they   They're going to buy a new typewriter.
               we   We're going to buy a new typewriter.
               you   You're going to buy a new typewriter.
               I   I'm going to buy a new typewriter.

5. M1T Rep: He's going to buy a new car.
       Sub: radio   S: He's going to buy a new radio.
               get   He's going to get a new radio.
               I   I'm going to get a new radio.
               house   I'm going to get a new house.
               have   I'm going to have a new house.
               we   We're going to have a new house.
               you   You're going to have a new house.
               look for   You're going to look for a new house.
               suit   You're going to look for a new suit.

(exercise continued on next page)

Sub: she

        buy

        coat

S: She's going to look for a new suit.

      She's going to buy a new suit.

      She's going to buy a new coat.

6. M2   Situation: You have $50.00. The stores are having the end-of-season sales. What are you going to buy?

        T: What are you going to buy?

        S1:   I'm going to buy (a coat).

        S2:   I'm going to buy a coat and (a hat).

        S3:   I'm going to buy a coat and a hat and (a scarf).

        S4:   I'm going to buy a coat and a hat and a scarf and (a   ).

7. M2   Situation: You have $3000. You want to take a trip. Where are you going to travel?

        T: Where are you going to travel?

        S1:   I'm going to travel to (Mexico).

        S2:   He's going to travel to Mexico. I'm going to travel to (Paris).

        S3:   He's going to travel to Mexico. She's going to travel to Paris. I'm going to travel to (Caracas).

        S4:   (etc.)

Part B.   *Questions/Negative*

Model: Are you going to buy a camera? No, I'm not.

1. M1   Listen: John is going to buy a new car.

             Is John   going to buy a new car?

             The boys are going to walk downtown.

           Are the boys   going to walk downtown?

        Rep: Is John going to buy a new car?

        Sub: camera

             the girl

             coat

             the boys

             car

             we

             TV

             you

S: Is John going to buy a new camera?

      Is the girl going to buy a new camera?

      Is the girl going to buy a new coat?

      Are the boys going to buy a new coat?

      Are the boys going to buy a new car?

      Are we going to buy a new car?

      Are we going to buy a new TV?

      Are you going to buy a new TV?

GENERALIZATION

Lesson One: The man |is| a professor.

                                               Answer
                |Is| the man   a professor?   Yes, he is. No, he isn't.

Lesson Two: The man |is| walking downtown.

                |Is| the man   walking downtown?   Yes he is. No, he isn't.

Lesson Three: The man |is| going to walk downtown.

                |Is| the man   going to walk downtown?   Yes, he is. No, he isn't.

---

2. M1T   T: The student is going to buy a new suit.   S: Is the student going to buy a new suit?
              The boys are going to drive downtown.   Are the boys going to drive downtown?
              She's going to look for a camera.   Is she going to look for a camera?
              We're going to take a bus to school.   Are we going to take a bus to school?
              You're going to buy a new radio.   Are you going to buy a new radio?
              The men are going to travel to Canada.   Are the men going to travel to Canada?
              John is going to take a bus downtown.   Is John going to take a bus downtown?
              Carlos and Chen are going to look for a   Are Carlos and Chen going to look for
                new apartment.   a new apartment?

☐ Model: I'm not going to buy a camera.

3. M1   Rep: I'm not going to buy a camera.
        Sub: house   S: I'm not going to buy a house.
              car   I'm not going to buy a car.
              radio   I'm not going to buy a radio.
              TV   I'm not going to buy a TV.
              coat   I'm not going to buy a coat.
              suit   I'm not going to buy a suit.
              jacket   I'm not going to buy a jacket.

***4. M1   Rep: I'm not going to buy a camera.
          Sub: he   S: He isn't going to buy a camera.
                she   She isn't going to buy a camera.
                they   They aren't going to buy a camera.
                we   We aren't going to buy a camera.
                you   You aren't going to buy a camera.

GENERALIZATION

   The negative of the "going to" future tense is formed the same way as the negative in Lessons One and Two.

I'm not going to travel to California.
He isn't going to buy a new camera.   or   He's not going to buy a new camera.

58

5. C   T: Ask ( ) if she's going to buy a new coat.   S1:   Are you going to buy a new coat?
                                                                 S2:   (No, I'm not. I'm going to buy (a
                                                                       new dress).) (Yes, I am.)

        T: Ask ( ) if he and ( ) are going to travel to   S1:   Are you and ( ) going to travel to
                Caracas.   Caracas?
                                                                 S2:   (Yes, we are.) (No, we aren't. We're
                                                                       going to travel to (Paris).)

        T: Ask ( ) if she's going to take a bus downtown.
                Ask ( ) if she and ( ) are going to watch TV tonight.
                Ask ( ) if he's going to eat lunch at the department store.
                Ask ( ) if he and ( ) are going to buy a car.
                Ask ( ) if he's going to study engineering.
                Ask ( ) if ( ) is going to buy a Cadillac.
                Ask ( ) if ( ) is going to get a VW.
                Ask ( ) if ( ) and ( ) are going to study business.
                Ask ( ) if ( ) and ( ) are going to see the new movie.
                Ask ( ) if ( ) is going to play bridge tonight.

Part C.   *Wh Questions*

Model: What are you going to buy? A radio.

1. M1   Rep: What is the girl going to buy?
        Sub: sell   S: What is the girl going to sell?
                study   What is the girl going to study?
                cook   What is the girl going to cook?
                eat   What is the girl going to eat?
                buy   What is the girl going to buy?

2. M1   Rep: What are the boys going to study?
        Sub: you   S: What are you going to study?
                buy   What are you going to buy?
                the girl   What is the girl going to buy?
                study   What is the girl going to study?
                the men   What are the men going to study?

```
GENERALIZATION

        Is John going to buy    something  ?

        What  is John going to buy?              Answer:  A camera.
```

3. M1   T: Is Jane going to buy something?   S: What is she going to buy?
                Are the boys going to see something?   What are they going to see?
                Are you and I going to do something?   What are we going to do?
                Is Mrs. Jackson going to cook something?   What is she going to cook?
                Are the girls going to buy something?   What are they going to buy?
                Is Bill going to eat something?   What is he going to eat?
                Are Chen and Carlos going to study something? What are they going to study?

59

4. M1T T: ( ) is going to do something.   S: What is he going to do?
              ( ) and ( ) are going to buy something.   What are they going to buy?
              I'm going to cook something.   What are you going to cook?
              We're going to study something.   What are you going to study?
              ( ) is going to eat something.   What is he going to eat?
              ( ) and ( ) are going to study something. What are they going to study?

5. M2 T: Ask ( ) what he's going to study.   S1:   What are you going to study?
                                                S2:   I'm going to study (computer science).

        T: Ask ( ) what he's going to buy.
              Ask ( ) what he's going to have for dinner.
              Ask ( ) what he's going to do.
              Ask ( ) what he's going to write.
              Ask ( ) what he's going to read.
              Ask ( ) what he's going to cook.
              Ask ( ) shat he's going to have for lunch.
              Ask ( ) what he's going to do next weekend.

Notice: *Where*

                    Is Chen going to travel | someplace | ?

  | Where | is Chen going to travel?   Answer: To Paris.

---

6. M1 T: Chen is going to travel someplace.   S: Where is Chen going to travel?
              Chen is going to study someplace.   Where is Chen going to study?
              Bill is going to have dinner someplace.   Where is Bill going to have dinner?
              I'm going to buy a new coat someplace.   Where are you going to buy a new coat?
              We're going to have lunch someplace.   Where are we going to have lunch?
              They're going to buy a book someplace.   Where are they going to buy a book?
              Bill and Carlos are going to have a snack   Where are Bill and Carlos going to have
                someplace.   a snack?

7. M1T T: Chen is going to do something.   S: What is he going to do?
              Chen is going to study someplace.   Where is he going to study?
              The boys are going to travel someplace.   Where are they going to travel?
              The girls are going to buy something.   What are they going to buy?
              The man is going to cook something.   What is he going to cook?
              The women are going to have lunch someplace. Where are they going to have lunch?
              I'm going to buy something.   What are you going to buy?
              Chen and Carlos are going to have coffee   Where are they going to have coffee?
                someplace.

8. M2 T: Ask ( ) where he's going to have dinner. S1:   Where are you going to have dinner?
                                                S2:   I'm going to have dinner (at home).

              Ask ( ) where he's going to study.
              Ask ( ) where he's going to travel in April.
              Ask ( ) where he's going to buy a camera.

(exercise continued on next page)

T: Ask ( ) where he's going to have coffee.
          Ask ( ) where he's going to have lunch.
          Ask ( ) where he's going to study in April.
          Ask ( ) where he's going to buy a new coat.
          Ask ( ) where he's going to have a snack.
          Ask ( ) where he's going to play bridge.
          Ask ( ) where he's going to live next term.
          Ask ( ) where he's going to travel next summer.

Notice: *When*

          Is Chen going to buy a camera | sometime | ?

| When | is Chen going to buy a camera?   Answer: Today.

---

9. M1   Rep: When is Carlos going to buy a camera?

    Sub: a car   S: When is Carlos going to buy a car?

           Chen   When is Chen going to buy a car?

           the boys   When are the boys going to buy a car?

           a new motorcycle   When are the boys going to buy a new motorcycle?

           the girl   When is the girl going to buy a new motorcycle?

           a new dress   When is the girl going to buy a new dress?

           the ladies   When are the ladies going to buy a new dress?

           jacket   When are the ladies going to buy a new jacket?

           you   When are you going to buy a new jacket?

10. M1T   T: We're going to fly to Paris sometime.   S: When are you going to fly to Paris?

               We're going to travel someplace.   Where are you going to travel?

               We're going to buy something.   What are you going to buy?

               Chen is going to study something.   What is he going to study?

               Chen is going to have lunch sometime.   When is he going to have lunch?

               Chen is going to fly somewhere.   Where is he going to fly?

               The boys are going to have lunch somewhere.   Where are they going to have lunch?

               The boys are going to study sometime.   When are they going to study?

               The boys are going to buy a car someplace.   Where are they going to buy a car?

11. M1   Notice the expressions of future time:

    Rep: I'm going to fly to Paris next year.

    Sub: month   S: I'm going to fly to Paris next month.

           week   I'm going to fly to Paris next week.

           weekend   I'm going to fly to Paris next weekend.

           Tuesday   I'm going to fly to Paris next Tuesday.

           summer   I'm going to fly to Paris next summer.

           year   I'm going to fly to Paris next year.

           April   I'm going to fly to Paris next April.

(exercise continued on next page)

Rep:	He's going to buy a camera soon.		
Sub:	in a couple of weeks	S:	He's going to buy a camera in a couple of weeks.
	tomorrow		He's going to buy a camera tomorrow.
	in a couple of months		He's going to buy a camera in a couple of months.
	soon		He's going to buy a camera soon.
	in a couple of days		He's going to buy a camera in a couple of days.

Rep:	I'm going to return home in a few years.		
Sub:	in a few months	S:	I'm going to return home in a few months.
	in a few days		I'm going to return home in a few days.
	the day after tomorrow		I'm going to return home the day after tomorrow.
	the week after next		I'm going to return home the week after next.
	*this weekend.		I'm going to return home this weekend.
	*next weekend		I'm going to return home next weekend.

*Note:　The use of these terms is not consistent among native speakers. Be sure to set a date if there is confusion.

***12. M2　T:　Ask ( ) if he's going to buy a new car.　　S1:　Are you going to buy a new car?
　　　　　　　　　　　　　　　　　　　　　　　　　　　　S2:　Yes, I am.

　　　　　T:　Ask when.　　　　　　　　　　　　　　　S1:　When are you going to buy a new car?
　　　　　　　　　　　　　　　　　　　　　　　　　　　　S2:　I'm going to buy a new car (in a few years).

　　　　　T:　Ask ( ) if he's going to drive downtown.
　　　　　　　Ask ( ) if he's going to fly to Paris.
　　　　　　　Ask ( ) if he's going to leave (Pittsburgh).
　　　　　　　Ask ( ) if he's going to travel to (country).
　　　　　　　Ask ( ) if he's going to have lunch.
　　　　　　　Ask ( ) if he's going to practice in the language lab.
　　　　　　　Ask ( ) if he's going to study computer science.
　　　　　　　Ask ( ) if he's going to study engineering.
　　　　　　　Ask ( ) if he's going to buy a camera.
　　　　　　　Ask ( ) if he's going to study in the library.
　　　　　　　Ask ( ) if he's going to graduate.
　　　　　　　Ask ( ) if he's going to visit his friend.

Notice: *Who*

Someone	is going to buy a camera.	
Who	is going to buy a camera?	Answer:　Chen is.

---

13. M1　T:　Someone is going to fly to Paris.　　　　　S:　Who is going to fly to Paris?
　　　　　　　Someone is going to buy a Cadillac.　　　　　Who is going to buy a Cadillac?
　　　　　　　Someone is going to study engineering.　　　Who is going to study engineering?
　　　　　　　Someone is going to take a bus downtown.　　Who is going to take a bus downtown?
　　　　　　　Someone is going to have lunch in the Student　　Who is going to have lunch in the Student
　　　　　　　　Union.　　　　　　　　　　　　　　　　　　　Union?

(exercise continued on next page)

T: Someone is going to walk to the
language lab.
Someone is going to drive home.

S: Who is going to walk to the
language lab?
Who is going to drive home?

14. M2 T: Someone is going to travel to Paris.

S1: Who is going to travel to Paris?
S2: (Carlos) is.
S3: I'm not going to travel to Paris.
I'm going to travel to (London).

T: Someone is going to study computer science.
Someone is going to travel to (San Francisco).
Someone is going to take a bus downtown.
Someone is going to travel to (Hong Kong).
Someone is going to cook dinner.
Someone is going to travel to (Chicago).
Someone is going to travel to (Caracas).
Someone is going to buy a Cadillac.
Someone is going to buy a VW.
Someone is going to play bridge.

***15. M2   T: Someone is going to do something,
someplace, sometime.

S1: Who is going to do something,
someplace, sometime?
S2: ( ) is going to do something,
someplace, sometime.
S1: What is ( ) going to do someplace
sometime?
S2: ( ) is going to (buy a new coat)
someplace sometime.
S1: Where is ( ) going to buy a new coat
sometime?
S2: He's going to buy a new coat (at
Sears) sometime.
S1: When is he going to buy a new coat
at Sears?
S2: He's going to buy a new coat at
Sears (tomorrow).

16. C T: When are you going to buy a Rolls-Royce?
When are you going to visit Hollywood?
What are you going to do Saturday?
Where are you going to travel next year?
Who is going to visit you next weekend?
What are you going to do after class?
When are you going to get an airplane?
Where are you going to travel?
When are you going to travel to France?
When are you going to finish your work?
When are you going to see the new movie?
Who is going to help you next term?

S: (Never.) (In ten years.)

17. C   Situation: You and your friends have planned a surprise birthday party for "X" on Saturday. He knows there is to be a party and wonders why he has not been invited. You meet "X" in the Student Union. "X" tries to find out about the party by asking your plans for the weekend. You try to evade the questions.

         Example: "X":   (What are you going to do this weekend?)
                   You: (I don't know. How about you?)
                   "X":   (Are you going to study?)
                   You: (Probably. Professor ( ) is giving an exam next week.)
                   "X":   (Are you and "Y" going to see the new movie Saturday?)
                   You: (I don't know. Are you?)

SECTION TWO

POSSESSIVE ADJECTIVES AND PRONOUNS

Part A.   *Adjectives*

Vocabulary

           Nouns

chair	coins	notebook
change	gloves	purse
	nickel	

Model: Where are my gloves? Here they are.

1. M1   Listen: The black Ford is my car.
                 The blue Ford is your car.
                 The red Ford is her car.
                 The green Chevrolet is his car.
                 The white Chevrolet is our car.
                 The yellow Rolls-Royce is their car.

2. M1   Rep: The tall boy is my brother.

Sub:		S:	
her			The tall boy is her brother.
his			The tall boy is his brother.
our			The tall boy is our brother.
your			The tall boy is your brother.
their			The tall boy is their brother.
my			The tall boy is my brother.

GENERALIZATION

The possessive forms do not change from singular to plural and depend in all cases on the possessor.

---

3. M1   Rep: The boys are my friends.
         Sub: our   S: The boys are our friends.
                 my   The boys are my friends.
                 your   The boys are your friends.
                 their   The boys are their friends.
                 her   The boys are her friends.
                 his   The boys are his friends.

4. M1T   T: The book belongs to Bill.   S: It's his book.
                 The hat belongs to Nancy.   It's her hat.
                 The car belongs to me.   It's my car.
                 The gloves belong to us.   They're our gloves.
                 The cars belong to the boys.   They're their cars.
                 The house belongs to us.   It's our house.
                 The book belongs to you.   It's your book.

***5. M1T Rep: It's our class.
           Sub: (Bill's)   S: It's his class.
                  (Laura's)   It's her class.
                  (Sally's)   It's her class.
                  (Carlos and Chen's)   It's their class.
                  (the class and ( )'s)   It's our class.
                  (( )'s)   It's your class.

***6. M2   T: Is this your book?   S: (No, it's his book.)
                  Whose coat is this?   (It's my coat.)
                  Is this my glove?
                  Are those your books?
                  Whose hat is this?
                  Whose pens are these?
                  etc.

7. C   T: Which man is your teacher?   S: ( ) is my teacher.
                 Which boys are your friends?   ( ) and ( ) are my friends.
                 Which women are Laura's teachers?   ( ) and ( ) are her teachers.
                 Which room is our classroom?
                 Which girls are ( ) friends?
                 Which book is ( )'s English book?
                 Which paper is ( )'s homework paper?
                 Which glove is my right glove?
                 Which car is your car?
                 Which room is ( )'s room?
                 Which bus is your bus?

Part B   *Possessive Pronouns*

Model: Are these yours? Yes, they are.

1. M1   Listen: The blue Ford is my car.—The blue Ford is *mine.*
                   The blue Ford is her car.—The blue Ford is *hers.*
                   The blue Ford is our car.—The blue Ford is *ours.*

(exercise continued on next page)

The blue Ford is their car.—The blue Ford is *theirs.*
The blue Ford is your car.—The blue Ford is *yours.*
The blue Ford is his car.—The blue Ford is *his.*

2. M1 T: | The books are mine. | S: | They're mine. |
|-------------------------|----|----------------|
| The books are his. | | They're his. |
| The gloves are ours. | | They're ours. |
| The pencils are theirs. | | They're theirs.|
| The pennies are yours. | | They're yours. |
| The gloves are hers. | | They're hers. |

GENERALIZATION

These substitute words show possession. Note the ones which are different from the Adjectives:

my book—mine	our book—ours
his book—his	your book—yours
her book—hers	their book—theirs

---

3. M1T T: | The blue VW is my car. | It's mine. |
|---------------------------|-------------|
| The blue VW is her car. | It's hers. |
| The blue VW is our car. | It's ours. |
| The blue VW is their car. | It's theirs.|
| The blue VW is your car. | It's yours. |
| The blue VW is his car. | It's his. |
| The blue VW is my car. | It's mine. |

4. M1T T: | It's my class. | S: | It's mine. |
|-------------------|----|-------------|
| It's her class. | | It's hers. |
| It's his class. | | It's his. |
| It's our class. | | It's ours. |
| It's their class. | | It's theirs.|
| It's your class. | | It's yours. |

5. M1T T: | The blue book is Laura's. | S: | It's hers. |
|---------------------------------|----|-------------|
| The red book is ( )'s. | | It's his. |
| The black notebook is ( )'s. | | It's yours. |
| The brown coat is ( )'s. | | It's his. |
| The yellow pencil is ( ) and ( )'s. | | It's theirs.|
| The green book is ( ) and yours.| | It's ours. |

***6. M2 T: | Whose notebook is this/that? | S: | It's (hers). |
|------------------------------|----|---------------|
| Whose class is this? | | It's (ours). |
| Whose coat is this? | | |
| Whose books are these? | | |
| Whose pen is this? | | |
| Whose papers are those? | | |
| etc. | | |

66

Part C.   *Whose?*

Model: Whose gloves are on the seat? Mine.

1. M1   Rep: Whose pen is on the table?
         Sub: pens   S: Whose pens are on the table?
                 book   Whose book is on the table?
                 books   Whose books are on the table?
                 hat   Whose hat is on the table?
                 glove   Whose glove is on the table?
                 papers   Whose papers are on the table?

GENERALIZATION

> *Someone's* camera is on the table.
> *Whose*   camera is on the table?   Answer: Chen's.

Whose is the question word indicating possession. If the subject is known to everyone,
whose can be used as a substitute (pronoun).

> "I have my camera. Whose (camera) is on the table?"

---

2. M2   T: change/on the table   S1:   Whose change is on the table?
                                                     S2:   It's (hers).
                coats/on the chair   S1:   Whose coats are on the chair?
                                                     S2:   They're (theirs).
                book/on the floor
                notebooks/on the table
                coat/in the corner
                chairs/near the table
                pencil/on the floor
                papers/in the basket
                books/under the table
                pens/under the book
                scarf/on the chair
                paper/in the book

3. C   Situation: At the end of a very large party, before the guests have left, you find a number
                      of things—sweaters, coats, gloves, purses, combs, etc. Bring the things to your
                      guests and find out who they belong to.

Part D.   *Who's/Whose*

Note: The pronunciation of *who's* (Pronoun + BE) and *whose* (Possessive) is the same.
You must listen to the rest of the sentence and think about the context to be sure
which one is being used. *Who's* will be followed by an *-ing* form of the verb or an
adjective or a noun phrase. (Who's going?) (Who's a lawyer?) The possessive *whose*
will be followed by a noun. (Whose book?) or BE (Whose is this?)

***A.   Someone's going.   B.   Someone's book.
Who's   going?   John.   Whose   book? John's.

Someone's late.
Who's   late?   John.

Someone's from Libya.
Who's   from Libya?   Ali.

---

1. M1   Listen to the following sentences. Say A or B to indicate which pattern you hear.

T:		S:	
	Who's late?		(A)
	Whose book?		(B)
	Who's from the U.S.?		(A)
	Whose friends?		(B)
	Who's going?		(A)
	Whose papers?		(B)
	Whose coats?		(B)
	Whose letter?		(B)
	Who's in the class?		(A)
	Who's a dentist?		(A)

2. M1T Listen to the following questions. Say *Possession* if the question asks *whose*. Say
Person if the question asks *who*.

T:		S:	
	Whose book is this?		(Possession)
	Who's going downtown?		(Person)
	Whose is this?		(Possession)
	Who's a doctor?		(Person)
	Whose is the VW?		(Possession)
	Who's a teacher?		(Person)
	Who's the tall girl?		(Person)
	Whose pen is on the table?		(Possession)
	Who's going to buy a book?		(Person)
	Whose friends are here?		(Possession)
	Who's the tall man?		(Person)
	Whose are on the chair?		(Possession)
	Who's late?		(Person)

3. M2 T: Who's late?   S: (John)
           Whose books?   (Mine)
           Who's going to buy a Rolls-Royce?
           Whose VW?
           Who's going to have lunch?
           Whose paper?
           Who's always on time?
           Who's never late?
           Whose friend is going to come?
           Who's the tall man?
           Who's from the Middle East?
           Whose car is the VW?
           Who's in the class?
           Whose are those nickels?

4. C   T: Find out if anyone is from Iran.   S1: Who's from Iran?
                                                 S2: (Sherazi and Kambiz.)
       T: Find out who the books belong to.   S1: Whose books are (on the table)?
                                                 S2: (Mine.)
       T: Find out if anyone is going to buy a Rolls-Royce.
           Fine out who owns the coat.
           Find out who the blue VW belongs to.
           Find out who is having coffee after class.
           Find out if anyone is living with a family.
           Find out if anyone is going to travel to New York this weekend.
           Find out if anyone is from South America.
           Find out who the change belongs to.
           Find out who is going to the party on Saturday.
           Find out if anyone is going to be an engineer.
           Find out who is studying ( ).
           Find out if the coins belong to anyone.

SECTION THREE

DEMONSTRATIVE ADJECTIVES AND PRONOUNS

Part A.   *Demonstrative Adjectives and Pronouns*

Vocabulary

Nouns

box   hat
cufflink   ring
earring   scarf
*gadget   sweater
                        *thing

*Use these words to ask about small objects for which
you don't know the vocabulary.

Model: This bus is ours.
              That car is mine.

Previous Pattern: *The* car is a VW.
    New Pattern: *This* car is a VW.

***1. M1   Listen: This book is a grammar book.
                     That book is a reading book.
                     This pencil is hers.
                     That pencil is his.

2. M1   Rep: This big book on the table is mine.

Sub:	S:
small	This small book on the table is mine.
that	That small book on the table is mine.
box	That small box on the table is mine.
this	This small box on the table is mine.
on the desk	This small box on the desk is mine.
that	That small box on the desk is mine.
yours	That small box on the desk is yours.
this	This small box on the desk is yours.

GENERALIZATION

    this = near the speaker
    that = far from the speaker

These words substitute for *the* to indicate location of the object. They are generally used with (things) except in the phrase for introductions: "This is my friend, Tom."

---

3. M2   T: notebook   S: (This/that) notebook is mine. (That/this) is (his).
              pen   (That) pen is mine. (This) is hers.
              coat
              pencil
              book
              scarf
              purse
              etc.

4. M1   Rep: This car is mine.   These cars are mine.
                   This book is hers.   These books are hers.
                   This coat is his.   These coats are his.

                   That pen is yours.   Those pens are yours.
                   That glove is hers.   Those gloves are hers.
                   That car is ours.   Those cars are ours.
                   That book is theirs. Those books are theirs.

GENERALIZATION

Singular	Plural
this	these
that	those

this/that; these/those can be used as substitute words when the subject is known to everyone. They substitute for *things* except in introductions: "These are my parents, Mr. and Mrs. Newton."

---

5. M1T   T: This car is mine.   S: These cars are mine.
                That book is mine.   Those books are mine.
                That car is mine.   Those cars are mine.
                That book is mine.   Those books are mine.
                This pen is mine.   These pens are mine.
                This coat is mine.   These coats are mine.
                That glove is mine.   Those gloves are mine.

***6. M1T   T: VW—here—a good car.   S: This new VW is a good car.
                   Cadillac—there   That new Cadillac is a good car.
                   Chevys—here   These new Chevys are good cars.
                   Ford—here   This new Ford is a good car.
                   Datsuns—there   Those new Datsuns are good cars.
                   Rambler—there   That new Rambler is a good car.
                   Fiats—here   These new Fiats are good cars.
                   Volvos—there   Those new Volvos are good cars.
                   Oldsmobile—here   This new Oldsmobile is a good car.

7. M2   Model: This is my friend, Nancy.
                   These are my friends, Chen and Carlos.

         T: Introduce the person next to you.   S: This is (Laura). She's from
               Tell something about him.   Colombia. She's studying (English)
                                                              now. She's going to study (home
                                                              economics) next year.

         T: Introduce two people to someone. Say
               something about them.
               etc.

***8. M2   Listen: What's this?   It's a cufflink.
                     What's that?   It's an earring.
                     What are these?   They're earrings.
                     What are those?   They're cufflinks.

            Note: Use this pattern to expand your vocabulary.

            (Picture Cue)
            S1:   What's this?   S2: It's a (   ).
                   What's this gadget?
                   What's this thing?
                   What are these?
                   What are those?

Part B.   *Which?*

1. M1 T: This car is mine.   S: Which car is his?
                These papers are mine.   Which papers are his?
                This book is mine.   Which book is his?
                These notebooks are mine.   Which notebooks are his?
                This hat is mine.   Which hat is his?
                Those cufflinks are mine.   Which cufflinks are his?
                That pen is mine.   Which pen is his?
                Those rings are mine.   Which rings are his?

GENERALIZATION

This   book is mine.
Which   book is yours?

The question *which* precedes a noun or substitutes for it (*which is yours?*). There is always a choice of items implied.

---

2. M2 T: books   S1:   (These) books are (mine). Which
                                                        books are (yours)?
                                      S2:   (These) are.

      T: book   S1:   (This) book is (his). Which book is
                                                            (yours)?
                                      S2:   (This) is.

      T: pencil
                hat
                gloves
                ring
                notebook
                pen
                pencils
                coat
                sweater
                English book

***3. C   (Picture Cue)
         Situation: You inherited a lot of money. Which things are you going to buy?

        S1:   (I'm going to buy that big house and these white boots.) (Which things are
                you going to buy?)
        S2:   (This blue VW and those dresses.)
                etc.

***4. C T: Here are a lot of cars.   S1:   Which car (are you going to buy) (are you
                                                      buying)?
                                          S2:   (The VW.) (The big car.) (The blue VW.)
      T: There are a lot of houses for sale.
                Here are some new novels.

(exercise continued on next page)

T: There are a lot of apartments for rent.
         There are some movies in the paper.
         Here is a list of restaurants.
         There are a lot of coats on the bed.
         Here are some scarves.
         Here are some cars for sale.
         There are a lot of books on the table.
         There are a lot of TV programs tonight.

***SUMMARY DIALOGUE

Situation: Two old friends meet after several years. The conversation is something
   like this:

Chen: Bill Jackson! How are you? *

Bill: Just fine, Chen. How are you? *

Chen: Great, thanks. What are you doing now?

Bill: I'm taking courses for a Masters in business. How about you? *

Chen: I'm finishing my Masters in engineering. I'm going to graduate in April.

Bill: That's great! What are you going to do then?

Chen: I'm going to return home. How about you? * When are you going to get your
            degree?

Bill: In August. Chen, I'm going to be late for class. Are you living in the same apartment? **

Chen: Yes, I am. See you later.

Bill: O.K. So long.

*Note: When the exact words of greetings or questions are used by a second speaker, the
          intonation changes. Listen carefully. Also note that "How are you" is a greeting
          for friends you haven't seen for some time. It is not usually in inquiry about
          health unless you know the person has been sick.

**Note: When this question follows the excuse for leaving, the speaker implies that he will
          call the other person.

LESSON THREE – SUMMARY OF PATTERNS

	Subject	BE	Going to	Verb	Completer	Short Answer
Statement	Chen	is	going to	buy	a camera.	
	I	am	going to	travel	to France.	
Question (Who)	Who	is	going to	buy	a house?	Mr. Jones is.
BE — Question (Yes/No)	Are · you		going to	visit	your friend?	Yes, I am. / No, I'm not.
QW — Question (When)	When · are · you		going to	visit	your friend?	Next week.
(Where)	Where · are · you		going to	travel?		To Paris.

DEMONSTRATIVES

Adjectives		
This book	is	a good novel.
That book	is	an English book.

Pronouns		
This/That	is	an English book.

Questions		
Which (book)	is	a good novel?

POSSESSIVES

Adjectives		
My book	is	blue.

Pronouns		
Mine	is	blue.

Questions		
Whose (book)	is	blue?

LESSON FOUR

INTRODUCTION   Bill Jackson's family

    Bill Jackson lives with his family in a suburb of the city. Bill commutes to school every day; he takes a street car and a bus, and he arrives at the university at nine o'clock. He stays at the university until five o'clock and then he goes home again. Bill works at a gas station on weekends. He likes science classes, sports, parties and girls. He doesn't like English class.

5   He studies hard, but he doesn't get good grades in English.

    Bill has a younger sister. Her name is Jane. She's a sophomore in high school. Jane is going to go to the university in three years.

    Mrs. Jackson teaches in the elementary school of their suburb and Mr. Jackson works in an office downtown. They have a car, but Mr. Jackson doesn't drive downtown. The traffic is

10   terrible, and parking places are very expensive. Besides, the Jackson's car doesn't increase the pollution in the city.

    Bill is studying in the living room. He is writing a composition for English class . . .

Bill: Do you have the dictionary, Jane? How do you spell "metamorphosis"?

Jane: I don't know. What does it mean?

15   Bill: Never mind the meaning . . . I want the spelling.

Jane: You always use big words, but they don't impress your professors. *Everyone knows that.*

Bill: O.K., O.K. I don't need a lecture.

OUTLINE OF PATTERNS   Example

      Section One   Simple Present Tense

          Part A   Third Person Singular
              Statement   Bill lives with his family.
              Interrogative and Short Answers   Does he . . . ? Yes, he does.
              Negative   He doesn't drive . . .
          Part B   Third Person Plural
              Statement   The boys study hard.
              Interrogative and Short Answers   Do they . . . ? No, they don't.
              Negative   Big words don't impress . . .

      Section Two   *Wh* Questions

          Who?   Who studies English?
          What?   What does it mean?
          Where?   Where does Bill live?
          When?   When does Bill study?

      Section Three   Tag Questions

          Part A   Type I   He doesn't drive, does he?
          Part B   Type II   They speak English, don't they?

      Section Four   Indefinite Pronouns

       Every-/no- in subject position
          Part A   Statements   Everyone knows that. No one is here.
          Part B   *Yes/No* Questions   Does anyone have . . . ?

COMPREHENSION QUESTIONS

  1. Does Bill live in the dorm?

  2. What does Bill do every day?

  3. How does he commute to school?

  4. What does he do at 5:00?

  5. Does Bill like English? (*Why?)

  6. What does Bill do on the weekends?

  7. Does Bill have an older or a younger sister?

  8. Is Jane at the university now? When is she going to go?

  9. What does Mrs. Jackson do?

10. Where does Mr. Jackson work?

11. Does he drive a car to work? (*Why? 3 reasons.)

12. What is Bill doing now?

*13. What does Bill ask Jane?

*14. Do professors like big words?

*15. What does Jane think?

*16. What do you think?

*17. Discuss students' families.

NOTES

Line 2: Clock time can be written in two ways: nine o'clock or 9:00, nine-thirty or 9:30. In the exercises which follow, it is written with numbers.

*** See Instructor's Manual

SECTION ONE

SIMPLE PRESENT TENSE

Part A   *Third Person Singular*

Vocabulary

Nouns		Verbs	Adjectives	Adverb
bicycle	mile	commute	older	hard
commercial	mink coat	increase	younger	
composition	mistake	make		
daughter	pollution	please		
dog	sister	want		
elementary	sports	wash		
school	suburb			
gas station	watch			
job				
lecture				

□ Statement

Model: Bill Jackson lives with his family.

1. M1 Rep: Bill Jackson lives with his family.
       Sub: stays at school until 5:00.   S: Bill Jackson stays at school until 5:00.
              lives in a suburb   Bill Jackson lives in a suburb.
              studies engineering   Bill Jackson studies engineering.
              has a sister   Bill Jackson has a sister.
              rides on the street car   Bill Jackson rides on the street car.
              drives the family car   Bill Jackson drives the family car.
              arrives at 9:00   Bill Jackson arrives at 9:00.

2. M1 Rep: Jane likes English class.
       Sub: writes compositions   S: Jane writes compositions.
              walks a mile every day   Jane walks a mile every day.
              works on weekends   Jane works on weekends.
              takes a bus to school   Jane takes a bus to school.
              commutes to school   Jane commutes to school.

3. M1 Rep: Mrs. Jackson teaches elementary school.
       Sub: watches TV in the evening   S: Mrs. Jackson watches TV in the evening.
             washes the clothes on Saturday   Mrs. Jackson washes the clothes on
                                                          Saturday.

             teaches her daughter to cook   Mrs. Jackson teaches her daughter to cook.
             pleases the children in her class   Mrs. Jackson pleases the children in
                                                          her class.

             watches all the commercials on TV   Mrs. Jackson watches all the commercials
                                                          on TV.

***GENERALIZATION

The simple present tense, third person, (he, she, it) has three pronunciations:
[z] , [s] , [iz] .

Example: he arrives   [z]
              he works   [s]
              he watches   [iz]

---

4. M1 Rep: Bill lives with his family.
       Sub: Jane   S: Jane lives with her family.
             Chen   Chen lives with his family.
             Sally   Sally lives with her family.
             the boy   The boy lives with his family.
             the girl   The girl lives with her family.
             Mary   Mary lives with her family.
             Carlos   Carlos lives with his family.
             Alice   Alice lives with her family.

5. M1 Rep: Bill has a sister.
       Sub: a car   S: Bill has a car.
             a dog   Bill has a dog.
             a job   Bill has a job.
             a thousand dollars   Bill has a thousand dollars.
             a Rolls-Royce   Bill has a Rolls-Royce.
             a Ford   Bill has a Ford.

6. M1T Rep: Mary commutes to school every day.
       Sub: drive downtown   S: Mary drives downtown every day.
             watch TV   Mary watches TV every day.
             go to school   Mary goes to school every day.
             study hard   Mary studies hard every day.
             walk a mile   Mary walks a mile every day.
             work in an office   Mary works in an office every day.
             have lunch at home   Mary has lunch at home every day.
             take a street car   Mary takes a street car every day.
             arrive at 9:00   Mary arrives at 9:00 every day.

GENERALIZATION

Previous Patterns

Lesson One:	Bill Jackson	is a student.
Lesson Two:	Bill	is studying in the living room.
Lesson Three:	Jane	is going to study at the university.

New Pattern

| Lesson Four: | Bill | studies hard. |

The Simple Present tense is used for actions which are habitual. It differs from the Present Continuous which in Lesson Two denotes actions which are happening now.

Most verbs add -s or -es to the simple verb for the third person. Note that *have* is irregular: Bill has a job.

***7. M1T Situation: Turn to Introduction to Lesson Four. These questions are about the Jacksons. Answer "yes" or "no."

T:	Does Bill take a street car to school?	S:	Yes.
	Is he going to school right now?		No.
	Does Bill work at a gas station?		Yes.
	Is he working at a gas station now?		No.
	Does Bill study English?		Yes.
	Is he studying English now?		Yes.
	Does Mrs. Jackson teach school?		Yes.
	Is she teaching now?		No.
	Does Mr. Jackson work downtown?		Yes.
	Is he working now?		No.

8. M1T   T: Does Jane go to school or to work every day?   S: She goes to school every day.

Does Mr. Jackson work at home or in an office?
Does Bill arrive at 9:00 or 10:00 every day?
Does Bill have a younger sister or an older sister?
Does Mr. Jackson have a car or an airplane?
Does Bill live with his family or in the dorm?
Does Jane go to high school or to the university?
Does Chen live with a family or in the dorm?
Does Carlos live in the dorm or with a family?
Does Mr. Jackson drive to work or take a bus every day?
Does Mrs. Jackson teach at a high school or an elementary school?

9. M1T   Rep: Bill works downtown every day.
   Sub:

now	S:	Bill is working downtown now.
tomorrow		Bill is going to work downtown tomorrow.
every day		Bill works downtown every day.
next week		Bill is going to work downtown next week.

(exercise continued on next page)

Sub: on weekends   Bill works downtown on weekends.

every Saturday   Bill works downtown every Saturday.

the day after tomorrow   Bill is going to work downtown the
day after tomorrow.

10. M1T Rep: Mary commutes to school in the city.

Sub: now   S: Mary is commuting to school in the city now.

every day   Mary commutes to school in the city every day.

next month   Mary is going to commute to school in the city
next month.

on Mondays   Mary commutes to school in the city on Mondays.

on Tuesdays and Thursdays   Mary commutes to school in the city on Tuesdays
and Thursdays.

next year   Mary is going to commute to school in the city
next year.

***11. M2 T: What is Jane doing now?   S: (She's sitting in the living room.)

What does Jane do every day?   (She goes to high school.)

What does Bill do on weekends?

What does Bill do every day?

What is he doing now?

What is Jane going to do in two years?

What does Mr. Jackson do every day?

Where does Mrs. Jackson teach?

Where does Jane go to school?

What time does Bill arrive at the university?

What time does Bill go home?

12. C T: What does your father do?   S: (He works in an office in Bangkok.)

Does your father work at home or in an office?

What does ( ) study?

Where does ( ) live?

What time does ( ) begin classes every day?

Where does ( ) go to class?

Does ( ) walk or take a bus to class?

Does ( ) have a (VW) or a Rolls-Royce?

Does ( ) eat lunch at home or in the cafeteria?

Does ( ) live in the dorm or with a family?

Does ( ) study at home or in the library?

Does your family have an American car or a ( ) car?

Does ( ) have an American car or a foreign car?

☐ INTERROGATIVE AND SHORT ANSWERS

Model: Does Bill live in the dorm? No, he doesn't.

13. M1 Rep: Does Bill have a dog?   No, he doesn't.
               Does Bill have a younger sister?   Yes, he does.
               Does Mary work downtown?   No, she doesn't.
               Does Mr. Jackson drive to work?   No, he doesn't.
               Does the girl watch TV?   Yes, she does.
               Does the woman teach elementary school? Yes, she does.
               Does the boy go to work?   No, he doesn't.

GENERALIZATION

	Statement/Question	Short Answer
Lesson one:	The campus is confusing.	
	Is the campus confusing?	Yes, it is.
Lesson Two:	Bill is walking downtown.	
	Is Bill walking downtown?	Yes, he is.
Lesson Three:	The boys are going to study.	
	Are the boys going to study?	No, they aren't.
Lesson Four:	Bill work[s] at a gas station.	
	Do[es] Bill work at a gas station?	Yes, he does.
	Mary drive[s] to school.	
	Do[es] Mary drive to school?	No, she doesn't.
	The boy ha[s] a dog.	
	Do[es] the boy have a dog?	Yes, he does.

Previous Pattern: All the statement patterns with BE in Lessons One through Three form questions by placing the BE form in front of the subject.

New Pattern: Sentences with simple present verb forms form questions by placing *do* plus the 3rd singular verb ending (*does*) in front of the subject.

---

14. M1T T: Mary works in an office.   S: Does Mary work in an office?
               The boy works at a gas station.   Does the boy work at a gas station?
               Bill has a younger sister.   Does Bill have a younger sister?
               The girl watches TV every day.   Does the girl watch TV every day?
               The woman teaches high school.   Does the woman teach high school?
               Mr. Jackson drives to work.   Does Mr. Jackson drive to work?
               Jane goes to high school.   Does Jane go to high school?
               Bill likes English.   Does Bill like English?
               Mary has a watch.   Does Mary have a watch?
               The boy has a dog.   Does the boy have a dog?
               The lady has a mink coat.   Does the lady have a mink coat?
               Mr. Jackson has a small car.   Does Mr. Jackson have a small car?

15. M1T Rep: Does Mary work in an office?

Sub:

Bill	**S:**	Does Bill work in an office?
drive downtown		Does Bill drive downtown?
arrive at school at 9:00		Does Bill arrive at school at 9:00?
the boy		Does the boy arrive at school at 9:00?
Mary		Does Mary arrive at school at 9:00?
like English		Does Mary like English?
like sports		Does Mary like sports?
work at a gas station		Does Mary work at a gas station?
Bill		Does Bill work at a gas station?
the boy		Does the boy work at a gas station?
have a car		Does the boy have a car?
have a younger sister		Does the boy have a younger sister?
the girl		Does the girl have a younger sister?
Chen		Does Chen have a younger sister?

16. M1T T:

Does Mrs. Jackson teach school?	**S:** Yes, she does.
Does Mrs. Jackson teach high school?	No, she doesn't.
Does Mr. Jackson work downtown?	Yes, he does.
Does Mr. Jackson drive downtown?	No, he doesn't.
Does Jane like school?	Yes, she does.
Does Bill like science?	Yes, he does.
Does Bill like English?	No, he doesn't.
Does Mr. Jackson take a street car to work?	Yes, he does.
Does Bill arrive at school at 10:00?	No, he doesn't.
Does Bill arrive at school at 9:00?	Yes, he does.
Does Bill have an older sister?	No, he doesn't.
Does Jane have an older brother?	Yes, she does.

***17. M1T T:

The campus is confusing.	**G1:** Is the campus confusing?
	G2: Yes, it is.
The men are going to work.	**G1:** Are the men going to work?
	G2: Yes, they are.
Bill works in a gas station.	**G1:** Does Bill work in a gas station?
	G2: Yes, he does.
Jane goes to high school.	**G1:** Does Jane go to high school?
	G2: Yes, she does.
The man is driving to work.	**G1:** Is the man driving to work?
	G2: Yes, he is.
Bill is going to write a composition.	**G1:** Is Bill going to write a composition?
	G2: Yes, he is.
Mrs. Jackson teaches school.	**G1:** Does Mrs. Jackson teach school?
	G2: Yes, she does.
The streets are dirty.	**G1:** Are the streets dirty?
	G2: Yes, they are.
The car increases pollution.	**G1:** Does the car increase pollution?
	G2: Yes, it does.

18. M2 T: Does ( ) walk to school?   S: (Yes, she does.) (No, she doesn't.)
               Does ( ) live with a family?   (Yes, he does.) (No, he doesn't.)
               Is ( ) from Iran?   (Yes, he is.) (No, he isn't.)
               Does ( ) teach English?
               Does ( ) commute to school?
               Is ( ) speaking Spanish now?
               Does ( ) come from ( )?
               Does ( ) have an American car?
               Is ( ) living in the dorm?
               Does ( ) live near the university?
               Does ( ) have a car?
               Does ( ) have an English book?
               Is ( ) going to study engineering?

19. M2 T: Ask ( ) if ( ) commutes to school.   S1:   Does ( ) commute to school?
                                                           S2:   (Yes, she does.) (No, she doesn't. She
                                                                 lives in Oakland.)

               Ask ( ) if ( ) is going to study biology.   S1:   Is ( ) going to study biology?
                                                           S2:   (Yes, he is.) (No, he isn't. He's going
                                                                 to study chemistry.)

               Ask ( ) if ( ) is living in the dorm.   S1:   Is ( ) living in the dorm?
                                                           S2:   (Yes, he is.) (No, he isn't. He has an
                                                                 apartment.)

               Ask ( ) if ( ) has a Cadillac.
               Ask ( ) if ( ) works in a gas station.
               Ask ( ) if ( ) is learning Spanish.
               Ask ( ) if ( ) wants a bicycle.
               Ask ( ) if ( ) comes from ( ).
               Ask ( ) if ( ) is going to learn German.
               Ask ( ) if ( ) wants a Rolls-Royce.
               Ask ( ) if ( ) works in an office.
               Ask ( ) if ( ) is going to have lunch in the Student Union.
               Ask ( ) if ( ) walks to school.
               Ask ( ) if ( ) has a car.

□ NEGATIVE STATEMENTS

Model: Mr. Jackson doesn't drive to work.

20. M1 Rep: Mr. Jackson doesn't drive to work.
               Bill doesn't have a car.
               Mrs. Jackson doesn't teach high school.
               The woman doesn't want a mink coat.
               The woman doesn't need a Cadillac.
               The student doesn't like English.
               The car doesn't increase pollution.

GENERALIZATION

Lesson Two:	Affirmative	Bill is	driving downtown now.
	Negative	Bill isn't	driving downtown now.
Lesson Four:	Affirmative	Bill	drives to work every day.
	Negative	Bill doesn't	drive to work every day.

The third singular uses *does* + *not* to form negatives. It is usually pronounced (and written) [dəz nt] *doesn't*. It may also be pronounced (and written) *does not.*

21. M1 Rep: Mary doesn't walk downtown every day.
    Sub: go   S: Mary doesn't go downtown every day.
          take a taxi   Mary doesn't take a taxi downtown every day.

          drive   Mary doesn't drive downtown every day.
          take the bus   Mary doesn't take the bus downtown every day.

          eat lunch   Mary doesn't eat lunch downtown every day.

          walk   Mary doesn't walk downtown every day.

22. M1 Rep: The lady doesn't want a mink coat.
    Sub: man   S: The man doesn't want a mink coat.
          need   The man doesn't need a mink coat.
          Cadillac   The man doesn't need a Cadillac.
          student   The student doesn't need a Cadillac.
          drive   The student doesn't drive a Cadillac.
          VW   The student doesn't drive a VW.
          girl   The girl doesn't drive a VW.
          have   The girl doesn't have a **VW**.

23. M1T T: Bill makes mistakes.   S: Bill doesn't make mistakes.
            Chen lives with a family.   Chen doesn't live with a family.
            Carlos has a Rolls-Royce.   Carlos doesn't have a Rolls-Royce.
            Jane has a bicycle.   Jane doesn't have a bicycle.
            The bicycle increases pollution. The bicycle doesn't increase pollution.
            Chen speaks French.   Chen doesn't speak French.
            Mr. Jackson teaches school.   Mr. Jackson doesn't teach school.
            Mrs. Jackson wants a mink coat. Mrs. Jackson doesn't want a mink coat.
            Bill needs a lecture.   Bill doesn't need a lecture.

24. C T: Ask about ( ) and *school.*   S1: (Does ( ) commute to school?)
                                          S2: (Yes, she does.) (No, she doesn't. She lives in the dorm.)

           Ask about ( ) and *English.*   S1: (Does ( ) study English?)
                                          S2: (Yes, he does.)

           Ask about ( ) and *a family.*
           Ask about ( ) and *the dorm.*
           Ask about ( ) and *a gas station.*
                    (exercise continued on next page)

84

T: Ask about ( ) and *a car.*
        Ask about ( ) and *a younger sister.*
        Ask about ( ) and *downtown.*
        Ask about ( ) and *Oakland.*
        Ask about ( ) and *a bicycle.*
        Ask about ( ) and *a Cadillac.*
        Ask about ( ) and *a job.*
        Ask about ( ) and (country).
        Ask about ( ) and *an older brother.*

***25. C T: Ask about ( ) and *English now.*   S1:   (Is ( ) studying English now?)
                                                             S2:   (Yes, she is.)

          Ask about ( ) and *English next year.*   S1:   (Is ( ) going to study English next year?)
                                                             S2:   (No, she isn't. She's going to study physics.)

          Ask about ( ) and *school every day.*   S1:   (Does ( ) go to school every day?)
                                                             S2:   (No, she doesn't. She doesn't have class
                                                                    on Wednesdays.)

        Ask about ( ) and *a family* this week/next month.
        Ask about *the little car* and *pollution* all the time/next year.
        Ask about *the lady* and *a mink coat* next year/now.
        Ask about *the boy* and *the gas station* on weekends/on Monday evenings.
        Ask about *Mr. Jackson* and *work* every day/this morning.
        Ask about *the student* and *English* every day/next year.

Part B.   *Third Person Plural*

Vocabulary

Nouns		Verbs	Adjective
cake	liberation	break	thousand
date (appointment)	movies	impress	
dictionary	politics	like	
gas	question	need	
high school	science		

☐ STATEMENT

Model: The boy studies hard.   The boys study hard.
        The girl works downtown.   The girls work downtown.

1. M1   Listen: The girl teaches English.   The girls teach English.
                 The student walks to school.   The students walk to school.
                 The street car goes downtown.   The street cars go downtown.

GENERALIZATION

Singular:	The girl	teach*es* English.
Plural:	The girl*s*	teach English.

Note that there are two differences. The plural subject has an -s, the plural verb does
not. Listen for both.

---

2. M1T T: Listen to the following sentences. If you hear a singular verb, raise one hand; if you
hear a plural, raise two.

T: Bill studies hard.   S: (1)
Bill and Chen study hard.   (2)
The boy studies hard.   (1)
The girls study hard.   (2)
The men need a car.   (2)
The lady wants a mink coat.   (1)
The women want liberation.   (2)
The men drive VWs.   (2)
The cars increase pollution.   (2)
The big car increases pollution.   (1)

3. M1 Rep: The men drive home at 5:00.
Sub: go   S: The men go home at 5:00.
walk   The men walk home at 5:00.
take a bus   The men take a bus home at 5:00.
take a street car   The men take a street car home at 5:00.
take a taxi   The men take a taxi home at 5:00.

4. M1 Rep: The women want a Rolls-Royce.
Sub: have   S: The women have a Rolls-Royce.
a VW   The women have a VW.
students   The students have a VW.
need   The students need a VW.
a bus   The students need a bus.
the men   The men need a bus.
drive   The men drive a bus.
a Ford   The men drive a Ford.

5. M1T T: The man drives to work.   S: The men drive to work.
The car needs gas.   The cars need gas.
The lady teaches school.   The ladies teach school.
The girl studies hard.   The girls study hard.
The boy makes mistakes.   The boys make mistakes.
The lady makes cakes.   The ladies make cakes.
The girl breaks dates.   The girls break dates.

6. M1T Rep: The man drives to work.
Sub: students   S: The students drive to work.
take a taxi   The students take a taxi to work.
to school   The students take a taxi to school.
boy   The boy takes a taxi to school.

(exercise continued on next page)

go	The boy goes to school.
to high school	The boy goes to high school.
girls	The girls go to high school.
take a bus	The girls take a bus to high school.
to work	The girls take a bus to work.
women	The women take a bus to work.

7. M1T   Rep: The men drive to work every day.

Sub:		S:	
now			The men are driving to work now.
tomorrow			The men are going to drive to work tomorrow.
girls			The girls are going to drive to work tomorrow.
every day			The girls drive to work every day.
now			The girls are driving to work now.
next week			The girls are going to drive to work next week.
professors			The professors are going to drive to work next week.
now			The professors are driving to work now.
every day			The professors drive to work every day.

☐ INTERROGATIVE AND SHORT ANSWERS

Model: Do the Jacksons have a car? Yes, they do.

8. M1   Rep:

Do professors like big words?	No, they don't.
Do the students like parties?	Yes, they do.
Do the students like exams?	No, they don't.
Do the Jacksons live in the city?	No, they don't.
Do the girls have an apartment?	Yes, they do.
Do the boys want a bicycle?	No, they don't.
Do the Jacksons have a car?	Yes, they do.

9. M1   Rep: Do the boys commute to school?

Sub:	S:
study English	Do the boys study English?
live in the dorm	Do the boys live in the dorm?
arrive at school at 9:00	Do the boys arrive at school at 9:00?
go home at 5:00	Do the boys go home at 5:00?
take the bus downtown	Do the boys take the bus downtown?
drive to work	Do the boys drive to work?
have a VW	Do the boys have a VW?
need a thousand dollars	Do the boys need a thousand dollars?
want an airplane	Do the boys want an airplane?

GENERALIZATION

Singular	The boy studies English.	
	Does the boy study English?	Yes, he does. No, he doesn't.
Plural	The boys study English.	
	Do the boys study English?	Yes, they do. No, they don't.

10. M1T   Rep: Does the boy need a haircut?
       Sub: boys   S: Do the boys need a haircut?
            want a VW   Do the boys want a VW?
            student   Does the student want a VW?
            students   Do the students want a VW?
            go to school   Do the students go to school?
            child   Does the child go to school?
            children   Do the children go to school?
            have a dog   Do the children have a dog?

***11. M1T   T: Do the boys study hard?   S: Yes, they do.
             Do the girls walk to school?   No, they don't.
             Does the child have a dog?   No, he doesn't.
             Does the boy walk downtown every day?   Yes, he does.
             Do the women work downtown?   Yes, they do.
             Does the girl like school?   Yes, she does.
             Do the boys have a bicycle?   No, they don't.
             Does the lady commute to school?   Yes, she does.
             Do the students live in the dorm?   Yes, they do.
             Do the men drive to work?   No, they don't.

□ NEGATIVE STATEMENT

Model: Big words don't impress your professors.

12. M1   Rep: Big words don't impress your professors.
              The little cars don't increase pollution.
              The students don't like English.
              The professors don't watch TV.
              Carlos and Chen don't live with a family.

GENERALIZATION

Singular:	The man *doesn't* drive to work.
Plural:	The men *don't* drive to work.

The plural uses *do + not* to form negatives. *do + not* is usually pronounced [dont] and written *don't.* It may also be pronounced and written *do not.*

13. M1   Rep: People don't read California newspapers.
          Sub: like   S: People don't like California newspapers.
               New York   People don't like New York newspapers.
               politicians   People don't like New York politicians.
               believe   People don't believe New York politicians.
               Washington   People don't believe Washington
                                                              politicians.
               newspapers   People don't believe Washington
                                                              newspapers.

14. M1T   T: The men like politics.   S: The men don't like politics.
               Girls like science.   Girls don't like science.
               Professors want Cadillacs.   Professors don't want Cadillacs.
               Girls ask those questions.   Girls don't ask those questions.
               Cars increase pollution.   Cars don't increase pollution.
               The girls have friends.   The girls don't have friends.
               The boys have an airplane.   The boys don't have an airplane.

15. M1T   T: The cars increase pollution.   S: The cars don't increase pollution.
               The car increases pollution.   The car doesn't increase pollution.
               The woman commutes to work.   The woman doesn't commute to work.
               The students take the bus.   The students don't take the bus.
               The student likes science.   The student doesn't like science.
               The boys need a dictionary.   The boys don't need a dictionary.
               The child goes to elementary school.   The child doesn't go to elementary school.
               The woman wants a mink coat.   The woman doesn't want a mink coat.
               The girl has a VW.   The girl doesn't have a VW.
               The students commute to school every day.   The students don't commute to school
                                                              every day.

16. M2   T: ( ) lives in the dorm.   S: ( ) doesn't live in the dorm. She lives
                                                              (with a family).
               ( ) wants a VW.   ( ) doesn't want a VW. He wants (a
                                                              Rolls-Royce).
               ( ) speaks French.
               ( ) and ( ) come from Turkey.
               ( ) studies engineering.
               ( ) and ( ) speak Portuguese.
               ( ) likes cold weather.
               ( ) takes the bus to school.
               ( ) wants a bicycle.
               ( ) lives in the dorm.
               ( ) has a mink coat.
               ( ) comes from a big country.
               ( ) likes (city).

17. C   T: Ask if ( ) lives in the dorm.   S1:   Does ( ) live in the dorm?
                                                       S2:   (Yes, she does.) (No, she doesn't. She
                                                              lives with a family.)

               Ask if ( ) and ( ) have a car.   S1:   Do ( ) and ( ) have a car?
                                                       S2:   (Yes, they do.) (No, they don't. They
                                                              walk to school.)

(exercise continued on next page)

T: Ask if ( ) and ( ) commute to school.
Ask if ( ) **works** at a gas station.
Ask if ( ) and ( ) speak Spanish.
Ask if ( ) likes movies.
Ask if ( ) likes girls.
Ask if ( ) and ( ) live in the dorm.
Ask if ( ) comes from Venezuela.
Ask if ( ) and ( ) come from Libya.
Ask if ( ) studies computer science.
Ask if ( ) and ( ) have a Rolls-Royce.
Ask if ( ) has an apartment.

Part C.   *First and Second Person*

Model: We commute to school every day.

1. M1   Listen: I commute to school every day.
John and I commute to school every day.
We commute to school every day.
You commute to school every day.

2. M1   Rep: The boys have a camera.

Sub:		S:	
the girls			The girls have a camera.
they			They have a camera.
I			I have a camera.
we			We have a camera.
you			You have a camera.
you and John			You and John have a camera.
The girls and he			The girls and he have a camera.
You and I			You and I have a camera.

GENERALIZATION

The Question, Short Answer and Negative forms are the same as Third Person Plural.

Question/Short Answer

Do you have a bicycle?   Yes, we do.
Do you commute to school?   No, I don't.

Negative

We don't have a Rolls-Royce.
I don't like computers.

---

3. M1T   Rep: I want a new car.

Sub:		S:	
we			We want a new car.
the boy			The boy wants a new car.
they			They want a new car.
the girls			The girls want a new car.

(exercise continued on next page)

the woman	The woman wants a new car.
the student	The student wants a new car.
the students	The students want a new car.

4. M1T   Rep: The boys have a car.
          Sub: boy   S: The boy has a car.
               I   I have a car.
               we   We have a car.
               the girl   The girl has a car.
               Mr. Jones   Mr. Jones has a car.
               Mr. and Mrs. Green   Mr. and Mrs. Green have a car.

5. M1T   Rep: We don't like little cars.
          Sub: I   S: I don't like little cars.
               the girl   The girl doesn't like little cars.
               the girls   The girls don't like little cars.
               she   She doesn't like little cars.
               we   We don't like little cars.
               Bill   Bill doesn't like little cars.

6. M1T   Rep: Does Chen have a bicycle?
          Sub: the boys   S: Do the boys have a bicycle?
               a car   Do the boys have a car?
               Mary   Does Mary have a car?
               the girls   Do the girls have a car?
               an apartment   Do the girls have an apartment?
               Jane   Does Jane have an apartment?
               you   Do you have an apartment?

***7. M1T T: Do the Jacksons live in the city?   S: No, they don't.
               Are Bill and Jane studying now?   Yes, they are.
               Does Bill like science?   Yes, he does.
               Is Bill studying science now?   No, he isn't.
               Is Jane going to go to the university?   Yes, she is.
               Does she go to the university this year?   No, she doesn't.
               Do Mr. and Mrs. Jackson work?   Yes, they do.
               Are they working now?   No, they aren't.

8. M2   T: Does ( ) drive to school or take a bus?   S1: Do you drive to school or take a bus?
                                                          S2: I (take a bus).

               Do ( ) and ( ) live in an apartment or in the   S1: Do you and ( ) live in an apartment or in
               dorm?   the dorm?
                                                          S2: We live (in the dorm).

               Are ( ) and ( ) studying Spanish or English? S1: Are you and ( ) studying Spanish or
                                                                   English?
                                                          S2: We're studying English.

               Do ( ) speak ( ) or ( ).
               Is ( ) speaking English or ( )?
               Does ( ) study science or math?
               Is ( ) learning English or ( )?
               Do ( ) and ( ) come from ( ) or ( )?
               Does ( ) like big cars or little cars?

(exercise continued on next page)

91

T: Do ( ) and ( ) want a VW or a Rolls-Royce?

Are you and ( ) learning spelling or grammar now?

Do ( ) and I like big cars or small cars?

Does ( ) have an apartment or a room?

Do ( ) and ( ) live near or far from the university?

Are ( ) and ( ) speaking English or ( )?

Does ( ) speak ( )?

9. C   T: Ask ( ) if he drives to school.   S1:   Do you drive to school?
                                                       S2:   (Yes, I do.) (No, I don't I take a bus.)
         Ask ( ) if he's studying math.   S1:   Are you studying math?
                                                       S2:   (Yes, I am.) (No, I'm not. I'm going to
                                                             study math next year.) (No, I'm not.
                                                             I hate math.)

         Ask ( ) if ( ) wants a VW.

         Ask ( ) if he speaks Spanish.

         Ask ( ) if he is speaking Spanish now.

         Ask ( ) if he has lunch in the cafeteria.

         Ask ( ) if ( ) is having coffee now.

         Ask ( ) if he wants an airplane.

         Ask ( ) if he's going to New York next weekend.

         Ask ( ) if he takes a trip every weekend.

         Ask ( ) if he and ( ) have a Rolls-Royce.

         Ask ( ) if ( ) and ( ) speak Arabic.

         Ask ( ) if he has class on Saturdays.

         Ask ( ) if ( ) and ( ) are buying a car.

SECTION TWO

WH QUESTIONS

Vocabulary

Nouns	Verbs
cigar	mean
laundry	smoke
newspaper	spell
	take (with transportation)

☐ *WHO?*

Note: Someone wants a Rolls-Royce.
         Who   wants a Rolls-Royce?   (Chen) does.

1. M1   T: Someone commutes to work.   S: Who commutes to work?
               Someone studies English.   Who studies English?
               Someone goes to school every day.   Who goes to school every day?
               Someone teaches elementary school.   Who teaches elementary school?

(exercise continued on next page)

T:	Someone works downtown.	S:	Who works downtown?
	Someone takes a bus to school.		Who takes a bus to school?

REMEMBER

Who has either singular or plural referent, but the verb form is almost always 3rd singular when *who* is its subject.

2. M2   T: Someone commutes to school.   S1:   Who commutes to school?
                                                S2:   ( ) does. ( ) and ( ) do.

Someone wants a Rolls-Royce.
Someone studies English.
Someone lives with an American family.
Someone lives in the dorm.
Someone takes a bus to school.
Someone has a new coat.
Someone walks to school.
Someone speaks Thai.
Someone speaks Arabic.
Someone teaches school.
Someone likes girls.
Someone comes from El Salvador.

□ *WHAT?*

Model: What does "metamorphosis" mean?   It means "change."

3. M1   Rep: What does it mean?
               What does John want?
               What do the girls need?
               What do you drive?
               What do we need?
               What does Carlos study?
               What does "metamorphosis" mean?

GENERALIZATION

Statement: John want[s]   something.

Yes/No Question: Do[es] John want   [something] ?   Answer: Yes, he does.

Wh Question: [What] does John want?   A Rolls-Royce.

4. M1T   T: John needs something.   G1:   Does John need something?

                                                       G2:   What does John need?

                 The girls want something.   G1:   Do the girls want something?

                                                        G2:   What do the girls want?

                 We need something.   G1:   Do we need something?

                                                        G2:   What do we need?

                 Chen has something.   G1:   Does Chen have something?

                                                        G2:   What does Chen have?

                 Chen studies something.   G1:   Does Chen study something?

                                                        G2:   What does Chen study?

                 The word means something.   G1:   Does the word mean something?

                                                        G2:   What does the word mean?

                 They have something.   G1:   Do they have something?

                                                        G2:   What do they have?

                 Jane wants something.   G1:   Does Jane want something?

                                                        G2:   What does Jane want?

                 Jane and Bill study something.   G1:   Do Jane and Bill study something?

                                                        G2:   What do Jane and Bill study?

5. M1T   T: John needs something.   S: What does he need?

                 John and Chen study something.   What do they study?

                 She likes something.   What does she like?

                 Chen has something.   What does he have?

                 They want something.   What do they want?

                 We need something.   What do we need?

                 Bill likes something.   What does he like?

                 She needs something.   What does she need?

                 You want something.   What you do want?

6. C   T: Ask ( ) what he wants.   S1:   What do you want?

                                                        S2:   I want (a new camera).

                 Ask ( ) what ( ) wants.   S1:   What does ( ) want?

                                                        S2:   He wants (a new car).

                 Ask ( ) what ( ) and ( ) need.

                 Ask ( ) what he drives.*

                 Ask ( ) what ( ) needs.

                 Ask ( ) what ( ) and ( ) want.

                 Ask ( ) what I want.

                 Ask ( ) what he studies.

                 Ask ( ) what ( ) teaches.

                 Ask ( ) what ( ) drives.

                 Ask ( ) what he smokes.**

        *   This refers to the make of car (e.g., VW, Chevrolet).

       **This refers to pipe, cigar or brand of cigarettes.

☐ *WHERE?*

Model: Where does Bill live?   With his family.

```
NOTE:

   Statement:                        Bill lives somewhere.
   Yes/No Question:         Does Bill live  somewhere?    Answer: Yes, he does.
   Wh Question:        Where    does Bill live?                      In the suburbs.
```

7. M1   T: Mary lives somewhere.   S: Where does Mary live?
               Mary studies somewhere every day.   Where does Mary study every day?
               The students go somewhere every day.   Where do the students go every day?
               The girls take a bus somewhere every day.   Where do the girls take a bus every day?
               The girl walks somewhere every day.   Where does the girl walk every day?
               The boys go somewhere every Saturday.   Where do the boys go every Saturday?
               Chen studies somewhere every night.   Where does Chen study every night?
               The boys go somewhere every weekend.   Where do the boys go every weekend?

8. M2   T: Ask ( ) where she lives.   S1:   Where do you live?
                                                         S2:   (In the dorm.) (On ( ) Street.)
               Ask ( ) where ( ) lives.
               Ask ( ) where ( ) and ( ) live.
               Ask ( ) where ( ) comes from.
               Ask ( ) where he comes from.
               Ask ( ) where ( ) and ( ) come from.
               Ask ( ) where he studies.
               Ask ( ) where ( ) studies.
               Ask ( ) where he goes every day at 3:00.
               Ask ( ) where ( ) goes every day at 10:00.
               Ask ( ) where he waits for the bus.
               Ask ( ) where ( ) lives.
               Ask ( ) where he eats dinner.
               Ask ( ) where ( ) goes on weekends.

☐ WHEN?

Model: When does Bill go to school?   Every day.

```
NOTE:

   Statement:                         Bill goes to school sometime.
   Yes/No Question:          Does Bill go to school sometime?    Yes, he does.
   Wh Question:        When    does Bill go to school?            Every day.
```

9. M1   T: Mary drives to school sometime.   S: When does Mary drive to school?
               The men commute to work sometime.   When do the men commute to work?
               The lady goes to school sometime.   When does the lady go to school?
               The children walk to school sometime.   When do the children walk to school?
               The women go to class sometime.   When do the women go to class?
               The girl studies sometime.   When does the girl study?
               The students read sometime.   When do the students read?
               The boy drives to school sometime.   When does the boy drive to school?

10. M2   T: Ask ( ) when she does her homework.   S1:   When do you do your homework?
                                                            S2:   (In the morning.)

                Ask ( ) when she reads the newspaper.
                Ask ( ) when he writes letters.
                Ask ( ) when he speaks English.
                Ask ( ) when he speaks (native language).
                Ask ( ) when he goes to school.
                Ask ( ) when he goes to the movies.
                Ask ( ) when he reads (Spanish) newspapers.
                Ask ( ) when he studies.
                Ask ( ) when he has lunch.
                Ask ( ) when he does his laundry.
                Ask ( ) when he watches TV.
                Ask ( ) when he listens to the radio.

***11. M2   T: Ask ( ) who studies English.   S1:   Who studies English?
                                                            S2:   (Jose) does.
                                                            S3:   Does Jose study English?
                                                            S4:   No, he doesn't.
                                                            S3:   What does he study?
                                                            S4:   He studies (economics).
                                                            S3:   Where does he study?
                                                            S4:   (At the university.)
                                                            S3:   When does he study?
                                                            S4:   (Every day.)

                Ask who lives with a family.
                Ask who wants a Rolls-Royce.
                Ask who likes American food.
                Ask who goes to history class.
                Ask who takes a bus to school.
                Ask who drives to school.
                Ask who lives in the dorm.
                Ask who has a car.
                Ask who speaks Arabic.
                Ask who drives a VW.
                Ask who comes from Thailand.
                Ask who smokes cigars.
                Ask who has an apartment.

12. C   T: What are you studying?   S: (I'm studying English.)
               Who commutes to school?
               Who takes the bus to school?
               Where do you study?
               What does ( ) study?
               When do you study?
               Where are you going to study next year?
               What are you going to study next year?
               Who is going to study ( )?
               Do you study every day? What? When?
               Where do you have lunch?
               Do you speak ( ) sometimes? When?

13. C   T: Find out when ( ) eats dinner.   S1:   (When do you eat dinner?)
                                                           S2:   (Around 6:00.)

Find out where ( ) and ( ) have lunch.   S1:   (Where do you and ( ) have lunch?)
                                                           S2:   (At the Student Union cafeteria.) (We go to a different place every day.)

Find out what ( ) does on weekends.
Find out what ( ) is going to do tomorrow after class.
Find out where ( ) and ( ) study.
Find out when ( ) and ( ) watch TV.
Find out where ( ) is going after class.
Find out what ( ) drives.
Find out who is going to visit the class next week.
Find out what ( ) does in his spare time.
Find out who eats lunch at the Student Union.
Find out were ( ) and ( ) live.
Find out when ( ) reads newspapers in his language.
Find out what ( ) reads for pleasure.

14. C   Situation: You are at a party. You don't know many of the people. Using the patterns you have learned, introduce yourself to someone near you and find out about him.

☐ NOTICE THE QUESTION: HOW DO YOU SPELL "METAMORPHOSIS"?

15. M1   Rep: How do you spell "metamorphosos"?
          Sub: pollution   S: How do you spell "pollution"?
                 street car   How do you spell "street car"?
                 hibernate   How do you spell "hibernate"?
                 commute   How do you spell "commute"?
                 weather   How do you spell "weather"?

> NOTE:
>
> Use this pattern when you want to know a spelling. *You* in this question is *impersonal* and not answered by *I,* but merely by giving the spelling. Other examples of impersonal *you:* "How do you get downtown?" "You take a bus." "Which bus do you take to get downtown?" "No. 75, 76 or 79."

16. M1T T: dictionary   S1:   How do you spell "dictionary"?
                                            S2:   D-I-C-T-I-O-N-A-R-Y.

                office   S1:   How do you spell "office"?
                                              S2:   O-F-F-I-C-E.

                cigar   S1:   How do you spell "cigar"?
                                                S2:   C-I-G-A-R.

                movies   S1:   How do you spell "movies"?
                                              S2:   M-O-V-I-E-S.

                bicycle   S1:   How do you spell "bicycle"?
                                          S2:   B-I-C-Y-C-L-E.

(exercise continued on next page)

T:	lecture	S1:	How do you spell "lecture"?
		S2:	L-E-C-T-U-R-E.
	politics	S1:	How do you spell "politics"?
		S2:	P-O-L-I-T-I-C-S.
	suburb	S1:	How do you spell "suburb"?
		S2:	S-U-B-U-R-B.

SECTION THREE

TAG QUESTIONS

Part A.   *Type I*

Model: Lesson Two: It isn't crowded, is it? No, it isn't.
        Lesson Four: He doesn't drive downtown, does he? No, he doesn't.

1. M1   Rep: He doesn't come from Spain, does he?   No, he doesn't.
                 She doesn't drive an Oldsmobile, does she?   No, she doesn't.
                 It doesn't often snow, does it?   No, it doesn't.
                 They don't speak English, do they?   No, they don't.
                 Mr. and Mrs. Jackson don't have an apartment,
                   do they?   No, they don't.
                 The ladies don't play bridge, do they?   No, they don't.
                 You don't come from the U.S., do you?   No, I don't.

GENERALIZATION

The pattern is the same as with *BE* Type I tags.

It isn't crowded,	is it?	No, it isn't.
He doesn't drive downtown,	does he?	No, he doesn't.
—	+	—

---

2. M1T   T: Mary doesn't work every day.   G1: Mary doesn't work every day, does she?
                                                         G2: No, she doesn't.

               Bill and Jane don't live on campus.   G1: Bill and Jane don't live on campus, do they?
                                                         G2: No, they don't.

               The Jacksons don't drive to work.   G1: The Jacksons don't drive to work, do they?
                                                         G2: No, they don't.

               We don't have class on Wednesdays.   G1: We don't have class on Wednesdays, do we?
                                                         G2: No, we don't.

               He doesn't speak Finnish.   G1: He doesn't speak Finnish, does he?
                                                         G2: No, he doesn't.

               You don't come from Canada.   G1: You don't come from Canada, do you?
                                                         G2: No, I don't.

(exercise continued on next page)

T:	They don't read the morning newspaper.	G1:	They don't read the morning newspaper, do they?
		G2:	No, they don't.
	You don't live in the dorm.	G1:	You don't live in the dorm, do you?
		G2:	No, I don't.
	Mrs. Bruder doesn't like computers.	G1:	Mrs. Bruder doesn't like computers, does she?
		G2:	No, she doesn't.
	Bicycles don't increase pollution.	G1:	Bicycles don't increase pollution, do they?
		G2:	No, they don't.
	The students don't read *Time.*	G1:	The students don't read *Time,* do they?
		G2:	No, they don't.
	You don't come from England.	G1:	You don't come from England, do you?
		G2:	No, I don't.
	She doesn't like the food in the cafeteria.	G1:	She doesn't like the food in the cafeteria, does she?
		G2:	No, she doesn't.

3. C   T: Make a conversational statement to your   S1: (You don't speak Arabic, do you?)
            neighbor and add a tag.   S2: No, I don't.

Part B.   *Type II*

Model: Lesson Two: You're studying engineering, aren't you?   Yes, I am.
        Lesson Four: Bill lives with his family, doesn't he?   Yes, he does.

1. M1   Rep: Big cars increase pollution, don't they?   Yes, they do.
               The boys need haircuts, don't they?   Yes, they do.
               Women like mink coats, don't they?   Yes, they do.
               He has a VW, doesn't he?   Yes, he does.
               You come from Libya, don't you?   Yes, I do.
               The weather gets hot, doesn't it?   Yes, it does.

GENERALIZATION

The tags with the simple present tense follow the same pattern as Type II with BE.

You're studying engineering, aren't you?   Yes, I am.
Bill lives with his family,   doesn't he?   Yes, he does.
          +   −   +

---

2. M1   T: He studies English.   G1: He studies English, doesn't he?
                                          G2: Yes, he does.
              We take bus 73.   G1: We take bus 73, don't we?
                                          G2: Yes, we do.
              She has a big car.   G1: She has a big car, doesn't she?
                                          G2: Yes, she does.
              They speak Arabic.   G1: They speak Arabic, don't they?
                                          G2: Yes, they do.

(exercise continued on next page)

T:		G1:	

T: It gets hot in the summer.

G1: It gets hot in the summer, doesn't it?
G2: Yes, it does.

She has a VW.

G1: She has a VW, doesn't she?
G2: Yes, she does.

Mr. and Mrs. Jackson work.

G1: Mr. and Mrs. Jackson work, don't they?
G2: Yes, they do.

Carlos comes from Latin America.

G1: Carlos comes from Latin America, doesn't he?
G2: Yes, he does.

We have time for a cup of coffee.

G1: We have time for a cup of coffee, don't we?
G2: Yes, we do.

You study engineering.

G1: You study engineering, don't you?
G2: Yes, I do.

You have an apartment in Oakland.

G1: You have an apartment in Oakland, don't you?
G2: Yes, I do.

They come from Southeast Asia.

G1: They come from Southeast Asia, don't they?
G2: Yes, they do.

Bill and Chen play bridge.

G1: Bill and Chen play bridge, don't they?
G2: Yes, they do.

3. C Make a conversational statement to your neighbor. Add a tag.

4. C Situation: You're at a party with many different people you don't know. Use a tag question and start a conversation.

S1: (You're in the English class, aren't you?)
S2: (Yes, I am.)

S1: (You don't speak Korean, do you?)
S2: (No, I don't. I speak (Thai.))

SECTION FOUR

INDEFINITE PRONOUNS *every/no* — IN SUBJECT POSITION

Vocabulary

Nouns		Adjectives	Verb
corruption	peace	sunny	hate
government	war	rainy	
losing	winning	honest	
match	fish	dishonest	

Part A.   *Statements*

Model: Everyone knows that.
         No one likes pollution.

1. M1   Rep: Everyone likes As; no one likes Fs.
          Sub: clean air/pollution   S: Everyone likes clean air; no one likes
                                                        pollution.

                sunny days/rainy days   Everyone likes sunny days; no one likes
                                                        rainy days.

                honest men/dishonest men   Everyone likes honest men; no one
                                                        likes dishonest men.

                good government/corruption   Everyone likes good government; no
                                                        one likes corruption.

                peace/war   Everyone likes peace; no one likes war.
                winning/losing   Everyone likes winning; no one likes losing.

GENERALIZATION

Every (which means *all*) and *no* (which means *none*) form compound words with
indefinite nouns such as *one, thing, place,* etc. They have opposite meanings and
are usually written as one word.

everyone, everybody	no one, nobody
everywhere, every place	nowhere, no place
everything	nothing [ˈnəθiŋ]

Note that *no one* is two words and *nothing* is pronounced differently from the other
no- words. Listen carefully as your teacher pronounces the words. When these
words are the subject of the sentence, the verb is singular.

---

2. M1T   T: All of the people are coming.   S: Everyone is coming.
                 All of the people like Coke.   Everyone likes Coke.
                 All of the people want clean air.   Everyone wants clean air.
                 All of the people are happy.   Everyone is happy.
                 All of the people work hard.   Everyone works hard.
                 All of the people speak English.   Everyone speaks English.
                 All of the people have change.   Everyone has change.
                 All of the people go home at 5:00.   Everyone goes home at 5:00.

3. M1T   T: Are all of the people coming?   S: Yes, everyone is coming.
                 Do all of the people like clean air?   Yes, everyone likes clean air.
                 Are all of the things here?   Yes, everything is here.
                 Are all of the students learning English? Yes, everyone is learning English.
                 Do all of the guests drink beer?   Yes, everyone drinks beer?
                 Are all of the things ready?   Yes, everything is ready.
                 Do all of the students go to the lab?   Yes, everyone goes to the lab?
                 Do all of the people want dinner?   Yes, everyone wants dinner.

4. M1T   T: Do any of the students speak Irish?   S: No, no one speaks Irish.

                       Are any of the students absent?   No, no one is absent.

                       Do any of the students have a Rolls-Royce?   No, no one has a Rolls-Royce.

                       Are any of the students going downtown?   No, no one is going downtown.

                       Do any of the students drink beer?   No, no one drinks beer.

                       Do any of the students study German?   No, no one studies German.

                       Do any of the students have a plane?   No, no one has a plane.

5. M2   T: pollution   S1:   Does everyone (hate) pollution?

                                              S2:   (Yes. No one likes pollution.)

                       dirty air   S1:   Does everyone (dislike) dirty air?

                                              S2:   (Yes. No one wants dirty air.)

                       war

                       crime

                       bad government

                       dangerous cities

                       violence

                       dishonest men

                       taxes

                       dirty streets

                       dirty cities

6. C   Make a generalization about people in your country.

           Ex: (Everyone in ( ) speaks Spanish.)

                  (No one in ( ) drives to work.)

Part B.   *Yes/No Questions*

Model: Does everyone want peace? Yes, they do.

           Does anyone like taxes? No, they don't.

1. M1   Rep: Does everyone like peace?

                    Does everyone like clean air?

                    Does everyone like safe cities?

                    Does everyone like good government?

                    Does anyone like violence?

                    Does anyone like war?

                    Does anyone like taxes?

                    Does anyone like pollution?

GENERALIZATION

The indefinite pronouns with *no* are not usually used in *yes/no* questions. In questions, use the form *any-*.

Is anything ready?	Nothing is ready.
Is anyone going?	No one is going.
Does anyone speak Thai?	No one speaks Thai.

The answer to the *yes/no* questions may be either *yes* or *no*, depending upon the situation.

Is anyone coming?	Yes, everyone is coming.
	No, no one is coming.
	Yes, John and Bill are.

---

2. M1   T: I need a dollar.   S: Does anyone have a dollar?
             I need a book.   Does anyone have a book?
             I need a car.   Does anyone have a car?
             I need a dime.   Does anyone have a dime?
             I need a pencil.   Does anyone have a pencil?
             I need a pen.   Does anyone have a pen?
             I need a match.   Does anyone have a match?

3. M1T T: People in Colombia speak Spanish.   S: Does everyone speak Spanish?
             People in the U.S. commute to work.   Does everyone commute to work?
             People in Canada speak English.   Does everyone speak English?
             People in Boston eat fish.   Does everyone eat fish?
             People in Washington work for the government.   Does everyone work for the government?
             People in Sweden speak Swedish.   Does everyone speak Swedish?
             People in Germany drink beer.   Does everyone drink beer?

NOTE:

The choice of *any-* or *every-* in the question depends on the expected answer. Use *every-* when the answer will probably be *yes*. Use *any-* when you don't know whether the answer will be *yes* or *no*.

Is everyone ready?	Yes, everyone is ready.
Is anyone ready?	Yes, everyone is ready. No, no one is ready.

You may get *no* answers with *every,* but it is not the expected answer.

---

4. M2   Situation: You are a teacher taking 30 ten-year-old children to the museum. It is a cold day and they need warm clothes. The admission is 50 cents. Ask questions to see if all the children have what they need.

        Ex: (Does everyone have fifty cents?)

***5. M2   Situation: You're with a group of friends at the Student Union. You have only a ten
            dollar bill.
            A.   You want to make a phone call.   S: (Does anyone have a dime?)
            B.   You want a pack of cigarettes.
            C.   You want to go downtown on the bus.
            D.   You want to buy a candy bar.

***6. M2   Situation: The students in the English class are going to have a test. Every student must
            have a pen, a pencil, an eraser, and a piece of paper.
            A.   You are the teacher. Find out if all the   S: (Does everyone have a pen?)
                  students have all the things they need,
                  if they are ready to begin and if they
                  understand the test directions.
            B.   You are a student in the class. You are   S: (Does anyone have a pen?)
                  very absent-minded and don't have the
                  things you need. Ask the other students.

7. C   You have heard many things about the United States. Using the questions in Section
            Four, ask your teacher if they are true.
            S1:   (Does everyone in the U.S. have a car?)   T: (Most people have cars, but not everyone.)
            S2:   (Does anyone in the U.S. understand the   T: (?)
                  government?)

***SUMMARY DIALOGUE

Carlos: You drive a VW, don't you?

Bill: Yes, I do. Why?*

Carlos: I see you every afternoon. I wait for the bus near the parking lot.

Bill: Do you live north or south of the city?

Carlos: North.

Bill: Oh, too bad. I live south.

Carlos: That's O.K. I enjoy the bus ride. I meet lots of interesting people.

*Note: A response to a tag question is often accompanied by the question *Why?*,
meaning "Why do you ask?" or "Why do you want to know?" It keeps the conversation going because the first person then explains.

LESSON FOUR – SUMMARY OF PATTERNS

	Subject	Verb	Completer	Short Answer
Statement	Bill	lives	with his family.	
Question (Who)	Who	lives	with his family?	Bill (does).

	Aux.	Subject	Verb	Completer	Short Answer
Question (yes/no)	Do	the men	drive	a VW?	Yes, they do. No, they don't.
	Does	Bill	live	in the dorm?	Yes, he does. No, he doesn't.

	QW	Subject	Verb	Completer	Short Answer
Question (when)	When do	the men	drive	to work?	In the morning.
(Where)	Where does	Bill	live?		With his family.

	Subject	Predicate	Tag	Short Answer
Tag Questions				
I	Bill	doesn't live in the dorm,	does he?	No, he doesn't.
II	Bill	lives at home,	doesn't he?	Yes, he does.

Indefinite Pronouns

	Subject	Verb	Completer	Short Answer
Statement	Everyone	speaks	English.	
	No one	speaks	Basque.	

	Aux.	Subject	Verb	Completer	Short Answer
yes/no	Does	everyone	play	bridge?	Yes, we do.
	Does	anyone	play	cribbage?	No, no one does.

NOTES

LESSON FIVE

Chen needs some advice.

Chen: Bill, *please give me some advice.*

Bill: Sure, Chen. What's the problem?

Chen: I'm going to have dinner at the Wilson's and I need a gift. *Do you have any ideas?*

5   Bill: A hostess gift? Buy something nice and inexpensive.

Chen: Sure. But what? *How many things* are nice *and* inexpensive in this country?

Bill: O.K., you're right, not many. How much money are you going to spend?

Chen: Between $5.00 and $10.00.

Bill: Oh, no! Don't spend that much. Expensive gifts embarrass the hostess. Let's keep
10   the amount under $5.00.

Chen: That's fine with me. How about a few suggestions?

Bill: My mother likes flowers. *A few roses* aren't very expensive. Or . . . buy some candy—
everyone likes candy.

Chen: I don't know, Bill. Please come to the gift shop. They have *a lot of things.*

15   Bill: O.K. Shall we go now?

Chen: Yes, let's. The invitation is for tomorrow night.

(At the gift shop.)

Bill: These coasters are nice.

Chen: Yes, but maybe they're the wrong color.

20   Bill: This is a pretty vase.

Chen: Maybe she doesn't need a vase.

Bill: How about a few candles? My mother loves candles. We have them on the dinner
table every night.

Chen: No, I don't like that idea.

25   Bill: You don't like any of my ideas. Let's get out of here.

Chen: I'm sorry, Bill. Don't be angry. Your customs are so different. I don't understand
these gifts. *They don't mean anything* to me.

Bill: I'm sorry, too, Chen. I'm not angry. But you don't have anything for Mrs. Wilson.
         Wait, I have an idea . . . do you have any things from your country?

30   Chen: Yes, of course. I have a small carving. Is it all right?

      Bill: It's perfect. Have a good time.

      Chen: Thanks, and thanks for the help.

      Bill: That's O.K.

OUTLINE OF PATTERNS   Example

      Section One   Count/Non-Count Nouns

          Part A   *Some/any*

                    Affirmative   some advice.
                    Interrogative/Negative   any ideas?

          Part B   Expressions of Quantity

                    a lot of   a lot of things
                    much/many   not much beer
                                                          not many ideas

                    a little/a few   a little money
                                                          a few candles

                    Wh Questions   How many things?
                                                          How much money?

      Section Two   Request/Suggestion Forms

          Part A   Request   Please give me some advice.

          Part B   Suggestion (self-included)

                    Let's   Let's go to the gift shop.
                    Shall   Shall we go?
                    Wh + shall   Where shall we go?

      Section Three   Indefinite Pronouns

          every/no in Object Position   They don't mean anything . . .

COMPREHENSION QUESTIONS

*1. What does Chen need from Bill?

2. What is Chen going to do?

3. What does Chen need?

*4. What is Bill's advice about the kind of gift?

5. How much is Chen going to spend?

*6. Why does Bill say "no" to that amount?
(How much does Bill suggest?)

*7. Why does Bill suggest flowers?
(What does Bill suggest to buy?)

8. Where do they go? Why?

9. When is the invitation?

10. What does Bill suggest first?

11. Why does Chen refuse the suggestion?

12. What does Chen say about the vase?

13. Why does Bill suggest candles?
(What does Bill's mother have on the table every night?)

*14. Why is Bill angry?

15. Why doesn't Chen like Bill's ideas?

16. What is Chen going to take as a hostess gift?

*17. What is the custom in your country in a similar situation?

NOTE

The customs about "hostess gifts" vary in different parts of the United States. Where hostess gifts are customary, the gift depends on the type of invitation and how well you know the host or hostess. Ask your teacher.

SECTION ONE

COUNT/NON-COUNT NOUNS

Vocabulary

Nouns				Verbs
advice	cup	ink	scarf	drink
bacon	egg	key	soap	spend
beer	exercise	macaroni	spaghetti	
bread	flower	magazine	spoon	*Adjective*
candy	free time	match	sugar	fresh (not stale)
candy bar	fruit	milk	suggestion	
cigarette	help	music	time	
clothes	ice cream	napkin	vegetable	
coaster	ice cream cone	potato chip		
coffee	information	rice		

Part A.   *some/any*

□ AFFIRMATIVE

NOTE:		
Previous Pattern:	I need a book.	
New Pattern:	I need some books.	(some = *a quantity of*)

1. M1 Rep: I need some books.
       Sub: glasses   S: I need some glasses.
             eggs   I need some eggs.
             coasters   I need some coasters.
             ideas   I need some ideas.
             flowers   I need some flowers.
             suggestions   I need some suggestions.
             candles   I need some candles.

2. M1 Rep: I want some advice.
       Sub: help   S: I want some help.
             milk   I want some milk.
             ink   I want some ink.
             bacon   I want some bacon.
             information   I want some information.
             beer   I want some beer.
             money   I want some money.
             change   I want some change.

GENERALIZATION

I need some books.
I need some help.

There are two main groups of nouns in English:
1. Count nouns — those which can be counted.
   They have singular and plural forms — *book/books*
2. Non-count (mass) nouns — those which cannot be counted.
   They have only one form — *advice, help.*

3. M1T   Rep: I have some books.
          Sub: idea   S: I have some ideas.
               money   I have some money.
               cigarette   I have some cigarettes.
               milk   I have some milk.
               carving   I have some carvings.
               help   I have some help.
               pencil   I have some pencils.
               change   I have some change.
               time   I have some time.

SOME COMMON NON-COUNT NOUNS

Add other nouns like these when you find them.

milk	rice	ice cream	money	air
butter	macaroni	beer	change	help
sugar	spaghetti	food	homework	advice
tea	soup	soap	mail	information
coffee	meat	toothpaste	music	time
bread	fruit	ink	water	
lettuce	spinach			

NOTE: These nouns may be counted by adding a countable noun.

milk	a bottle of milk	two bottles of milk
butter	a pound of butter	two pounds of butter

***4. M2   T: What do you have?   S1:   I have some (books).
                                                 S2:   He has some books and I have some (money).
                                                 S3:   He has some books, she has some money
                                                       and I have some (letters).

***5. C   T: We're going to have a party. What do we   S1:   We need (some music).
                 need?   S2:   We need (some beer).
                                                            etc.

☐ INTERROGATIVE/NEGATIVE

Previous Pattern: Do you have an idea? No, I don't have an idea.
New Pattern: Do you have *any* ideas? No, I don't have *any* ideas.
                      Do you have *some* ideas?

6. M1   Rep: Do you have any money?
           Sub: beer   S: Do you have any beer?
                change   Do you have any change?
                help   Do you have any help?
                suggestions   Do you have any suggestions?
                milk   Do you have any milk?
                cigarettes   Do you have any cigarettes?
                sugar   Do you have any sugar?
                matches   Do you have any matches?

7. M1   Rep: No, we don't have any money.
           Sub: beer   S: No, we don't have any beer.
                change   No, we don't have any change.
                help   No, we don't have any help.
                suggestions   No, we don't have any suggestions.
                milk   No, we don't have any milk.
                cigarettes   No, we don't have any cigarettes.
                sugar   No, we don't have any sugar.
                matches   No, we don't have any matches.

+---+
| |
| GENERALIZATION |
| |
| I need some money/books. |
| Do you   need ⎰some⎱money/books? |
| ⎱any ⎰ |
| I don't   need any money/books. |
| |
| *Some* is used in Affirmative and, in some cases, in Interrogative sentences.*** |
| *Any* is used in Negative and Interrogative, and means an indefinite *quantity of.* |
| Both are used with both count and non-count nouns. |
| |
+---+

***8. M1T   Situation: You're in a grocery store late Saturday afternoon. The store is out of many
                things. Ask the clerk.
             T: fresh vegetables   S1:   Do you have any fresh vegetables?
                  spinach and lettuce   S2:   We have some spinach and lettuce.

                  fresh bread   S1:   Do you have any fresh bread?
                  no   S2:   No, we don't have any fresh bread.

                  fresh fruit/apples and oranges
                  fresh eggs/no

9. M2   T: Bill doesn't have any money.   S1:   Bill doesn't need any money.
                                                     S2:   Yes, he does. He needs some (for lunch).
                 We don't have any time.   S1:   We don't need any time.
                                                     S2:   Yes, we do. We need some (for the test).

                 Mrs. Jackson doesn't have any rice.
                 I don't have any change.
                 We don't have any beer.
                 Chen doesn't have any coffee.
                 The cook doesn't have any eggs.
                 We don't have any milk.
                 Mrs. Wilson doesn't have any gasoline.

Part B.   *Expressions of Quantity*

☐ *A LOT OF*

Model: Chen needs a lot of help.

1. M1   Rep: He needs a lot of money.
           Sub: eggs   S: He needs a lot of eggs.
                 change   He needs a lot of change.
                 ideas   He needs a lot of ideas.
                 advice   He needs a lot of advice.
                 milk   He needs a lot of milk.
                 pictures   He needs a lot of pictures.
                 candy bars   He needs a lot of candy bars.
                 beer   He needs a lot of beer.
                 cigars   He needs a lot of cigars.

GENERALIZATION

I need some help.
I need a lot of help.
Do you read a lot of magazines?

a lot of = a large quantity. The expression is used with count and mass nouns in
affirmative statements and questions. It is not usually used with negatives.

---

2. M1T   T: I need help.   S: Do you need a lot of help?
                 He eats rice.   Does he eat a lot of rice?
                 They drink beer.   Do they drink a lot of beer?
                 She buys clothes.   Does she buy a lot of clothes?
                 We have problems.   Do we have a lot of problems?
                 You need time.   Do you need a lot of time?
                 She uses eggs.   Does she use a lot of eggs?
                 He smokes cigarettes.   Does he smoke a lot of cigarettes?

3. M2   T: rice

          magazines

          cigarettes
          beer
          money
          eggs
          meat
          newspapers
          homework
          milk
          advice
          coffee
          tea

S1:   Do you (eat) a lot of rice?
S2:   Yes, I (use) a lot of rice.
S1:   Do you (buy) a lot of magazines?
S2:   Yes, I (read) a lot of magazines.

□ *MUCH/MANY*

Model: He doesn't drink much milk.
          He doesn't smoke many cigarettes.

4. M1   Rep: He doesn't drink much beer.
        Sub: have—money
             buy—milk
             have—homework
             use—paper
             eat—rice
             have—time
             need—advice

S: He doesn't have much money.
     He doesn't buy much milk.
     He doesn't have much homework.
     He doesn't use much paper.
     He doesn't eat much rice.
     He doesn't have much time.
     He doesn't need much advice.

5. M1T   Rep: We don't smoke many cigars.
        Sub: eat—vegetables
             use—eggs
             read—papers
             buy—magazines
             eat—potato chips
             buy—flowers
             read—books

S: We don't eat many vegetables.
     We don't use many eggs.
     We don't read many papers.
     We don't buy many magazines.
     We don't eat many potato chips.
     We don't buy many flowers.
     We don't read many books.

GENERALIZATION

Much and *many* are similar in meaning to *a lot of.*

Much and *many* are used in Questions and Negative Statements.

     Note: Question: Do you need {a lot of / much} help?

               Affirmative: Yes, I need a lot of help.
               Negative: No, I don't need much help.

What kinds of nouns are preceded by *much?* ((Non-count)) What kinds of nouns are preceded by *many?* ((Count))

6. M1   T: Do you drink much milk?   S: No, I don't drink much milk.
               Do you read many newspapers?   No, I don't read many newspapers.
               Do you have much money?   No, I don't have much money.
               Do you smoke many cigarettes?   No, I don't smoke many cigarettes.
               Do you drink much beer?   No, I don't drink much beer.
               Do you have many books?   No, I don't have many books.
               Do you have much homework?   No, I don't have much homework.

7. M1T   T: Do you eat a lot of rice?   S: No, I don't eat much rice.
               Do you read a lot of books?   No, I don't read many books.
               Do you drink a lot of milk?   No, I don't drink much milk.
               Do you spend a lot of money?   No, I don't spend much money.
               Do you give a lot of advice?   No, I don't give much advice.
               Do you have a lot of ideas?   No, I don't have many ideas.
               Do you see a lot of movies?   No, I don't see many movies.
               Do you buy a lot of bread?   No, I don't buy much bread.
               Do you buy a lot of cigarettes?   No, I don't buy many cigarettes.
               Do you need a lot of help?   No, I don't need much help.

8. M2   T: use   S: I use a lot of (paper); I don't use (many
                                                          pencils).
               need   I need a lot of (money); I don't need
                                                          (much advice).
               want
               have
               spend
               drink
               smoke
               watch
               buy
               get
               lose
               cook
               eat
               meet

9. C   You are going to get $1,000,000 from a lottery ticket. Tell the class what you're going to
         do with it and what you aren't going to do.

         S: (I'm going to buy a lot of cars. I'm not going to do much work.)

□ *A LITTLE/A FEW*

Model: I don't eat much rice. I eat a little rice.
        I don't read many books. I read a few books.

10. M1   T: I eat a lot of rice.   S: I eat a little rice.
                I drink a lot of beer.   I drink a little beer.
                I buy a lot of bread.   I buy a little bread.
                I use a lot of spaghetti.   I use a little spaghetti.
                I have a lot of homework.   I have a little homework.
                I spend a lot of money.   I spend a little money.
                I drink a lot of coffee.   I drink a little coffee.

       T: I read a lot of books.   S: I read a few books.
                I read a lot of magazines.   I read a few magazines.
                I see a lot of movies.   I see a few movies.
                I have a lot of ideas.   I have a few ideas.
                I smoke a lot of cigarettes.   I smoke a few cigarettes.
                I buy a lot of candy bars.   I buy a few candy bars.

GENERALIZATION

Much/many/a lot of are opposite in meaning from *a little/a few*. *A little* and *a few* are used mainly in Affirmative Statements:

     I need a few dollars.   They have a little money.

Which expression is used with count nouns? ((*a few*))
Which expression is used with non-count nouns? ((*a little*))

Count: a lot of/many/a few
Non-count: a lot of/much/a little

---

11. M1T   T: time   S: I have a little time.
                minutes   I have a few minutes.
                money   I have a little money.
                coffee   I have a little coffee.
                magazines   I have a few magazines.
                ideas   I have a few ideas.
                advice   I have a little advice.
                information   I have a little information.
                cigarettes   I have a few cigarettes.
                homework   I have a little homework.

12. M2   T: ( ) uses a few ( ).   S: (Carlos) uses a few (eggs).
                ( ) doesn't smoke many ( ).
                ( ) wants a little ( ).
                ( ) doesn't watch much ( ).
                ( ) spends a little ( ).
                ( ) doesn't buy many ( ).
                ( ) uses a little ( ).
                ( ) doesn't have much ( ).
                ( ) buys a few ( ).
                ( ) eats a little ( ).
                ( ) drinks a little ( ).
                ( ) cooks a few ( ).

□ *WH* QUESTIONS

Model: How many things are nice and inexpensive? Not many.
         How much money are you going to spend? About five dollars.

13. M1   Rep: How much money do you need?
           Sub: time   S: How much time do you need?
                help   How much help do you need?
                change   How much change do you need?
                bread   How much bread do you need?
                fruit   How much fruit do you need?
                beer   How much beer do you need?
                macaroni   How much macaroni do you need?
                bacon   How much bacon do you need?

14. M1   Rep: How many books do you need?
           Sub: scarves   S: How many scarves do you need?
                pictures   How many pictures do you need?
                cigarettes   How many cigarettes do you need?
                eggs   How many eggs do you need?
                newspapers   How many newspapers do you need?
                matches   How many matches do you need?
                napkins   How many napkins do you need?
                spoons   How many spoons do you need?

+---+
| GENERALIZATION |
| |
| The *Wh* questions for all the expressions of quantity are: |
| how much |
| how many |
| Which one is used for count nouns? ((How many?)) |
| Which one is used for non-count nouns? ((How much?)) |
| How many things . . .? |
| How much money . . .? |
+---+

15. M1T   T: matches   S: How many matches does he need?
                money   How much money does he need?
                eggs   How many eggs does he need?
                milk   How much milk does he need?
                bread   How much bread does he need?
                cigars   How many cigars does he need?
                rice   How much rice does he need?
                candy bars   How many candy bars does he need?
                apples   How many applies does he need?

117

16. M2   T: How much money do you need ( )?   S1:   How much money do you need (for
                                                                 tuition)?
                                                         S2:   You need ( ) for tuition.
               How many people do you need ( )?   S1:   How many people do you need (for
                                                                 a party)?
                                                         S2:   You need ( ) for a party.

               How much candy ( )?
               How many flowers ( )?
               How much money ( )?
               How many books ( )?
               How much pollution ( )?
               How many cups ( )?
               How many potato chips ( )?
               How much beer. ( )?
               How many glasses ( )?
               How much time ( )?
               How many songs ( )?
               How much music ( )?
               How many records ( )?

17. C   T: money . . .   S1:   How much money do you (need) for a
                                                                 (haircut)?
                                                         S2:   (About $2.50.)
               people . . .   S1:   How many people (do you need for a
                                                                 bridge game?)
                                                         S2:   (Four.)
               time . . .
               meat . . .
               flowers . . .
               gas . . .
               eggs . . .
               books . . .
               help . . .
               beer . . .
               money . . .
               records . . .

18. C   T: Ask ( ) how much rice he eats.   S1:   How much rice do you eat?
                                                         S2:   (A lot.) (I don't like rice.)
               Ask ( ) how many pencils he has.   S1:   How many pencils do you have?
                                                         S2:   (Three.) (None.)
         Ask ( ) how many newspapers he reads every day.
         Ask ( ) how much change she needs for the bus every week.
         Ask ( ) how many letters he gets every day.
         Ask ( ) how many cars he has.
         Ask ( ) how much macaroni he eats.
         Ask ( ) how much coffee he drinks.
         Ask ( ) how many books he reads every week.
         Ask ( ) how many pencils he uses every year.
         Ask ( ) how many miles he drives every year.
         Ask ( ) how many movies he sees every month.
         Ask ( ) how much beer he drinks every week.

19. C   T: free time—have

                              S1:   How much free time do you have (every day)?

                              S2:   (I don't have any free time.) (I don't have much free time.) (A few hours.)

                cigarettes—smoke

                              S1:   How many cigarettes do you smoke (every week)?

                              S2:   (I smoke a lot of (a few) cigarettes.) (I don't smoke.)

                rice—eat
                books—read
                help—need
                money—spend
                ideas—have
                newspapers—read
                beer—drink
                bread—buy
                coffee—drink
                magazines—read
                clothes—buy
                gas—use
                miles—drive
                trips—take

SECTION TWO

REQUEST/SUGGESTION FORMS

Vocabulary			
Nouns	**Verbs**	**Adjectives**	**Adverbs**
dancing	begin	angry	clearly
noise	bring	late	fast
seat	call (telephone)	nervous	slowly
	close	prompt	
	eat out	upset	
	print		
	sign		

Part A.   *Request****

Model: Please give me some advice.

1. M1   Rep: Please give me some advice.
                   Please speak English.
                   Please come to class on time.

(exercise continued on next page)

Please do the homework.
Please be prompt.
Please open the window.
Please close the door.
Please write clearly.

2. M1T   T: Ask ( ) to speak English in Class.   S1:   Please speak English in class.
                ( ) answer O.K.   S2:   O.K.
                Ask ( ) to be on time to class.   S: Please be on time to class.
                Ask ( ) to close the door.   Please close the door.
                Ask ( ) to wait a minute.   Please wait a minute.
                Ask ( ) to finish her homework.   Please finish your homework.
                Ask ( ) to bring his car.   Please bring your car.
                Ask ( ) to come at 5:00.   Please come at 5:00.
                Ask ( ) to print his name.   Please print your name.
                Ask ( ) to sign his name.   Please sign your name.
                Ask ( ) to drive slowly.   Please drive slowly.
                Ask ( ) to speak English.   Please speak English.
                Ask ( ) to speak slowly.   Please speak slowly.

GENERALIZATION

The request forms are identical with the *you* present tense of the verb except for
BE. (Please be on time.) (Please don't be angry.)

---

3. M1   Rep: Please don't be angry.
              Please don't speak Spanish.
              Please don't make so much noise.
              Please don't lose your books.
              Please don't walk so fast.

4. M1T   T: Ask ( ) not to speak (native language)   S1:   Please don't speak (Persian) in class.
                in class.   S2:   O.K.
                Ask ( ) not to be late.   S: Please don't be late.
                Ask ( ) not to walk so fast.   Please don't walk so fast.
                Ask ( ) not to spend so much money.   Please don't spend so much money.
                Ask ( ) not to be angry.   Please don't be angry.
                Ask ( ) not to lose his money.   Please don't lose your money.
                Ask ( ) not to drink so much beer.   Please don't drink so much beer.
                Ask ( ) not to dance so fast.   Please don't dance so fast.
                Ask ( ) not to speak so fast.   Please don't speak so fast.
                Ask ( ) not to drive so fast.   Please don't drive so fast.
                Ask ( ) not to be upset.   Please don't be upset.
                Ask ( ) not to be nervous.   Please don't be nervous.
                Ask ( ) not to do his homework in class.   Please don't do your homework in class.

5. M2   T: Ask your friend not to do something.   S: (Please don't drive so fast.)
               Ask your friend to do something.   (Please get me some soap.)
               etc.

6. C   Situation: Your only son/daughter or best friend is going away to school in a foreign
                    country. As a parent (friend) what would you tell your child/friend?
               S: (Study hard.)
                     (Don't lose your money.)
                     etc.

Part B.   *Suggestion (self-included)*

☐ LET'S

Model: Let's go to the gift shop.

1. M1   Rep: Let's go downtown.
               Let's go to the movies.
               Let's have a party.
               Let's get a cup of coffee.
               Let's do the homework.
               Let's have lunch at the cafeteria.

2. M1   Situation: You don't agree to the suggestion.
         Rep: Let's not go downtown.
               Let's not have a party.
               Let's not have lunch at the cafeteria.
               Let's not do the homework.

GENERALIZATION

This pattern is used for suggestions. Agreement in conversations is made by saying:
O.K., Sure, Great. Disagreement is made by saying: *Let's not,* and offering an
alternative suggestion. (It's impolite to say, "Let's not" and not offer another
suggestion.)

In formal styles, the full form is frequent: "Let us consider the ramifications of . . ."

---

3. M2   T: Make a suggestion. The next student   S1:   Let's (go downtown).
               will disagree.   S2:   Let's not go downtown. Let's (go
                                                                 to Shadyside).
                                                           S3:   Let's not go to Shadyside. Let's
                                                                 (get a cup of coffee).

☐ SHALL

Model: Shall we go now? Yes, let's.

4. M1   Rep: Shall we go?
           Sub: begin   S: Shall we begin?
                leave   Shall we leave?
                stop   Shall we stop?
                do the exercise   Shall we do the exercise?
                go now   Shall we go now?
                call Bill   Shall we call Bill?

GENERALIZATION

This pattern with *shall* is an alternate for *Let's* and can be used in *formal* and *informal* situations. It has the question (rising) intonation and is the *only common use* of the word *shall* in American English.

---

5. M1   T: Let's go.   S: Shall we go?
                Let's stop.   Shall we stop?
                Let's do the homework.   Shall we do the homework?
                Let's leave.   Shall we leave?
                Let's have a party.   Shall we have a party?
                Let's get some coffee.   Shall we get some coffee?

NOTE: Short answers for the *shall* pattern.

Shall we go?   Yes, let's.
               No, let's not.   (Let's stay a while.)

---

6. M2   T: go now   S1: Shall we go now?
                                               S2: Yes, let's.
                                               S3: No, let's not. (Let's stay here.)
                have lunch at the cafeteria   S1: Shall we have lunch at the cafeteria?
                                               S2: Yes, let's.
                                               S3: No, let's not. (Let's have lunch at
                                                        MacDonalds.)

                go get an ice cream cone
                go downtown
                do the homework
                take a taxi
                take a bus
                speak English
                buy some candy
                play bridge

7. C   T: Make a suggestion—use shall. S2 will   S1:   Shall (we go to the Student Union
                agree or disagree.   for a cup of coffee)?
                                                          S2:   (Sure, let's go.) (No, let's get coffee
                                                                  at MacDonalds.)

           etc.

☐ *WH* + SHALL

Model: Where shall we go? Let's go to the gift shop.

8. M1   T: Shall we go somewhere?   S: Where shall we go?
                Shall we eat somewhere?   Where shall we eat?
                Shall we sit somewhere?   Where shall we sit?
                Shall we stop somewhere?   Where shall we stop?
                Shall we walk somewhere?   Where shall we walk?
                Shall we drive somewhere?   Where shall we drive?

9. M2   T: go   S1:   Where shall we go?
                                                          S2:   Let's go (to New York).
                eat dinner
                sit down
                stop for coffee
                get an ice cream cone
                buy a record
                go shopping
                eat lunch
                get some coffee
                take some pictures
                go dancing
                take a walk

GENERALIZATION

The *Wh* questions for the suggestion patterns use *shall*. "What shall we do?" "Where
shall we go?" In rapid informal speech, *what shall* is often contracted to ['hwɑt͜ʃl]
or ['hwət·l]. You should listen to your teacher when he pronounces these forms.

---

10. M1   T: Shall we do something?   S: What shall we do?
                Shall we eat something?   What shall we eat?
                Shall we buy something?   What shall we buy?
                Shall we cook something?   What shall we cook?
                Shall we make something?   What shall we make?

11. M2   T: do   S1:   What shall we do?
                                                          S2:   Let's (have a party).
                make   S1:   What shall we make?
                                                          S2:   Let's make (a cake).

(exercise continued on next page)

123

T: study
     begin
     wash
     practice
     get
     buy
     see
     play
     write
     sing

12. M1   T: Shall we go downtown sometime?   S: When shall we go downtown?
              Shall we have lunch sometime?   When shall we have lunch?
              Shall we do the work sometime?   When shall we do the work?
              Shall we finish the lesson sometime?   When shall we finish the lesson?
              Shall we eat out sometime?   When shall we eat out?
              Shall we make a cake sometime?   When shall we make a cake?

13. C   Situation: It's Saturday night. You and your roommate are bored. Discuss what you want
         to do and make suggestions for activities. Use *what, where,* etc. and the request forms.
         If you don't like the idea suggested say *no* and suggest something else.

SECTION THREE

INDEFINITE PRONOUNS — *every/no* — IN OBJECT POSITION

Vocabulary		
Nouns	Verb	Adjectives
gift	give	correct
carving		hostess
candle		

Model: The gift shop has everything.
         You don't have anything for Mrs. Wilson.

1. M1   Rep: He needs everything; he doesn't have anything.
         Sub: look at/buy   S: He looks at everything; he doesn't buy anything.
               have/need   He has everything; he doesn't need anything.
               drink/eat   He drinks everything; he doesn't eat anything.
               buy/sell   He buys everything; he doesn't sell anything.
               want/need   He wants everything; he doesn't need anything.
               see/hear   He sees everything; he doesn't hear anything.
               eat/drink   He eats everything; he doesn't drink anything.

124

2. M1   Rep: I'm not going to travel anywhere.
           Sub: see anyone   S: I'm not going to see anyone.
                buy anything   I'm not going to buy anything.
                go anywhere   I'm not going to go anywhere.
                write to anyone   I'm not going to write to anyone.
                sell anything   I'm not going to sell anything.
                talk to anyone   I'm not going to talk to anyone.
                do anything   I'm not going to do anything.

GENERALIZATION

Lesson Four: Everyone likes clean air.
                  No one likes pollution.

Lesson Five: He likes everyone.
                  He doesn't like anyone.

When the *no-* words occur in object position the spoken form is negative verb + *any-*
(anyone, anything).

        Nothing — He does*n't* know *any*thing.
        No one — He does*n't* like *any*one.
        No where— He does*n't* go *any*where.

You may read "He wants nothing." or "He listens to no one." but the forms are not
common in speech.

---

3. M1T   T: nothing—need   S: He doesn't need anything.
                no one—see   He doesn't see anyone.
                nowhere—drive   He doesn't drive anywhere.
                nowhere—go   He doesn't go anywhere.
                nothing—want   He doesn't want anything.
                nothing—drink   He doesn't drink anything.
                no one—like   He doesn't like anyone.

***4. M1T   T: Everyone is here.   S: No one is here.
                She speaks to everyone.   She doesn't speak to anyone.
                Everything is correct.   Nothing is correct.
                She has everything.   She doesn't have anything.
                Everyone is going to come.   No one is going to come.
                She's going to see everyone.   She isn't going to see anyone.
                Everyone is walking home.   No one is walking home.
                She's telling everyone.   She isn't telling anyone.

5. M2   T: see someone   S1: (Are you going to see someone tomorrow?)
                                          S2: No, I'm not going to see anyone.

                someone give you flowers   S1: (Does someone give you flowers every week?)
                                          S2: No. No one gives me flowers.

(exercise continued on next page)

125

T: drive someone home

S1:   (Are you driving someone home this afternoon?)

S2:   No, I'm not driving anyone home.

someone tell you a story
give someone a gift
someone take you to the movies
someone drive you to school
buy someone a gift
send someone a letter
someone teach you Spanish
send someone flowers
someone bring you a carving
buy someone a few candles

6. C   T: Who helps you with your homework?   S: (No one.) (My roommate.)
Do you live with a family?
Who drives you to school every day?
Who are you going to visit next weekend?
Where are you going next weekend?
What are you going to do tonight?
Where do you walk every day?
Who calls you every night?
Who sends you a letter every week?
Do you drink milk with your meals?
Do you talk to someone every evening?
Where do you go on weekends?
Who is going to send you money next week?
Do you take something to the hostess in your country?

SUMMARY DIALOGUE

Jane: Bill, do you have a few minutes? I need some help.

Bill: Sure, Jane. What's the problem?

Jane: Tomorrow is Chen's birthday. Do you have any ideas for a gift?

Bill: How many people are going to chip in?*

Jane: Six, including you.

Bill: How much?

Jane: A dollar each.

Bill: Six dollars. Let's go to the camera shop and look around.

Jane: Good idea. Shall we go now?

Bill: O.K. Let's.

*chip in = contribute

SUMMARY OF PATTERNS

EXPRESSIONS OF QUANTITY

		Count	*Non-count*
Statement (Affirmative)			
I want		some books.	some candy.
		a lot of eggs.	a lot of money.
		a few flowers.	a little rice.
Statement (Negative)			
I don't need		any cigarettes.	any help.
		many friends.	much beer.
Question (*yes/no*)			
Do you have		any ideas?	any soup?
		some roses?	some tea?
		many friends.?	much homework?
Question (Wh)			
		How many eggs do you need?	How much milk do you want?

Request Pattern (speaking to others)

			Count	*Non-count*
Affirmative	Please		come	on time.
			be	prompt.
Negative	Please	don't	come	late.
		don't	be	angry.

Suggestion Pattern (self-included)

A. *Let's* type

Affirmative	Let's		go	home.
Negative	Let's	not	go	downtown.

B. *Shall we* type

Yes/No	Shall we		have	dinner out?

        Short Answer: Yes, let's. No, let's not.

Wh + shall	Where shall we	have	dinner?

        Short Answer: Let's go to Bimbo's.

Indefinite Pronouns (*every/no* in object position)

He wants everything.

He doesn't need anything.

NOTES

LESSON SIX

INTRODUCTION   Planning a party

Some foreign students *in the Institute* are planning a party. They're going to invite a lot of American friends. They're discussing the plans with Bill and with Nancy, a girl in their biology class.

Nancy: How often do you have parties?

5   Laura: This is *the first one.* Please give us your ideas.

Nancy: O.K., but we need some information. When is the party?

Jose: A week from Saturday at eight o'clock.

Bill: Where?

Farimeh: In the recreation room of the Student Union.

10   Nancy: How many people are coming?

Shirazi: About thirty.

Bill: That's a lot. Are you going to have refreshments?

Laura: Sure! What do *you* have at parties?

Nancy: *We always have* snacks—potato chips, pretzels, and stuff. Everyone is always hungry
15   at parties.

Bill: And music—we never have a party without music. Who has a record player?

Jose: I do and I have records from my country.

Nancy: Are you going to have decorations?

Shirazi: Decorations? Oh, yes. What do we need?

20   Nancy: Some balloons, a few *feet* of ribbon and some flowers. The florist near my house
            has nice ones and they're cheap.

Jose: What are we going to have to drink?

Bill: How about soft drinks and beer?

Jose: That sounds good. This is going to be a great party!

129

OUTLINE OF PATTERNS   Example

Section One	Post-Nominal Prepositional Phrases	Students *in the Institute.*
Section Two	Irregular Noun Plurals	a few feet.
Section Three	Frequency Adverbs in:	
Part A	Statements with Affirmative Verb	We always have snacks.
Part B	*Yes/No* Questions	Are you ever late?
Part C	Negative Statements	We never have parties without music.
Part D	*Wh* Questions	How often do you have parties?
Section Four	Indefinite Pronouns—*one/ones*	This is the first one. The florist has some nice ones.

COMPREHENSION QUESTIONS

1. Who is planning a party?

2. Whom are they going to invite?

*3. Who is helping them?

4. Do they have parties often?

5. When is the party?

6. Where is the party?

7. How many people are coming?

8. What are they going to have for refreshments?

9. What do they always have at parties?

10. What is Jose going to bring?

11. What do they need for decorations?

*12. Why does Nancy suggest the florist near her house?

13. What are they going to have to drink?

14. Does Jose like the idea?

15. What are the customs at parties in your country? How do you invite people? Do people stand up or sit down? What kind of parties are common among students? Do people dance?

NOTES:

Line 10:   What tense is used?
                What *time* is meant?

                When the context is clear, remember that the Present Continuous is often used
                to express an action in the future time.

Line 12   *refreshments* and *decorations* are usually in the plural.
and 19:

Note: Americans feel uncomfortable about going to a party to which they have not been
         specifically invited. The invitation may be verbal, but should include specific informa-
         tion such as time, place, who is giving the party and the occasion if any.

SECTION ONE

POST-NOMINAL PREPOSITIONAL PHRASES

```
Vocabulary

    Nouns                          Adjectives

    bakery                         blonde
    block (distance)               leather
    collar                         torn
    cover
    painting
```

Model: The florist near my house has some nice ones.

Previous pattern: I want the *big* book.
New pattern: I want the   book *with the red cover.*
Combination: I want the *big* book *with the red cover.*

1. M1   Rep: The florist near my house has nice flowers.
        Sub: _on the corner   S: The florist on the corner has nice flowers.
               down the street   The florist down the street has nice
                                                          flowers.

               across from my house   The florist across from my house has nice
                                                          flowers.

               near the bakery   The florist near the bakery has nice
                                                          flowers.

               next to the church   The florist next to the church has nice
                                                          flowers.

               near my office   The florist near my office has nice flowers.
               two blocks down   The florist two blocks down has nice
                                                          flowers.

***2. M1　　Rep: The tall girl is studying physics.
　　　　　Sub: short　　　　　　　　　　　　　　　S: The short girl is studying physics.
　　　　　　　　fat　　　　　　　　　　　　　　　　The fat girl is studying physics.
　　　　　　　　pretty　　　　　　　　　　　　　　The pretty girl is studying physics.
　　　　　　　　thin　　　　　　　　　　　　　　　The thin girl is studying physics.
　　　　　　　　blonde　　　　　　　　　　　　　The glonde girl is studying physics.
　　　　　　　　Mexican　　　　　　　　　　　　The Mexican girl is studying physics.
　　　　　　　　Persian　　　　　　　　　　　　The Persian girl is studying physics.

GENERALIZATION

Single-word modifiers (*fat*) precede the noun; phrases (*in my class*) follow the noun.

---

3. M1T　　Rep: The tall boy with the broken arm is going to have a party.
　　　　　Sub: short　　　　　　　　　　　　S: The short boy with the broken arm is going to have
　　　　　　　　　　　　　　　　　　　　　　　　a party.
　　　　　　with the broken leg　　　　　　　The short boy with the broken leg is going to have
　　　　　　　　　　　　　　　　　　　　　　　　a party.
　　　　　　fat　　　　　　　　　　　　　　　　The fat boy with the broken leg is going to have
　　　　　　　　　　　　　　　　　　　　　　　　a party.
　　　　　　in my class　　　　　　　　　　　The fat boy in my class is going to have a party.
　　　　　　thin　　　　　　　　　　　　　　　The thin boy in my class is going to have a party.
　　　　　　in the blue shirt　　　　　　　　The thin boy in the blue shirt is going to have a
　　　　　　　　　　　　　　　　　　　　　　　　party.
　　　　　　tall　　　　　　　　　　　　　　　The tall boy in the blue shirt is going to have a party.
　　　　　　with long hair　　　　　　　　　The tall boy with long hair is going to have a party.

4. M2　　T: The (green) book (with the torn cover)　　S1: The (small) book (with the black cover)
　　　　　　　is mine. Which book is yours?　　　　　　　is mine. Which book is yours?
　　　　　　　　　　　　　　　　　　　　　　　　S2: The (blue) book (without a cover) is
　　　　　　　　　　　　　　　　　　　　　　　　　mine. Which book is yours?

5. C　　　T: Which boy is in your class?　　　　　　S: The (tall) boy (with blond hair) is in
　　　　　　　　　　　　　　　　　　　　　　　　　my class.

　　　　　　Which car is yours?
　　　　　　Which girl is from Persia?
　　　　　　Which book is mine?
　　　　　　Which purse is ( )'s?
　　　　　　Which jacket is ( )'s?
　　　　　　Which notebook is yours?
　　　　　　Which man is your reading teacher?
　　　　　　Which building is the Student Union?
　　　　　　Which coat is yours?
　　　　　　Which man is your brother?
　　　　　　Which woman is your professor?
　　　　　　Which house is yours?

6. C   T: What kind of books do you like?   S: (I like exciting books with a lot of action.)
                      What kind of weather do you like?
                      What kind of classes do you like?
                      What kind of parties do you like?
                      What kind of paintings do you like?
                      What kind of cities do you like?
                      What kind of houses do you like?
                      What kind of people do you like?
                      What kind of food do you like?
                      What kind of movies do you like?
                      What kind of cars do you like?
                      What kind of flowers do you like?

7. C   Situation: You're in a department store. You need to buy some things, but you don't see what you want. Ask the clerk. Describe what you want using this pattern.
           Example: (I want a leather purse with lots of room.)
                     (I want a black coat with a fur collar.)

8. C   Situation: You and your friend are going to have dinner. You are waiting for him/her in the restaurant. He/she is fifteen minutes late. Tell the people near you:
           S: I'm looking for my friend. (He's a tall man with blond hair.) (She's a short girl with blue eyes and blonde hair.)

9. C   Situation: You walk to your car in the morning and it's gone. Describe it to the police.
           S: (It's a blue VW with Pennsylvania license plates.)

SECTION TWO

IRREGULAR NOUN PLURALS

Vocabulary

Nouns			Verb	Adjectives
diet	**loaf	**tooth	admire	high
**half	plant	umbrella		liberated
kitchen	poet	**wife		loose
**knife	ribbon	wisdom tooth		missing
**leaf	**shelf			sharp
	**Irregular plural			

Model: We'll need a few feet of ribbon.

1. M1   Rep: one child—two children
                  one man—two men
                  one woman—two women
                  one loaf—two loaves
                  one wife—two wives
                  one half—two halves
                  one life—two lives
                  one knife—two knives
                  one leaf—two leaves
                  one shelf—two shelves
                  one foot—two feet
                  one tooth—two teeth
                  one person—two people

NOTE: Usually the word *children* refers to young people, but it can mean *offspring* of any
         age. Ex: There are two children in my family, my brother (34 years old) and
         myself.

GENERALIZATION

These are the most common irregular nouns, but you will find others in your reading.
Note that *person/people* are not S/Pl of the same word, but usage usually puts the
two together, since *person* usually is not plural and *people* does not have a singular
form.

---

2. M1T   T: The fat woman is going on a diet.   S: The fat women are going on a diet.
                The student's wife is studying English.   The students' wives are studying English.
                The knife in the kitchen is very sharp.   The knives in the kitchen are very sharp.
                The leaf is turning red.   The leaves are turning red.
                The big shelf at the bottom is for plants.   The big shelves at the bottom are for
                                                                  plants.

                The person in front of me has an umbrella.   The people in front of me have umbrellas.
                The life of the poet is interesting.   The lives of the poets are interesting.

3. M2   T: The fat woman . . .   S: The fat woman (with the big hat is
                                                                  breaking the chair).
                The tall men . . .   The tall men (in the corner have new cars).
                The knives . . .
                The shelf . . .
                The people . . .
                The leaves . . .
                The life . . .
                The big loaf . . .
                The student's wife . . .
                The low shelves . . .
                The person . . .

4. M2   T: people   S1:   How many people (do we need for a
                                                         party) (are going to the party)?
                                                S2:   (Any number.) (Fifteen or twenty.)
               shelves   S1:   How many shelves (do we need for
                                                         the books)?
                                                S2:   (Three or four.)

               children
               men
               women
               loaves of bread
               feet of ribbon

5. C   T: When do children lose their first teeth?   S: (At five years.)
               When do people get their wisdom teeth?
               What do you put on a high shelf in your room?
               Do you have bookshelves? Are they full? Of what?
               How many books do you have on your shelves?
               Do you admire the life of any person? Who?
               When do the leaves turn color? Here? In your country?
               Do the trees lose their leaves in your country?
               Are women in your country liberated?
               What do you think of liberated women?
               How many people are there in your family?
               How many children are there in your family?

6. C   Situation: You're at a social gathering—a party or a reception. Use the patterns you know
               and find out about the other people.
         S: (Who is the tall man with the blue suit?)
               (Who is the short girl near the people in the corner?)
               (Who are the men near the bar?)

SECTION THREE

FREQUENCY ADVERBS

Vocabulary			
Nouns	**Verbs**	**Adjectives**	**Expressions**
breakfast	listen to	absent	go shopping
headache	stay up	early	go swimming
midnight		hungry	
nap		sick	
trouble		sleepy	
		tired	

Model: We *always* have snacks.
         We *never*   have a party without music.
         We   are *never* late for a party.

Part A.   *Statement with Affirmative Verb*

1. M1   Rep: We always have snacks at a party.
           Sub: sometimes   S: We sometimes have snacks at a party.
                usually   We usually have snacks at a party.
                often   We often have snacks at a party.
                occasionally   We occasionally have snacks at a party.
                never   We never have snacks at a party.
                seldom   We seldom have snacks at a party.
                rarely   We rarely have snacks at a party.

GENERALIZATION

100% of the time	always
	usually
	often
	frequently
50%	sometimes
	occasionally

{ rarely
  seldom } ————————→ Negative
  never }

0%

Note: The percentages are only an approximation. *Rarely, seldom* and *never* are negatives and are never used when the verb is in the negative form.

Ex: We don't often have parties. We rarely have parties.

---

2. M1   Rep: We never have parties without snacks.
           Sub: usually   S: We usually have parties without snacks.
                always   We always have parties without snacks.
                seldom   We seldom have parties without snacks.
                often   We often have parties without snacks.
                occasionally   We occasionally have parties without
                                                         snacks.
                sometimes   We sometimes have parties without
                                                         snacks.

3. M1   Rep: He is never late for parties.
         Sub: always   S: He is always late for parties.
              usually   He is usually late for parties.
              sometimes   He is sometimes late for parties.
              rarely   He is rarely late for parties.
              often   He is often late for parties.
              seldom   He is seldom late for parties.

GENERALIZATION

The adverbs of frequency usually follow the verb BE but precede other verbs:

He is *always* late.
He *always* has a good time.

---

4. M1T   T: The boys are late for class. (always)   S: The boys are always late for class.
               I'm on time for lunch. (never)   I'm never on time for lunch.
               We're absent from class. (rarely)   We're rarely absent from class.
               They're on time for appointments. (usually)   They're usually on time for appointments.
               You're tired in class. (seldom)   You're seldom tired in class.
               Bill is helpful to the foreign students. (always)   Bill is always helpful to the foreign students.
               Nancy is sleepy at midnight. (often)   Nancy is often sleepy at midnight.
               We're hungry at noon. (sometimes)   We're sometimes hungry at noon.

5. M1T   T: Bill helps Chen and Carlos. (often)   S: Bill often helps Chen and Carlos.
               We have snacks at parties. (always)   We always have snacks at parties.
               The girls cook dinner at home. (occasionally)   The girls occasionally cook dinner at home.
               The students speak Farci. (never)   The students never speak Farci.
               The lawyers drive VWs. (rarely)   The lawyers rarely drive VWs.
               I walk to school. (usually)   I usually walk to school.
               Mr. Jackson drives to work. (rarely)   Mr. Jackson rarely drives to work.
               You ask a lot of questions. (always)   You always ask a lot of questions.

6. M1T   T: ( ) is late for class. (never)   S: ( ) is never late for class.
               ( ) drinks beer. (never)   ( ) never drinks beer.
               ( ) is on time. (never)   ( ) is never on time.
               ( ) walks to school. (always)   ( ) always walks to school.
               ( ) works in a restaurant. (often)   ( ) often works in a restaurant.
               ( ) is tired. (often)   ( ) is often tired.
               ( ) has a headache. (sometimes)   ( ) sometimes has a headache.
               ( ) speaks Persian. (rarely)   ( ) rarely speaks Persian.
               ( ) is late. (seldom)   ( ) is seldom late.
               ( ) cooks dinner. (always)   ( ) always cooks dinner.
               ( ) speaks Persian. (never)   ( ) never speaks Persian.
               ( ) is absent. (sometimes)   ( ) is sometimes absent.
               ( ) asks questions. (often)   ( ) often asks questions.

7. M2   T: ( ) is late to class.   S: ( ) is (always) late to class.
                ( ) eats ice cream cones.
                ( ) works in a gas station.
                ( ) drives to school.
                ( ) is absent.
                ( ) speaks Thai.
                ( ) goes to the movies on week nights.
                ( ) is sick.
                ( ) has lots of dates.
                ( ) takes a bus to school.
                ( ) studies in the library.
                ( ) does his homework.

8. C   T: Are you often late for class?   S: (Yes, I'm often late.) (No, I'm seldom late.)

                Do you always do your homework?
                Do you often buy flowers for your friend?
                Are you often sick?
                Are you often in trouble with your teachers?
                Do you always have music at your parties?
                Do you always listen to the radio at night?
                Are you often hungry in the afternoon?
                Do you usually get up at 5:00 in the morning?
                Are you often sleepy in class?
                Do you always watch TV in the evening?
                Do you sometimes take a nap in the afternoon?
                When do you usually do your homework?
                What do you usually have for breakfast?

Part B.   *Yes/No Questions*

Model: Are you ever late for class? No, never.

1. M1   Rep: Are you ever late for class?
            Sub: often   S: Are you often late for class?
                  usually   Are you usually late for class?
                  sometimes   Are you sometimes late for class?
                  occasionally   Are you occasionally late for class?
                  always   Are you always late for class?

2. M1   Rep: Do you ever have parties without beer?
            Sub: often   S: Do you often have parties without beer?
                  usually   Do you usually have parties without beer?
                  sometimes   Do you sometimes have parties
                                                                      without beer?
                  ever   Do you ever have parties without beer?

GENERALIZATION

Frequency adverbs can be used in Yes/No questions. Most require a simple *Yes* or *No* answer but *ever* (at any time) usually requires a fuller response:

Are you sometimes late for class?	Yes, I am.
Are you ever late for class?	No, I'm never late.
Do you ever have parties without beer?	No, we usually have beer.

***3. C   T: Ask if ( ) is ever late to class.   S1:   Are you ever late to class?
                                                            S2:   (No, I'm never late.) (Yes, I'm
                                                                    sometimes late.)

           Ask if ( ) ever has parties without beer.   S1:   Do you ever have parties without beer?
                                                            S2:   (Yes, we occasionally have parties
                                                                    without beer.) (No, we never have
                                                                    parties without beer.)

           Ask if ( ) is ever sleepy in class.
           Ask if ( ) often eats in a restaurant.
           Ask if ( ) is sometimes on time for class.
           Ask if ( ) usually takes a taxi to school.
           Ask if ( ) often has coffee at 10:00.
           Ask if ( ) always walks to school.
           Ask if ( ) is usually late for language laboratory.
           Ask if ( ) ever buys flowers for his friend.
           Ask if ( ) ever walks to school.
           Ask if ( ) is ever awake at 4:00 a.m.
           Ask if ( ) ever drives to class.
           Ask if ( ) usually drinks beer at parties.

Part C.   *Negative Statements*

Model: We never have parties without beer.

1. M1   Rep: We never have parties without beer.
         Sub: rarely   S: We rarely have parties without beer.
              seldom   We seldom have parties without beer.
              don't usually   We don't usually have parties without
                                                          beer.
              don't often   We don't often have parties without beer.
              never   We never have parties without beer.

2. M1   Rep: She is never late to class.
         Sub: rarely   S: She is rarely late to class.
              seldom   She is seldom late to class.
              isn't usually   She isn't usually late to class.
              isn't often   She isn't often late to class.
              isn't always   She isn't always late to class.

GENERALIZATION

Rarely, seldom and *never* are not used with a verb in the negative form, since their meaning is already negative.

---

3. M2   T: How often do you forget your homework?   S: I (rarely) forget my homework.
                                                                       I (don't often) forget my homework.

How often are you sleepy at noon?   I'm (seldom) sleepy at noon. I'm (not often) sleepy at noon.

How often are you late to class?
How often do you stay up until 4:00 a.m.?
How often are you hungry at 1:00 in the afternoon?
How often do you go downtown?
How often are you sick?
How often do you go swimming?
How often do you buy flowers?
How often do you go to parties?
How often do you go to the movies?
How often do you watch TV?
How often are you absent from class?

Part D.   *Wh Question—How Often?*

Model: How often do you have parties? Every weekend.

1. M1   Rep: How often do you go downtown?
          Sub: have parties   S: How often do you have parties?
               buy flowers for your friend   How often do you buy flowers for your friend?
               take a taxi to school   How often do you take a taxi to school?
               forget your homework   How often do you forget your homework?
               stay up until midnight   How often do you stay up until midnight?

2. M1   Rep: How often are you late for class?
          Sub: sleepy in the morning   S: How often are you sleepy in the morning?
               hungry at 1:00   How often are you hungry at 1:00?
               late for work   How often are you late for work?
               early for class   How often are you early for class?
               tired in grammar class   How often are you tired in grammar class?

GENERALIZATION

Do you |often| have parties?   Yes, we often have them.

|How often| do you   have parties?   We have them every week.

Are you |usually| late for class?   No, I'm rarely late.

|How often| are you   late?   Only once a month.

The *Wh* question of frequency is *How often?*

---

3. M1T   T: go downtown   S: How often do the boys go downtown?
                late for class   How often are the boys late for class?
                do the work   How often do the boys do the work?
                hungry at midnight   How often are the boys hungry at midnight?
                walk home   How often do the boys walk home?
                sleepy in lab   How often are the boys sleepy in lab?
                sleep in class   How often do the boys sleep in class?

4. M2   T: She's late today.   S1:   How often is she late?
                                               S2:   She's (seldom) late. (She's always late.)

                She's taking a bus now.   S1:   How often does she take a bus?
                                               S2:   She (seldom) takes a bus. (She usually
                                                        takes a bus.)

                She's absent from class today.
                She's walking downtown now.
                She's buying flowers now.
                She's late for work today.
                She's speaking English now.
                She's going to a party tonight.
                She's late for her job today.
                She's buying some beer now.
                She's going downtown this afternoon.
                She's doing the laundry today.
                She's nervous now.

5. C   T: Ask how often (he) walks to school.   S1:   How often do you walk to school?
                                                       S2:   I (always) walk to school.

                Ask how often ( ) is late for school.
                Ask how often ( ) is early for class.
                Ask how often ( ) goes to a party.
                Ask how often ( ) is hungry at midnight.
                Ask how often ( ) eats in a restaurant.
                Ask how often ( ) buys beer.
                Ask how often ( ) is sleepy at 3:00 in the afternoon.
                Ask how often ( ) takes a taxi to school.
                Ask how often ( ) is absent from class.
                Ask how often ( ) goes shopping.
                Ask how often ( ) cooks dinner.
                Ask how often ( ) eats out.

SECTION FOUR

INDEFINITE PRONOUNS — ONE/ONES

```
┌ ─ ─ ─ ─ ─ ─ ─ ─ ─ ─ ─ ─ ─ ─ ─ ─ ┐
│    Vocabulary                            │
│                                          │
│    Nouns                Adjectives       │
│    bathroom             new              │
│    bedroom              ugly             │
│    boat                                  │
│    raincoat                              │
│    shirt                                 │
│    telephone                             │
└ ─ ─ ─ ─ ─ ─ ─ ─ ─ ─ ─ ─ ─ ─ ─ ─ ┘
```

Model: How often do you have parties?   This is the first one.
        We need some flowers. The florist near my house has some nice ones.

***1. M1   T: Situation: two cars; a VW and a Rolls-Royce.
             Rep: I want the cheap one; ( ) wants the
                  expensive one.
             Sub: little/big   S: I want the little one; ( ) wants the big one.
                  yellow/black   I want the yellow one; ( ) wants the black
                                                     one.
                  short/long   I want the short one; ( ) wants the long one.
                  small/big   I want the small one; ( ) wants the big one.
                  ugly/beautiful   I want the ugly one; ( ) wants the beautiful
                                                     one.

2. M1   Situation: The bookstore is having a sale of many types of books. Which topics are you
              interested in?
          Rep: I'm going to look at the ones on Latin
               American geography.
          Sub: English grammar   S: I'm going to look at the ones on English grammar.
               travel in the United States   I'm going to look at the ones on travel in the
                                                  United States.
               U.S. history   I'm going to look at the ones on U.S. history.
               economics   I'm going to look at the ones on economics.
               World War II   I'm going to look at the ones on World War II.
               Canadian government   I'm going to look at the ones on Canadian
                                                  government.
               American Indian languages   I'm going to look at the ones on American
                                                  Indian languages.

3. M1   Rep: I'm going to buy this camera; he's going
               to buy that one.
          Sub: hat   S: I'm going to buy this hat; he's going to buy
                                                 that one.
               car   I'm going to buy this car; he's going to buy
                                                 that one.

(exercise continued on next page)

Sub:	house		I'm going to buy this house; he's going to buy that one.
	coat		I'm going to buy this coat; he's going to buy that one.
	overcoat		I'm going to buy this overcoat; he's going to buy that one.
	jacket		I'm going to buy this jacket; he's going to buy that one.
	shirt		I'm going to buy this shirt; he's going to buy that one.

4. M1   Rep: She wants these old hats; I want these
                    new ones.

Sub:	cars	S:	She wants these old cars; I want these new ones.
	gloves		She wants these old gloves; I want these new ones.
	books		She wants these old books; I want these new ones.
	sweaters		She wants these old sweaters; I want these new ones.
	blouses		She wants these old blouses; I want these new ones.

GENERALIZATION

One (singular) and *ones* (plural) can be substituted for any count noun. They are
often used in conversation to avoid repetition of a noun previously mentioned. They
may follow adjectives ("big one/ones") and the singular may follow demonstratives
("this one"); for plural, use "*these, those.*"

---

5. M1T   T: Bill is going to get a new car.   S: He isn't going to get an old one.
                  Please buy pretty flowers.   Please don't buy ugly ones.
                  We want to see the new movie.   We don't want to see the old one.
                  Chen is buying an expensive camera.   He isn't buying a cheap one.
                  Let's go to the new restaurant.   Let's not go to the old one.
                  They're buying expensive gloves.   They aren't buying cheap ones.
                  Carlos likes difficult assignments.   He doesn't like easy ones.

6. M2   T: flowers   S1:   (I like red ones. What color do you like?)
                                                  S2:   (I like yellow ones.)
                 hostess gifts   S2:   (I buy inexpensive ones. What kind do
                                                        you buy?)
                                                  S3:   (I usually get little ones.)
                 car   S3:   (I want a little one. Do you have a car?)
                                                  S4:   (No, I don't have one.)

                 ice cream cones
                 raincoat
                 houses
                 candy bar
                 magazines
                 parties
                 class
                 movies

NOTE: *One/ones* may not be used in the following patterns (Drills 7, 8, 9).
          Try to guess the generalization.

---

7. M1   Rep: I want these books; he wants those.
          Sub: flowers   S: I want these flowers; he wants those.
               hats   I want these hats; he wants those.
               gloves   I want these gloves; he wants those.
               pencils   I want these pencils; he wants those.
               books   I want these books; he wants those.

8. M1   Rep: We have one car; the Jacksons have two.
          Sub: cat/three   S: We have one cat; the Jacksons have three.
               bedroom/four   We have one bedroom; the Jacksons have four.
               telephone/five   We have one telephone; the Jacksons have five.
               dog/two   We have one dog; the Jacksons have two.
               bathroom/three   We have one bathroom; the Jacksons have three.
               TV set/four   We have one TV set; the Jacksons have four.

9. M1   Rep: This is her new coat. Where is yours?
          Sub: his books   S: These are his new books. Where are yours?
               my car   This is my new car. Where is yours?
               our painting   This is our new painting. Where is yours?
               their boots   These are their new boots. Where are yours?
               her sweater   This is her new sweater. Where is yours?
               our gloves   These are our new gloves. Where are yours?

GENERALIZATION

One/Ones are *not* used immediately following:

1. Numbers:		I have two.
	but:	I have two big ones.
2. Plural demonstrative Adjectives:		these
	but:	These big ones.
3. Possessive Adjectives & Pronouns		It's theirs.
	but:	It's their big one.

---

10. M1T   T: I'm going to buy a new car.   S: I'm going to buy a new one.
                I'm going to buy this car.   I'm going to buy this one.
                I'm going to buy that car.   I'm going to buy that one.
                I'm going to buy five new cars.   I'm going to buy five new ones.
                I'm going to buy these cars.   I'm going to buy these.
                I'm going to buy those cars.   I'm going to buy those.
                I'm going to buy five houses.   I'm going to buy five.
                I'm going to buy your cars.   I'm going to buy yours.
                I'm going to buy that hat.   I'm going to buy that one.
                I'm going to buy those hats.   I'm going to buy those.
                I'm going to buy these flowers.   I'm going to buy these.
                I'm going to buy those pretty flowers.   I'm going to buy those pretty ones.

144

11. M2   T: a pencil   S1:   (I need a pencil.) (Does anyone have a pencil?)
                                  S2:   (Take this one.) (I have one.)

                flowers   S1:   (We need some flowers for the party.)
                                  S2:   (The florist near the office has cheap ones.)

                car   S1:   (Are you going to buy a car?)
                                  S2:   (No, I don't need one.)

                party
                candles
                gift
                telephone
                TV set
                coasters
                roses
                apartment
                magazines
                gifts
                sweater

12. M2   T: Next term all the students in the   S1:   I'm going to look at the courses in (engineering).
                Institute can choose an academic   S2:   He's going to look at the courses in engineering;
                course in addition to the English   I'm going to look at the ones in (biology).
                course. What department are   S3:   He's going to look at the courses in engineering;
                you going to consider for courses?   she's going to look at the ones in biology, and
                                                             I'm going to (take one in public health).
                                                       etc.

13. M2   Situation: You have $50,000. What kind of house are you going to buy?
          S: I'm going to buy (a big) one (with 15 rooms).
                I'm going to buy a (small) one (with a lot of windows).

14. C   (Picture Cues)
          T: Here are pictures of similar items (houses,   S1:   (I like the white one. How much is it?)
                cars). You want to buy one, but you   S2:   (How many rooms does the big one have?)
                need more information. Ask the
                salesman.

SUMMARY DIALOGUE

Jose: The students in the Institute are going to have a party. You're invited.

Nancy: Thanks. Do you often have parties?

Jose: No. This is the first one this term. We're going to have a good time.

Nancy: Yes, I'm sure. Parties with the Institute students are always fun.

Jose: It's at the Student Union on Friday, the 22nd, at 8:00. All the students will be there.

Nancy: O.K. Thanks again. See you then.

LESSON SIX — SUMMARY OF PATTERNS

Noun Modification

	The	boy	is having a party.
Single word	The tall	boy	is having a party.
Phrase	The tall	boy from Peru	is having a party.

Frequency Adverbs

Affirmative	BE	He is always late.
	Verb	He always drives to school.

Yes/No Questions	Are you always late?	Answer:	Yes, I am.
	Do you always drive to school?		No, I don't.

Wh Questions	How often are you late?	Answer:	Never.
	How often do you have parties?		Every week.

Negative	We never have parties without beer.
	We don't usually have parties without beer.

LESSON SEVEN

INTRODUCTION   Daylight Saving Time

Carlos is describing a bad day to Nancy.

Carlos: Yesterday was a terrible day!

Nancy: Why? Were you in some kind of trouble?

Carlos: I certainly was. *I was an hour late* for all my appointments. I usually go to church
5   at 10:00. When I got there, *everyone was leaving;* the service was over. I don't know what
           happened. It was a beautiful day, so later I was walking in the park before my dinner
           invitation at two o'clock. When I arrived, Mrs. Newton was a little upset. It was three
           o'clock on her clock, and I was very embarrassed. I guess my watch was wrong, but I don't
           understand it.

10   Nancy: (laughing) All your trouble was because of Daylight Saving Time.

Carlos: What's that?

Nancy: On the last Sunday in April, everyone turns his clock ahead one hour. On the last
          Sunday in October, the clocks are turned back to Standard Time.

Carlos: It sounds crazy to me. Why do you do that?

15   Nancy: You get more hours of daylight during the summer. The more hours of daylight
          there were the less electricity people needed. After a while, everyone was used to it and
          people liked the long summer days, so Daylight Saving Time is now a part of every
          summer.

Carlos: Do all the states have it?

20   Nancy: Almost all of them do. The state legislatures decided for each state.

Carlos: I guess it's a good idea, but I was really confused yesterday.

Nancy: It was terrible when I was little. In the summer, small children have to go to bed
          while it's still light.

Carlos: How do you remember which way to turn the clock?

25   Nancy: The expression is pretty dumb, but I remember it by the phrase "spring ahead; fall
          behind."

Carlos: I see what you mean. But anything is better than another day like yesterday.

147

OUTLINE OF PATTERNS   Example

Section One	BE Past Tense	
Part A	Affirmative	I was an hour late.
Part B	*Yes/No* Questions	Were you in trouble?
Part C	*Wh* Questions	Where were you?
Part D	Time expressions with *When?*	in January/on Monday
Part E	*How long?* and Time expressions	How long were you there? For ten years.

Section Two	Past Continuous	Everyone was leaving.

Section Three	Tag Questions	
Part A	Type I	was it?
Part B	Type II	wasn't it?

COMPREHENSION QUESTIONS

1. What kind of day was it for Carlos?
2. What happened?
3. Why was Carlos late?
4. When are the clocks turned ahead? back?
5. Why?
6. Do all the states have Daylight Saving Time (DST)?
7. Why didn't Nancy like DST when she was little?
8. Why don't small children like DST?
9. How does Nancy remember which way to turn the clock?
*10. Why is it dumb?
*11. Do you have Daylight Saving Time in your country?

Vocabulary

Nouns		Verbs	Adjectives	Expression
accident	phrase	clean	arrested	mow the lawn
birthday	synagogue	happen	right	
country (rural)	theater		serious	
jail	war		wrong	
	writing			

SECTION ONE

BE — PAST TENSE

Part A.   *Affirmative*

Model: I was an hour late for all my appointments.

***1. M1   Rep: I was in Paris yesterday.
   Sub: London   S: I was in London yesterday.
       Hong Kong   I was in Hong Kong yesterday.
       Caracas   I was in Caracas yesterday.
       Teheran   I was in Teheran yesterday.
       Washington   I was in Washington yesterday.
       New York   I was in New York yesterday.

2. M1   Rep: I was at home yesterday.
   Sub: John   S: John was at home yesterday.
       Mary   Mary was at home yesterday.
       the man   The man was at home yesterday.
       the woman   The woman was at home yesterday.
       the child   The child was at home yesterday.
       ( )   ( ) was at home yesterday.
       ( )   ( ) was at home yesterday.
       ( )   ( ) was at home yesterday.

3. M1   Rep: My friend was at home yesterday.
   Sub: I   S: I was at home yesterday.
       in Paris   I was in Paris yesterday.
       the boy   The boy was in Paris yesterday.
       downtown   The boy was downtown yesterday.
       my sister   My sister was downtown yesterday.
       in New York   My sister was in New York yesterday.
       I   I was in New York yesterday.

4. M1   Rep: My friend and I were at home last night.
   Sub: downtown   S: My friend and I were downtown last night.
       at school   My friend and I were at school last night.
       at the synagogue   My friend and I were at the synagogue last night.
       at the movies   My friend and I were at the movies last night.
       at Bill's house   My friend and I were at Bill's house last night.

5. M1   Rep: My friend and I were in New York City last weekend.
   Sub: We   S: We were in New York City last weekend.
       my friends   My friends were in New York City last weekend.
       they   They were in New York City last weekend.
       the men and women The men and women were in New York City last weekend.
       the students   The students were in New York City last weekend.
       you and your friends You and your friends were in New York City last weekend.
       you   You were in New York City last weekend.

GENERALIZATION

I, he, she, it + was   (Singular)
We, they, you + were   (Plural)

Note: When referring to someone else and yourself, the other person is mentioned first:

My friend and I.   *John and I.*

---

6. M1T   Rep: The boys were sleepy in class last Friday.
         Sub: I   S: I was sleepy in class last Friday.
              the teacher   The teacher was sleepy in class last Friday.
              the girls   The girls were sleepy in class last Friday.
              we   We were sleepy in class last Friday.
              they   They were sleepy in class last Friday.
              Miss Gottlieb   Miss Gottlieb was sleepy in class last Friday.
              Miss Gottlieb and I   Miss Gottlieb and I were sleepy in class
                                                    last Friday.

              you and your friend   You and your friend were sleepy in class
                                                    last Friday.

7. M1T   Rep: I was in Paris last summer.
         Sub: John and Bill   S: John and Bill were in Paris last summer.
              in Colombia   John and Bill were in Colombia last summer.
              last month   John and Bill were in Colombia last month.
              Mary   Mary was in Colombia last month.
              in the country   Mary was in the country last month.
              Mr. and Mrs. Jones   Mr. and Mrs. Jones were in the country last
                                                    month.

              at the theater   Mr. and Mrs. Jones were at the theater last
                                                    month.

8. M2   T: I/last week   S: I was (in New York City) last week.
              John and Bill/last year   John and Bill were (at the university) last year.
              ( )/last weekend
              ( )/yesterday
              we/last Friday
              ( ) and ( )/last Tuesday
              ( )/yesterday at noon
              I/in January 1968
              ( )/last March
              ( ) and ( )/the day before yesterday
              I/this morning
              Chen/two months ago
              Mr. Jackson/last Wednesday

9. C   T: Where were you at 10:00 yesterday?   S: (In grammar class.) (At home.)
              Where were ( ) and ( ) at noon yesterday?
              When were you downtown the last time?
              How was the weather in your country last month?
              Where was ( ) at 3:00 yesterday?
                            (exercise continued on next page)

When was ( ) absent?
When were you late?
Who was the teacher last week?
When was ( ) sleepy in lab?
When were you in New York?
Where were ( ) and ( ) yesterday morning?
Who was with you on your last vacation?
How was your dinner last night?
When were you absent from class?

Part B.   *Yes/No Questions*

Model: Were you in some kind of trouble? I certainly was.

Note:

		Short Answer
Present (Lesson One):	Is the boy at home today?	Yes, he is. No, he isn't.
Past (Lesson Seven):	Was the boy home yesterday?	Yes, he was. No, he wasn't.
Present (Lesson One):	Are they here today?	Yes, they are. No, they aren't.
Past (Lesson Seven):	Were they here yesterday?	Yes, they were. No, they weren't.

The *Yes/No* questions for BE—past have the same formation as BE—present.

---

1. M1T   T: I'm tired today.   S: Were you tired yesterday?
                The boy is late for class today.   Was he late for class yesterday?
                The girls are busy today.   Were they busy yesterday?
                We're on time today.   Were you on time yesterday?
                Bill is busy today.   Was he busy yesterday?
                Carlos is sick today.   Was he sick yesterday?
                Chen and Nancy are late today.   Were they late yesterday?
                Charlie is absent today.   Was he absent yesterday?

2. M2   T: Ask ( ) if he was tired yesterday.   S1:   Were you tired yesterday?
                                                           S2:   (Yes, I was.) (No, I wasn't.)

                Ask ( ) if he was at home last night.
                Ask ( ) if ( ) and ( ) were in Paris last month.
                Ask ( ) if he was in Teheran last year.
                Ask ( ) if ( ) and ( ) were late to class on Friday.
                Ask ( ) if I was sick yesterday.
                Ask ( ) if ( ) was in New York last weekend.
                Ask ( ) if he and his friend were at the movies last night.
                Ask ( ) if ( ) and ( ) were at the library last night.

151

3. M2   T: tired in lab   S1:   Were you tired in lab (yesterday)?
                                                   S2:   Yes, I was. I'm (always tired in lab).

              in New York   S1:   Were you in New York (last weekend)?
                                                   S2:   Yes, I was. I (always go to New York
                                                          on weekends).

              hungry at noon   S1:   Were you hungry at noon (last week)?
                                                   S2:   No, I wasn't. I'm (never hungry at noon).

              in the library   S1:   Were you in the library (last night)?
                                                   S2:   No, I wasn't. I (never go to the library).

              at the cafeteria
              sleepy in grammar class
              at home
              tired after class
              at the party
              in church
              busy at home
              hungry at midnight
              in Washington
              sleepy in the afternoon

4. C   T: Ask ( ) if ( ) and ( ) were in Paris last   S1:   Were ( ) and ( ) in Paris last month?
               month.   S2:   I don't know. (to S3) Were you and ( )
                                                                    in Paris last month?
                                                             S3:   (Yes, I was.)
                                                             S2:   (Yes, she was.)

               Ask ( ) if I was in Washington last week.   S1:   Was she in Washington last week?
                                                             S2:   I don't know. Were you in Washington
                                                                    last week?
         S3:   Yes, I was.   S2:   Yes, she was.
               Ask ( ) if ( ) was in New York two months ago.
               Ask ( ) if ( ) was an hour late for an appointment last week.
               Ask ( ) if ( ) was in an accident last year.
               Ask ( ) if ( ) and ( ) were in the White House.
               Ask ( ) if ( ) was in jail last year.
               Ask ( ) if ( ) and ( ) were at the theater last month.
               Ask ( ) if ( ) was in a movie in (country).
               Ask ( ) if ( ) was in a fight last weekend.
               Ask ( ) if ( ) and ( ) were in ( ) last year.
               Ask ( ) if ( ) was in ( ) last month.

Part C.   *WH Questions*

Model: Where were you? In class.

152

NOTE: The formation of the *Wh* questions is the same as in previous lessons. When the *some* word is in subject position, the word order of the question is the same as the statement. When the *some* word is in the object position, the subject and verb are inverted.

		Short Answer
Someone	was in New York yesterday.	
Who	was in New York yesterday?	Chen was.
Were you *someplace*	yesterday?	Yes, I was.
Where were you	yesterday?	In New York.
Were you in New York *sometime?*		Yes, I was.
When were you in New York?		Yesterday.

1. M2   T: Someone was in New York yesterday.   S1:   Who was in New York yesterday?
                                                           S2:   ( ) was.
                                                           S3:   I wasn't in New York. I was in ( ).

Someone was late for class last Friday.
Someone was absent from class last week.
Someone was sleepy in lab yesterday.
Someone was sick last week.
Someone was in Teheran three months ago.
Someone was in Michigan last year.
Someone was a teacher last year.
Someone was in New York City last weekend.

2. M2   T: ( ) was someplace yesterday.   S1:   Where were you yesterday?
                                                           S2:   (At home.)

( ) was someplace last night.
( ) was someplace last weekend.
( ) was someplace three days ago.
( ) was someplace yesterday afternoon.
( ) was someplace yesterday morning.
( ) was someplace the day before yesterday.
( ) was someplace two hours ago.

3. M2   T: late for class   S1:   When were you late for class?
                                                           S2:   (Last week.) (Never.)

sleepy in the lab
absent from class
busy with the homework
downtown
in Teheran
in Hong Kong
in Washington, D.C.
sick
at the lab
at the movies
in the cafeteria
in Rome

4. C   T: Were you ever in London? (When?)
                     Where were you yesterday at 3:00?
                     When were you downtown?
                     Were you at a party last week? (Was it fun?)
                     Who was late for class last week? (Why?)
                     Was anyone absent last week? (Who?)
                     Were you ever late for a dinner invitation? (Why?)
                     Who was sleepy in lab last week?
                     Where were you last weekend?
                     When were you very tired? (Why?)
                     Who was very busy last week? (Why?)
                     Where were you at 9:00 this morning?

***5. C   Situation: You are a police detective interviewing someone who is suspected of robbing a bank in Syracuse, New York, on May 12, 1972, at 2:15 p.m. Find out if the person was ever there, when, who he was with, where he was on the day of the robbery, etc.

Part D.   *Time Expressions — answers to When?*

Model: I was in Paris in the spring.

1. M1   Rep: I was in Paris in 1965.
              Sub: April   S: I was in Paris in April.
                    the spring   I was in Paris in the spring.
                    June   I was in Paris in June.
                    1967   I was in Paris in 1967.
                    December   I was in Paris in December.
                    the fall   I was in Paris in the fall.

2. M1   Rep: I was in London on Monday.
              Sub: June 27   S: I was in London on June 27.
                    Thursday   I was in London on Thursday.
                    April 29   I was in London on April 29.
                    July 10, 1964   I was in London on July 10, 1964.
                    Saturday   I was in London on Saturday.
                    my birthday   I was in London on my birthday.

3. M1   Rep: I was in Hong Kong during 1967.
              Sub: the war   S: I was in Hong Kong during the war.
                    the summer   I was in Hong Kong during the summer.
                    the spring   I was in Hong Kong during the spring.
                    the fall   I was in Hong Kong during the fall.
                    1970   I was in Hong Kong during 1970.

GENERALIZATION

In answer to the question *When,* use *in* with general times ("in April"); use *on* with specific times such as dates or days ("on June 27"); use *during* to emphasize the length of time ("during the war").

In and *during* are used with the same expressions.

On preceding days and dates may be omitted:
"I was in Washington June 23."

***4. M1T   T: Paris—1970   S1:   When were you in Paris?
                                               S2:   I was in Paris *in* 1970.

                  Paris—June 12   S1:   When were you in Paris?
                                               S2:   I was in Paris *on* June 12.

                  London—May   S1:   When were you in London?
                                               S2:   I was in London in May.

                  New York—1950   S1:   When were you in New York?
                                               S2:   I was in New York in 1950.

                  Caracas—February 23   S1:   When were you in Caracas?
                                               S2:   I was in Caracas on February 23.

                  Teheran—the summer   S1:   When were you in Teheran?
                                               S2:   I was in Teheran in the summer.

                  Hong Kong—1969   S1:   When were you in Hong Kong?
                                               S2:   I was in Hong Kong in 1969.

                  Washington, D.C.—January 12   S1:   When were you in Washington, D.C.?
                                               S2:   I was in Washington, D.C. on January 12.

                  Pittsburgh—the winter   S1:   When were you in Pittsburgh?
                                               S2:   I was in Pittsburgh in the winter.

                  Madrid—March   S1:   When were you in Madrid?
                                               S2:   I was in Madrid in March.

5. M2   T: the spring   S: (My country is beautiful in the spring.)
               Monday   (I do my laundry on Monday.)
               June 25
               1970
               the winter
               Saturday
               the summer
               November 23
               September
               Tuesday
               January
               the fall

6. C   T: When did you arrive here?   S: (In June.) (On April 25.)
               When does the next term begin?
               When are you going to leave here?
               Where were you on your birthday last year?
               What month is your birthday?
               When is the weather nice in (country)?

(exercise continued on next page)

T: Is the weather ever bad in ( )? When?
      What date is your national holiday?
      What month is an important religious holiday?
      What season do people take vacations in ( )?
      What day do you usually do your shopping?
      When does it rain a lot in ( )?
      Does it ever snow in ( )? When?

Part E.   *How long? and Time responses*

Model: How long were you in Paris? For a year.

NOTE: Were you in Paris   for a long time   ?

How long   were you in Paris?

---

1. M1   T: Were you in London for a long time?   S: How long were you in London?
               Were you in Hong Kong for a long time?   How long were you in Hong Kong?
               Were you in Teheran for a long time?   How long were you in Teheran?
               Were you in Colombia for a long time?   How long were you in Colombia?
               Were you in Venezuela for a long time?   How long were you in Venezuela?
               Were you in New York for a long time?   How long were you in New York?
               Were you in Europe for a long time?   How long were you in Europe?
               Were you in Asia for a long time?   How long were you in Asia?
               Were you in Africa for a long time?   How long were you in Africa?

2. M1   T: Notice the answers to the question *How long.*
         Rep: I was in London for two weeks.
         Sub: three months   S: I was in London for three months.
               two years   I was in London for two years.
               ten days   I was in London for ten days.
               a week   I was in London for a week.
               a month   I was in London for a month.
               a year   I was in London for a year.

GENERALIZATION

When were you in Paris?   *In* the summer.
                                             On August 15.
                                             During August.

How long were you in Paris?   *For* three days.

Use the word *there* to avoid repeating the name of a place.
   Ex: I was there for three weeks.

---

3. M2   T: What city (other than this one) were you   S1: (Paris.)
                in last year?   S2: How long were you in Paris?
                                                                 S1: I was there for three weeks.
                etc.

***4. M1T   T: Paris—three weeks   S1: *How long* were you in Paris?
                                                                 S2: I was there *for* three weeks.

                Paris—1965   S1: *When* were you in Paris?
                                                                 S2: I was there *in* 1965.

                Paris—April 5   S1: *When* were you in Paris?
                                                                 S2: I was there *on* April 5.

                London—July 14   S1: When were you in London?
                                                                 S2: I was there on July 14.

                Caracas—a month   S1: How long were you in Caracas?
                                                                 S2: I was there for a month.

                New York—two days   S1: How long were you in New York?
                                                                 S2: I was there for two days.

                San Francisco—June   S1: When were you in San Francisco?
                                                                 S2: I was there in June.

                Los Angeles—May 3   S1: When were you in Los Angeles?
                                                                 S2: I was there on May 3.

                St. Louis—two weeks   S1: How long were you in St. Louis?
                                                                 S2: I was there for two weeks.

                Boston—December 31   S1: When were you in Boston?
                                                                 S2: I was there on December 31.

                Bangkok—May   S1: When were you in Bangkok?
                                                                 S2: I was there in May.

                Mexico City—my birthday   S1: When were you in Mexico City?
                                                                 S2: I was there on my birthday.

                New Zealand—three years   S1: How long were you in New Zealand?
                                                                 S2: I was there for three years.

***5. C   T: Paris   S1: Were you in Paris (last year)?
                                                                 S2: (No, I wasn't.)

                London   S1: Were you in London (last year)?
                                                                 S2: (Yes, I was.)
                                                                 S1: When were you there?
                                                                 S2: (In the spring.) (On April 12.) (During April.)
                                                                 S1: How long were you there?
                                                                 S2: (For three days.)

SECTION TWO

PAST CONTINUOUS

Model: Everyone was leaving.

NOTE: Previous Pattern:	I'm studying English now.
New Pattern:	I was studying English last week.

1. M1   Rep: I was studying English last week.
                He was watching TV at ten o'clock last night.
                We were walking to school at 8:30 yesterday.
                They were working in the library yesterday afternoon.
                Laura was playing bridge in the Student Union last night.
                Carlos was driving home at 4:00 yesterday.

GENERALIZATION

Formation of Past Continuous: *was/were* + verb *-ing*.

Use: To indicate an action at a *specific time* or a *continuing* action in the past.

---

2. M1   Rep: I was watching TV at 10:00 last night.
         Sub: we   S: We were watching TV at 10:00 last night.
              sleeping   We were sleeping at 10:00 last night.
              11:00   We were sleeping at 11:00 last night.
              yesterday   We were sleeping at 11:00 yesterday.
              the children   The children were sleeping at 11:00
                                                                  yesterday.
              playing tennis   The children were playing tennis at
                                                                  11:00 yesterday.
              2:00   The children were playing tennis at 2:00
                                                                  yesterday.
              yesterday afternoon   The children were playing tennis at 2:00
                                                                  yesterday afternoon.
              the boy   The boy was playing tennis at 2:00 yesterday
                                                                  afternoon.
              playing bridge   The boy was playing bridge at 2:00 yesterday
                                                                  afternoon.

3. M1T   T: I'm cooking dinner now.   S: Were you cooking dinner at the same time
                                                                  yesterday?

              Jane is writing a letter now.   Was she writing a letter at the same time
                                                                  yesterday?

              Carlos is walking home now.   Was he walking home at the same time
                                                                  yesterday?

              Chen and Judy are waiting for a bus now.   Were they waiting for a bus at the same time
                                                                  yesterday?

              Mrs. Newton is cleaning the house now.   Was she cleaning the house at the same time
                                                                  yesterday?

              Mr. and Mrs. Newton are driving downtown now.   Were they driving downtown at the same
                                                                  time yesterday?

              Bill is mowing the lawn now.   Was he mowing the lawn at the same time
                                                                  yesterday?

              Nancy is listening to records now.   Was she listening to records at the same time
                                                                  yesterday?

              Sam and Jake are playing cards now.   Were they playing cards at the same time
                                                                  yesterday?

4. M2   T: Yesterday at 6:00 I was cooking dinner.   S1:   Yesterday at 6:00 (Mrs. Bruder) was
               What were you doing?   cooking dinner, and I was (driving
                                                                  downtown). What were you doing?
                                                         S2:   Yesterday at 6:00 (Mrs. Bruder) was
                                                                  cooking dinner; ( ) was driving downtown,
                                                                  and I was (sitting in the Student Union.)
                                                                  What were you doing?

5. M2   T: Ask ( ) if he was sleeping at 2:00   S1:   Were you sleeping at 2:00 yesterday afternoon?
               yesterday afternoon.   S2:   No, I wasn't. I was (studying in the library).
               Ask ( ) if he was watching TV last night.
               Ask ( ) if he was playing tennis/skiing yesterday afternoon.
               Ask ( ) if he was walking to school at 8:30 yesterday.
               Ask ( ) if he was studying grammar yesterday.
               Ask ( ) if he was driving home at noon yesterday.
               Ask ( ) if he was playing bridge in the Student Union yesterday.
               Ask ( ) if he was taking a bus home yesterday afternoon.
               Ask ( ) if he was walking downtown at midnight yesterday.
               Ask ( ) if he was flying to London at noon a week ago.
               Ask ( ) if he was driving a Rolls-Royce yesterday afternoon.
               Ask ( ) if he was mowing the lawn yesterday afternoon.
               Ask ( ) if he was eating dinner at 3:30 yesterday.

6. C   T: What were you doing last night at midnight?   S: (Sleeping.) (Finishing my homework.)
               Where were you at 3:30 yesterday?   (In Room 113.)
               What was ( ) doing at 8:00 last night?   S1:   I don't know. What were you doing
                                                                     at 8:00 yesterday?
                                                              S2:   (Eating dinner.) (Watching TV.)

               Where were you going at 8:30 yesterday morning?
               What were you doing yesterday morning?
               Where were ( ) and ( ) this morning?
               What was ( ) doing at 4:30 yesterday?
               Where were you going last Friday?
               When were you studying reading yesterday?
               When were you studying grammar yesterday?
               When were you studying writing yesterday?
               Were you doing your homework at 4:00 this morning?
               Where were you at 9:00 yesterday?
               When was ( ) in (city)?

SECTION THREE

TAG QUESTIONS

Part A.   *Type I.*

Model: It wasn't late, was it? No, it wasn't.
          They weren't leaving, were they? No, they weren't.

159

1. M1   Rep: It wasn't late, was it? No, it wasn't.
                 They weren't leaving, were they? No, they weren't.
                 She wasn't sleeping, was she? No, she wasn't.
                 It wasn't hot, was it? No, it wasn't.
                 He wasn't busy, was he? No, he wasn't.
                 The service wasn't over, was it? No, it wasn't.
                 You weren't eating dinner, were you? No, I wasn't.

GENERALIZATION

The tag questions for BE—past and Past Continuous follow the same pattern as for
the present. (Lesson Two)

Statement	Tag	Response
It wasn't late,	was it?	No, it wasn't.
They weren't leaving,	were they?	No, they weren't.
—	+	—

---

2. M1T   T: She wasn't sleeping.   G1:   She wasn't sleeping, was she?
                                                  G2:   No, she wasn't.
                He wasn't busy.   G1:   He wasn't busy, was he?
                                                  G2:   No, he wasn't.
                They weren't eating.   G1:   They weren't eating, were they?
                                                  G2:   No, they weren't.
                The weather wasn't hot.   G1:   The weather wasn't hot, was it?
                                                  G2:   No, it wasn't.
                The people weren't waiting.   G1:   The people weren't waiting, were they?
                                                  G2:   No, they weren't.
                The service wasn't over.   G1:   The service wasn't over, was it?
                                                  G2:   No, it wasn't.
                The man wasn't angry.   G1:   The man wasn't angry, was he?
                                                  G2:   No, he wasn't.

3. M2   Situation: You called a friend on the phone. He seems annoyed. Use a tag question to find
                out if you've interrupted him.
           S1:   (You weren't eating, were you?)
           S2:   (No, I wasn't; I was taking a nap.)
           S1:   (Oh, I'm sorry.)
           S2:   (That's O.K.)

Part B.   *Type II*

Model: You were late, weren't you? Yes, I was.
        He was sleeping, wasn't he? Yes, he was.

1. M1T   T: You were eating.   G1: You were eating, weren't you?
                                                        G2: Yes, I was.

               He was late.   G1: He was late, wasn't he?
                                                        G2: Yes, he was.

               Nancy was sleeping.   G1: Nancy was sleeping, wasn't she?
                                                        G2: Yes, she was.

               They were dancing.   G1: They were dancing, weren't they?
                                                        G2: Yes, they were.

               It was hot.   G1: It was hot, wasn't it?
                                                        G2: Yes, it was.

               Mrs. Newton was upset.   G1: Mrs. Newton was upset, wasn't she?
                                                        G2: Yes, she was.

               Carlos was an hour late.   G1: Carlos was an hour late, wasn't he?
                                                        G2: Yes, he was.

               The students were playing bridge.   G1: The students were playing bridge, weren't they?
                                                        G2: Yes, they were.

GENERALIZATION

This follows the same pattern as Type II in Lesson Two.

Statement	Tag	Response
You were late,	weren't you?	Yes, I was.
He was sleeping,	wasn't he?	Yes, he was.
+	−	+

---

2. M2   Situation: Your friend asked you to call at 3:00. He answers after nine rings. You are
               afraid you've bothered him. Use a tag question to find out.
          S1: (You were working, weren't you? I'm sorry.)
          S2: (I was outside, but that's O.K.)

NOTE: Type II tags are frequently used as a mild apology when you think you've interrupted
someone. Note the difference in position of "I'm sorry" in Type I (3) and Type II (2).
Both types are also used to begin conversations as discussed in Lesson II.

---

3. C   Situation: You're at a party. You meet someone you have met before, but you can't quite
               remember where. Use a tag question to find out where.
          S1: (You were at the ELI party last week, weren't you?)
          S2: (Yes, I was.)
          S2: (You weren't playing bridge at the Union yesterday, were you?)
          S3: (No, I wasn't.)

SUMMARY DIALOGUE

Nancy: Where were you yesterday? Everyone was worried.

Chen: I was in the library all day. We're going to have a big exam next week.

Nancy: You weren't studying at three o'clock. You were having coffee with a pretty girl.

Chen: Oh. We were just taking a break.

Nancy: I see.

LESSON SEVEN – SUMMARY OF PATTERNS

		Subject	BE	Verb -ing	Completer	Short Answer
Statement		Carlos	was	walking	in the park.	
Question (Who?)		Who	was	driving	downtown?	Chen was.
Question (Yes/No)	BE — Was	Carlos		walking	in the park?	Yes, he was. / No, he wasn't.
Question (Wh)	QW — When / BE — was	Carlos		walking	in the park?	At 2:00.
	QW — How long / BE — was	Carlos		reading?		For two hours.

163

NOTES

***STYLES OF LANGUAGE

To the Student:

Probably you have noticed that you can understand the teachers in the classroom much easier than you can your American friends at a party. This is because people speak different *styles* of language in different situations. Think about how you use your own language. Do you speak in the same manner to your friends as you do to your teachers?

In *formal* situations, the language spoken is most nearly like the written language. In *informal* situations there are more contractions, words are omitted, and some verb tenses are not used.

The style you should use is the style taught in the classroom, but you should be able to understand a more informal style. Following are two conversations about the same topic in different styles. Your teacher will help you find the differences.

Variations on a Theme No. 1

Last weekend Bill went to see a very popular movie, starring one of his favorite actors and a beautiful young actress. He's discussing it with Nancy.

Nancy: Hey, Bill. What did you do over the weekend?

Bill: Saw the new flick with Peck and Welch.

5   Nancy: Oh, yeah? How was it?

Bill: Peck was great as usual, and well, you don't go to see great acting from Raquel.

Nancy: Know what you mean. All the guys go to watch Raquel. For me Peck is the drawing card. Gotta go to class—see you later.

Bill: So long.

10   On the way home on the bus, Bill sits next to a lady who lives down the street. She is a good friend of Bill's parents.

Mrs. Cassetti: Did you have a pleasant weekend, Bill?

Bill: Yes, thank you. I studied quite a bit, but Saturday I took the evening off and went to the new movie with Gregory Peck and Raquel Welch.

15   Mrs. Cassetti: Oh, did you? Did you enjoy it?

Bill: Gregory Peck was very good—he always is. Raquel Welch isn't expected to be a great actress, I guess.

Mrs. Cassetti: Yes, I suppose you're right. All of the young men certainly seem to enjoy her movies. From my point of view Gregory Peck would be the reason for going. I have to get
20   off here. It was nice to see you, Bill.

Bill: It was nice talking to you. Goodbye, Mrs. Cassetti.

Variations on a Theme No. 2

Bill and Frank are planning a Saturday evening.

Bill: What'll we do tonight, Frank? Got any good ideas?

Frank: I don't know. How about the baseball game?

Bill: Nah, the Pirates are lousy this year. How about the new flick at the Strand?

5   Frank: Saw it already. Sorry about that.

Bill: Let's go over to Shadyside and see who's around.

Frank: Good idea. You driving?

Bill: O.K. Pick you up at 8:00.

Bill and Sally (a new girl in class) are discussing plans for their Saturday night date.

10   Bill: What would you like to do tonight, Sally? Is there any place special you'd like to go?

Sally: Not really, unless maybe a baseball game.

Bill: We can go, if you like, but the Pirates are pretty bad this year. How about the new flick at the Strand?

Sally: I've already seen it, I'm sorry. I'll watch it again, though, if you want to see it.

15   Bill: No, that's O.K. Would you like to go to Shadyside? There are always people from school around, and the music in the night clubs is great.

Sally: That sounds like a good idea.

Bill: Good. I'll pick you up at 8:00.

LESSON EIGHT

INTRODUCTION　　　　　***The telephone

Chen is telling Nancy and Bill about a strange incident.

Chen:　　It was really odd.

Bill:　　What happened?

Chen:　　Well, I was reading a novel *in the living room about four o'clock. A character in the*
5　　　　*book reminded me* of my friend in California, so I decided to call him.

Nancy:　At four o'clock in the afternoon?! That's expensive.

Bill:　　That's right. Why did you call then?

Chen:　　I didn't realize the expense. But it's O.K., I never completed the call.

Nancy:　Why not?

10　　Chen:　　I dialed the Operator and waited . . . and waited. It was a long time. She finally
　　　　answered.

(The conversation between Chen and the Operator.)

Operator (Local): Operator.

Chen:　　I want to call California.

15　　Operator: Yes, sir. What number please?

Chen:　　I don't have the number. I have the name and address.

Operator: Is this a person-to-person call?

Chen:　　No, station-to-station.

Operator: What city is it?

20　　Chen:　　San Francisco.

Operator: Dial Area Code 415, then 555-1212. It's a toll-free call. The California operator
　　　　has the number. Then hang up and dial the number.

Chen:　　Thank you, Operator. (He hangs up; then, he dials the California number.)

Operator (California): Directory assistance for what city please?

25　　Chen:　　San Francisco.

Operator: Yes, may I help you?

167

Chen: Please give me the number for Dan Talbert *at 415 Madison Street.*

Operator: How do you spell the name?

Chen: Talbert, T-A-L-B-E-R-T.

30   Operator: Thank you. One moment please. The number is 683-5210.

Chen: 683-5210. Thank you, Operator.

Operator: You're welcome.

Chen: I dialed the number, but it was busy. I tried later, and a girl answered. It was a wrong number. The third time it rang and then a woman said, "the number you have dialed has been
35   dis-" Something I didn't understand. "Please check your directory and dial again." I gave up. I never did talk to my friend.

Nancy: Disconnected?

Chen: Yes, that's it. What does it mean?

Nancy: The number is disconnected. Your friend isn't using it.

40   Chen: Oh, I see. Maybe he moved. I'm going to write him a letter. How much do I pay for all the calls?

Bill: The information call and the disconnected number are free. Call the operator and explain about the wrong number and it's free too.

NOTES:

Line 21:   The Directory Assistance number for long distance calls is always the same. Just dial the Area Code first.

Line 33:   Chen probably dialed a wrong number when the girl answered. The computerized telephone system makes some mistakes, but not very often. Make sure to call the operator if you call long distance and dial incorrectly. Also, check your monthly bill to make sure the computer has all your charges correct.

Lesson Eight

OUTLINE OF PATTERNS

Section One   *in/on/at* + place

in California
at 115 Madison Street.

Section Two   Using the Telephone

    Part A.   Numbers

    Part B.   Situations

    Part C.   Practice

Section Three   Simple Past Tense

    Part A.   Affirmative

I dialed the number.

    Part B.   Interrogative and Short Answers

Did you call your friend?
Yes, I did./No, I didn't.

    Part C.   Negative Statements

I didn't complete the call.

    Part D.   *Wh* Questions
                 Whom

What happened?
Whom did you call?

Section Four   Time and Place Expressions

. . . in the living room about four o'clock.

COMPREHENSION QUESTIONS

1. Who is telling the story?

2. What was he doing at about 4:00?

3. What reminded him of a friend?

4. What did he decide to do?

5. Which operator did he talk to first?

6. What kind of call did he want to make?

7. Where does his friend live?

8. What is the San Francisco area code?

9. What is the long distance Directory Assistance number?

10. What is his friend's address?

11. How many times did he call?

12. What happened the first time? (the second?) (the third?)

13. What does "disconnected" mean?

14. Which calls does Chen pay for?

```
┌ ─ ─ ─ ─ ─ ─ ─ ─ ─ ─ ─ ─ ─ ─ ─ ─ ─ ─ ─ ┐
│   Vocabulary                                                        │
│                                                                     │
│   Nouns              Verbs            Adjectives   Expressions      │
│                                                                     │
│   baseball game  expense    describe   receive   loud   information call │
│   biography      message    explain    remind            person-to-person │
│   boulevard      package    mail       ring              station-to-station │
│   drive          place      pick up    sound             toll-free call │
│   excitement     sandwich   pronounce  weigh             wrong number │
│                             realize                                 │
└ ─ ─ ─ ─ ─ ─ ─ ─ ─ ─ ─ ─ ─ ─ ─ ─ ─ ─ ─ ┘
```

SECTION ONE

IN/ON/AT + PLACE

1. M1   Rep: He lives *in* California.
         Sub: Pennsylvania   S: He lives in Pennsylvania.
              New York   He lives in New York.
              Pittsburgh   He lives in Pittsburgh.
              San Francisco   He lives in San Francisco.
              Washington, D.C.   He lives in Washington, D.C.
              the United States   He lives in the United States.
              Iran   He lives in Iran.
              Oakland   He lives in Oakland.
              Penn Hills   He lives in Penn Hills.
              Beaver Falls, Pa.   He lives in Beaver Falls, Pa.
              Homer, New York   He lives in Homer, New York.

2. M1   Rep: He lives *on* Centre Avenue.
         Sub: Forbes Avenue   S: He lives on Forbes Avenue.
              Fifth Avenue   He lives on Fifth Avenue.
              Meyran Street   He lives on Meyran Street.
              Baum Boulevard   He lives on Baum Boulevard.
              Jefferson Drive   He lives on Jefferson Drive.
              Park Place   He lives on Park Place.

3. M1   Rep: He lives *at* 115 Centre Avenue.
         Sub: 225 Forbes Avenue   S: He lives at 225 Forbes Avenue.
              2535 Fifth Avenue   He lives at 2535 Fifth Avenue.
              101 Main Street   He lives at 101 Main Street.
              139 Jefferson Drive   He lives at 139 Jefferson Drive.
              1137 Atwood Street   He lives at 1137 Atwood Street.
              4756 Baum Boulevard   He lives at 4756 Baum Boulevard.
              25 Park Place   He lives at 25 Park Place.

170

GENERALIZATION

Use *in* with states, cities, countries, and towns.
Use *on* with streets (etc.) when the house humber is not given.
Use *at* with house numbers.

NOTE: Written abbreviations:

Avenue	Ave.	Place	Pl.
Street	St.	Square	Sq.
Boulevard	Blvd.	Circle	Cir.
Drive	Dr.	Road	Rd.

NOTE: Numbers in addresses are spoken in groups of two if possible:

25	=	twenty-five	2535	=	twenty-five thirty-five
139	=	one thirty-nine	1137	=	eleven thirty-seven

but 101 = one oh one (an exception)

4. M1T   (See Instructor's Manual)

5. M2   (See Instructor's Manual)

6. C   T: Where do you live?   S: (In Oakland.)
              What is your address?   (381 Jefferson Drive.)
              What street do you live on?
              Where does your family live? (city, country)
              What is your friend's address?
              Where does the President of the United States live?
              Where does the leader of your country live?
              Where is the ELI office?
              Where does ( ) live?
              What street does ( ) live on?
              Do all your friends live in ( )?

SECTION TWO

USING THE TELEPHONE

Part A.   *Numbers*

***1. M1   Rep: 624-5900
            (401) 963-2456
            834-9725
            441-5134
            731-3052
            922-4893
            343-0160
            (412) 624-5900 Extension 6562

171

NOTE: Telephone numbers in the U.S. consist of a three digit Area Code (used when calling long distance), a three digit local area number and a four digit specific "station" number. Thus, a number in Pittsburgh might be:

Area Code 412 343-0165

Telephone numbers are spoken in groups, usually with each number spoken separately. A person calling the number above would say: "Area Code four-one-two (pause) three-four-three (pause) oh-one-six-five." Large round numbers are sometimes spoken as wholes; thus: 621-3500 is sometimes read as six-two-one (pause) three five hundred.

In large organizations such as a business, or a university, each office has a separate extension. This number is indicated by Ext. and another number.

XYZ Corporation:	621-3500
Production Department:	621-3500 Ext. 6562

***2. M1T   T: Write the following:
(412) 321-4889
673-4695
883-0415
391-2600 Ext. 519
531-5065
471-3213
481-4476
991-1900
828-3027
281-5015

***3. M1T   T: Read the following:
621-3500
731-3052
391-2600 Ext. 519
(412) 321-4889
441-5134
922-4893
834-9725
991-1900
531-5065
621-3500 Ext. 6562
(607) 749-2216 Ext. 2

4. C   T: My number is 343-0160. What's your number?   S1:   My number is ( ). What's your number? etc.

NOTE: The *Yellow Pages* is a list of businesses and services in the local community. You can find almost anything available by looking in the index. For example, if you are in a new city and want to go to a nearby Italian restaurant, look in the section "Restaurants," find one with an Italian name, then look at the address.

Part B.   *Situations********

1. Wrong Number
   - A.   Hello.
   - B.   May I speak to Bill Jackson?
   - A.   You must have the wrong number. There's no Bill Jackson here.
   - B.   I'm sorry.
   - A.   That's O.K.
          (Hang up and dial again.)'

   - C.   Hello.
   - B.   May I speak to Nancy please?
   - C.   You must have the wrong number.
   - B.   Is this 695-4826?
   - C.   No, it isn't.
   - B.   I'm sorry.
   - C.   That's O.K.
          (Hang up.)

   NOTE: Do not give your number to a person who has dialed incorrectly.

   - D.   Hello.
   - B.   May I speak to Jane please?
   - D.   You have the wrong number.
   - B.   Is this 483-6191?
   - D.   Yes, it is, but there's no one named Jane here.
   - B.   I'm sorry to have bothered you.
          (Hang up. Ask Jane her telephone number or call the operator to find out if the
             number has been changed.)

2. Person not in.
   - E.   Linguistics.
   - B.   May I speak to Professor Paulston, please.
   - E.   She's not in right now. May I take a message?
   - B.   No, I'll call back. What time do you expect her?
   - E.   Sometime after 10:00.
   - B.   Thank you, I'll try then.

   - F.   Hello.
   - B.   May I speak to Judy, please.
   - F.   She's not here. Do you want to leave a message?
   - B.   This is Carlos. Will you ask her to call me back?
   - F.   Sure. Does she have your number?
   - B.   Yes, she does. Thank you.
   - F.   You're welcome. Bye.
   - B.   Bye.

173

3. Salesman
        B.   Hello.
        S.   Mr. Jackson?
        B.   Yes.
        S.   Mr. Jackson, I'm calling for the Rest Easy Company. I'm sure you'll be happy to
                  have one of our salesmen who will be on your street this week stop in and show
                  you our newest line of goods which is the finest money can buy east of the
                  Pacific or west of the Atlantic. (pause for breath)
        B.   Thank you, but I'm not interested. (Hang up.)

Part C.   *Practice*

T: 1.   Call Directory Assistance and get the number for John Hastings at 215 Maple Avenue.
     2.   Call Directory Assistance and get the number for Judy Wilson on Meadow Lane in Los
           Angeles.
     3.   Call the Operator and report that you have dialed long distance incorrectly.
     4.   Your baby just swallowed some lighter fluid. Call the Operator and get the number for the
           Poison Control Center. (They will tell you the first aid to use while waiting for an
           ambulance.)
     5.   Call the Operator and report a fire in your apartment.
     6.   Call the Police and report a stolen car.
     7.   Call a taxi.
     8.   Call the bank and report the loss of your check book.
     9.   Call the nearest department store and find out if they have London Fog raincoats.
   10.   Call the English Language Institute and leave a message that you will be absent from class.

SECTION THREE

SIMPLE PAST TENSE

Part A.   *Affirmative*

Model: I dialed the number.

1. M1   Listen: I study the lesson every day.
                 I studied the lesson yesterday.
                 He watches TV every day.
                 He watched TV yesterday.
                 They need the English book every day.
                 They needed the English book yesterday.

***GENERALIZATION**

There is only one form of the verb in the past tense for both singular and plural
subjects. The spelling is usually *-ed,* but note that there are three different
pronunciations: [-id] —*needed,* [-d] —*learned,* and [-t] —*washed.*

---

2. M1T   T: If you hear a verb in the present, raise one hand; if past, raise two.

He studies engineering.	S:	(1)
He studied engineering.		(2)
We watch a movie.		(1)
We watched a movie.		(2)
They needed a dollar.		(2)
They need a dollar.		(1)
We watched a movie.		(2)
He needs a dollar.		(1)
She studied English.		(2)
They learned a song.		(2)
We play bridge.		(1)
He described Pittsburgh.		(2)
They finish in April.		(1)
She pronounced a word.		(2)
It weighs 50 pounds.		(1)
He translated a poem.		(2)
She washed an apple.		(2)
They need a nickle.		(1)
He practices English.		(1)
He practiced German.		(2)

3. M1   T:

need a dollar	S:	I needed a dollar.
start an exercise		I started an exercise.
translate a poem		I translated a poem.
attend a concert		I attended a concert.
want a letter		I wanted a letter.
complete an exercise		I completed an exercise.
wait an hour		I waited an hour.

4. M1   T:

play a song	S:	He played a song.
call a friend		He called a friend.
dial a number		He dialed a number.
answer a question		He answered a question.
explain a problem		He explained a problem.
describe a city		He described a city.
move a house		He moved a house.
mail a letter		He mailed a letter.

5. M1   T:

talk a long time	S:	They talked a long time.
watch a movie		They watched a movie.
practice English		They practiced English.
pronounce a word		They pronounced a word.
finish a lesson		They finished a lesson.
walk a mile		They walked a mile.
wash a floor		They washed a floor.
smoke a cigar		They smoked a cigar.

GENERALIZATION

Previous Pattern:	I was studying	the lesson at 2:00	yesterday.
New pattern:	I studied	the lesson	yesterday.

The Simple Past is used to denote any past action when the continuousness of the action is not important.

6. M1T   T: He watches a movie every day.   S: He watched a movie yesterday.
He practices English every night.   He practiced English last night.
We attend a concert every week.   We attended a concert last week.
They call home every month.   They called home last month.
She studies her lesson every day.   She studied her lesson yesterday.
They move every year.   They moved last year.
She needs a dollar every day.   She needed a dollar yesterday.
They want a letter every day.   They wanted a letter yesterday.
He washes his shirts every week.   He washed his shirts last week.
They practice in the lab every day.   They practiced in the lab yesterday.

7. M1T   T: finish a book   S: I finished a book yesterday.
smoke a cigar at 2:00   I was smoking a cigar at 2:00 yesterday.
walk a mile   I walked a mile yesterday.
practice English at noon   I was practicing English at noon yesterday.
watch TV at 10:00   I was watching TV at 10:00 yesterday.
mail a package   I mailed a package yesterday.
wash the dishes at 8:00   I was washing the dishes at 8:00 yesterday.
attend a concert   I attended a concert yesterday.
talk on the phone at 4:00   I was talking on the phone at 4:00 yesterday.

8. M1T   Rep: He practices in the lab every day.
Sub: tomorrow   S: He is going to practice in the lab tomorrow.
yesterday   He practiced in the lab yesterday.
every day   He practices in the lab every day.
now   He is practicing in the lab now.
at 2:00 yesterday   He was practicing in the lab at 2:00 yesterday.
we   We were practicing in the lab at 2:00 yesterday.

tomorrow   We are going to practice in the lab at 2:00 tomorrow.

9. M1T   Rep: They play bridge every Monday.
Sub: last Monday   S: They played bridge last Monday.
next Monday   They're going to play bridge next Monday.
we   We're going to play bridge next Monday.
yesterday   We played bridge yesterday.
at 5:00 yesterday   We were playing bridge at 5:00 yesterday.
every day   We play bridge every day.
the boys   The boys play bridge every day.
tomorrow   The boys are going to play bridge tomorrow.

10. M1T   Rep: I need a dollar every day.
           Sub: yesterday   S: I needed a dollar yesterday.
                next Tuesday   I'm going to need a dollar next Tuesday.
                you   You're going to need a dollar next Tuesday.
                last week   You needed a dollar last week.
                every morning   You need a dollar every morning.
                the girl   The girl needs a dollar every morning.
                yesterday   The girl needed a dollar yesterday.
                next Friday   The girl is going to need a dollar next Friday.

***11. M2   T: What did Chen do yesterday?   S: (He called California.)
                  What was he doing at 4:00?   (He was reading a novel in the living room.)
                  Was he reading a biography?
                  Why did he call California?
                  Which operator did he talk to first?
                  Was Chen making a person-to-person call?
                  Where was he calling?
                  Which number did he dial next?
                  What did Chen spell for the operator?
                  Did Chen talk to his friend the first time? Why not?

Part B.   *Interrogative and Short Answers*

Model: Did you call your friend?   Yes, I did.
                                        No, I didn't.

1. M1   Rep: Did you call your friend last night?
           Sub: dial a number   S: Did you dial a number last night?
                answer a question   Did you answer a question last night?
                talk to your sister   Did you talk to your sister last night?
                ask the operator   Did you ask the operator last night?
                watch a movie   Did you watch a movie last night?
                finish a novel   Did you finish a novel last night?
                want some excitement   Did you want some excitement last night?

2. M1   Rep: Did Bill talk to his friend in Washington?
           Sub: call   S: Did Bill call his friend in Washington?
                friends   Did Bill call his friends in Washington?
                Chicago   Did Bill call his friends in Chicago?
                Carlos   Did Carlos call his friends in Chicago?
                write to   Did Carlos write to his friends in Chicago?
                girlfriend   Did Carlos write to his girlfriend in Chicago?
                San Francisco   Did Carlos write to his girlfriend in San
                                                     Francisco?

GENERALIZATION

Previous Pattern:		He walk[s]	downtown every day.	Short Answer
	Do[es]	he walk	downtown every day?	Yes, he does./No, he doesn't.
New Pattern:		He walk[ed]	downtown yesterday.	
	D[id]	he walk	downtown yesterday?	Yes, he did./No, he didn't.

3. M1T   T: He calls his friend every day.   S: Did he call his friend yesterday?
                I attend a concert every month.   Did you attend a concert last month?
                She needs a dollar every Friday.   Did she need a dollar last Friday?
                They finish a lesson every week.   Did they finish a lesson last week?
                I watch a movie on TV every weekend.   Did you watch a movie on TV last weekend?
                The man walks a mile every morning.   Did he walk a mile yesterday morning?
                The girl calls a friend every week.   Did she call a friend last week?
                I study a new language every year.   Did you study a new language last year?
                The lady washes the clothes every   Did she wash the clothes last Saturday?
                  Saturday.
                The boys play a game every afternoon.   Did they play a game yesterday afternoon?
                The girls need a ride every day.   Did they need a ride yesterday?

4. M1   T: Did the lady wash the clothes?   S: No, she didn't.
                Did the man attend the concert?   No, he didn't.
                Did the boys need a thousand dollars?   No, they didn't.
                Did we study the present tense today?   No, we didn't.
                Did Chen need some money last week?   No, he didn't.

5. M1   T: Did Chen call his friends?   S: Yes, he did.
                Did the novel remind him of a friend?   Yes, it did.
                Did we use the telephone yesterday?   Yes, we did.
                Did Bill and Nancy explain the phone
                  calls to Chen?   Yes, they did.
                Did Mr. Hastings go downtown?   Yes, he did.

6. M2   T: Walk, downtown . . . every day.   S1:   Do you walk downtown every day?
                                                             S2:   (Yes, I do./No, I don't.)

                yesterday   S1:   Did you walk downtown yesterday?
                                                             S2:   (Yes, I did./No, I didn't.)

                attend a concert . . . every week/last week
                wash your clothes . . . every weekend/last weekend
                play tennis . . . every Monday/last Monday
                practice English . . . every morning/yesterday morning
                need a dollar . . . every day/yesterday
                want an ice cream cone . . . every afternoon/yesterday afternoon
                call your friend . . . every week/last week
                finish your homework . . . every day/yesterday

---

NOTE: Do not confuse the Lesson Seven patterns (BE + Adjective and Past Continuous)
   with the Simple Past tense.

   Lesson Seven: I was late.
                    I was trying to call my friend.

   Lesson Eight: I tried to call California.

---

7. M1T   T: She's in class every day.   S: Was she in class yesterday?
                He works every weekend.   Did he work last weekend?
                They are sick every day.   Were they sick yesterday?
                She studies every Monday.   Did she study last Monday?
                They watch TV at night.   Did they watch TV last night?
                I'm late for class now.   Were you late for class yesterday?
                I wash the clothes on Monday.   Did you wash the clothes last Monday?
                We finish a lesson every week.   Did we finish a lesson last week?
                They're busy today.   Were they busy yesterday?
                He's sleepy today.   Was he sleepy yesterday?
                He calls his friend every weekend.   Did he call his friend last weekend?
                We start a new lesson on Tuesdays.   Did we start a new lesson last Tuesday?

***8. M2   T: walk to school at 8:00 yesterday   S1:   (Were you) (Was ( )) walking to school at
                                                              8:00 yesterday?
                                                      S2:   (Yes, I was./No, I wasn't. I was sleeping.)
                                                              (Yes, he was./No, he wasn't. He was having
                                                              breakfast.)

                  late to class yesterday   S1:   (Were you) (Was ( )) late to class yesterday?
                                                      S2:   (Yes, I was./No, I wasn't.) (Yes, he was./No,
                                                              he wasn't.)

                  call California last weekend   S1:   (Did you) (Did ( )) call California last
                                                              weekend?
                                                      S2:   (Yes, I did./No, I didn't. I called Mexico.)
                                                              (Yes, he did./No, he didn't. He didn't
                                                              call anyone.)

                  sick last week
                  finish the book yesterday
                  sleepy at midnight last night
                  start a novel last week
                  watch TV last night
                  busy yesterday
                  sleepy yesterday
                  watch TV at 8:00 last night
                  play tennis last week
                  practice in the lab at 4:00 yesterday
                  call your family last month
                  attend a concert last weekend

Part C.   *Negative Statement*

Model: I didn't call my friend.

        Listen: I don't study every day.
                  I didn't study yesterday.
                  He doesn't watch TV every day.
                  He didn't watch TV yesterday.

1. M1   Rep: I didn't call my friend last week.
          Sub: he   S: He didn't call his friend last week.
               last Friday   He didn't call his friend last Friday.
               the girls   The girls didn't call their friend last Friday.
               last week   The girls didn't call their friend last week.
               we   We didn't call our friend last week.
               last month   We didn't call our friend last month.
               you   You didn't call your friend last month.
               yesterday afternoon   You didn't call your friend yesterday afternoon.
               I   I didn't call my friend yesterday afternoon.

2. M1   Rep: I didn't practice in the lab yesterday.
          Sub: he   S: He didn't practice in the lab yesterday.
               last Friday   He didn't practice in the lab last Friday.
               the girls   The girls didn't practice in the lab last Friday.
               last week   The girls didn't practice in the lab last week.
               we   We didn't practice in the lab last week.
               last month   We didn't practice in the lab last month.
               you   You didn't practice in the lab last month.
               yesterday afternoon   You didn't practice in the lab yesterday afternoon.
               I   I didn't practice in the lab yesterday afternoon.

```
GENERALIZATION

    Lesson Four:      He             studies   every day.
                      He doesn't     study     every day.

    Lesson Eight:     He             studied   yesterday.
                      He didn't      study     yesterday.
```

***3. M1T   T: I worked yesterday.   S: I didn't work yesterday.
                 He was looking for something.   He wasn't looking for anything.
                 John was sleeping at midnight.   John wasn't sleeping at midnight.
                 Chen was late yesterday.   Chen wasn't late yesterday.
                 They mailed the letter last week.   They didn't mail the letter last week.
                 We watched TV last Tuesday.   We didn't watch TV last Tuesday.
                 I was looking for someone.   I wasn't looking for anyone.
                 She was tired last night.   She wasn't tired last night.
                 I waited for the bus.   I didn't wait for the bus.
                 We needed some money.   We didn't need any money.
                 I called someone yesterday.   I didn't call anyone yesterday.

***4. M2   T: Who called (X) yesterday?   S1:   (Y) called (X) yesterday.
                                                     X: (Y) didn't call me yesterday. (Z called me
                                                           yesterday.) (Y called me last week.)
                  When did ( ) wait for a bus?   S1:   He waited for a bus (this morning).
                                                     S2:   I didn't wait for a bus this morning. (I
                                                           waited for one yesterday morning.)

                      (exercise continued on next page)

180

T: Where did ( ) wait for the bus?
       Who was late yesterday?
       What did ( ) study yesterday?
       How much money did ( ) need yesterday?
       Who was sleeping at 3:00 yesterday afternoon?
       Who explained the problem?
       Who attended the concert?
       Who was absent last week?
       What did ( ) practice yesterday?
       Who watched TV last night?
       Who needed some money yesterday?
       Who weighed the package?
       Where did ( ) watch the movie?
       When was ( ) in Washington, D.C.?
       How many sandwiches did ( ) want for lunch?

Part D.   *Wh Questions*

Model: What happened? I called three wrong numbers.

Previous Pattern: Who works downtown?   Where does the man work?
New Pattern: Who worked downtown? Where did the man work?

1. C   T: Ask ( ) what he studied yesterday.   S1:   What did you study yesterday?
                                              S2:   (History.) (English grammar.)

            Ask ( ) who waited for the bus.   S1:   Who waited for the bus?
                                                S2:   ( ) did.

            Ask ( ) when he watched TV.
            Ask ( ) when he attended a concert.
            Ask ( ) where he washed the clothes.
            Ask ( ) where he moved two months ago.
            Ask ( ) when he watched the girls in the park.
            Ask ( ) when he mailed the letter.
            Ask ( ) how many times he called home last month.
            Ask ( ) how many cigars he smoked last week.
            Ask ( ) where he mailed the package.
            Ask ( ) how much money he needed last month.
            Ask ( ) how many books he needed for class.

□ ***WHOM

2. M1   T: Did you call someone?   S: Whom did you call?
            Did you need someone?   Whom did you need?
            Did he watch someone?   Whom did he watch?
            Did she describe someone?   Whom did she describe?
            Did you ask someone?   Whom did you ask?
            Did they want someone?   Whom did they want?

3. M1   T: Did you want someone?   S: Whom did you want?
               Did you want something?   What did you want?
               Did you call someone?   Whom did you call?
               Did you dial someone?   Whom did you dial?
               Did you move something?   What did you move?
               Did you need someone?   Whom did you need?

GENERALIZATION

Previous Pattern A: *Someone*   attended the concert.

                          Who   attended the concert?

                        Something   is confusing.

                          What   is confusing?

Previous Pattern B: Did you want *something?*

                          What   did you want?

New Pattern: Did you want *someone?*

                          Whom   did you want?

Remember: When the *some* word is in object position, the subject and verb are inverted. The *Wh* word for people is *whom* in formal styles. You will almost never hear it in casual speech where *who* is used for both the subject and object pronoun.

Formal	Informal
Who studied?	Who studied?
Whom did you call?	Who did you call?

---

4. M1   T: You called someone.   S: Whom did you call?
               You needed someone.   Whom did you need?
               He watched someone.   Whom did he watch?
               She described someone.   Whom did she describe?
               You asked someone.   Whom did you ask?
               They wanted someone.   Whom did they want?

5. M1T   T: You called someone.   S: Whom did you call?
               Someone called home.   Who called home?
               You needed someone.   Whom did you need?
               Someone needed a dollar.   Who needed a dollar?
               Someone described the city.   Who described the city?
               He wanted someone.   Whom did he want?
               Someone watched TV.   Who watched TV?
               She asked someone.   Whom did she ask?
               Someone weighed the package.   Who weighed the package?
               They dialed someone.   Whom did they dial?
               Someone finished the lesson.   Who finished the lesson?

6. M2   T: Someone finished the lesson.   S1:   Who finished the lesson?
                                                     S2:   ( ) did.

         when   S1:   When did he finish it?
                                                     S2:   He finished it (last week).

         ( ) called someone.   S1:   Who(m) did ( ) call?
                                                     S2:   He called ( ).

         when   S1:   When did he call him?
                                                     S2:   He called him (last night).

         someone needed some money—how much
         ( ) invited someone for dinner—when
         someone received a package—when
         ( ) described someone—when
         someone answered the question—where
         someone watched TV—where
         ( ) called someone—when
         someone wanted some beer—how much
         ( ) dialed someone—when
         ( ) asked someone—what

7. C   T: Find out when ( ) called long distance and   S1:   When did you call long distance?
                   what kind of call it was.   S2:   (Last week I called Venezuela.)
                                                           S1:   (Did you call person-to-person?)
                                                           S2:   (No. Station-to-station.)
         Find out when ( ) called long distance and who dialed the number, ( ) or the operator.
         Find out if ( ) ever called a wrong number long distance and what happened.
         Find out who helped ( ) with his first long distance call in this country.
         Find out when someone called ( ) long distance and who it was.
         Find out if ( ) needed some money and how much.
         Find out when ( ) watched TV and if the program was good.
         Find out when someone asked ( ) for advice and what the person wanted.
         Find out when ( ) received a package and what it was.

8. C   T: When did you arrive (in Pittsburgh)?   S: (Last month.)
         Did you call someone yesterday? Whom? When?
         Were you late for class yesterday?
         Where were you at midnight yesterday? What were you doing?
         Where did you live in 1965?
         What were you doing at 6:00 last night?
         Did someone call you last week? Who? When?
         Did you receive a package yesterday?
         How much money did you need for the bus yesterday?
         How often were you late for class last week?
         Where did you walk yesterday?
         What were you doing at the Student Union yesterday?

SECTION FOUR

PLACE + TIME

Listen: I watched TV at home last night.
     He studied English in class yesterday.
     They attended the concert downtown last week.

1. M1 Rep: We watched TV at home last night.
     Sub: in the Student Union   S: We watched TV in the Student Union last night.
       in the living room   We watched TV in the living room last night.
       in the recreation room   We watched TV in the recreation room last night.
       in the kitchen   We watched TV in the kitchen last night.
       in my apartment   We watched TV in my apartment last night.

2. M1 Rep: We washed the clothes at home last night.
     Sub: yesterday   S: We washed the clothes at home yesterday.
       last weekend   We washed the clothes at home last weekend.
       yesterday morning   We washed the clothes at home yesterday morning.
       yesterday afternoon   We washed the clothes at home yesterday afternoon.
       the day before yesterday   We washed the clothes at home the day before yesterday.

3. M1 Rep: They mailed a letter at the post office yesterday.
     Sub: I   S: I mailed a letter at the post office yesterday.
       pick up   I picked up a letter at the post office yesterday.
       package   I picked up a package at the post office yesterday.
       last week   I picked up a package at the post office last week.
       Carlos   Carlos picked up a package at the post office last week.
       mail   Carlos mailed a package at the post office last week.
       a letter   Carlos mailed a letter at the post office last week.
       Monday   Carlos mailed a letter at the post office last Monday.

GENERALIZATION

	Place	Specific Time	General Time
We watched TV	in the living room	at 4:00	yesterday.

NOTE: You may hear different orders, but you will not be wrong if you use this order.

---

4. M1T Rep: I attended a concert in Oakland last Saturday.
     Sub: we   S: We attended a concert in Oakland last Saturday.
       a movie   We attended a movie in Oakland last Saturday.
       downtown   We attended a movie downtown last Saturday.

(exercise continued on next page)

Sub:	last night	S:	We attended a movie downtown last night.
	the boys		The boys attended a movie downtown last night.
	a baseball game		The boys attended a baseball game downtown last night.
	in Pittsburgh		The boys attended a baseball game in Pittsburgh last night.
	yesterday		The boys attended a baseball game in Pittsburgh yesterday.

5. M2   T: I mailed a letter . . .   S: I mailed a letter (at the Post Office yesterday).
              I watched TV . . .
              ( ) attended a concert . . .
              ( ) is going to a movie . . .
              ( ) washed his clothes . . .
              ( ) is going to mail a package . . .
              ( ) and ( ) are studying English . . .
              We finished the lesson . . .
              The teacher answered the question . . .
              The students pronounced the new words . . .
              ( ) and ( ) needed a dollar . . .

6. C   Situation: A friend has just arrived from your country and is curious about your routine in the United States.

         T: eat lunch   S: (I eat lunch (in the cafeteria at noon).)
             write letters   (I rarely write letters.)
             watch TV
             attend class
             study English
             cook dinner
             have breakfast
             wait for the bus
             go shopping
             do the laundry

SUMMARY DIALOGUE

Chen: Hello.

Nancy: Hi, Chen. This is Nancy. I called your number six times yesterday and no one answered. Where were you?

Chen: I walked to the park in the morning. Bill phoned in the afternoon and we played cards.

Nancy: You played cards without me?

Chen: We dialed you, but the line was busy. I called again a little later and got a wrong number.

Nancy: Well, it's O.K. I was busy anyway.

LESSON EIGHT – SUMMARY OF PATTERNS

	QW	Aux.	Subject	*Verb + -ed*	*Completer*	*Short Answer*
Statement			Chen	dialed	the number.	
Question (Who)			Who	dialed	the number?	Chen did.
Question (Yes/No)		Did	Chen	*Verb* call	his friend?	Yes, he did./No, he didn't.
Question (Wh)	Whom	did	Chen	call	last weekend?	His friend.

LESSON NINE

INTRODUCTION   Bank accounts

Chen is asking Nancy about bank accounts.

Chen: I received a check from home yesterday. *Where can I cash it?*

Nancy: Do you have a bank account?

Chen: No, I don't. Should I open one?

5   Nancy: Yes, you should. Most banks won't cash checks for people without accounts.

Chen: O.K. What should I do?

Nancy: Do you want a savings account or a checking account?

Chen: A checking account, I guess. It's more convenient. Which bank should I go to?

Nancy: Well, it depends. You want a bank near you. You also want a bank with a small
10   service charge. Some banks give you the checks free with a minimum balance of 300 or
         500 dollars. Others charge a little for the checks and don't require a minimum balance.

Chen: Inexpensive checks and no charges, that's *for me.* I'll never be able to keep 300
         dollars in the bank.

Nancy: O.K. Go to the bank on the corner of Main and Forbes. Tell them what you need.
15   A bank official will help you fill out the forms.

Chen: When will I get the checks?

Nancy: They'll give you some checks right away. You can use them until your personal
         checks are ready.

Chen: Will the checks have my name on them?

20   Nancy: Yes, of course.

Chen: How will I know how much money I have? I'll never remember from month to month.

Nancy: For one thing, you write down each check and deposit in your checkbook. And then
         the bank will send you a statement with the canceled checks once a month. You balance your
         checkbook and compare it with the statement.

25   Chen: What if they're different?

Nancy: Then you figure it out again. If it doesn't balance, you call the bank and ask them.

Chen: Should I keep the canceled checks?

Nancy: Oh, yes! They're a record of payment and proof if there is any question.

Chen: Thanks a lot, Nancy. That's a big help.

30   Nancy: That's O.K., Chen.

NOTE: If you bring a large amount of money to the United States—enough for a year or more, you should think of using a savings account in addition to a checking account. Ask someone about the bank with best interest rates in your area. Things to consider are the percentage of interest and the frequency with which the bank computes the interest.

OUTLINE OF PATTERNS   Example

Section One	Modals	
Part A.	*can*	
	Affirmative	you can use . . .
	Negative	I can't remember . . .
	Interrogative	where can I . . .
Part B.	*will*	
	Affirmative, Negative, Interrogative	A bank official will help you.
	Request form	Will you open the door?
Part C.	*should*	You should open an account.
Section Two	Articles	
Part A.	*a/the*	a bank/the bank
Part B.	no article/*the* (Object/Activity)	go to church/the church
Section Three	*Other*-Adjective/Pronoun	
Part A.	Adjective	Other banks have free checks.
Part B.	Pronoun	Others charge for checks.
Section Four	Object Pronouns—Personal	. . . that's for me.

COMPREHENSION QUESTIONS

1. When did Chen receive a check?

2. Does he have a bank account?

3. Should he open one? Why?

188

4. What kinds of bank accounts are available?

5. What kind does Chen want? Why?

*6. What should you consider when you choose a bank?

*7. Describe three possible types of checking accounts.

8. Where is the bank?

9. Who will help Chen at the bank?

10. When will he get the checks?

11. Will the checks have his name on them?

12. How will he know how much money he has?

*13. What is a "bank statement"?

*14. What is a "canceled check"?

15. Should he keep the canceled checks? *Why?

*16. How do you balance a bank statement?***

Expressions

balance your check book	minimum balance	make a deposit
bank statement	open an account	deposit some money
canceled check	overdraw an account	withdraw (v) withdrawal (n)
checking account	savings account	make a withdrawal
close an account	service charge	withdraw some money
		buy traveler's checks

Vocabulary

Nouns		Verbs		Adjectives	
ashtray	meal	borrow	help	accurate	lazy
bill	paper (news)	charge	lead	boring	minimum
convertible	pipe	choose	lend	brunette	million
drill	sedan	copy	pass	comfortable	passing
emergency	song	depend (on)	require	correct	personal
form	snow	deposit	skip	corrupt	studious
golf	tape recorder	figure out	start	delicious	stupid
government	teller	fill out	stay up	dull	thousand
hospital	topcoat	find out	withdraw	fun	vacant
loan	window			helpful	wise
mayor	withdrawal				

SECTION ONE

MODAL VERBS

Part A.   *Can*

☐ AFFIRMATIVE

Model: You can cash the check at the bank.

1. M1 Rep: Chen can cash his check at the bank.
      Sub: call his friend in California   S: Chen can call his friend in California.
             walk downtown in half an hour   Chen can walk downtown in half an hour.
             open an account at the bank   Chen can open an account at the bank.
             speak English very well   Chen can speak English very well.
             deposit his check in his account   Chen can deposit his check in his account.
             withdraw a hundred dollars   Chen can withdraw a hundred dollars.
             drive a car in the United States   Chen can drive a car in the United States.

2. M1 Rep: Carlos can drive a car in the United States.
      Sub: I   S: I can drive a car in the United States.
             the girl   The girl can drive a car in the United States.
             the boys   The boys can drive a car in the United States.
             we   We can drive a car in the United States.
             they   They can drive a car in the United States.
             he   He can drive a car in the United States.
             we   We can drive a car in the United States.

GENERALIZATION

Can is called a modal verb and it comes before the main verb of the sentence:

> Chen has a bank account.
> He *can* cash a check at the bank.

Can adds the meaning of "ability to do something." It has only one form for all persons (unlike BE and DO), and when it is used, the main verb is always in its simple form.

Can is used with both present and future time words, but not with past time:

> I can go with you now/tomorrow.

---

3. M1T T: speak English   S: I can speak English; I'm speaking English now.
            speak (Spanish)   I can speak Spanish; I'm not speaking Spanish
                                                          now.

            study English   I can study English; I'm studying English now.
            ride a bicycle   I can ride a bicycle; I'm not riding a bicycle now.
            walk downtown   I can walk downtown; I'm not walking downtown
                                                          now.

            open an account   I can open an account; I'm not opening an
                                                          account now.

(exercise continued on next page)

T:	learn English grammar	S:	I can learn English grammar; I'm learning English grammar now.
	cash a check		I can cash a check; I'm not cashing a check now.

☐ NEGATIVE STATEMENTS

Model: Chen can't cash a check for a million dollars.

4. M1   Listen: Bill can drive; I can't drive.
              Bill can go downtown; I can't go downtown.
              Bill can ride a bicycle; I can't ride a bicycle.

NOTE: The modal is not usually stressed in the affirmative:

   I can [kən] drive.   (The stress is on the main verb.)

In a negative sentence, the modal usually receives more stress:

   I can't [kæn] drive.

The contraction is used in speech, the full form more often in writing.

Spoken Form	Written Form
I can't support the policy.	I cannot support the policy.

---

5. M1T   Raise one hand for positive, two for negative.

T:	I can go.	S:	(1)
	I can't go.		(2)
	I can't drive.		(2)
	I can drive.		(1)
	I can swim.		(1)
	I can't dive.		(2)
	I can speak English.		(1)
	Carlos can't speak Spanish.		(2)
	Bill can't cash a check.		(2)
	We can go downtown.		(1)
	They can't have a dollar.		(2)

6. M1T

T:	Chen can cash a check.	S:	Chen can't cash a check.
	We can open an account.		We can't open an account.
	He can withdraw a thousand dollars.		He can't withdraw a thousand dollars.
	I can speak Farci.		I can't speak Farci.
	They can finish the homework.		They can't finish the homework.
	She can teach English.		She can't teach English.
	You can sing the song.		You can't sing the song.

191

7. M2   T: Tell me what you can and cannot do.
              ride in a plane—fly a plane   S: I can ride in a plane; I can't fly a plane.
              speak Spanish—speak Persian
              watch TV—be on TV
              ride on a bus—drive a bus
              build a house—buy a house
              stop the snow—watch the snow
              open an account—own a bank
              make a telephone—make a telephone call
              buy a VW—buy a Rolls-Royce
              cook dinner—eat dinner
              write a letter—write a book

☐ INTERROGATIVE

8. M1   T: You can speak English.   S: Can you speak English?
              He can cash a check.   Can he cash a check?
              We can drive downtown.   Can we drive downtown?
              She can withdraw a million dollars.   Can she withdraw a million dollars?
              Bill can fly a plane.   Can Bill fly a plane?
              Jane and Nancy can understand Spanish.   Can Jane and Nancy understand Spanish?
              Mr. Jones can buy a Rolls-Royce.   Can Mr. Jones buy a Rolls-Royce?
              Judy can help her friends.   Can Judy help her friends?

GENERALIZATION

The modal verbs form questions in the same way as the sentences with BE, by inverting the subject and verb.

BE			He's studying something here.	
Yes/No		Is he	studying something here?	Yes, he is.
Wh	What is	he	studying?	English.
Modal			He can study something here.	
Yes/No		Can he	study something here?	Yes, he can. (No, he can't.)
Wh	What can	he	study?	English.

***9. M2   T: Ask ( ) if you can open a savings account.   S1:   Can I open a savings account?
                                                             S2:   (Yes, you can.) (Sure, go and speak
                                                                    to the bank officer.)

              Ask ( ) if he can go to the movies this afternoon.
              Ask ( ) if he can speak French.
              Ask ( ) if you can swim in the university pool.
              Ask ( ) if he can ski.
              Ask ( ) if you can help him with his bank statement.
              Ask ( ) if he can drive a car.
              Ask ( ) if he can fly an airplane.
              Ask ( ) if you can depend on his help.
              Ask ( ) if he can lend you a dollar.

(exercise continued on next page)

T: Ask ( ) if he can come to dinner tonight.
        Ask ( ) if you can cash a check at the drug store.
        Ask ( ) if he can deposit some money.
        Ask ( ) if he can withdraw a thousand dollars.

10. M1   Rep: Where can I cash a check?
            Sub: Bill   S: Where can Bill cash a check?
                 get some money   Where can Bill get some money?
                 when   When can Bill get some money?
                 Carlos   When can Carlos get some money?
                 make a deposit   When can Carlos make a deposit?
                 where   Where can Carlos make a deposit?
                 Jane   Where can Jane make a deposit?
                 borrow a dollar   Where can Jane borrow a dollar?

***11. M2   T: Ask ( ) where you can get an inexpensive   S1:   Where can I get an inexpensive meal?
                  meal.   S2:   You can get an inexpensive meal at
                                                                     (MacDonald's).

            Ask ( ) where you can mail a letter.
            Ask ( ) where you can buy some stamps.
            Ask ( ) where you can buy some toothpaste.
            Ask ( ) where you can get a good used car.
            Ask ( ) where you can cash a check.
            Ask ( ) when he can help you with the homework.
            Ask ( ) when he can go downtown.
            Ask ( ) when he can leave (Pittsburgh).
            Ask ( ) where he can find out about the TOEFL test.
            Ask ( ) when he can go to the concert.
            Ask ( ) where you can borrow some money.

NOTE: *Borrow* and *lend* are "one-way" verbs in English.

The one who *takes* — *borrows*.
The one who *gives* — *lends*.

Can I borrow a dollar?   } Sure. Here.   { Thanks. I'll pay you
Can you lend me a dollar? }   { back tomorrow.

Part B.   *Will*

□ AFFIRMATIVE, NEGATIVE, INTERROGATIVE

Model: The bank official will help you.

1. M1   Rep: I'll do the work tomorrow.
                 He'll finish the homework tomorrow.
                 We'll buy the tickets tomorrow.
                 She'll open the account tomorrow.
                 They'll give you some checks tomorrow.
                 You'll have it tomorrow.

2. M1   Rep: I'll finish the work next week.
          Sub: he   S: He'll finish the work next week.
               do   He'll do the work next week.
               the lesson   He'll do the lesson next week.
               we   We'll do the lesson next week.
               start   We'll start the lesson next week.
               the book   We'll start the book next week.
               the day after tomorrow   We'll start the book the day after
                                                            tomorrow.
               she   She'll start the book the day after
                                                            tomorrow.
               read   She'll read the book the day after
                                                            tomorrow.
               the paper   She'll read the paper the day after
                                                            tomorrow.
               next Monday   She'll read the paper next Monday.

GENERALIZATION

Will indicates an action in the future; there is an element of promise, determination or
inevitability. The pattern is the same as for *can*.

	Spoken Form			Written Form	
She'll	come to class.		**She will**	come to class.	
She won't	come to class.		She will not	come to class.	

---

3. M1   T: He'll do the work.   S: He won't do the work.
                 She'll read the paper.   She won't read the paper.
                 We'll finish the lesson.   We won't finish the lesson.
                 He'll do it.   He won't do it.
                 We'll finish it.   We won't finish it.
                 They'll read it.   They won't read it.
                 She'll listen to it.   She won't listen to it.
                 I'll buy it.   I won't buy it.

4. M2   T: Will you finish the book sometime?   S1:   Yes, I will.
                                                        S2:   When will you finish it?
                                                        S1:   I'll finish it (next week).

                 Will you go somewhere tomorrow?   S1:   Yes, I will.
                                                        S2:   Where will you go?
                                                        S1:   I'll go (to class).

                 Will you see the girl sometime?
                 Will you open an account sometime?
                 Will you finish something next week?
                 Will you do the work sometime?
                 Will you cash a check somewhere?
                 Will you go to New York sometime?
                 Will you get the answer sometime?
                 Will you call someone?
                 Will you ask someone for dinner?

5. M2   T: finish the lesson   S1:   Will you finish the lesson (tomorrow)?
                                                  S2:   (Yes, I will.) (No, I won't have time.)
                   read the novel   S1:   Will you read the novel (next week)?
                                                  S2:   (Yes, I will.) (No, I never read novels.)

                   come to dinner
                   have the money
                   bring the book
                   find the paper
                   call California
                   be on time

6. C   T: Where will you be tomorrow afternoon?   S: (I'll be at home after 3:00.)
                   When will you see your advisor?
                   Where will you open an account?
                   How will you find your friend's house?
                   How many people will we need for the soccer game?
                   How much money will you need for your trip?
                   When will the new students arrive?
                   What will you show your friends in the city?
                   Where will you eat dinner?
                   How long will you be in the United States?
                   When will your friends arrive?
                   How will you contact your family?

☐ REQUEST FORM***

7. M1   T: Please open the door.   S: Will you please open the door?
                   Please pass the butter.   Will you please pass the butter?
                   Please close the window.   Will you please close the window?
                   Please sit down.   Will you please sit down?
                   Please hand in the homework.   Will you please hand in the homework?
                   Please be on time.   Will you please be on time?
                   Please have your money ready.   Will you please have your money ready?

8. M1   Rep: Please don't be late.   Will you please not be late?
                   Please don't hurry.   Will you please not hurry?
                   Please don't drive so fast.   Will you please not drive so fast?

┌───┐
│   │
│   NOTE: This request pattern is an alternate to the pattern in Lesson Five. │
│   │
│   Lesson Five: Please open the door.   │
│   Lesson Nine: Will you please open the door?   │
│   │
└───┘

9. M1T   T: Ask ( ) to open the window.   S: Will you please open the window?
                   Ask ( ) to close the door.   Will you please close the door?
                   Ask ( ) to pass the sugar.   Will you please pass the sugar?
                   Ask ( ) not to be late.   Will you please not be late?

(exercise continued on next page)

195

T:	Ask ( ) not to drive so fast.	S:	Will you please not drive so fast?
	Ask ( ) to be on time.		Will you please be on time?
	Ask ( ) to speak slowly.		Will you please speak slowly?
	Ask ( ) to have the money ready.		Will you please have the money ready?
	Ask ( ) to drive slowly.		Will you please drive slowly?
	Ask ( ) to find the tape recorder.		Will you please find the tape recorder?
	Ask ( ) to buy some pencils.		Will you please buy some pencils?
	Ask ( ) to get some flowers.		Will you please get some flowers?
	Ask ( ) to bring some records.		Will you please bring some records?
	Ask ( ) to borrow a record player.		Will you please borrow a record player?

Part C.   *Should*

Model: You should open an account at the bank.

1. M1   Rep: Chen should open an account.
          Sub: I   S: I should open an account.
               we   We should open an account.
               she   She should open an account.
               they   They should open an account.
               the man   The man should open an account.
               you   You should open an account.

2. M1   Rep: I should study for the test.
          Sub: he   S: He should study for the test.
               come to class on time   He should come to class on time.
               the girls   The girls should come to class on time.
               do their homework every day   The girls should do their homework every day.
               the student   The student should do his homework every day.
               pay the bill right away The student should pay the bill right away.
               I   I should pay the bill right away.

GENERALIZATION

Should indicates that *it is a good idea* to do something, that to perform the action in the future is desirable:

Ex: My parents live in another city; I should write them every week.
         Chen was absent from class; I should call tonight and give him the assignment.

The pattern is the same as *can* and *will.*

Spoken Form	Written Form
She should learn to drive.	She should learn to drive.
She shouldn't learn to drive.	She should not learn to drive.

3. M1   Rep: Chen shouldn't spend all his money.

           Sub: buy a car   S: Chen shouldn't buy a car.

                go to the movies   Chen shouldn't go to the movies.

                be late   Chen shouldn't be late.

                walk downtown   Chen shouldn't walk downtown.

                take a taxi   Chen shouldn't take a taxi.

                call California   Chen shouldn't call California.

***4. M1T   T: It is a good idea to pay bills on time.   S: You should pay bills on time.

               It is not a good idea to be late for dinner.   You shouldn't be late for dinner.

               It is not a good idea to drive fast.   You shouldn't drive fast.

               It is a good idea to write home often.   You should write home often.

               It is a good idea to do the homework every day.   You should do the homework every day.

               It is not a good idea to forget appointments.   You shouldn't forget appointments.

               It is a good idea to open a savings account.   You should open a savings account.

               It is not a good idea to borrow a lot of money.   You shouldn't borrow a lot of money.

5. M2   Tell what is a good idea in the following situations.

          T: I'm going to have a test on Friday.   S: You (should study). You (shouldn't go to the movies).

            It's raining.   (You should take your umbrella.) (You shouldn't go out.)

            It's snowing.

            I borrowed ten dollars from Bill last week.

            My parents wrote to me last week.

            I want to cash a check.

            I want to learn English.

            He has a million dollars at his house.

            Lots of children are playing in the street. I'm driving a car.

6. M2   What is proper in the following situations?

          T: If you have a test, should you go to the movies?   S: (No, you shouldn't; you should study.) (Yes, you should relax before a test.)

            If you have a test, should you copy from your friend?

            If you have a test, should you bring your book to class?

            If you have a test, should you talk to your friend?

            If you have a test, should you stay up all night?

            If you need money, should you borrow it from a friend?

            If you have a problem, should you stay in your room?

            If you have a question, should you be quiet?

            If you have a test, should you drink a lot of beer?

            If you have a test, should you watch TV?

            If you have an appointment, should you be late?

7. C   T: Tell some things you should/shouldn't do in the United States/your country.

        S: (You should learn to speak English) in the United States.

           (You shouldn't be late for appointments) in the United States.

           (You should write a thank-you note for an invitation) in the United States.

           (You shouldn't be absent from class without calling the teacher.)

           (In my country, you should learn to speak ( ).)

8. M2   T: Using the modals *can, will, should,* make statements about the following situations.

Bill is a very good student at the university. He gets good grades. His friend Jack is not a good student. He goes to parties every night, and cuts class often. Professor Johnson is going to give a test on Friday.

S: (Jack should study.) (Bill can go to the movies, but he probably won't.)

Judy is a very pretty girl. She has lots of new clothes and always has lots of money. She lends money to her friends all the time. They sometimes forget to pay her back. At the end of the month she is sometimes broke.

9. C   T: When can you open an account?   S: (Tomorrow.) (I opened an account last week.)

What should you look for in a bank?
Where will you go between semesters?
When will you do the exercises?
Whom can you ask for help?
Where should you keep your money in ( )?
Where can we get a good meal?
What should we see in ( )?
When will ( ) buy a Rolls-Royce?
Whom should you call in an emergency?
What can we do this weekend?
Where should we look for a new coat?

SECTION TWO

ARTICLES

Part A.   *a/the*

1. M1   Rep: He wants a bank.   The bank on the corner is good.
               He wants a car.   The little VW is cheap.
               He wants a book.   The blue book is good.
               He needs an apartment.   The apartment next to mine is vacant.
               He wants a camera.   The German camera is good.

GENERALIZATION

As you have seen, all singular count nouns are preceded by a definite article *the* or an indefinite article *a/an.* The choice of article depends on the context. When you refer to a noun that has been mentioned previously, it is preceded by a definite article:

"I opened *an account* yesterday."
"*The account* is at Pittsburgh National Bank."

---

2. M2   T: Chen opened an account.   S: (The account is at Mellon Bank.)
                   Chen is going to see a movie.   (The movie is at the Strand.)
                   Chen is going to buy a gift.   (The gift is for his girlfriend.)
                   A new girl is in the class.
                   We have a new teacher.
                   I'm going to buy a novel.
                   There's a new movie in town.
                   Bill is going to buy a car.
                   Carlos rented an apartment.
                   Bill has a job.
                   Mr. Jackson is buying a gift.

***3. M2   (Picture Cue)
           T: What's this?   S: It's a cigarette lighter. (The lighter is a cheap one.)
                   etc.

4. C   T: Tell where you live and describe S: (I live in an apartment. It's near here. The apartment
                   it.   has three rooms and a bath.)
                                                           (I live in a room in the dorm. The room is large and
                                                                   pleasant.)

Part B.   *no article/the (activity/object words)*

1. M1   Rep: We go to church every Sunday.   The church is beautiful.
                  He goes to bed at 8:00.   The bed is very comfortable.
                  We have dinner at 6:00.   The dinner last night was delicious.
                  I go to school every day.   The school is near my house.
                  We're in class now.   The class is in the Cathedral of Learning.
                  I go home by bus.   The home of the President is beautiful.

GENERALIZATION

Words like *home, school,* etc. take the definite article (*the*) if they are an object, not
if they are part of an activity:

go to school	—	Activity
The school is big.	—	Object

---

2. M1T   T: Tell if the situation describes an object or an activity.
                   We go to church on Sundays.   S: Activity
                   The church on the corner is small.   Object
                   I'm going home now.   Activity
                   The home of the President is the
                       White House.   Object
                   Our children go to the school around
                       the corner.   Object
                   The school is very new.   Object
                   She's going to school next year.   Activity

3. C   T: How often do you go to church?   S: (I go to church (every Sunday).)
              Where is it?   (The church is near my house.)
              What is it like?
              How many days a week do you go to school?
                Where is it? How do you get there?
              How many days a week do you have class? Where does it meet? What is it like?
              What time do you have dinner?
              How often do you have dinner at a restaurant?
              Where do you have lunch? How was lunch yesterday?

SECTION THREE

INDEFINITE ADJECTIVE/PRONOUN — *OTHER*

Part A.   *Adjective*

Model: The other bank gives free checks.
           Other banks charge for checks.

1. M1   Rep: This girl is from Spain. The other girl is from France.

	Sub: man	S:	This man is from Spain. The other man is from France.
	student		This student is from Spain. The other student is from France.
	woman		This woman is from Spain. The other woman is from France.
	professor		This professor is from Spain. The other professor is from France.
	car		This car is from Spain. The other car is from France.
	book		This book is from Spain. The other book is from France.
	hat		This hat is from Spain. The other hat is from France.

2. M1   Rep: One student is studying; another student is playing bridge.

Sub: man	S:	One man is studying; another man is playing bridge.
cutting the grass/eating dinner		One man is cutting the grass; another man is eating dinner.
woman		One woman is cutting the grass; another woman is eating dinner.
making lunch/writing checks		One woman is making lunch; another woman is writing checks.
girl		One girl is making lunch; another girl is writing checks.
studying English/reading a book		One girl is studying English; another girl is reading a book.
professor		One professor is studying English; another professor is reading a book.
from Korea/from Lebanon		One professor is from Korea; another professor is from Lebanon.

GENERALIZATION

Other can modify definite nouns: the   other   girl
                                           the   other   girls

                and indefinite nouns: an   other   student
                                                 other   students

Note that the indefinite *an* joins with the adjective in spelling: *another*

NOTE: *One/ones* (Lesson Six) often are used instead of repeating the second definite noun or the singular indefinite noun:

This book is from France; the other one is from Spain.
This book is from France; the other ones are from Spain.
One book is from France; another one is from Spain.

---

3. M1   Rep: These drills are fun; the other drills are dull.
         Sub: long/short   S: These drills are long; the other drills are short.
               easy/hard   These drills are easy; the other drills are hard.
               simple/confusing   These drills are simple; the other drills are confusing.
               helpful/stupid   These drills are helpful; the other drills are stupid.
               interesting/boring   These drills are interesting; the other drills are boring.
               useful/bad   These drills are useful; the other drills are bad.

4. M1   T: Some books are good. (bad)   S: Other books are bad.
              Some men are wise. (stupid)   Other men are stupid.
              Some watches are accurate. (slow)   Other watches are slow.
              Some men smoke cigarettes. (cigars) Other men smoke cigars.
              Some cars are ugly. (beautiful)   Other cars are beautiful.
              Some people drive to work. (walk)   Other people walk to work.
              Some students have savings accounts.
                 (checking)   Other students have checking accounts.

5. M1T   T: Two students
              Israel/France   S: This student is from Israel; the other student is from France.
              studying English/studying   This student is studying English; the other student is studying
                 computer science   computer science.
              interested/bored   This student is interested; the other student is bored.
              a graduate/an undergraduate   This student is a graduate; the other student is an under-
                                                 graduate.
              good/bad   This student is good; the other student is bad.
              has good grades/has poor   This student has good grades; the other student has poor
                 grades   grades.
              Asia/Africa   This student is from Asia; the other student is from Africa.

***6. M1T T: Four cars
              three Japanese/American S: Three cars are Japanese; the other car is American.
              two French/Canadian   Two cars are French; the other cars are Canadian.
              three fast/slow   Three cars are fast; the other car is slow.
              one expensive/inexpensive   One car is expensive; the other cars are inexpensive.
              two beautiful/ugly   Two cars are beautiful; the other cars are ugly.
              three slow/fast   Three cars are slow; the other car is fast.
              one big/little   One car is big; the other cars are little.

201

***7. M2   (Picture Cue)
              T: Here are some students. One   S1:   (Another student is playing bridge.)
                   student is studying.   S2:   (Another student is going to have lunch.)
                                                       S3:   (Another student has a date for the movies.)
                                                             etc.

8. M2   T: Is Mr. Brown coming?   S: No, another (professor) is coming.
              Is Jane going to play the piano?   No, another (student) is going to play the piano.
              Is Mrs. Casetti speaking today?   No, another (teacher) is speaking.
              Is Michael driving?
              Is Bill working at the gas station?
              Is Mr. Mooney driving the bus?
              Is George mowing the lawn?
              Is Mr. Allen going to be President?
              Is Dr. Paulston talking to the students?
              Is Mr. Bruder going to Maine?
              Is Suzie going to the hospital?
              Is Mr. Cameron playing golf?

9. M2   T: Are all books interesting?   S: No, some books are interesting; other books
                                                        are (dull).
              Are all leaders wise?   No, some leaders are wise; other leaders are
                                                        (stupid).
              Are all cities beautiful?
              Are all professors absent-minded?
              Do all cars pollute the air?
              Are all women liberated?
              Do all Americans have checking accounts?
              Do all bank accounts give interest?
              Do all Americans speak Spanish?
              Do all students study hard?
              Do all people borrow money from their friends?

10. C   T: Does everyone from (Libya) speak   S: (No, some people speak Classical Arabic;
                (Classical Arabic)?   other people speak Colloquial Arabic.)
              Does everyone in ( ) keep his money in   (No, some people keep their money in
                the bank?   banks; other people keep their money at
                                                            home.)
              Do you have any brothers? Do they (both) live at home?
              Do all banks in your country have checking accounts?
              Do all banks in your country have savings accounts?
              Are all women in your country liberated?
              Are all tellers in banks helpful?
              Does everyone in your country drive to work?
              Are all your friends interesting?
              Can everyone balance a checkbook?
              Should everyone have a savings account?
              Does everyone borrow money from a finance company?
              Will everyone pass this course?

Part B.   *Pronoun*

Model: Others charge a little for the checks.

***1. M1   (Picture Cue — Here are two boys)

T:	tall/short	S:	One is tall; the other is short.
	fat/thin		One is fat; the other is thin.
	has blue eyes/has brown eyes		One has blue eyes; the other has brown eyes.
	has blond hair/has black hair		One has blond hair; the other has black hair.
	lives in the dorm/has an apartment		One lives in the dorm; the other has an apartment.
	has a VW/has a Ford		One has a VW; the other has a Ford.
	speaks Swedish/speaks Arabic		One speaks Swedish; the other speaks Arabic.

2. M1   (Picture Cue — Here are some students)

T:	One is reading. (playing bridge)	S:	Another is playing bridge.
	One is sleeping. (making lunch)		Another is making lunch.
	One is opening a savings account. (checking account)		Another is opening a checking account.
	One is studying English. (French)		Another is studying French.
	One is taking a nap. (having a snack)		Another is having a snack.
	One is watching TV. (listening to the radio)		Another is listening to the radio.
	One is going downtown. (to the movies)		Another is going to the movies.
	One is writing checks. (balancing his checkbook)		Another is balancing his checkbook.

GENERALIZATION

Other (singular) and *others* (plural) may be substitute words (pronouns) when the referent is known.

	Adjective	The other car	is blue.
	Pronoun	The other	is blue.
Definite			
	Adjective	The other	car[s] are blue.
	Pronoun	The other[s]	are blue.

	Adjective	Another car	is blue.
	Pronoun	Another	is blue.
Indefinite			
	Adjective	Other	car[s] are blue.
	Pronoun	Other[s]	are blue.

In conversational speech, the singular pronouns are not common. The adjective + *one* is more usual. See Part A.

The other is blue.	The other one is blue.
Another is blue.	Another one is blue.

---

3. M1   (Picture Cue — Here are five cars)

T:	yellow/green	S:	Two are yellow; the others are green.
	big/small		Two are big; the others are small.

(exercise continued on next page)

	T:	convertibles/sedans		S:	Two are convertibles; the others are sedans.
		expensive/cheap			Two are expensive; the others are cheap.
		long/short			Two are long; the others are short.
		VWs/Rolls-Royces			Two are VWs; the others are Rolls-Royces.
		yellow/black			Two are yellow; the others are black.

4. M1   T: Some books are bad. (good)   S: Others are good.
         Some men are wise. (stupid)   Others are stupid.
         Some watches are accurate. (slow)   Others are slow.
         Some students have checking accounts.
            (savings accounts)   Others have savings accounts.
         Some women work at home. (in an office)   Others work in an office.
         Some people drive small cars. (big)   Others drive big cars.
         Some men smoke cigars. (pipes)   Others smoke pipes.
         Some students study at the library. (at home)   Others study at home.

***5. M1T   T: Ten people
         Some are from the United States.   S: Others are from Latin America and
            (Latin America and Asia)   Asia.
         Five are from the United States.
            (Latin America)   The others are from Latin America.
         Nine are from the United States.
            (Latin America)   The other is from Latin America.
         A few speak English. (Spanish and German)   Others speak Spanish and German.
         Three are students. (businessmen)   The others are businessmen.
         Some are drinking coke. (beer)   Others are drinking beer.
         Nine are women. (man)   The other is a man.
         Two are arguing. (listening)   The others are listening.

6. M2   T: Three people — Two are from Asia.   S: The other is from (Latin America).
         Three people — One is from Latin America.   The others are from (Asia).
         Four watches — Two are made in the United States.
         Five airplanes — Four are going to San Francisco.
         Three students — One speaks English.
         Six people — Four are passing.
         Two movies — One has Sophia Loren.
         Three books — One is a biography.
         Two classes — One is dull.
         Six people — Four are my friends.

7. M2   T: What's the matter with this pen? (out   S: It's out of ink. (I need another one.)
            of ink)
         What's the matter with this pencil? (broken)   It's broken. (Please give me another one.)
         What's the matter with this book? (torn)   It's torn. (I'm going to buy another one.)
         What's the matter with this rug? (the wrong color)
         What's the matter with this government? (corrupt)
         What's the matter with that bank? (gives low interest)
         What's the matter with that car? (ashtray is full)
         What's the matter with that cup of coffee? (cold)
         What's the matter with that radio? (broken)
         What's the matter with that book? (boring)
         What's the matter with that drill? (dull)

(exercise continued on next page)

T: What's the matter with that dress? (the wrong color)

        What's the matter with that movie? (stupid)

8. C   T: Is your account in Mellon bank?   S: (Yes, it is.) (No, it's in another bank.) (Yes, and I have an account in the other bank.)

                Do you have a savings account?   (Yes, I do.) (No, I have another kind of account.) (Yes, and another one—a checking account.)

                Is your apartment on Forbes Avenue?

                Does she like these coats?

                Did you travel to Paris?

                Can you use this pen?

                Are you going to buy a VW?

                Is ( ) living in the dorm?

                Will the professor be in the office tomorrow?

                Should we open an account at that bank?

                Can we buy these cigars?

                Should ( ) get this apartment?

                Do you like romantic stories?

SECTION FOUR

OBJECT PRONOUNS — PERSONAL

Model: Chen has the check. He has it.

1. M1   Rep: John sees the book.   He sees it.

                John sees the man.   He sees him.

                John sees the woman.   He sees her.

                John sees the men.   He sees them.

                John sees you and the boys. He sees you.

                John sees you and me.   He sees us.

                John sees (the teacher).   He sees me.

GENERALIZATION

Most of the subject pronouns have different forms when they are the object of the verb.

Subject	Object
I	me
we	us
you	you
it	it
he	him
she	her
they	them

205

2. M1T   T: I can pay the bill.   S: I can pay it.
                I can pay the man.   I can pay him.
                I can pay the boys.   I can pay them.
                I can pay the woman.   I can pay her.
                He can pay you and me.   He can pay us.
                He can pay you and Bill.   He can pay you.
                He can pay Bill and Jane.   He can pay them.

3. M2   T: When can you see Bill and Jane?   S: I can see them (tomorrow).
                When can Bill bring the book?   He can bring it (next week).
                When did you call your friend?   I called (him) (last night).
                When did Mary telephone you?
                When can he see you and Jane?
                When did you talk to Mr. Jones?
                Where did the boys wait for the girls?
                When will you call Mr. Cassetti?
                When are you going to pay the invoice?

4. C   T: When did you last talk to your friend?   S: (I called him yesterday.)
                Are you going to go to the new movie? When? Where?
                Did you call your friend? When?
                How often do you read the (local newspaper)?
                How often do you write to your family?
                How often does your family write to you?
                When are you going to pay the invoice?
                How often do you see your friend?
                Where did you see the movie?
                Did you like the (baseball game)?
                How often do you call your friends?
                When will you write your parents?
                When should you balance your checkbook?
                Should you throw away the canceled checks?

SUMMARY DIALOGUE

Carlos: I'd like to open an account. Can you help me?

Bank Official: Of course, will you please have a seat?

Carlos: Thank you.

Official: Do you want a checking account or a savings account?

Carlos: Which is better?

Official: It depends on what you need. A checking account is convenient—you can pay your bills by check.

Carlos: What are the charges?

Official: You pay 10 cents for each check.

Carlos: Is that all? Are there monthly charges?

Official: No, that's all.

Carlos: O.K. I want a checking account.

Official: How much will you deposit?

Carlos: Five hundred dollars.

Official: Very good. Excuse me, I'll get the forms to fill out.

LESSON NINE – SUMMARY OF PATTERNS

	QW	Modal	Subject	Modal	Verb	Completer	Short Answer
Statement			Carlos	can	open	an account.	
Question (who/what)			Who	can	cash	a check?	Chen can.
Question (yes/no)		Will	Carlos		open	an account?	Yes, he will. No, he won't.
Question (Wh)	When	should	Chen		withdraw	some money?	Tomorrow.

LESSON TEN

INTRODUCTION   Weekend

Some of the students are having coffee and discussing the past weekend.

Bill: Did you have a good weekend, Chen?

Chen: Oh, yes! The weather was beautiful and I spent all day Saturday at the park.

Bill: That's a long way. Who *took* you?

5   Chen: I met an American family during my first week here. They invited me.

Nancy: Did you take a picnic lunch?

Chen: Yes. *Mrs. Brown's daughter* made a salad and a cake. Their son's wife brought hot
          dogs, and I bought some potato chips for snacks. We roasted the hot dogs over a fire and
          we had toasted marshmallows for dessert.

10   Nancy: Stop! I'm getting hungry.

Chen: The children taught me a new game. The *name of the game* is "Frisbee." One person
          throws a round plastic disk, and another person catches it with one hand. I tried very hard,
          but the children always won.

Bill: You'll do better next time. What did you do, Nancy?

15   Nancy: I have exams in *most of my courses* next week. I read almost all weekend.

Chen: You didn't leave your room all weekend? How terrible!

Nancy: *I was going to study all weekend,* but I found time for a walk on Sunday afternoon.
          On Saturday night my roommate's brother lent us his car. I lost a little of my study time
          then.

20   Bill: Ah ha! I knew it. You didn't *read* all weekend.

Nancy: I said "almost all weekend." You probably slept all weekend.

Bill: No, I didn't. I caught up on my correspondence. I sat under a tree near the dorm,
          fed the pigeons and squirrels, and wrote ten letters. A real weekend's work!

Nancy: I'll be happy at the end of the term. I can never study in good weather.

OUTLINE OF PATTERNS   Example

Section One		Irregular Past (1)	
	Part A	Vowel [ɔ] in Past; *make, have*	caught, made, had
		Statement	She made a cake.
		Wh Questions	What did he bring?
	Part B	Vowel [ε] in Past, Final Consonant	
		Change	read, spent
	Part C	Unpredictable	won
Section Two		Possessive	
	Part A	's	
		Names	Mrs. Brown's daughter . . .
		Nouns	My roommate's brother . . .
	Part B	—of the—	The name of the game . . .
Section Three		Prearticles (Quantifiers)	
	Part A	Count nouns	. . . most of my classes . . .
	Part B	Non-count nouns	. . . a little of my time . . .
Section Four		BE (past) + *going to*	I was going to study all weekend.

COMPREHENSION QUESTIONS

1. What are the students doing? What are the students discussing?

2. How was the weather last weekend?

3. What did Chen do last Saturday? Where did Chen spend last Saturday?

4. How did Chen go to the park? Who took Chen to the park?

5. Did they take a picnic lunch?

6. What did Mrs. Brown's daughter make?

7. Who brought hot dogs?

8. How did they cook the hot dogs?

9. What did they have for dessert?

*10. Why did Nancy say "Stop"?

11. What game did the children teach Chen?

12. How do you play Frisbee?

13. What was Nancy going to do? What did she do?

14. Did she stay in the dorm all weekend? What else did she do?

15. What did Bill do?

16. Why will Nancy be happy at the end of the term?

*17. Can you study in good weather?

Vocabulary

Nouns		Verbs		Adjective
assignment	size	build	point	past
corner	skyscraper	catch up on	say	
course	sound	find	sit on	Adverb
flavor	story	fix	sleep in	almost
kitten	taste	hear	stand on	
length	term	hold	sweep	
magazine	title	light	tell	
odor	trunk (car)			
prize	wife		Expression	
rent		in front of ("in the presence of")		

SECTION ONE

***IRREGULAR PAST TENSE (1)

Part A.   *Vowel [ɔ]; make, have*

☐ STATEMENT

Model: She made the cake.

1. M1   Rep: He made it.
       Sub: had   S: He had it.
              taught   He taught it.
              thought   He thought it.
              brought   He brought it.
              bought   He bought it.
              caught   He caught it.

2. M1   Rep: The girls bought a lot of dresses.
       Sub: the women   S: The women bought a lot of dresses.
              made   The women made a lot of dresses.
              cakes   The women made a lot of cakes.
              woman   The woman made a lot of cakes.
              brought   The woman brought a lot of cakes.
              marshmallows   The woman brought a lot of marshmallows.

(exercise continued on next page)

boys   The boys brought a lot of marshmallows.
had   The boys had a lot of marshmallows.
hot dogs   The boys had a lot of hot dogs.

GENERALIZATION

The verbs in this group, except for *have* and *make* have the vowel sound [ɔ] in the past tense.

Present	Past
make	made
have	had
teach	taught
think	thought
bring	brought
buy	bought
catch	caught

---

3. M1T   T: He teaches English every day.   S: He taught English yesterday.
              She makes a cake every week.   She made a cake last week.
              The women have a bridge party every month.   They had a bridge party last month.
              Bill brings his notebook to class every day.   He brought his notebook to class yesterday.
              Nancy thinks about her classes every night.   She thought about her classes last night.
              Mrs. Jackson teaches school every day.   She taught school yesterday.
              Bill catches up on his sleep every Sunday.   He caught up on his sleep last Sunday.
              Bill and Nancy have a picnic every weekend.   They had a picnic last weekend.
              Nancy has a date every Saturday.   She had a date last Saturday.
              Chen makes a phone call every weekend.   He made a phone call last weekend.

☐ WH QUESTIONS

Model: What did he bring? Potato chips.

***4. M2   T: make a new dress   G1:   Someone made a new dress.
                                          G2:   Who made a new dress?
                                          S: (My sister did.)

                teach English   G1:   Someone taught English.
                                          G2:   Who taught English?
                                          S: ( ) did.

                catch the frisbee   G1:   Someone caught the frisbee.
                                          G2:   Who caught the frisbee?
                                          S: ( ) did.

                buy hot dogs   G1:   Someone bought hot dogs.
                                          G2:   Who bought hot dogs?

                bring marshmallows   G1:   Someone brought marshmallows.
                                          G2:   Who brought marshmallows?

                have a new car   G1:   Someone had a new car.
                                          G2:   Who had a new car?

(exercise continued on next page)

T:	think about a Rolls-Royce	G1:	Someone thought about a Rolls-Royce.
		G2:	Who thought about a Rolls-Royce?
	make a salad	G1:	Someone made a salad.
		G2:	Who made a salad?
	catch up on his work	G1:	Someone caught up on his work.
		G2:	Who caught up on his work?

5. M1   T:

T:		S:	
Did he make something?			What did he make?
Did he think something?			What did he think?
Did he bring something?			What did he bring?
Did he buy something?			What did he buy?
Did he teach something?			What did he teach?
Did he have something?			What did he have?
Did he catch something?			What did he catch?
Did he think about something?			What did he think about?

GENERALIZATION

Pattern A.

(*Wh* word in Subject Position)

Present:	Someone	catches the ball.
	Who	catches the ball?
		(Chen)

Past:	Someone	caught the ball.
	Who	caught the ball?
		(Chen)

Pattern B.

(*Wh* word in Object Position)

	He catch es something.
Do es	he catch	something?
		(Yes, he does.)
What	does	he catch? (The ball.)

	He ca ught something.
D id	he catch	something?
		(Yes, he did.)
What	did	he catch? (The ball.)

The formation of *Wh* questions is the same as in Lessons Four and Eight. Try to answer the following questions without looking at the answers at the bottom of the next page.

1. When the *some*-word is in the object position, how is the question different from the statement? (Two ways.)

2. Which word indicates time in the statement?

3. Which word indicates time in the question?

***6. M1T   T:

T:		S:	
They caught something.			What did they catch?
They had something.			What did they have?
They taught something.			What did they teach?
They bought something.			What did they buy?
The brought something.			What did they bring?
They thought something.			What did they think?
They made something.			What did they make?
The thought about something.			What did they think about?

7. M1T   T: I brought marshmallows sometime.   S: When did you bring marshmallows?
              I had a party sometime.   When did you have a party?
              I made a cake sometime.   When did you make a cake?
              I thought about Paris sometime.   When did you think about Paris?
              I caught a plane sometime.   When did you catch a plane?
              I bought a car sometime.   When did you buy a car?

8. M2   T: Someone bought hot dogs.   S1: Who bought hot dogs?
                                                         S2: ( ) did.
              John brought something.   S1: What did he bring?
                                                         S2: (Marshmallows.)
              The boys taught something.   S: What did they teach?
              Someone had a dollar.   Who had a dollar?
              Mrs. Newton made something.   What did she make?
              The girl caught something.   What did she catch?
              Someone made a salad.   Who made a salad?
              Someone brought marshmallows.   Who brought marshmallows?
              Mrs. Orlove made something.   What did she make?
              Mr. Bruder bought something.   What did he buy?
              Suzie taught something.   What did she teach?
              Someone caught up on his sleep.   Who caught up on his sleep?

***9. M2 T: He teaches the class every day.   S1: Then he taught the class yesterday.
                                                         S2: No, he didn't teach it yesterday.
                                                         S1: Why not?
                                                         S2: (He was sick.)
                                                         S1: When *did* he teach it?
                                                         S2: He taught it (the day before yesterday).
              She makes a cake every week.   S1: Then she made a cake last week.
                                                         S2: No, she didn't make one last week.
                                                         S1: Why not?
                                                         S2: (She was busy.)
                                                         S1: When *did* she make one?
                                                         S2: She made one (the week before last).

              He buys an ice cream cone every day.
              The ladies have a bridge party every month.
              Bill brings his notebook to class every day.
              Nancy thinks about her classes every night.
              Mrs. Jackson teaches school every day.
              Bill catches up on his sleep every Saturday.
              Nancy has a date every weekend.
              Chen makes a long distance phone call every weekend.

Answers:

1. Word order and the auxiliary.
2. The verb.
3. The auxiliary.

10 C   T: Ask ( ) what he bought yesterday.   S1:   What did you buy yesterday?
                                                         S2:   I bought (an ice cream cone). (I didn't
                                                                buy anything.)

          Ask ( ) when he made a telephone call.
          Ask ( ) when he caught up on his sleep.
          Ask ( ) what he thought about last night.
          Ask ( ) when he had an ice cream cone.
          Ask ( ) when he taught his friend a new game.
          Ask ( ) where he bought his car.
          Ask ( ) how many telephone calls he made last week.
          Ask ( ) how much beer he had at the last party.
          Ask ( ) how many long distance phone calls he made last month.
          Ask ( ) how many exams he had last week.
          Ask ( ) where he bought his ( ).
          Ask ( ) when he bought his ( ).
          Ask ( ) who caught up on his sleep last weekend.
          Ask ( ) who made a cake for the party.

Part B.   *Vowel [ɛ] in Past, Final Consonant Change*

Model: He reads a book every week. He read one last week.

1. M1   Rep: He read it.
          Sub: fed   S: He fed it.
               swept   He swept it.
               left   He left it.
               kept   He kept it.
               meant   He meant it.
               felt   He felt it.
               lent   He lent it.
               sent   He sent it.
               spent   He spent it.
               built   He built it.

2. M1   Rep: The men spent a lot of money last week.
          Sub: lent   S: The men lent a lot of money last week.
               books   The men lent a lot of books last week.
               read   The men read a lot of books last week.
               magazines   The men read a lot of magazines last week.
               kept   The men kept a lot of magazines last week.
               letters   The men kept a lot of letters last week.
               sent   The men sent a lot of letters last week.

215

GENERALIZATION

The verbs in this group have the vowel [ɛ] in the past tense or end in the consonant _t_ in the past, or a combination of both.

Present	Past	Present	Past
feed	fed	read	read
build	built	spend	spent
lend	lent	send	sent
sweep	swept	leave	left
keep	kept	mean	meant
feel	felt		

***3. M1T   T: The girl reads the morning newspaper during breakfast every day.

S: She read the morning newspaper during breakfast yesterday.

The man sweeps the floor at home every day.

He swept the floor at home yesterday.

The girls spend ten dollars on books every month.

They spent ten dollars on books last last month.

The woman leaves home at ten o'clock every morning.

She left home at ten o'clock yesterday morning.

The student sends ten letters to his girlfriend every week.

He sent ten letters to his girlfriend last week.

The engineers build fifty skyscrapers every year.

They built fifty skyscrapers last year.

The boy lends a lot of money to his friend every week.

He lent a lot of money to his friend last week.

The little girl feeds her dog hamburger every day.

She fed her dog hamburger yesterday.

The teacher meets his students at lunch every Tuesday.

He met his students at lunch last Tuesday.

4. M2   T: read the newspaper

S1:   Did you read the newspaper (yesterday)?
S2:   No, I didn't. (I read it last week.) (I never read the newspaper.)

spend fifty dollars
sweep the floor
lend money to a friend
leave home at 8:00
keep your money in a savings account in your country
build a house
send a letter home
read a good book
feel happy
sleep all morning
meet your friend for lunch
keep your appointment

5. M2   T: ( ) read something   S1:   What did he read?
                                             S2:   He read a (magazine).

                 ( ) met someone   S1:   Whom did ( ) meet?
                 ( ) spent some money   How much money did ( ) spend?
                 ( ) left some books   How many books did ( ) leave?
                 ( ) built something   What did ( ) build?
                 ( ) read something   What did ( ) read?
                 ( ) met ( ) someplace   Where did ( ) meet ( )?
                 The boys met someone.   Whom did they meet?
                 The engineer built something.   What did he build?
                 ( ) and ( ) read something.   What did they read?
                 The engineers built something.   What did they build?
                 ( ) spent some money.   How much money did ( ) spend?
                 Someone spent $10.00.   Who spent $10.00?
                 Someone swept the floor.   Who swept the floor?

6. C   T: When did you read the newspaper?   S: (I read it this morning.) (Yesterday.)
                 How did you feel yesterday?
                 How long did you sleep last night?
                 When did you send a letter home?
                 Where did you keep your money at home?
                 How many papers did you read last week?
                 How many letters did you send home last week?
                 Whom did you meet during your first week here?
                 When did you leave your country?
                 Where did you meet your friend yesterday?
                 When did you last sleep in?
                 Who sent fifteen letters last week?

Part C.   *Unpredictable*

Model: He lights a fire every night. He lit the fire last night.

1. M1   Rep: I found it.
          Sub: said   S: I said it.
                heard   I heard it.
                told   I told it.
                sold   I sold it.
                won   I won it.
                lost   I lost it.
                held   I held it.
                stood on   I stood on it.
                sat on   I sat on it.

2. M1   Rep: Chen was lucky; he found a dollar in the park.
          Sub: unlucky/lost five dollars on the race   S: Chen was unlucky; he lost five dollars on
                                                                 the race.
                happy/sold his car for five hundred   Chen was happy; he sold his car for five
                  dollars   hundred dollars.
                unhappy/heard about the political   Chen was unhappy; he heard about the
                  situation in his country   political situation in his country.

(exercise continued on next page)

T:	lucky/found a five dollar bill on the sidewalk	S:	Chen was lucky; he found a five dollar bill on the sidewalk.
	upset/sat on a broken chair		Chen was upset; he sat on a broken chair.
	happy/won the ten dollar bet		Chen was happy; he won the ten dollar bet.
	unhappy/said a bad word in front of his professor's wife		Chen was unhappy; he said a bad word in front of his professor's wife.

GENERALIZATION

There is no "rule" for these irregular past tense forms. Learn them in sentences.

Present	Past		Present	Past
find	found		say	said
hear	heard		tell	told
sell	sold		win	won
lose	lost		hold	held
stand	stood		sit	sat

---

3. M1T | T: | find a dollar | S: | We found a dollar. |
|---|---|---|---|
| | lost a book | | We lost a book. |
| | hear the news | | We heard the news. |
| | sell the car | | We sold the car. |
| | tell a lie | | We told a lie. |
| | win the game | | We won the game. |
| | say "hello" | | We said "hello." |
| | light a match | | We lit a match. |

4. M1T

T:		G1:		T:		G2:	
	say		What did you say?		hello		I said "hello."
	hear		What did you hear?		a record		I heard a record.
	sell		What did you sell?		my car		I sold my car.
	lose		What did you lose?		my keys		I lost my keys.
	find		What did you find?		a dollar		I found a dollar.
	tell		What did you tell?		a story		I told a story.
	win		What did you win?		a prize		I won a prize.
	light		What did you light?		a candle		I lit a candle.
	stand on		What did you stand on?		a chair		I stood on a chair.
	sit on		What did you sit on?		a park bench		I sat on a park bench.
	hear		What did you hear?		an opera		I heard an opera.
	lose		What did you lose?		my favorite sweater		I lost my favorite sweater.

4. M2

T:	Ask ( ) what he found; add a place.	S1:	What did you find (in the park)?
		S2:	I found a (kitten) (dollar).

Ask ( ) if he lost any money; add a time.
Ask ( ) what he said to his teacher; add a time.
Ask ( ) if he found any money; add a place.

(exercise continued on next page)

T: Ask ( )how many records he heard; add a time.

Ask ( ) when he lit a fire; add a place.

Ask ( ) if he caught a cold; add a time.

Ask ( ) what he bought; add a place and time.

Ask ( ) whom he met; add a place and time.

Ask ( ) how much he spent; add a place and time.

Ask ( ) how many telephone calls he made; add a time.

***5. C   Summary

T: Using one of the verbs below, tell   S1:   I (bought a record).
      something you did last week.   S2:   He bought a record and I (heard it).
                                                   S3:   ( ) bought a record. ( ) heard it and
                                                          I slept during the record.
                                                          etc.

IRREGULAR VERBS — 1

Present Tense (Third Person Singular)	Past Tense (and Past Participle)*	Others (unpredictable)	
		finds	found
makes	made	lights	lit
has	had	stands	stood
teaches	taught	(understands/understood)	
thinks	thought	says	said
brings	brought	hears	heard
buys	bought	tells	told
catches	caught	sells	sold
reads	read	wins	won
meets	met	loses	lost
feeds	fed	sits	sat
keeps	kept	holds	held
sleeps	slept		
sweeps	swept		
leaves	left		
means	meant		
feels	felt		
lends	lent		
sends	sent		
spends	spent		
builds	built		

*In Lesson Fourteen, you will study a verb tense which uses the past participle. Some irregular verbs have a special form for the past participle, but these do not. The past and the past participle are the same form.

SECTION TWO

POSSESSIVE

Part A.   's

☐ NAMES

Model: Mrs. Brown's daughter made a salad.

***1. M1   Listen: Whose pen is this?   Rep: It's (Maria)'s pen.
                        Whose book is this?   It's (   )'s book.
                        Whose notebook is that?   It's (   )'s notebook.
                        Whose English book is that?   It's (   )'s English book.
                        Whose purse is that?   It's (   )'s purse.
                        Whose jacket is that?   It's (   )'s jacket.
                        Whose books are these?   They're (   )'s books.
                        Whose papers are these?   They're (   )'s papers.
                        Whose pens are these?   They're (   )'s pens.

GENERALIZATION

In *spelling*, add 's to names to show possession. The pronunciation will be [s], [z] or
[iz] depending on the final sound of the name (similar to the formation of plurals —
Lesson One).

        It's Joseph's book.   [-s]
        It's John's book.   [-z]
        It's Rose's book.   [-iz]

When the *spelling* of the name ends in s or z, there are two possibilities in spelling and
in sound:

        It's Mr. Jones' book.   [-z]   It's Mr. Jones's book.   [-ziz]
        It's Mr. Fernandez' book.   [-z]   It's Mr. Fernandez's book. [-ziz]

In the exercise four you will practice the first alternative, but you should listen to the
native speakers in your area to see which one they use.

***2. M1T   T: pencil—(Pablo)   S: It's (Pablo)'s pencil.
                   English book—(   )   It's (   )'s English book.
                   jacket—(   )   It's (   )'s jacket.
                   papers—(   )   They're (   )'s papers.
                   pens—(   )   They're (   )'s pens.
                   coat—(   )   It's (   )'s coat.
                   gloves—(   )   They're (   )'s gloves.
                   new book—(   )   It's (   )'s new book.
                   friends—(   )   They're (   )'s friends.

***3. M1T   T: It's her book.   S: It's ( )'s book.
                     They're his pens.   They're ( )'s pens.
                     It's his jacket.   It's ( )'s jacket.
                     It's my notebook.   It's ( )'s notebook.
                     They're her gloves.   They're ( )'s gloves.
                     It's her English book.   It's ( )'s English book.
                     They're his assignments.   They're ( )'s assignments.
                     It's her watch.   It's ( )'s watch.

4. M1   T: The book belongs to Mr. Jones   Rep: It's Mr. Jones' book.
                     The gloves belong to Mr. Fernandez.   They're Mr. Fernandez' gloves.
                     The paper belongs to Doris.   It's Doris' paper.
                     The car belongs to Gladys.   It's Gladys' car.
                     The hat belongs to Carlos.   It's Carlos' hat.
                     The papers belong to Luis.   They're Luis' papers.
                     The car belongs to Lois.   It's Lois' car.

***5. M2   T: books—(Maria)   S1:   Are those Maria's books?
                                                         S2:   No, they aren't. They're (Carlos') books.
                     jacket—(Luis)   S1:   Is that Luis' jacket?
                                                         S2:   No, it isn't. It's (Ali's) jacket.

                     pen—( )
                     gloves—( )
                     notebook—( )
                     pencils—( )
                     scarf—( )
                     book—( )
                     coat—( )
                     hat—( )
                     pencil—( )
                     pens—( )

□ NOUNS

Model: My roommate's brother lent us his car.

6. M1   Listen: Whose book is this?   Rep: It's the boy's book.
                    Whose pens are these?   They're the student's pens.
                    Whose gloves are these?   They're the woman's gloves.
                    Whose salad is this?   It's the lady's salad.
                    Whose hot dog is this?   It's the girl's hot dog.
                    Whose notebooks are these?   They're the professor's notebooks.
                    Whose papers are these?   They're the teacher's papers.
                    Whose car is this?   It's the man's car.

GENERALIZATION

To show possession in writing, add ' if the noun ends in *-s;* add 's if it does not.

boy	—	the boy's book
boys	—	the boys' book
man	—	the man's book
men	—	the men's book

In speech, there is no difference in sound between the singular and plural possessive of regular nouns. Only the context of the sentence will tell you if the possessive noun is singular or plural.

Example: The student is here. His book is on the table.
            The *student's* book is on the table.

            The students are here. Their book is on the table.
            The students' book is on the table.

---

7. M1T   T: The book belongs to the man.   S: It's the man's book.
                The book belongs to the men.   It's the men's book.
                The dog belongs to the child.   It's the child's dog.
                The dog belongs to the children.   It's the children's dog.
                The VW belongs to the woman.   It's the woman's VW.
                The VW belongs to the women.   It's the women's VW.

8. M1T   T: This book belongs to the boys.   S: It's the boys' book.
                These books belong to the boy.   They're the boy's books.
                This VW belongs to the girl.   It's the girl's VW.
                These gloves belong to the teacher.   They're the teacher's gloves.
                These notes belong to the professor.   They're the professor's notes.
                This TV belongs to the student.   It's the student's TV.
                These cars belong to the lawyer.   They're the lawyer's cars.

***9. M2   (Object Cue)
          T: Whose book is this?   S: It's ( )'s book.
                Whose coats are those?   They're (the boys') coats.
                etc.

10. C   T: Do you always have dinner at home? S: (No. Sometimes I have dinner at my
                                                                friend's house.)
                Whose car can you borrow?   (I can borrow my roommate's car.) (Ali's.)
                Did you hear (the President's) latest
                   speech? What did you think of it?
                Do many people give you advice? Whose advice do you follow?
                Is washing the dishes a man's job or a woman's job?
                What kinds of jobs are men's/women's jobs in ( )?
                Do children have any duties in ( )? What are they?
                What do you think are a teacher's responsibilities?
                What are a student's responsibilities?
                What are a friend's responsibilities?

NOTE: Some common time-words have possessive forms.

                    a   day's work
                    a   month's rent
                    two   years' time
                    two   days' pay
                    an   hour's work

        Example: How long will it take to fix my car?   It'll be about two hours' work.

Part B.   —*of the*—

Model: The name of the game is "Frisbee."

1. M1   Rep: the top of the table
                 the back of the chair
                 the arms of the chair
                 the legs of the table
                 the roof of the house
                 the corner of the room
                 the color of the hat
                 the length of the scarf
                 the name of the game

GENERALIZATION

Inanimate things usually use the following possession pattern:

Noun	*of the*	Noun
the top	of the	table
the back	of the	chair
the arms	of the	chair
the legs	of the	table

2. M1   T: cover—book   S: the cover of the book
                color—scarf   the color of the scarf
                trunk—car   the trunk of the car
                roof—house   the roof of the house
                back—bus   the back of the bus
                size—room   the size of the room
                length—room   the length of the room
                flavor—ice cream   the flavor of the ice cream
                sound—traffic   the sound of the traffic
                corner—room   the corner of the room

3. M1T   T: cover—book   S: the cover of the book
                John—book   John's book
                front—building   the front of the building
                Mr. Raven—building   Mr. Raven's building
                lady—purse   the lady's purse
                student—typewriter   the student's typewriter
                corner—house   the corner of the house
                name—magazine   the name of the magazine
                title—book   the title of the book
                George—date   George's date

4. C   T: Where do you usually sit in the bus?   S: (I usually sit in the (back) of the bus.)
                Where is your apartment (room) in
                   the building?   (It's in the front of the building.)
                Describe the roofs of the houses in
                   your country.   (The roofs of the houses are flat.)
                Describe a sound which is pleasant to you.
                Describe a sound which is unpleasant.
                Describe an odor which is pleasant.
                Describe a taste which is pleasant.
                Name a taste which you don't like.
                Where is your room in the dorm?
                Do you like the front or back of the room in class? Why?
                Which is most important—the length or color of a coat?
                Do you like marshmallows? Why?
                Do you like VWs? Why?

SECTION THREE

PREARTICLES (QUANTIFIERS)

Part A.   *Count Nouns*

Model: Most of my classes . . .

***1. M1   Rep: Some of the pens are red.
                    Five of the pens are red.
                    A few of the pens are red.
                    Half of the pens are red.
                    Many of the pens are red.
                    A lot of the pens are red.
                    All of the pens are red.
                    Not many of the pens are red.

GENERALIZATION

To indicate a *portion* of a quantity, the expressions of quantity (Lesson Five) precede the article and noun. When the context is clear, the article and noun may be omitted.

Example: I have a lot of friends. *Some of* my friends are from the United States. *Not many* are from Asia.

---

2. M1   Rep: A few of the students are from Latin America.
          Sub: three   S: Three of the students are from Latin America.
               professors   Three of the professors are from Latin America.
               Asia   Three of the professors are from Asia.
               half   Half of the professors are from Asia.
               books   Half of the books are from Asia.
               the United States   Half of the books are from the United States.
               many   Many of the books are from the United States.

3. M2   Situation: Here are five Cadillacs and five Rolls-Royces.
          T: cheap   S: (None of the cars are cheap.)
                imported   (Half of the cars are imported.) (Five of the cars are
                                            imported.)

                expensive
                made in the United States
                made in Great Britain
                ugly
                beautiful
                little
                economical
                made in Canada

4. M2   T: How many of the people in this class are   S: (Five of the people are from Iran.)
                  from Iran?
               How many of the people in this class are   (None of the people are from
                  from Venezuela?   Venezuela.)
               How many of the people in this class are from Colombia?
               How many of the people in this class are studying math?
               How many of the people in this class are from the U.S.?
               How many of the people in this class are from Libya?
               How many of the people in this class are studying English?
               How many of the people in this class have a car?
               How many of the people in this class are graduate students?
               How many of the people in this class commute to class?
               How many of the people in this class live in the dorm?

Part B.   *Non-count Nouns*

Model: . . . a little of my study time

***1. M1   Rep: Some of the money is from Mexico.
            A lot of the money is from Mexico.
            Half of the money is from Mexico.
            A little of the money is from the U.S.
            All of the money is from the U.S.
            None of the money is from the U.S.

GENERALIZATION

As you learned in Lesson Five, some expressions of quantity are used with count nouns, others with non-count nouns. The same is true of the prearticles.

Count		Non-count	
five		a little	
a few	} of the pens	(not) much	} of the money
(not) many			

Both Kinds of Nouns

Some
Half
A lot } of the { pens
All   { money
None

---

2. M1   Rep: Half of my money is in a savings account.
         Sub: some   S: Some of my money is in a savings account.
              a little   A little of my money is in a savings account.
              a lot   A lot of my money is in a savings account.
              not much   Not much of my money is in a savings account.
              all   All of my money is in a savings account.
              none   None of my money is in a savings account.

3. M1T   T: A lot of the pollution is from   S: A little of the pollution is from big cars.
             big cars.
             A lot of the people are from New York.   A few of the people are from New York.
             A lot of the students are from Asia.   A few of the students are from Asia.
             A lot of the food is good for you.   A little of the food is good for you.
             A lot of the people are coming to   A few of the people are coming to
             dinner.   dinner.
             A lot of my friends are from the   A few of my friends are from the United
             United States.   States.
             A lot of his money is in a checking   A little of his money is in a checking
             account.   account.

4. M1T   Rep: Not much of the pollution is from Canada.
          Sub: books   S: Not many of the books are from Canada.
               money   Not much of the money is from Canada.
               people   Not many of the people are from Canada.
               gasoline   Not much of the gasoline is from Canada.
               music   Not much of the music is from Canada.
               cars   Not many of the cars are from Canada.

5. M2   T: friends from the United States   S1: (Are all of your friends from the United States?)
                                               S2: (No. Most of my friends are from Libya.)
              money in a checking account   S1: (How much of your money is in a checking
                                                     account?)
                                               S2: (Most of it.)
              friend's advice   S1: (Do you follow all of your friend's advice?)
                                               S2: (Not all, but most of it.)

              friends live in the dorm
              teachers from the United States
              classes in this building
              money in a savings account
              friends live in apartments
              pollution from industry
              free time in the library
              friends speak English

6. Discussion

    Now that you have learned more about the United States, there may be some questions
    you want to ask. Use this pattern and ask the teacher.

    S: (Does it rain all of the time here?)   T: (Not all of the time, but in the spring
                                                        it rains a lot.)

         (There are the companies U.S. Steel,   (No. The government doesn't own any
         American Oil, American Broadcasting   of those companies. They're just
         Co. Does the government own most   names.)
         of the industry?)

SECTION FOUR

$$\left.\begin{matrix}WAS\\WERE\end{matrix}\right\} + GOING\ TO + VERB$$

Model: I was going to study all weekend.

1. M1   Rep: I was going to study all weekend.
          Sub: we   S: We were going to study all weekend.
               sleep   We were going to sleep all weekend.
               all day   We were going to sleep all day.
               Judy   Judy was going to sleep all day.
               work   Judy was going to work all day.
               all morning   Judy was going to work all morning.
               you   You were going to work all morning.

2. M1   Rep: When was the man going to fix your car?

Sub: where		S:	Where was the man going to fix your car?
drive			Where was the man going to drive your car?
take			Where was the man going to take your car?
why			Why was the man going to take your car?
when			When was the man going to take your car?
paint			When was the man going to paint your car?
use			When was the man going to use your car?
how			How was the man going to use your car?

GENERALIZATION

Lesson Three:	I'm going to study tomorrow.
Lesson Ten:	I was going to study all day.

The pattern in Lesson Three indicates *intentions* of future activities. The pattern in this lesson indicates past intentions. It means that plans were changed. The sentences are often combined with *but*.

"I was going to fly to Paris; I'm going to take a boat *instead.*"***
"I was going to fly to Paris; I'm going to London *instead.*"
"I was going to study English, but I'm studying French *instead.*"

Note the difference between this pattern and the other past tenses you have studied:

Lesson Eight:	Simple Past	I studied yesterday.
Lesson Seven:	Past Continuous	I was studying at 8:00 last night.
Lesson Ten:	New Pattern	I was going to study last night, but I didn't.

Note also the negative of the pattern:

I wasn't going to call him, but I did.

---

3. M1T   If you hear a sentence which describes a completed action in the past, say "I did it"; if uncompleted, say, "But I didn't."

T:	I was driving home.	S:	I did it.
	I drove home.		I did it.
	I was going to drive home.		But I didn't.
	I wrote home.		I did it.
	I was going to write a novel.		But I didn't.
	I was writing to John.		I did it.
	I was going to sleep all day.		But I didn't.
	I was working at midnight.		I did it.
	I was going to work all night.		But I didn't.

4. M1T   Tell what happened.

T:	I wasn't going to call him.	S:	I called him.
	I was going to write her.		I didn't write her.
	We were going to play bridge.		We didn't play bridge.
	They weren't going to pay the bill.		They paid the bill.
	He wasn't going to fly to New York.		He flew to New York.
	She was going to do the dishes.		She didn't do the dishes.
	We were going to quit smoking.		We didn't quit smoking.
	They weren't going to write the paper.		They wrote the paper.

228

5. M1T   T: fly to Paris/fly to London   S: I was going to fly to Paris; I'm going to fly to London instead.

study English/study French   I was going to study English. I'm going to study French instead.

read a novel/read a biography   I was going to read a novel. I'm going to read a biography instead.

buy a VW/buy a Chevrolet   I was going to buy a VW; I'm going to buy a Chevrolet instead.

work all day/sleep all day   I was going to work all day; I'm going to sleep all day instead.

take a nap/mow the lawn   I was going to take a nap; I'm going to mow the lawn instead.

open a checking account/open a   I was going to open a checking account; I'm going
  savings account   to open a savings account instead.

bring hot dogs/bring marshmallows   I was going to bring hot dogs; I'm going to bring marshmallows instead.

6. M2   T: The man was going to bring my S: The man was going to bring my car last week, but
                  car last week, but——   (he brought it yesterday instead).

                The students were going to bring   The students were going to bring hamburgers for
                  hamburgers for the pucnic,   the picnic, but (they brought hotdogs instead).
                  but——

                The men were going to paint the house last month, ——
                Our friends were going to call last weekend, ——
                Their daughter was going to make a salad, ——
                We were going to have a picnic last weekend, ——
                I was going to buy a VW, ——
                Jane was going to study Saturday night, ——
                Bill and Nancy were going to watch the baseball game, ——
                Their friends were going to travel in France this summer, ——
                They were going to buy a new house, ——
                Charles was going to work in New York, ——
                The Bruders were going to buy a plane, ——
                Suzie was going to sail to Spain, ——

7. C   T: Did you do everything you planned   S: (Not everything. I was going to go to the zoo,
                  for last weekend? What did you   but it rained. I played bridge at the Union.)
                  do instead?   (Almost everything. I was going to finish my
                                                            homework, but I didn't have time. I went
                                                            to a party.)
                Did anyone persuade you to do   (Yes. I wasn't going to study, but my room-
                  something that you planned not   mate told me about a test in biology.)
                  to do?

8. C   T: Tell about a time when you had some very important plans which you changed.

          S: (I was going to become a teacher. I studied engineering instead.) (I wasn't
                  going to come here, but I changed my mind.)

SUMMARY DIALOGUE

Chen: What are you going to do this weekend, Nancy?

Nancy: I was going to go to the park, but the weather looks bad. Maybe I'll call some friends
for a bridge game. Do you want to play?

Chen: Thanks. But some of my roommate's friends are coming. I'm going to take them to
the International Students' Party.

Nancy: Have fun.

Chen: Thanks. Good luck in the bridge game.

Nancy: I'll need it.

LESSON TEN — SUMMARY OF PATTERNS

		Aux	Subject	Verb	Completer	Short Answer
Statement			She	made	a cake.	
Question (Who)			Who	took	you?	The Hastings did.
Question (Yes/No)		Did	the lady	make	a cake?	Yes, she did. No, she didn't.
Question (Wh)	What	did	the man	buy?		A car.
Statement			I	was going to study English.		

LESSON ELEVEN

INTRODUCTION   Credit cards

Chen and Nancy are discussing credit cards.

Chen: Nancy, I have a problem. Can you help me?

Nancy: I'll try. What's the matter?

5   Chen: About a month ago, *I got a credit card* from one of the large department stores. I
         didn't know much about them—the cards—so I wrote for information, but I didn't
         understand the letter. I took the card and the letter and went to the store. I saw the
         manager, but he spoke very fast. Now, I have this card, but I can't use it.

Nancy: O.K. Where's the letter? Ask me the questions. I'll try to explain.

Chen: *Here it is. Do I have to pay for the card?*

10   Nancy: Not usually. Some of the national companies have a fee, department stores rarely do.

Chen: O.K. Let's suppose I find something in the store. I take it to the clerk.

Nancy: The clerk will usually say, "Is this cash or charge?" You'll say "charge." She'll write
         out the charge slip; you'll sign it and keep a copy. Once a month the store will send you a
         bill.

15   Chen: When do I have to pay?

Nancy: Usually it's within 25 days from the date on the bill. But you ought to pay right away,
         so you won't forget.

Chen: It's really convenient to have a credit card. I might see something really great, and I
         might not have the money.

20   Nancy: That's right, but you should always have the money in the bank. The store doesn't
         charge if you pay on time. But the charge is one and one-half percent per month if you're
         late.

Chen: That's 18% a year! I'll have to be careful. I don't want to pay a late charge.

Nancy: A few years ago not many people used to have credit cards. Now they're very common,
25   but you have to know the *disadvantages* as well as the *advantages.*

Chen: Thanks, Nancy. Kaufmann's is having a sale next week. I'll go there and try to use
         my card.

OUTLINE OF PATTERNS   Example

    Section One   Irregular Past Verbs — 2   gave, wore

    Section Two   *Here/There* Adverbials

        Part A.   Indication of Location   There's the letter. Here it is.

        Part B.   Pronoun for Place   I'll go there . . .

    Section Three   Modals

        Part A.   *ought to*   You ought to pay . . .

        Part B.   *might*   I might see something . . .

        Part C.   *have to*   Do I have to pay . . .?

    Section Four   *Used to* + Verb   Not many people used to have
                                                credit cards . . .

COMPREHENSION QUESTIONS

1. What are Nancy and Chen discussing?

2. Where did Chen get a credit card?

*3. Why did he write for information?

4. Why did he go to the store?

5. Whom did he see at the store?

6. Did he understand the manager? Why didn't he understand the manager?

7. Does he have to pay for the card?

8. What does the clerk in the store say?

9. What does the clerk write?

10. How often do they send a bill?

11. When does he have to pay?

12. When should he pay?

13. What is the charge if he doesn't pay on time?

*14. Do you have any credit cards?

*15. Are credit cards common in your country?

> NOTE: If you have credit cards, you should record the numbers and keep them in a safe place in case you have to notify the company of a loss. You should also know your responsibility in case someone charges things on your card after it has been lost or stolen.

Vocabulary

Nouns		Verbs		Adjectives
advisor	lettuce	blow	ride	handwritten
alma mater	manager	choose	ring	
boat	ocean	contribute	swim	
company	orange juice	*get	tear	
contribution	pizza	grow	type	
elevator	receipt	pay	wake	
fee	seashore	quit	wake up	
gas tank	shower			
invoice	slipper			
laundry	smoking	*He gets home at 8:00.		(arrive)
	tomato	He gets a letter every day.		(receive)

SECTION ONE

***IRREGULAR PAST — 2

Model: I got a credit card.

1. M1   T: gave   S: He gave it.
             tore   He tore it.
             broke   He broke it.
             saw   He saw it.
             chose   He chose it.
             drank   He drank it.
             rang   He rang it.

2. M1T   T: wear   S: We wore it.
             ring   We rang it.
             choose   We chose it.
             break   We broke it.
             give   We gave it.
             tear   We tore it.
             see   We saw it.
             drink   We drank it.

233

3. M1   T: threw   S: I threw it.

knew — I knew it.
grew — I grew it.
blew — I blew it.
took — I took it.
did — I did it.

4. M1T   T: She throws it.   S: She threw it.

She knows it. — She knew it.
She does it. — She did it.
She grows it. — She grew it.
She takes it. — She took it.
She blows it. — She blew it.

GENERALIZATION

These verbs, like those in Lesson Ten, have *irregular* past tense forms. They differ from the previous verbs in that there is a third part (Participle) which is different from the past and is used to form other tenses. The best way to memorize these irregular forms is to practice the sentences in drills 1-6.

---

5. M1   T: spoke   S: He spoke there.

woke up — He woke up there.
got — He got there.
went — He went there.
rode — He rode there.
drove — He drove there.
ate — He ate there.
swam — He swam there.
wrote — He wrote there.

6. M1T   T: I write a letter every day.   S: I wrote a letter yesterday.

They wake up at 5:00 every day. — They woke up at 5:00 yesterday.
He speaks Spanish every week. — He spoke Spanish last week.
She swims a mile every month. — She swam a mile last month.
They get up at noon every Saturday. — They got up at noon last Saturday.
They go downtown every day. — They went downtown yesterday.
We eat pizza every Sunday. — We ate pizza last Sunday.
He rides a bike every morning. — He rode a bike yesterday morning.
He drives a VW every day. — He drove a VW yesterday.

7. M1T   T: He gives his daughter a dime every day.   S: He gave his daughter a dime yesterday.

He eats an apple every day. — He ate an apple yesterday.
He drives 10,000 miles every year. — He drove 10,000 miles last year.
He writes five letters every week. — He wrote five letters last week.
He rides his bike to school every day. — He rode his bike to school yesterday.
He drinks orange juice every morning. — He drank orange juice yesterday morning.
He sings in the shower every night. — He sang in the shower last night.
He swims in the ocean every summer. — He swam in the ocean last summer.
He rings for the elevator every morning. — He rang for the elevator yesterday morning.

GENERALIZATION

Lesson Ten: Affirmative: She made a dress.

                 Yes/No Question: D[id] she make a dress?   Yes, she did.

                 Wh Question: When did she make a dress?   Last week.

Lesson Eleven: Affirmative: He dr[a]nk a scotch.

                 Yes/No Question: D[id] he drink a scotch?   Yes, he did.

                 Wh Question: When did he drink a scotch?   Last Saturday.

***8. M1T   T: He gives money to the government every year.

    S1:   Did he give money to the government last year?

    S2:   Of course he gave money to the government last year.

He eats a steak every Saturday.

    S1:   Did he eat a steak last Saturday?

    S2:   Of course he ate a steak last Saturday.

He drives to work every Monday.
He rides his horse every Saturday.
( ) writes a letter every week.
( ) drinks milk for breakfast every day.
He sings in church every Sunday.
The alarm rings at 8:00 every morning.
The girls swim in the ocean every summer.
( ) sees a movie every week.
( ) takes a thousand dollars out of the bank every day.
( ) swims a mile every week.
( ) rides his bike to school every day.

9. M1T   T: throw—book/pencil

    G1:   Did he throw the book?

    G2:   No, he didn't throw the book. He threw the pencil.

know—answer/question

    G1:   Did he know the answer?

    G2:   No, he didn't know the answer. He knew the question.

grow—tomatoes/lettuce
take—bus/taxi
go—home/downtown
do—dishes/laundry
see—movie/play
tear—shirt/jacket
wear—boots/slippers
choose—Mary/Jane
speak—English/Farci
break—his leg/his foot

***10. M2   T: Someone drank the beer.   G1:   Who drank the beer?
                                                      S1:   ( ) did.
                                                      G2:   When did he drink it?
                                                      S1:   He drank it (yesterday).

                    Someone sang a new song.   G1:   Who sang a new song?
                                                      S2:   ( ) did.
                                                      G2:   When did he sing it?
                                                      S2:   He sang it ( ).

                    Someone swam the Channel.   G1:   Who swam the Channel?
                                                      S3:   ( ) did.
                                                      G2:   When did he swim it?
                                                      S3:   He swam it ( ).

                    Someone rode a bike.   G1:   Who rode a bike?
                                                      S4:   ( ) did.
                                                      G2:   When did he ride it?
                                                      S4:   He rode it ( ).

                    Someone wrote a book.   G1:   Who wrote a book?
                                                      S5:   ( ) did.
                                                      G2:   When did he write it?
                                                      S5:   He wrote it ( ).

                    Someone drove the Rolls-Royce.   G1:   Who drove the Rolls-Royce?
                                                      S6:   ( ) did.
                                                      G2:   When did he drive it?
                                                      S6:   He drove it ( ).

                    Someone ate a pizza.   G1:   Who ate a pizza?
                                                      S7:   ( ) did.
                                                      G2:   When did he eat it?
                                                      S7:   He ate it ( ).

                    Someone gave a lecture.   G1:   Who gave a lecture?
                                                      S8:   ( ) did.
                                                      G2:   When did he give it?
                                                      S8:   He gave it ( ).

11. M2   T: He usually gets home *at 10:00.*   S1:   What time did he get home (yesterday)?
                 (What time?)   S2:   He got home at (9:00).
                 He usually wears a *jacket.* (What?)   S1:   What did he wear (last night)?
                                                       S2:   He wore (an overcoat).
                 He usually goes *downtown* after class. (Where?)
                 He usually does his laundry on *Saturday.* (When?)
                 He usually eats *four* hot dogs. (How many?)
                 He usually takes *a little* money to school. (How much?)
                 He usually rides ( )'s bicycle. (Whose?)
                 He usually writes *his parents.* (Whom?)
                 He usually wakes up *at noon.* (When?)
                 He usually sees his friend *at the cafeteria.* (Where?)

12. C   T: What time did you wake up this morning?   S: (6:00.) (The alarm went off at 7:30.)
                 Who did you write to yesterday?
                 Where did you go last weekend?
                 When did you do your laundry?

(exercise continued on next page)

236

T: When did you see a good movie? Where?
     Did you ever break your arm? How?
     Did you ever see a movie star? Where?
     How much money did you take on your trip? Where did you go?
     How many people did you know when you came here? Who?
     How often did you write home last week?
     What time did you get home yesterday?
     Did you get a letter yesterday?
     Did you ever swim in the ocean? Which one? When?

13. C   Use one of the verbs at the bottom of this page and tell something you did last week.

S1:   (I gave a lecture.)
S2:   He gave a lecture and I (went to a party).
S3:   He gave a lecture; she went to a party and I ( ).

IRREGULAR VERBS — 2 (All three parts different)

Third Person Singular—Present	Simple Past	*Past Participle
is	was	been
gives	gave	given
eats	ate	eaten
drives	drove	driven
rides	rode	ridden
writes	wrote	written
drinks	drank	drunk
sings	sang	sung
rings	rang	rung
swims	swam	swum
throws	threw	thrown
knows	knew	known
grows	grew	grown
blows	blew	blown
takes	took	taken
goes	went	gone
does	did	done
sees	saw	seen
tears	tore	torn
wears	wore	worn
chooses	chose	chosen
speaks	spoke	spoken
breaks	broke	broken
wakes	woke	***
gets	got	gotten

*The past participle is not used until Lesson Fourteen

SECTION TWO

HERE/THERE ADVERBIALS

Part A.   *Indication of Location*

Model: Where's the letter?
        Here it is. or *There* it is.

***1. M1   T: The book is on the table.   S: There's the book.
                  The hat is on the chair.   There's the hat.
                  The car is on the corner.   There's the car.
                  The store is down the street.   There's the store.
                  The office is down the hall.   There's the office.
                  The professor is near the door.   There's the professor.

***2. M1   T: The letters are on the desk.   S: Here are the letters.
                  The men are at the door.   Here are the men.
                  The keys are in the lock.   Here are the keys.
                  The girls are in the class.   Here are the girls.
                  The books are on the table.   Here are the books.
                  The papers are under the book.   Here are the papers.

3. M1   T: There's the book.   S: There it is.
               There's the man.   There he is.
               There's the girl.   There she is.
               There's the key.   There it is.
               There's the woman.   There she is.
               There's the letter.   There it is.

GENERALIZATION

Here/There refer to the location of items in the same manner as the demonstrative adjectives *this* and *that* (Lesson Three).

Here refers to something or someone near the speaker, and *there,* far from the speaker.

Note that the pattern with nouns is different from the pattern with pronouns:

Here/There	BE	Noun
Here	is	the book.
There	are	the keys.

Here/There	Pronoun	BE
Here	it	is.
There	they	are.

When *here* and *there* are at the end of the sentence, they often have the form: *right here* or *over there.*

I can't find the book.   It's right here.
                              It's over there.

238

4. M1T   T: Here's the book.   S: Here it is.

4. M1T	T:	Here's the book.	S:	Here it is.
		There's the key.		There it is.
		Here are the cards.		Here they are.
		There are the stores.		There they are.
		There's the girl.		There she is.
		Here's the woman.		Here she is.
		Here are the boys.		Here they are.
		There's the man.		There he is.

5. M2	T:	Where's your coat?	S:	(Here it is.) (There it is.) (Here's my coat.)
		Where are your papers?		(Here they are.) (There they are.) (There are my papers.)
		Where are ( )'s gloves?		
		Where is my book?		
		Where are my papers?		
		Where is my coat?		
		Where is ( )'s coat?		
		Where is ( )'s notebook?		
		Where are ( )'s books?		
		Where are ( )'s papers?		
		Where is ( )'s scarf?		
		Where is your coat?		

Part B.   *Pronoun for Place*

Model: I'll go there after dinner.

1. M1	T:	John was in Paris last week.	S:	John was there last week.
		John was in London last week.		John was there last week.
		John was in Thailand last week.		John was there last week.
		John was downtown last week.		John was there last week.
		John was in the country last week.		John was there last week.
		John was at the party last week.		John was there last week.

2. M1	Rep:	Bill will be here tomorrow.		
	Sub:	Bill and Chen	S:	Bill and Chen will be here tomorrow.
		next week		Bill and Chen will be here next week.
		The girl		The girl will be here next week.
		the day after tomorrow		The girl will be here the day after tomorrow.
		Nancy		Nancy will be here the day after tomorrow.
		the week after next		Nancy will be here the week after next.
		the men		The men will be here the week after next.

GENERALIZATION

Here and *there* substitute for places when the referent is known:

Did you visit New York?   Yes, I was there last month.

When will you see John?   He'll be here next week.

---

3. M1T   T: John was in class last week.   S: John was here last week.

                  Bill will be in Paris next month.   Bill will be there next month.

                  The boys will be in (Pittsburgh) tomorrow.   The boys will be here tomorrow.

                  The men went to London last month.   The men went there last month.

                  Charlie was in Puerto Rico yesterday.   Charlie was there yesterday.

                  Mary will be at the university next week.   Mary will be here next week.

                  Bill was in class yesterday.   Bill was here yesterday.

                  The men were in Mexico last week.   The men were there last week.

4. M2   T: Bill wants to go to ( ).   S: He can go there (next year).

                  Maria wants to come to ( ).   She'll come here (next week).

                  Chen and Nancy want to go to ( ).

                  I want to go to ( ).

                  ( ) wants to visit ( ).

                  ( ) wants to come to the U.S.

                  We want to visit ( ).

                  ( ) and ( ) want to visit this class.

                  ( ) and ( ) want to go to ( ).

                  ( ) wants to come to the university.

                  ( ) and ( ) want to go to ( ).

                  ( ) wants to come to our class.

***5. C   T: When is the best season to go to ( )?   S: (You should go there in April. That's carnival time.)

                  When is the worst time to go to ( )?   (You shouldn't go there in December. The weather is cold.)

                  When is the best time to come to ( )?   (People should come here in summer. In winter, it's awful.)

                  When is the worst time to come to ( )?

                  When should I visit ( )?

                  When should someone start school here?

                  When should someone not start school?

SECTION THREE

MODALS: *OUGHT TO, MIGHT, HAVE TO*

***Part A.   *Ought to*

Model: You ought to pay right away.

1. M1   Rep: I can go to the bank.

         Sub: should   S: I should go to the bank.

               will   I will go to the bank.

               might   I might go to the bank.

               ought to   I ought to go to the bank.

               have to   I have to go to the bank.

GENERALIZATION

Ought to is a "two-word" modal that means *should* and like *should* precedes the simple form of the verb:

        I should pay the bill.   I ought to pay the bill.

Even though the modals have the same meaning, *should* is much more common in negative statements and questions:

        Should we stay?   Yes, we ought to.
                            No, we shouldn't.

---

2. M1   **T:**   I ought to go now.   **S:**   I should go now.

                     You ought to pay the rent.   You should pay the rent.

                     He ought to open an account.   He should open an account.

                     We ought to pay the bill.   We should pay the bill.

                     She ought to do her work.   She should do her work.

                     They ought to have a savings account.   They should have a savings account.

                     I ought to study for the test.   I should study for the test.

                     He ought to get a haircut.   He should get a haircut.

3. M1T   **T:**   We ought to go.   Question   **S:**   Should we go?

                     He ought to leave.   Negative   He shouldn't leave.

                     They ought to pay the

                        bill.   Question   Should they pay the bill?

                     She ought to study.   Question   Should she study?

                     You ought to buy a car.   Negative   You shouldn't buy a car.

                     I ought to see my friend.   Negative   I shouldn't see my friend.

                     He ought to write home.   Question   Should he write home?

                     She ought to go to the

                        movies.   Negative   She shouldn't go to the movies.

4. M2   **T:**   It's late.   **S:**   (I should go home.) (We should leave.)

                     I have a test tomorrow.   (I should study.) (I shouldn't go to the movies.)

                     I got a letter from my friend a month ago.

                     The professor doesn't like handwritten papers.

                     The house is quite dirty.

                     The professor gave an assignment for tomorrow.

                     Smoking is bad for people.

                     The gas tank is almost empty.

                     The grass is very tall.

                     The windows are dirty.

                     Large cars increase pollution.

                     My alma mater is asking for contributions.

                     The bill is due in a few days.

Part B.   *Might*

Model: I might see something really great.

1. M1   T: Maybe I'll go to the movies.   S: I might go to the movies.
                 Maybe we'll stay home.   We might stay home.
                 Maybe he'll buy a VW.   He might buy a VW.
                 Maybe she'll study engineering.   She might study engineering.
                 Maybe we'll get a pizza.   We might get a pizza.
                 Maybe we'll be late.   We might be late.
                 Maybe they'll sing a song.   They might sing a song.
                 Maybe you'll win the prize.   You might win the prize.

GENERALIZATION

Might, which means possibility, indicates *present* or *future* time, depending on the context:

        Maybe I'll   go tomorrow.
            I might   go tomorrow.

        Maybe he is   sick today.
        He might be sick today.

As with the other modals, *might* precedes the simple form of the verb. *Not* is rarely contracted:

        I might not be on time.

---

2. M1   Rep: I might not go to class today.
           Sub: go shopping   S: I might not go shopping today.
                 do the laundry   I might not do the laundry today.
                 finish the lesson   I might not finish the lesson today.
                 have the money   I might not have the money today.
                 go home early   I might not go home early today.
                 see John   I might not see John today.
                 have time to do the assignment   I might not have time to do the assignment
                                                        today.

3. M1T   T: Maybe John is sick.   S: John might be sick.
                 Maybe I have a dime.   I might have a dime.
                 Maybe Jane is downtown.   Jane might be downtown.
                 Maybe they have a credit card.   They might have a credit card.
                 Maybe the car increases pollution.   The car might increase pollution.
                 Maybe smoking is bad.   Smoking might be bad.
                 Maybe the gloves are lost.   The gloves might be lost.
                 Maybe the rent is late.   The rent might be late.

4. M1T   T: Maybe John is sick.   S: John might be sick.
               Maybe John will come early.   John might come early.
               Maybe Jane isn't downtown.   Jane might not be downtown.
               Maybe the students will come.   The students might come.
               Maybe we won't finish on time.   We might not finish on time.
               Maybe Chen will meet his friends.   Chen might meet his friends.
               Maybe they aren't at home.   They might not be at home.
               Maybe she won't answer the phone.   She might not answer the phone.

5. M2   T: go to the park/the movies   S: (I might go to the park. I don't like movies.)
                                                         (I might go to the movies. It's going to rain.)

               read a book/a magazine
               call John/Mary
               write a letter/a book
               eat at home/eat out
               buy a suit/a coat
               buy a plane/a boat
               go to New York/San Francisco
               be on time/be late
               have a dinner party/picnic
               buy a typewriter/pen

6. C   T: Tell something you might do next weekend.   S: (I might write a paper.)

Part C.   *Have to*

Model: Do I have to pay for the card? Not usually.

GENERALIZATION

Have to is somewhat different from the other modals; it agrees with the third person
subject and has question and negative forms like the verb *have*.

	Should (etc.)			*Have to*	
Statement	He should	leave.		He	has to leave.
Negative	He shouldn't	leave.		He doesn't	have to leave.
Interrogative	Should	he	leave?	Does he	have to leave?
	Answer: Yes, he should.			Answer: Yes, he does.	

Have to indicates a requirement or an obligation: We have to pay the rent (or we'll
be evicted).

---

1. M1   Rep: I have to pay the rent.
          Sub: be on time   S: I have to be on time.
                 do my work every day   I have to do my work every day.
                 speak English in the U.S.   I have to speak English in the U.S.
                 report the accident   I have to report the accident.

(exercise continued on next page)

know the disadvantages of credit cards.   I have to know the disadvantages of credit cards.
call my friend   I have to call my friend.
quit smoking   I have to quit smoking.

2. M1   Rep: He has to study the lesson.
    Sub: go to bed   S: He has to go to bed.
    finish the homework   He has to finish the homework.
    type the paper   He has to type the paper.
    pay the rent   He has to pay the rent.
    get gas   He has to get gas.
    leave the country   He has to leave the country.
    attend class   He has to attend class.
    find the key   He has to find the key.
    be on time   He has to be on time.

3 M1   Rep: Does he have to pay the invoice today?
    Sub: finish the lesson   S: Does he have to finish the lesson today?
    get the book   Does he have to get the book today?
    type the paper   Does he have to type the paper today?
    answer the letter   Does he have to answer the letter today?
    send the application   Does he have to send the application today?
    go to the lab   Does he have to go to the lab today?
    quit smoking   Does he have to quit smoking today?
    leave early   Does he have to leave early today?

4. M1   Rep: We don't have to do the work today.
    Sub: pay the bill   S: We don't have to pay the bill today.
    go to class   We don't have to go to class today.
    send the application   We don't have to send the application today.
    talk to our advisor   We don't have to talk to our advisor today.
    be on time   We don't have to be on time today.
    get up early   We don't have to get up early today.
    cook dinner   We don't have to cook dinner today.

***5. M1T   T: go to our friends' party (Possibility)   S: We might go to our friends' party.
    write to my parents (Good idea)   I should write to my parents.
    pay his bills by Monday (Obligation)   He has to pay his bills by Monday.
    finish her work tomorrow (Possibility)   She might finish her work tomorrow.
    tell the police about their accident (Obligation)   They have to tell the police about their accident.
    finish my research paper this weekend (Good idea)   I should finish my research paper this weekend.
    take his license to the police (Obligation)   He has to take his license to the police.
    close their account today (Possibility)   They might close their account today.

***6. M2   T: I don't have to ——   S: I don't have to (pay the rent until next week).
    ( ) has to ——   ( ) has to (pay for his car).
    etc.

7. M2   T: Ask ( ) when he has to send the application for graduate school.   S1:   When do you have to send the application for graduate school?

S2:   (Next week.) (I sent it yesterday.)

Ask ( ) when he has to pay the invoice.
Ask ( ) when he has to pay the credit card bill.
Ask ( ) when he has to apply for grad school.
Ask ( ) when he has to take the TOEFL exam.
Ask ( ) where he has to wait for the bus.
Ask ( ) how often he has to cash a check.
Ask ( ) how much money he has to have every month.
Ask ( ) how often he has to go shopping.

8. C   T: Tell something you have to do today and when.   S: (I have to go to the bank this afternoon.)

Tell something you don't have to do next weekend.   (I don't have to study.)

9. M2   Use a modal to comment on the following situations:

T: John has a test tomorrow. His friends want him to go to the movies.   S: (He should study.) (He shouldn't go to the movies.) (He ought to stay home.)

Jane is very fat. She wants to reduce, but she loves candy.
It's raining. Bill has a headache. He also has a class at the university.
Bill needs some money for the weekend. It's 4:30; the bank closes at 5:00.
The invoice just came from the university. Jose doesn't have the money to pay for it.
Chen just got a credit card. Kaufmann's is having a sale, but Chen doesn't have any money.
Someone stole Jane's wallet with all her credit cards.
In a large city you are totally lost.
You are in a bank when a robber comes in with a gun.
You finish dinner in an expensive restaurant and discover you don't have your wallet.
A good friend advises you to do something you think is wrong.

10. C   T: What do you have to do every day? Why?   S: (Get up at 6:00.) (Write to my girlfriend.)
What do you have to do if you're broke?
What are you going to do this weekend? (might)
What should you do if you see a fire?/an accident?/a robbery?
What should you do if it's raining?
Do you have a credit card? How often do you have to pay?
Do you have to type your papers?
What are your plans for the weekend?
What are your plans for the summer?
Do you have to be on time to class? When?
Are there things you have to do every day? What?
Are there things you ought to do every day? What?
Who ought to study very hard?

SECTION FOUR

***USED TO + VERB

Model: Not many people used to have credit cards.

1. M1   Rep: I used to live in Boston.
                 They used to have a party every week.
                 The girl used to ride her bike to school.
                 Chen used to have a savings account.
                 The professor used to type his papers.
                 The students used to be on time.
                 The man used to quit smoking every year.
                 The men used to cook dinner every Sunday.
                 I used to speak French very well.

GENERALIZATION

Used to + verb is a *past* expression which indicates something which was *formerly* a
fact, but is no longer. "I used to live in Boston; now I live in Pittsburgh."

---

2. M1T   T: I don't live in Boston any longer.   S: You used to live in Boston.
                 They don't have a VW any longer.   They used to have a VW.
                 He doesn't drive to work any longer.   He used to drive to work.
                 She doesn't smoke cigars any longer.   She used to smoke cigars.
                 We don't speak French well any longer.   You used to speak French well.
                 He doesn't study hard any longer.   He used to study hard.
                 They don't get up early any longer.   They used to get up early.
                 They don't come on time any longer.   They used to come on time.

3. M2   T: I used to ——, but now I ——.   S1: I used to (live in Paris), but now I
                                                                (live in the U.S.).
                                                           S2: I used to (have a VW), but now I
                                                                (don't have a car).

4. C   T: Do you study the same way that you did   S: (No, I used to study with my friends.
                    when you came here?   Now I study alone.)
                 Do you live in the same place as when you first came?
                 Do you have a car? Is it the same kind that you had before?
                 Do you have a checking/savings account? What did you have at home? Are they in the
                    same bank as when you first came?
                 Do you have a lot of friends? As many as when you first came?
                 Do you eat the same kind of food here as at home (as when you first came)?
                 How did you get help when you first came? Is it the same now?
                 Do you read the U.S. newspapers? Did you when you first came?

SUMMARY DIALOGUE

Chen is shopping in a large department store. He chooses a scarf.

Clerk: May I help you?

Chen: Yes. I'd like this scarf.

Clerk: Yes, sir. Will that be cash or charge?

Chen: Charge. Here's my card.

Clerk: Sign here, please. (Chen signs.) Here's your receipt. Thank you, sir.

LESSON ELEVEN — SUMMARY OF PATTERNS

For Past Tense, see the Summary of Patterns for Lesson Eight

MODALS

	Aux.	Subject	Modal	Verb	Completer
Statement		Nancy	might	go	home.
		Chen	has to	pay	the bill.
		Carlos	ought to	pay	the rent.
Question *(have to)*	Does	Bill	have to	get	a credit card? Yes, he does.
	Modal				
(can)	Can	Bill		get	a credit card? Yes, he can.
Used to + Verb		Judy	used to	go	to school.

LESSON TWELVE

INTRODUCTION   Bills

On the way to a restaurant for a snack, Carlos is complaining to Nancy about the synonomous terms for money in English.

Carlos: I'll never understand this crazy language. You can't be satisfied with one word. *There are always dozens* for the same idea.

5   Nancy: What's bothering you now, Carlos? You *didn't get into trouble, did you?*

Carlos: No, I didn't. It's this capitalistic society and all the words for money. *The university sends me an invoice;* the waitress brings me a check; the doctor gives me a bill; and the lawyer charges a fee. *I didn't shut my checkbook* all weekend.

Nancy: Are you upset by the words or by the cost of living in this country?

10   Carlos: The cost of living, I guess. I put a lot of money in the bank and I was going to *buy myself a car* this month. Now I don't have the money. But, Nancy, do me a favor, will you, and explain some of the differences in these words?

Nancy: Sure, Carlos, but I have to make a phone call. Order me a cup of coffee, will you? I'll be right back. (Nancy soon returns.) How much was the coffee? Fifteen, twenty cents?

15   Carlos: Never mind, it's on me.

Nancy: Thanks, Carlos. That's very nice. Now where were we? Oh, yes, the words for money . . . well, there are two categories. One is the actual amount you have to pay—fee, charge, price, and the other is the written statement—check, bill, invoice.

Carlos: Well, that's easy enough, but how can I know the right context? How is a bill different
20   from an invoice?

Nancy: They're about the same, really. Technically, a bill is a statement of the amount owed; an invoice is a bill with the individual items listed, but people usually think of "invoice" as a business term.

Carlos: I see, I guess. There are other terms, though—*toll* and *fare,* for instance.

25   Nancy: A fare is the amount for some form of transportation—a bus fare, a taxi fare. A toll is the charge for using a public facility—a toll road, a toll bridge. The telephone company also charges *toll* calls, but that may be because they like to have people think they are a public service company.

Carlos: It's pretty confusing, you have to admit.

30   Nancy: I guess you're right. I never thought about it.

OUTLINE OF PATTERNS   Example

Section One	Irregular Past — 3		
	Part A.	All three parts of verb the same	shut
	Part B.	come, run	came, ran
	Part C.	Tag Questions — Past Tense	
		Type I	get into trouble, did you?
		Type II	found your purse, didn't you?

Section Two	*There* — Subject Position	

Section Three	Verb + Indirect Object + Direct Object	
	Group I	Order me a cup of coffee.
	Group II	The doctor sends me a bill.

Section Four	Reflexive Pronoun — Indirect Object	buy myself a car

Section Five	Comparison I	
	like	A bill is like an invoice.
	the same as	A fee is the same as a charge.
	different from	A fare is different from a toll.

COMPREHENSION QUESTIONS

1. Where are Carlos and Nancy going?

2. What is Carlos complaining about?

*3. What is bothering Carlos?

4. What does the university send?

5. What does the waitress bring?

6. What does the doctor send?

7. What does the lawyer charge?

*8. What really upsets Carlos?

9. What was Carlos going to buy? Why isn't he going to?

10. What does Nancy have to do?

*11. What is Nancy going to do for Carlos?

12. Who paid for the coffee?

13. What are the terms for the "amount" to be paid?

*14. What are the terms for "written statement"?

*15. What is a bill? What is an invoice? What is a fare? What is a toll?

*16. Are there as many terms for money in your language? Are the terms for the charge different from those for the written statement?

Vocabulary

Nouns			Verbs		
back	knee	police station	bet	cut	return
barber	ladies' room	powder room	bother	hurt	run
bathroom	landlord	race (competition)	come	let out	set
bet	leather	restroom	cost	put	
bird	lie	root beer			
block	lobby	sandwich		**Adjectives**	
bully	lounge	silk			
drug store	lunch counter	slide (film)	actual		synonymous
finger	men's room	society			
fog	pet	stairs		**Expressions**	
hamburger	phone booth	statement	cut class		drop a line
haze		wig			
horse					

SECTION ONE

IRREGULAR PAST — 3

Part A.   *All three parts of the verb are the same.*

Model: I never shut my checkbook all weekend.

1. M1   T: shut the window   S: He shut the window yesterday.
                  put it on the table   He put it on the table yesterday.
                  let the dog out   He let the dog out yesterday.
                  set the table   He set the table yesterday.
                  bet on the race   He bet on the race yesterday.
                  cut the meat   He cut the meat yesterday.

GENERALIZATION

The past tense of these verbs is the same as the simple form of the verb. The third part (past participle) is also the same.

Present Tense Third Singular	Past Tense (and Past Participle)
shuts	shut
puts	put
lets	let
sets	set
bets	bet
cuts	cut
costs	cost
hurts	hurt

2. M1T T: He shuts the window every morning.   S: He shut the window yesterday morning.
            He puts money in the bank every month.   He put money in the bank last month.
            He lets the cat out every morning.   He let the cat out yesterday morning.
            I set the table every morning.   I set the table yesterday morning.
            They bet on the horses every week.   They bet on the horses last week.
            Tuition costs a lot every year.   Tuition cost a lot last year.
            I cut class every week.   I cut class last week.
            He cuts the grass every week.   He cut the grass last week.

3. M1T T: Charlie and I let the cat out every day.   S: Did you let the cat out yesterday?
            John puts money in the bank every week.   Did he put money in the bank last week?
            John and Chen bet a dollar every month.   Did they bet a dollar last month?
            Mary sets the table every day.   Did she set the table yesterday?
            John bets $10 on the horse race every month.   Did he bet $10 on the horse race last month?
            The boy hurts his leg in the football game   Did he hurt his leg in the football game last
              every year.   year?
            Books cost more every year.   Did they cost more last year?
            The little girl sets the table every afternoon. Did she set the table yesterday afternoon?

4. M2   T: Someone hurt his back yesterday.   S1: Who hurt his back?
                                                        S2: (John) did.
            John bet some money on the race.   S1: How much money did he bet?
                                                        S2: (Twenty dollars.)
            The boys cut some classes last term.
            Something cost five thousand dollars in 1960.
            Someone shut the window last night.
            Jill hurt someone in the game.
            Carlos put some money in the bank.
            Someone let the cat out.
            The nurse set the glass somewhere.
            I cut the little girl's hair sometime.
            Someone bet $25 on the horse.

5. M2   T: Someone is going to bet $25 on the horse.   S1:   Who is going to bet $25 on the horse?
                                                            S2:   (Bill) is.

        The boys cut some classes every term.   S1:   How many classes do they cut?
                                                            S2:   They cut (ten or fifteen).

        Carlos put some money in the bank.
        Something costs $10,000.
        The hostess is setting something on the table.
        Someone was shutting the windows.
        Judy is putting some dishes on the table.
        Bill cut the grass sometime.
        Someone bet a lot of money on the Kentucky Derby.
        Jill cut class sometime.
        Someone is going to put on a play.
        Someone was setting the table.
        Mrs. Casetti is putting the car somewhere.

6. M2   T: Someone let the cat out.   S1:   Who let the cat out?
                                                            S2:   ( ) did.
                                                            S3:   I didn't let the cat out. I let (the dog) out.

        Something cost 25 dollars.   S1:   What cost $25?
                                                            S2:   The book did.
                                                            S3:   The book didn't cost $25, it cost ($).*

        Someone bet $100 on the race.
        Someone cut Bill's hair.
        Mrs. Hastings set something on the table.
        Someone cut the grass.
        Something shut the door.
        Jill bet some money on the race.
        Someone set the table.
        Mrs. Jones put the money somewhere.
        Someone shut his finger in the door.
        Someone hit the bully.
        Someone put a wet glass on Mrs. Hastings' new table.

> *NOTE: While it is customary to compare prices in general, it is considered impolite
> by many people in the U.S. to ask specific costs of personal objects or personal salaries.
> For example, it is O.K. to ask "How much does a telephone operator make?" but *not*
> "How much do you make?" It is O.K. to ask "How much are Persian rugs in this
> country?" but *not* "How much was that Persian rug?"

7. C   T: Do you ever bet on the horse races?   S: (Yes, often.) (What is "the numbers"?)
                the numbers?
        How much did a haircut cost in your country last year?
        Who set the table for dinner at home?
        Who sets the table now?
        Did you ever shut your finger in a door? When?
        Did anyone hurt his leg in the (soccer) game?
        How often do you put money in the bank?
        What kind of account do you put your money in?
        Who cuts the grass at home? Did you ever cut the grass at home?
        How much does a car cost in your country?
        How did you cut costs?

Part B.   *Come, run*

Model: The bill came last week.

1. M1   Rep: He came at 10:00.
              Sub: She   S: She came at 10:00.
                    we   We came at 10:00.
                    they   They came at 10:00.
                    you   You came at 10:00.
                    I   I came at 10:00.
                    the man   The man came at 10:00.

2. M1   Rep: He ran a mile every day last week.
              Sub: we   S: We ran a mile every day last week.
                    two miles   We ran two miles every day last week.
                    morning   We ran two miles every morning last week.
                    month   We ran two miles every morning last month.
                    I   I ran two miles every morning last month.
                    two blocks   I ran two blocks every morning last month.
                    summer   I ran two blocks every morning last summer.

GENERALIZATION

Come and *run* are different from the other irregular verbs. The present and the past participle are the same. The past is different.

Present	Past	Past Participle
run(s)	ran	run
come(s)	came	come

---

3. M1T   T: He runs a mile every afternoon.   S: He ran a mile yesterday afternoon.
                  She comes at 8:00 every morning.   She came at 8:00 yesterday morning.
                  We run to the bus stop every day.   We ran to the bus stop yesterday.
                  They come early every morning.   They came early yesterday morning.
                  The bill comes on Monday every month.   The bill came on Monday last month.
                  He runs around the block every morning.   He ran around the block yesterday morning.

4. M2   T: ( ) came ——   S: (( ) came to the U.S. in February. He started English
                                                          classes with me.)
                                                      (( ) came to class yesterday. He was absent the day before.)
                  ( ) ran ——   (( ) ran to class yesterday. It was raining.)
                                                      (( ) ran home at 10:00. He forgot his book.)
                  ( ) and ( ) bet ——
                  ( ) put ——
                  ( ) and ( ) cut ——
                  ( ) and I came ——
                  ( ) hit ——
                  ( ) and I cut ——
                  ( ) shut ——
                  ( ) and ( ) hurt ——

(exercise continued on next page)

T: ( ) ran ——
        ( ) and ( ) came ——

Part C.   *Tag Questions — Past Tense*

☐ TYPE I***

Model: You didn't get into trouble, did you? No, I didn't.

1. M1   Rep: You didn't hurt your foot, did you?
               He didn't write this book, did he?
               They didn't drive downtown, did they?
               The boys didn't need any money, did they?
               We didn't lose the game, did we?

GENERALIZATION

The pattern of Type I tag questions is the same as of the BE verbs in Lessons One and
Two, the present tense in Lesson Four, and past tense in Lesson Seven.

Previous Pattern: It wasn't late,   was it?   No, it wasn't.
Present Pattern: You didn't get into trouble, did you?   No, I didn't.
                        —   +   —

---

2. M1T   T: sell your car   G1: You didn't sell your car, did you?
                                          G2: No, I didn't.
               lose his money   G1: He didn't lose his money, did he?
                                          G2: No, he didn't.
               say "hello" to her friend G1: She didn't say "hello" to her friend, did she?
                                          G2: No, she didn't.
               hurt her arm   G1: She didn't hurt her arm, did she?
                                          G2: No, she didn't.
               make their sweaters   G1: They didn't make their sweaters, did they?
                                          G2: No, they didn't.
               do their homework   G1: They didn't do their homework, did they?
                                          G2: No, they didn't.
               find his dog   G1: He didn't find his dog, did he?
                                          G2: No, he didn't.
               lend their friends the   G1: They didn't lend their friends the money, did they?
               money   G2: No, they didn't.

3. C   T: Make a conversational statement to your neighbor using the past tense. Add a tag.
               The second student will answer and give a comment.

         S1:   (You didn't buy a car, did you?)
         S2:   (No, I didn't. It's too expensive.)

255

□ TYPE II

Model: You found your purse, didn't you? Yes, I did.

1. M1   Rep: You found your purse, didn't you?
                     You read the letter, didn't you?
                     He told the story, didn't he?
                     He won the bet, didn't he?
                     She ran to the bus stop, didn't she?
                     They caught the bus, didn't they?
                     They fed the birds, didn't they?

GENERALIZATION

The pattern is the same as Type II tags in earlier lessons.

Previous Pattern:	You were	late,	weren't you?	Yes, I was.
Present Pattern:	You found	your purse,	didn't you?	Yes, I did.
	+		−	+

***2. M1T   T: find your key   G1: You found your key, didn't you?
                                              G2: Yes, I did.

                     buy his paper   G1: He bought his paper, didn't he?
                                              G2: Yes, he did.

                     teach her lesson   G1: She taught her lesson, didn't she?
                                              G2: Yes, she did.

                     feed their pets   G1: They fed their pets, didn't they?
                                              G2: Yes, they did.

                     go to his class   G1: He went to his class, didn't he?
                                              G2: Yes, he did.

                     drive her VW to work   G1: She drove her VW to work, didn't she?
                                              G2: Yes, she did.

3. M1T   T: He lent his car.   G1: He lent his car, didn't he?
                                              G2: Yes, he did.

                     He didn't lose his keys. G1: He didn't lose his keys, did he?
                                              G2: No, he didn't.

                     She paid the bill.   G1: She paid the bill, didn't she?
                                              G2: Yes, she did.

                     They wanted some advice. G1: They wanted some advice, didn't they?
                                              G2: Yes, they did.

                     We met the host.   G1: We met the host, didn't we?
                                              G2: Yes, we did.

                     They didn't have the   G1: They didn't have the money, did they?
                       money.   G2: No, they didn't.

                     He had a cold.   G1: He had a cold, didn't he?
                                              G2: Yes, he did.

                     The man didn't call.   G1: The man didn't call, did he?
                                              G2: No, he didn't.

                     She understood the terms. G1: She understood the terms, didn't she?
                                              G2: Yes, she did.

***4. M1T   T: Bill's from the United States.   G1: Bill's from the United States, isn't he?
                                                      G2: Yes, he is.

                    Carlos isn't from Canada.   G1: Carlos isn't from Canada, is he?
                                                      G2: No, he isn't.

                    Jane wasn't late.   G1: Jane wasn't late, was she?
                                                      G2: No, she wasn't.

                    Nancy was in New York last   G1: Nancy was in New York last week, wasn't she?
                      week.   G2: Yes, she was.

                    Chen forgot the appointment.   G1: Chen forgot the appointment, didn't he?
                                                      G2: Yes, he did.

                    The Pirates won the game.   G1: The Pirates won the game, didn't they?
                                                      G2: Yes, they did.

                    The Steelers didn't come in   G1: The Steelers didn't come in first, did they?
                      first.   G2: No, they didn't.

                    The bank isn't far.   G1: The bank isn't far, is it?
                                                      G2: No, it isn't.

                    We met the hostess.   G1: We met the hostess, didn't we?
                                                      G2: Yes, we did.

                    You didn't forget the address.   G1: You didn't forget the address, did you?
                                                      G2: No, I didn't.

                    You were on time.   G1: You were on time, weren't you?
                                                      G2: Yes, I was.

                    You received the message.   G1: You received the message, didn't you?
                                                      G2: Yes, I did.

***5.   Situation: You are at a party. You remember having met the person before, but you can't
                    remember where. Use tag questions to find out about him.

        S1:   (You were in ( ) class at the university, weren't you?)
               (You didn't go to (university), did you?)

SECTION TWO

THERE — SUBJECT POSITION

Model: There are many words for the same idea.
        There is a good restaurant down the street.

1. M1   Rep: There's a good restaurant down the street.
                 There are many words for the same idea.
                 There's a drug store in the next block.
                 There are some new students in the class.
                 There's a lot of money in the bank account.
                 There are a few people on the bus.
                 There's a little bread on the table.
                 There are a lot of words for the same thing.

GENERALIZATION

Lesson Eleven: Where's my book?   There it is.

There is used as an introductory of "pointing word" to indicate the *location* of a *definite* object. Stress is on *there*.

Lesson Twelve: Where's a good restaurant?   There's one down the street.

There is used in subject position and precedes an indefinite noun or pronoun. In this pattern *there* indicates existence of an item, but does not point to it. Stress is not on *there*.

Indefinite pronouns are common in responses:

Where's a phone booth?	There's one down the hall.
Are there any new magazines?	There are some on the table.

---

2. M1T	T:	some letters on the desk	S:	There are some letters on the desk.
		a good restaurant near here		There's a good restaurant near here.
		a phone call for John		There's a phone call for John.
		some bills for you		There are some bills for you.
		some people at the door		There are some people at the door.
		a bakery across the street		There's a bakery across the street.
		ten people at the party		There are ten people at the party.
3. M1T	T:	any messages for me	S:	Are there any messages for me?
		a phone booth around here		Is there a phone booth around here?
		a restroom in this building		Is there a restroom in this building?
		any letters for us		Are there any letters for us?
		a mailbox near here		Is there a mailbox near here?
		any elevators in this building		Are there any elevators in this building?
		a bus stop near here		Is there a bus stop near here?
		any new students coming		Are there any new students coming?
		an assignment for tomorrow		Is there an assignment for tomorrow?
4. M2	T:	a phone booth	S1:	Is there a phone booth (around here)?
			S2:	There's one (around the corner).
		night clubs	S1:	Are there any night clubs (in this city)?
			S2:	There are some (in Shadyside).
		good restaurants		
		a post office		
		a restroom		
		a men's room		
		car dealers		
		a ladies' room		
		a police station		
		jewelry stores		
		a drug store		
		a barber		
		good hotels		
		a lunch counter		
		dress shops		

***NOTE: In a public place, the terms used for sanitary facilities are different from a
private home:

Public	Private
restroom	bathroom
men's room	powder room
ladies' room	

The question form "Where is the ———, please?" is appropriate to either private homes or
public places, but men usually do *not* ask for the "powder room."

5. M2   T: the accident   S1:   Where's the accident?
                                           S2:   It's (over there).

               a drug store   S1:   Where's a drug store?
                                           S2:   There's one (   ).

               the professor   S: Where's the professor?
               a cheap apartment   Where's a cheap apartment?
               a good restaurant   Where's a good restaurant?
               the Linguistics Department   Where's the Linguistics Department?
               some night clubs   Where are some night clubs?
               a good hairdresser   Where's a good hairdresser?
               my coat   Where's my coat?
               a good movie   Where's a good movie?
               the new doctor   Where's the new doctor?
               a good dentist   Where's a good dentist?
               a cheap barber shop   Where's a cheap barber shop?

6. C   T: Where can I make a phone call?   (There's a phone booth in the Student Union.)
               Where can I get a good cheap meal?   (You can get a cheap meal at MacDonald's.)
               Is there a hospital near here?
               Where's the nearest restroom?
               How can I find Professor (   )?
               I need a pack of cigarettes.
               Where can I cash a check?
               I need change for the bus.
               I need some vegetables for dinner.
               Is there a place I can buy a stamp?
               Where's the best place for a cup of coffee?
               I need to go downtown right away.
               Who can tell me about this building?

SECTION THREE

VERB + INDIRECT OBJECT + DIRECT OBJECT

□ ***GROUP I

Model: Order me a cup of coffee.

1. M1   T: send a bill   S: Did you send John a bill?

                     teach a new song   Did you teach John a new song?

                     take the invoice   Did you take John the invoice?

                     tell the story   Did you tell John the story?

                     throw the frisbee   Did you throw John the frisbee?

                     pay the rent   Did you pay John the rent?

                     show your new jacket   Did you show John your new jacket?

                     give a dollar   Did you give John a dollar?

                     read the letter   Did you read John the letter?

                     ask the question   Did you ask John the question?

GENERALIZATION

In this pattern there are two objects: *The doctor sent me a bill.* The first object *(me)* is the recipient of the second object *(a bill).* The first object may be a pronoun (her, him, me, etc.). The second is usually a noun or a substitute word like *one, other* (see drill 3, Part B.).

---

2. M2   T: tell   S: (I'm going to tell my friend a story tomorrow.)

                                                 (I told my roommate a legend yesterday.)

                                                 (I might tell the professor the story next week.)

                     show

                     give

                     read

                     ask

                     send

                     teach

                     take

                     throw

                     show

☐ GROUP II

3. M1   T: buy a car   S: When did you buy her a car?

                     do a favor   When did you do her a favor?

                     order a pizza   When did you order her a pizza?

                     make a dress   When did you make her a dress?

                     find an apartment   When did you find her an apartment?

                     leave the money   When did you leave her the money?

                     get an appointment   When did you get her an appointment?

                     save some time   When did you save her some time?

                     buy the new hat   When did you buy her the new hat?

NOTE: The difference between Group I verbs and Group II verbs will become clear in Lessons Nineteen and Twenty. In this lesson the patterns are the same.

---

4. M2   T: Did you order someone something?   S1:   Yes, I ordered (Mary a hamburger).
                                               S2:   (When) did you order her a hamburger?
                                               S1:   (Yesterday.)
             Are you going to buy someone   S1:   Yes. I'm going to buy (my friend a gift).
                something?   S2:   (Where) are you going to buy her a gift?
                                               S1:   (At Gimbel's.)
             Are you going to give someone something?
             Did you send someone something?
             Are you getting someone something?
             Did you leave someone something?
             Will you read someone something?
             Can you show someone something?
             Did you make someone something?
             Do you have to buy someone something?
             Did you throw someone something?
             Will you pay someone something?
             Can you take someone something?

5. M2   T: She needs a new dress.   S: I (bought) her one (last week).
             He wants a letter   I (wrote) him one (last night).
             They want some coffee.   I (took) them some (an hour ago).
             She wants some money.
             I want a new apartment.
             The doctor wants some money.
             The children want a story.
             The lady wants some bread.
             The little girl wants a new dress.
             The students want slides.
             Mr. Brown needs a favor.
             Mrs. Green wants an appointment.
             Suzie wants a record.

6. C   T: When did you write your family a letter?   S: (I wrote them one last week.)
             How often do you do your friends favors?   (I often do them favors.)
             When are you going to buy your friend a gift?
             When can you get me an appointment to see the President?
             When do you have to pay the landlord the rent?
             How often do you give your friends advice?
             When are you going to read your friend the letter?
             When will you show us your slides?
             When are you going to drop your friend a line?
             How often do you lend your friends money?
             When did the university send you the invoice?

SECTION FOUR

REFLEXIVE PRONOUN — INDIRECT OBJECT

Model: I was going to buy myself a car.

1. M1   Rep: I'm going to buy myself a car.
                He got himself a new apartment.
                She's buying herself a wig.
                We're going to save ourselves some money.
                They're doing themselves a favor.
                You can save yourself some time.
                You can save yourselves some money.

GENERALIZATION

The same pattern as Section Three can be used to show that the subject of the sentence is also the receiver of the object.

Previous Pattern:	I bought him a candy bar.
Present Pattern:	He bought himself a candy bar.

---

2. M1T   Rep: He told himself a lie.
            Sub: she   S: She told herself a lie.
                  they   They told themselves a lie.
                  we   We told ourselves a lie.
                  I   I told myself a lie.
                  you and Bill   You and Bill told yourselves a lie.
                  Carlos   Carlos told himself a lie.

3. M1T   T: Is Bill going to buy his brother a book?   S: No. He's going to buy himself a book.
                  Did Chen get his brother an appointment?   No. He got himself an appointment.
                  Did Mary do her brother a favor?   No. She did herself a favor.
                  Do Bill and Mary give their brother some money? No. They give themselves some money.
                  Did the girls write their brother a check?   No. They wrote themselves a check.
                  Did you teach your brother a new song?   No. I taught myself a new song.
                  Will Carlos order his brother some coffee?   No. He'll order himself some coffee.
                  Did Sally make her brother a drink?   No. She made herself a drink.
                  Did you and Chen save your brother some
                     money?   No. We saved ourselves some money.

4. M2   T: buy   S1:   I (bought) (my friend a book).
                                                S2:   What did you buy yourself?
                                                S1:   I bought myself (a hat).
               make   S1:   I('m going to) make (my friends a
                                                      hamburger.)
                                              S2:   What are you going to make yourself?
                                              S1:   I'm going to make myself a (sandwich).

               get
               send
               write
               order
               get
               make
               buy
               save
               give

***5. C   T: What did you buy yourself last week?   S: (I bought myself a new car.)
                         Did you tell someone something last week? What?
                         When did you teach someone something? What?
                         When did you write your family a letter?
                         Did you send someone something recently? When? What?
                         Did you drive someone somewhere last week? Whom? Where?
                         Did you make someone something last year? Whom? What?
                         Did someone give you something last year? Who? What?
                         Did someone buy you something last week? What? Who?
                         Are you going to write someone soon? What? Who?
                         Are you going to get someone a present soon? Who? What?
                         Are you teaching someone something? Who? What?

SECTION FIVE

COMPARISON I

□ *LIKE*

Model: A bill is like an invoice.

1. M1   Rep: The weather is like spring.
           Sub: my room—a freezer   S: My room is like a freezer.
                her car—a truck   Her car is like a truck.
                your hand—ice   Your hand is like ice.
                their house—an oven   Their house is like an oven.
                his room—a prison   His room is like a prison.
                a bill—an invoice   A bill is like an invoice.
                a fee—a charge   A fee is like a charge.
                that knife—a razor   That knife is like a razor.

NOTE: *like* is used to compare items, either *literally* as an explanation: A bill is like an
invoice, or *figuratively* as in descriptions: Your hands are like ice.

---

2. M1   T: How does the man act? (a two-year-old child)   S: He acts like a two-year-old child.
                  What does this flower feel like? (silk)   It feels like silk.
                  How does this weather seem? (fall)   It seems like fall.
                  What is your room like? (a prison)   It's like a prison.
                  What do her hands feel like? (ice)   Her hands feel like ice.
                  What does the car sound like? (a broken washing
                     machine)   It sounds like a broken washing machine.
                  What is the man's skin like? (leather)   It's like leather.

***3. M2   T: root beer   S1:   What's root beer?
                                                     S2:   Root beer is like (coke. It's not like beer).
                  a check in a restaurant.   S1:   What's a check in a restaurant?
                                                     S2:   It's like (a bill. It's not like a check at the bank).
                       (exercise continued on next page)
                                  263

T: Pepsi-Cola
an expressway
an alley
bourbon
toll
Volvo
a lunch counter
a hail storm
haze
sleet
a thunder storm
a powder room
fog

4. M2   T: Describe the place you live.   S: (My room is like a palace.) (It's like a prison.)
Describe the weather here in winter.   (It's like Alaska.) (It's like winter in my country.)
Describe a beautiful song.
Describe a very handsome man.
Describe a very beautiful woman.
Describe a very noisy car.
Describe a delicious dinner.
Describe a terrible storm.
Describe a terrible driver.
Describe a person with poor manners.
Describe a beautiful flower.
Describe a terrible actor.

☐ *THE SAME AS*

Model: A fee is the same as a charge.

5. M1   Rep: A fee is the same as a charge.
        Sub: a cocktail lounge—a bar   S: A cocktail lounge is the same as a bar.
            a bathroom—a restroom   A bathroom is the same as a restroom.
            a toll—a charge   A toll is the same as a charge.
            a fare—a charge   A fare is the same as a charge.
            autumn—fall   Autumn is the same as fall.

NOTE: Use *like* to compare *similar* items: A bill is like an invoice, and *the same as* to compare *equal* items: A fee is the same as a charge.

Often the difference in equal items is in the usage. For example: A restroom is *the same as* a bathroom, but restrooms are found in public places and bathrooms in private homes.

---

6. M1T   T: Pepsi—Coke   S: Pepsi is like Coke.
            autumn—fall   Autumn is the same as fall
            frozen water—ice   Frozen water is the same as ice.
            bill—invoice   A bill is like an invoice.

(exercise continued on next page)

T:	fee—charge	S:	A fee is the same as a charge.
	VW—Volvo		A VW is like a Volvo.
	a cocktail lounge—a bar		A cocktail lounge is the same as a bar.
	haze—fog		Haze is like fog.

☐ *DIFFERENT FROM*

Model: A fare is different from a toll.

7. M1   Rep: Our customs are different from England's.

Sub:	seasons	S:	Our seasons are different from England's.
	Thailand's		Our seasons are different from Thailand's.
	weather		Our weather is different from Thailand's.
	Mexico's		Our weather is different from Mexico's.
	prices		Our prices are different from Mexico's.
	Japan's		Our prices are different from Japan's.
	cars		Our cars are different from Japan's.

> NOTE: Use *different from* to compare items which are not the same. You may hear
> *different than* in this pattern, but in formal speech and in writing *different than* com-
> bines *clauses:*
>
>   Their weather is *different from* ours.
>   They have *different* weather *than* we do.

8. M1T   T:

a trolley—a street car	S:	A trolley is the same as a street car.
a trolley—a bus		A trolley is different from a bus.
autumn—fall		Autumn is the same as fall.
a taxi—a cab		A taxi is the same as a cab.
a VW—a Rolls-Royce		A VW is different from a Rolls-Royce.
a dictionary—an encyclopedia		A dictionary is different from an encyclopedia.
a fare—a toll		A fare is different from a toll.
a street—an avenue		A street is the same as an avenue.

9. M2   T: He's from New York City; she's from
             Syracuse, New York.   S: (They come from the same state.)

Chen has Mr. Jackson for a teacher;   (Chen's teacher is different from Bill's.)
   Bill has Miss Wilson.   (Chen and Bill don't have the same teacher.)
We're going to the movie at 7:00; they're going at 9:30.
I bought a VW; Bill bought a Ford.
We come from New England; they come from the mid-West.
Bill likes sports cars; Carlos likes sports cars.
Nancy likes science; Chen likes languages.
Carlos studies English in room 136; Chen studies English in room 129.
Nancy likes adventure stories; Bill likes science fiction.
Bill comes to school by bus; Chen drives to school.
Charlie likes big cities; Mary likes small towns.

10. C   T: The price of a haircut   S1:   (Is the price of a haircut in (country) the same
                                                           as here?)
                                                 S2:   (Yes, it's the same.) (No, it's very different from
                                                           my country.)

              the price of a newspaper
              the political situation
              the weather
              the seasons
              students
              winter
              the food
              pollution
              customs
              cities
              traffic
              the position of women

SUMMARY DIALOGUE

Nancy: I have to make a phone call. Order me a cup of coffee, will you?

Carlos: Sure. What do you want in it?

Nancy: A little cream, no sugar.

Carlos: That's right—Americans never have sugar in their coffee.

Nancy: That's not true. Lots of Americans have their coffee with sugar; but I'm on a diet
         and sugar is fattening.

SUMMARY OF PATTERNS

Past Tense (see Lesson Eight)

Tag Question 1:   You didn't get   into trouble,   did you?   No, I didn't.
                                 —   +   —

Tag Question 2:   You   got   into trouble,   didn't you?   Yes, I did.
                                    +   —   +

Two Objects

	Subject	*Verb*	+ *Indirect Object*	+ *Direct Object*
	I	bought	him	a radio.
Reflexive	She	wrote	herself	a letter.

266

LESSON THIRTEEN

INTRODUCTION   Bargaining for a car

Mr. Jackson bought a car three years ago, but now it has 50,000 miles and he wants a new one. It's a good year for the buyer because business is slow, and car prices are down. He should be able to get a good deal by careful planning and *by bargaining shrewdly* with the dealer. He can finance the car with a loan from the bank, but he *may use* the dealer's
5   financing plan. It will depend on the costs. He visited several dealers last weekend and he read the newspaper ads; then he made a decision.

It's Saturday. Mr. Jackson decided *a week ago* on a small blue sedan at the dealer near his house. Today he's going to discuss the price, the trade-in and the options with the salesman. The sticker price is $2,500, but with the allowance for his car and some talking, he shouldn't
10   have to pay more than $1,400. At the car lot:

Salesman: Good morning, sir. May I help you?

Mr. Jackson: Yes, maybe. I'm thinking of a new sedan. The old one is still good, but you know how women are. They have to keep in style.

Salesman: I know what you mean. My wife is the same way. Are you going to trade in the
15   old one?

Mr. Jackson: Yes, I guess so.

Salesman: O.K. The mechanic will check it out and then I can tell you how much we'll allow. (Mr. Jackson gives him the keys and the mechanic drives the car away.) Did you have any particular color in mind?

20   Mr. Jackson: Not really, but my wife prefers blue.

Salesman: We just happen to have a dark blue one on the lot. It's right over here. It has automatic transmission, radio, whitewalls. Your wife will love it.

Mr. Jackson: I can do without the automatic transmission, but it looks pretty good. How much is it?

25   Salesman: The sticker price is $2,500. With a good trade-in on your car, it'll probably be about $2,000.

Mr. Jackson: That's more than I was going to spend. Only $500 for my car?

Salesman: That's the going rate right now, but if it's in good shape, we may be able to do a little better.

30   Mr. Jackson: I was hoping to get one for around a thousand.

Salesman: Well, I may be able to let you have it for $1,800 and your car.

Mr. Jackson: That's really more than I want to spend. I guess I'll have to look around a little more. A friend of mine got one from a dealer across town for quite a lot less.

35   Salesman: Oh, really? Well, I'll have to talk to the boss. And the *mechanic must be back* by
          now; I'll look at his report. Excuse me a minute.

          Mr. Jackson: Sure. (The salesman leaves for about ten minutes. He looks at the mechanic's
          report and talks briefly with the owner.)

          Salesman: Sorry to keep you waiting. We can let you have it for $1,650 and your car.

          Mr. Jackson: Well, I'm willing to go $1,250.

40   Salesman: How about $1,600—that's with automatic transmission, remember.

          Mr. Jackson: I'll have to think about it and refigure my budget. Can I call you later this
          afternoon?

          Salesman: Of course. Just ask for Ed Brown. Here's my card.

          Mr. Jackson: Thanks. (He goes home, and about an hour later he calls the dealer.) Mr. Brown?
45   This is Joe Jackson. I'm calling about the blue sedan. I talked to you a little while ago.

          Salesman: Oh, yes, Mr. Jackson. I talked with the boss, we can come down to $1,500 and
          you're getting a great deal.

          Mr. Jackson: Really. My budget can go the $1,300, but . . .

          Salesman: O.K. Will you split the difference? $1,400? I'll have to take a loss, but you know
50   how things are.

          Mr. Jackson: I guess I may be able to do that. Maybe my wife can serve hamburger a little
          more often. I'll be down in an hour and we'll settle it.

          Salesman: Fine. Thank you very much, Mr. Jackson.

NOTE: It is often said that people in the U.S. don't bargain, and while it is true in department
stores and small retail shops, it is not true in all cases as the conversation above shows. The sale
of a house usually involves bargaining; high-priced items such as carpeting, TVs, stereos, etc.,
can be bargained for in stores which deal exclusively in those items.

The list price ("sticker price" on cars) is the price asked. As a rule of thumb, to start the bargaining offer about 25% less than the list price. You can usually find out if bargaining is
possible by asking the price and then stating that it is "more than I had in mind." The salesman will then either show you less expensive merchandise or ask how much you "had in mind."
The second often means negotiation is possible and you're on your own. If in doubt about
items you can bargain for, ask a native of the area whose business sense you respect. Americans,
like everyone, love to get "bargains" and are usually happy to share information.

Beware, however, the salesman who offers you a ridiculously low price. The merchandise may
be defective or "hot."*

*I am indebted to Charles E. Bruder for the information and sequence of events in
this introduction.

268

OUTLINE OF PATTERNS

Example

Section One	*How* and Manner Expressions	
Part A.	*How?*	How did Mr. Jackson bargain?
Part B.	Answers *-ly*	Shrewdly.
Part C.	Answers *by* + N/V -ing	By getting a loan.
Part D.	Answers *with/without* + Noun	. . . with a loan from the bank.

Section Two	*It* in Subject Position	
Part A.	With time/weather/people	It's Saturday.
Part B.	In place of a noun phrase	It's easy to bargain for a car.

Section Three	Modals	
Part A.	*may*	Mr. Jackson may use . . .
Part B.	*must*	The mechanic must be back . . .

Section Four	Past Time + *ago*	Mr. Jackson decided a week ago.

COMPREHENSION QUESTIONS

1. When did Mr. Jackson last buy a car?

2. How many miles does his car have on it?

3. Why is it a good year for the buyer?

*4. How can he get a good deal?

*5. How can he finance the car?

6. What did he do before he made his decision? *Why?

7. When did he decide on the car?

8. Where is he going to buy the car?

9. What is the sticker price?

10. How much does Mr. Jackson want to pay?

269

*11. Why does he say he needs a new car?

*12. Why does he say his wife prefers blue?

13. What options does the car have?

*14. Why does he say he can do without the automatic transmission?

15. How much of a trade-in will they give for Mr. Jackson's car?

*16. Why does Mr. Jackson mention his friend?

*17. Why does the salesman leave?

18. Why does Mr. Jackson leave the lot?

*19. When the two offers are $200 apart, what does the salesman suggest?

*20. Why will Mrs. Jackson have to serve hamburger?

*21. Discuss the concept of bargaining in other situations.

*22. Discuss bargaining processes in other countries. (items, people involved, etc.)

Vocabulary

Nouns		Adjectives	
air letter	notes	careful	quick
air mail	opener	drunk	quiet
argument	picture phone	enthusiastic	rapid
article (news)	phone	hard	reckless
bottle	pound	honest	shrewd
cablegram	safe	industrious	straight
campfire	shooting match	patient	
church key	special delivery		
competition	speech	Adverbs	
dynamite	storm	beautifully	patiently
hill	strike (stop of work)	carefully	quickly
janitor	system	enthusiastically	quietly
machine	telegram	excellently	rapidly
marijuana	test	fast	shrewdly
messenger	trade-in	honestly	slowly
	try out	industriously	well

Verbs		Expression
communicate	rattle	get in touch with (someone)
contact	scratch	
debate	sew	
look on	shoot	
rain	shut down	

SECTION ONE

HOW? + MANNER EXPRESSIONS

Part A.   *How?*

Model: How did Mr. Jackson bargain?   Shrewdly.
         How can Mr. Jackson get a good deal?   By bargaining.
         How can he finance the car?   With a loan from the bank.

1. M1   Rep: How can I get downtown?
        Sub: learn to drive   S: How can I learn to drive?
                lose ten pounds   How can I lose ten pounds?
                pay my bill   How can I pay my bill?
                learn to bargain   How can I learn to bargain?
                find an apartment   How can I find an apartment?
                get a driver's license   How can I get a driver's license?
                meet American students   How can I meet American students?

GENERALIZATION

How is considered a *Wh* question because it has the same pattern of Subject and Verb inversion as *where, when,* etc. *How* asks about the *manner* of doing something. It may be answered in one of the three ways discussed below.

---

2. M1T   T: learn English somehow   S: How are you going to learn English?
                learn something   What are you going to learn?
                travel someplace   Where are you going to travel?
                buy something   What are you going to buy?
                go downtown somehow   How are you going to go downtown?
                buy a Rolls-Royce sometime   When are you going to buy a Rolls-Royce?
                learn to bargain somehow   How are you going to learn to bargain?
                work somewhere   Where are you going to work?
                learn Arabic sometime   When are you going to learn Arabic?
                get a license somehow   How are you going to get a license?

***3. M2   T: How can ——?   S: How can (I pay my tuition)?
                How did ——?   How did (you learn to drive)?
                How should ——?
                How will ——?
                How are ——?
                How is ——?
                etc.

Part B.   *Answers -ly*

Model: Mr. Jackson bargained shrewdly.

1. M1   Rep: He bargained shrewdly.
          Sub: fast   S: He bargained fast.
               hard   He bargained hard.
               slowly   He bargained slowly.
               well   He bargained well.
               carefully   He bargained carefully.
               quickly   He bargained quickly.
               quietly   He bargained quietly.
               patiently   He bargained patiently.
               honestly   He bargained honestly.

GENERALIZATION

The manner adverbs are formed by adding *-ly* to the Adjective:

    slow   —   slowly

There are a few exceptions:

Adjective	Adverb
fast	fast
hard	hard
good	well
straight	straight

The adverbs follow the verb if there is no direct object.

    The man speaks well.
    The man speaks English well.

---

2. M1   Rep: He's a good reader.   He reads well.
               He's a fast driver.   He drives fast.
               He's a hard bargainer.   He bargains hard.
               He's a straight shooter.   He shoots straight.

3. M1T T: John is a slow thinker.   S: He thinks slowly.
            Mr. Jackson is a careful bargainer.   He bargains carefully.
            Bill is an excellent swimmer.   He swims excellently.
            Nancy is an industrious student.   She studies industriously.
            Jill is a rapid reader.   She reads rapidly.
            Jean is a patient shopper.   She shops patiently.
            Mr. Cosby is an enthusiastic
               entertainer.   He entertains enthusiastically.
            Miss Streisand is a beautiful
               singer.   She sings beautifully.

4. M1T T: He's a slow driver.   S: He drives slowly.
            He's a rapid worker.   He works rapidly.
            He's a hard worker.   He works hard.
            He's a good reader.   He reads well.
            He's a patient listener.   He listens patiently.
            He's a reckless driver.   He drives recklessly.
            He's a straight shooter.   He shoots straight.
            He's an enthusiastic student.   He studies enthusiastically.

272

5. M1T   T: He shoots straight.   S: He's a straight shooter.
                He's a careful driver.   He drives carefully.
                You're a good driver.   You drive well.
                They're shrewd bargainers.   They bargain shrewdly.
                She's a patient listener.   She listens patiently.
                You read well.   You're a good reader.
                He drives fast.   He's a fast driver.
                They're industrious workers.   They work industriously.

6. M2   T: Listen to some results and then explain.
                He lost the argument.   S: He (argued carelessly).
                He had an accident with the car.   He (drove recklessly).
                She won the swimming competition.
                They won the shooting match.
                We lost the debate.
                He passed the test.
                He failed the test.
                We didn't understand the child.
                She didn't understand the foreign student.
                We made the thousand mile trip with no difficulties.
                She lost the race.
                I didn't finish the exam.

***7. M2   T: drive VWs   S1:   (Women drive VWs poorly.)
                                                 S2:   (That's not always true. My sister has a VW and she drives
                                                        well.)

                prepare meals   S1:   (Men prepare meals badly.)
                                                 S2:   (Maybe sometimes, but my roommate is a great cook.)

                learn English
                speak Spanish
                clean the house
                balance checkbooks
                sing popular music
                paint pictures
                write poetry
                produce movies
                direct companies
                debate the issues
                sail boats

8. C   T: Describe yourself as a driver.   S: (I'm a good driver.) (I drive fast.) (I don't drive.)
                Describe yourself as a singer.
                Describe yourself as a listener.
                Describe yourself as a student.
                Describe yourself as a reader.
                Describe yourself as a worker.
                Describe the people in your country as drivers.
                Describe the people in your country as voters.
                Describe the people in your country as workers.
                Describe the people in your country as businessmen.
                Describe your friends as students.
                Describe your friends as listeners.
                Describe your friends as cooks.

Part C.   *by* + N/V *-ing*

☐ BY N

1. M1   Rep: How did they go to Paris?   They went by plane.
                 How did he send the letter?   He sent it by air mail.
                 How did she sew the dress?   She sewed it by machine.

2. M1   Listen: How did he send the message?
           Rep: He sent it by mail.
           Sub: letter   S: He sent it by letter.
                 messenger   He sent it by messenger.
                 air mail   He sent it by air mail.
                 special delivery   He sent it by special delivery.
                 air letter   He sent it by air letter.
                 air mail special delivery   He sent it by air mail special delivery.
                 radio   He sent it by radio.

GENERALIZATION

One answer to the question *how* is *by* + Noun.

    Question: How do you get to school?   Answer: By bus.

Short answers which do not contain a subject and verb are common in speech.

---

3. M2   T: contact your family   S1: How (do you) contact your family?
                                             How (are you going to) contact your family?
                                        S2: (By phone.) (By telegram.)
                locate your friend   S1: How (did you) locate your friend?
                                        S2: (By letter.)

                send money to your friend
                get to the United States
                travel to Europe
                make a reservation at a hotel
                come to this country
                find a room
                send messages home
                make a reservation at a restaurant
                send important messages home
                contact your family
                talk to your friends

***4. C   T: How do you usually communicate with your family?   S: (By letter.)
                How do you usually communicate with your friends?
                How do I get to (capitol of country)?
                How can I get downtown?
                How can I get to (Shadyside)?
                How does the President of the U.S. communicate with the people/Senators?
                How can you tell embarrassment?
                How can I get to San Francisco? How else?
                How can I communicate with my sister-in-law in Okinawa? (3 ways)

☐ *BY + V -ING*

5. M1   Listen: How did she get in touch with her husband?
         Rep: She got in touch with him by sending a telegram.

Sub:		S:	
writing a letter			She got in touch with him by writing a letter.
calling long distance			She got in touch with him by calling long distance.
sending a telegram			She got in touch with him by sending a telegram.
using a messenger			She got in touch with him by using a messenger.
sending an air letter			She got in touch with him by sending an air letter.
calling his secretary			She got in touch with him by calling his secretary.
sending a cablegram			She got in touch with him by sending a cablegram.
using the picture phone			She got in touch with him by using the picture phone.

GENERALIZATION

The question *How?* can also be answered with *by + -ing* form of the verb.

How?	By + Noun
How did you contact her?	By telephone.
	By + V -ing
	By calling on the phone.

---

6. M1T   T: How did you get the information?

	S:	
call on the phone		By calling on the phone.
a telegram to my brother		By a telegram to my brother.
ask someone		By asking someone.
watch movies		By watching movies.
call the operator		By calling the operator.
listen to records		By listening to records.

7. M2   T: letter

                                       S1: How (did you contact your friend)?
                                       S2: I contacted him by letter (last week).

        looking in the newspaper   S1: How (did you find your apartment)?
                                       S2: I found it by looking in the newspaper (every day).

        telephone
        asking someone
        plane
        calling the operator
        bargaining
        car
        reading novels
        watching movies
        dieting
        listening to the radio
        check

8. M2   Ask advice about the following items:

    T: losing ten pounds   S1: How can I lose ten pounds?
                                           S2: (By dieting.) (By not eating candy.)

             getting a good deal on a car
             opening a savings account
             contacting a friend
             learning a language fast
             finding an apartment
             getting a date for the weekend
             meeting the professor
             finishing the exam in time
             buying a car
             finding a recipe for "shish-ka-bob"
             getting downtown

Part D.   *With/without + Noun*

Model: He can finance the car with a loan from the bank.
          He can finance the car without a loan.

1. M1   Rep: He opened the door with a key.
        Sub: can—church key   S: He opened the can with a church key.
             bottle—opener   He opened the bottle with an opener.
             window—baseball bat   He opened the window with a baseball bat.
             box—his teeth   He opened the box with his teeth.
             letter—knife   He opened the letter with a knife.
             door—credit card   He opened the door with a credit card.
             book—pencil   He opened the book with a pencil.

2. M1   Rep: He opened the door without a key.
        Sub: bottle—opener   S: He opened the bottle without an opener.
             letter—knife   He opened the letter without a knife.
             box—knife   He opened the box without a knife.
             can—opener   He opened the can without an opener.
             safe—dynamite   He opened the safe without dynamite.

GENERALIZATION

The third way of explaining the manner of doing something or answering the question *How?* is by using *with* or *without* + a noun.

      Example: How did he open the bottle?   With a church key.
                    He calmed the crowd without a word.

---

3. M1T   T: He used a plane to go there.   S: He went there by plane.
            He used his teeth to open it.   He opened it with his teeth.
            He used a telegram to answer it.   He answered it by telegram.
            He used a key to unlock it.   He unlocked it with a key.
            He used a phone to contact her.   He contacted her by phone.

(exercise continued on next page)

	T:	He used a smile to calm them.	S:	He calmed them with a smile.
		He used the radio to talk to them.		He talked to them by radio.
		He used his knife to open it.		He opened it with his knife.

*4. M2   T: open a bottle   S1: How do you open a bottle?
                                        S2: (With an opener.)

finance a car   S1: How do you finance a car?
                                        S2: (With a loan from the bank.) (By getting a loan.)

light a campfire   S1: How do you light a campfire?
sharpen a pencil   How do you sharpen a pencil?
make a sandwich   How do you make a sandwich
answer a question   How do you answer a question?
pay a bill   How do you pay a bill?
paint a house   How do you paint a house?
finish a dinner   How do you finish a dinner?
begin a dinner   How do you begin a dinner?
record a speech   How do you record a speech?
take notes   How do you take notes?

*NOTE: *You* in the questions is the general, not the specific *you.*

5. M2   T: The girl listened ——   S: The girl listened (patiently)(without a smile).
             He opened the bottle ——   He opened the bottle (with an opener) (quickly).
             He got in touch with his friend ——
             He flew to Paris ——
             The ladies discussed the party ——
             The students talked about the test——
             The salesman wrote out the bill ——
             The buyer bargained ——
             I called my friend ——
             He financed the car ——
             The young men drove the car ——
             The child opened the box ——
             The man mowed the lawn ——
             The lady cleaned the house ——
             The man got a good deal on the car ——

6. C   T: How do you usually send letters to your country?   S: (By surface mail.)
            How can I get to (capital of country)?   (By taking a plane to ——).
            How can I get a good deal on a car in (country)?
            How do people in ( ) pay their bills?
            How do you pay your bills here?
            How did you find your apartment/room?
            How did you find out about the English Language Institute?
            How will you go on your next vacation?
            How does your friend listen to your problems?
            How can I find a good restaurant?
            How do you study?
            How do people in ( ) buy cars? (Do they bargain?)

SECTION TWO

IT IN SUBJECT POSITION

Part A.   *With time/weather/people*

Model: It's Saturday.

1. M1   Rep: It's Saturday.
           Sub: 10:00   S: It's 10:00.
                raining   It's raining.
                going to snow   It's going to snow.
                was Tuesday   It was Tuesday.
                will be late   It will be late.
                is going to be nice tomorrow   It is going to be nice tomorrow.
                might be raining now   It might be raining now.
                is Marie on the phone   It is Marie on the phone.

GENERALIZATION

In Lesson One *it* was used as a substitute word (pronoun): The book is on the table. *It's* on the table.

In this lesson *it* is in Subject position, but is not a substitute word. *It* introduces expressions of *time, weather,* and sometimes *people.*

"Who's on the phone?"   "It's John."
"Who's at the door?"   "It's a man and a woman."

---

2. M2   T: Someone's on the phone.   S1:   Who's on the phone?
                                             S2:   It's (Mary).

                Someone was at the door.   S1:   Who was at the door?
                                             S2:   It was (a salesman).

                Someone called you.   S1:   Who called me?
                                             S2:   It was (Chen).

                Someone sent him a telegram.
                Someone is going to call back at 10:00.
                Someone is coming down the hill.
                Someone is going to treat us to an ice cream cone.
                Someone got a good deal on a car.
                Someone knows the bargaining system.
                Someone listens to the baseball games.
                Someone went to Latin America.

3. C   T: What is the weather like in ( )?   S: (It's always sunny.)
                What time is it?
                Who's at the door?
                Who called you last night?
                What will the weather be tomorrow?
                          (exercise continued on next page)

278

T: What is the weather like in spring (month/season) in ( )?
        What time did you get here this morning?
        Did anyone ever call you late at night? What time was it? Who?
        What day did you arrive in the U.S.? Month? Season?
        What was the weather like when you arrived here?

Part B.   *In Place of a Noun Phrase*

Model: It's easy to bargain for a car.

1. M1   Listen: Bargaining for a car is fun.   Rep: It's fun to bargain for a car.
                    Buying a house was a lot of work.   It was a lot of work to buy a house.
                    Learning English is hard work.   It's hard work to learn English.
                    Talking to the professor was   It was interesting to talk to the professor.
                      interesting.
                    Learning about U.S. politics took a   It took a long time to learn about U.S.
                      long time.   politics.
                    Planning the party was a lot of work.   It was a lot of work to plan the party.

GENERALIZATION

Many verbs in English can be made into nouns by adding *-ing* as you have seen in previous
lessons: Lesson Six — Planning a party, and Lesson Thirteen — Bargaining for a car.

The noun + *-ing*, when it is the subject of the sentence, is often replaced by *it*, and the
noun + *-ing* becomes *to* + verb after the main verb in the sentence.

Example: *Bargaining for the car*   was fun.

               It   was fun *to bargain for the car.*

---

2. M1   Situation: Mr. Hastings is telling his friends about his experience buying the car.
           Rep: It was fun to bargain for a car.
           Sub: interesting—talk to the mechanic   S: It was interesting to talk to the mechanic.
                 necessary—see the boss   It was necessary to see the boss.
                 good—talk it over with my wife   It was good to talk it over with my wife.
                 possible—try out the car on Saturday   It was possible to try out the car on Saturday.
                 necessary—drive the car for a few days   It was necessary to drive the car for a few days.
                 good—ask the salesman about the car   It was good to ask the salesman about the car.
                 impossible—buy the car right away   It was impossible to buy the car right away.

3. M1T   T: Buying a car in the U.S. is easy.   S: It's easy to buy a car in the U.S.
                Getting a license here takes time.   It takes time to get a license here.
                Talking on the phone in English is hard.   It's hard to talk on the phone in English.
                Bargaining for a car is hard work.   It's hard work to bargain for a car.
                Learning the customs of a foreign   It takes a long time to learn the customs of a
                  country takes a long time.   foreign country.
                Driving fast in the city is dangerous.   It's dangerous to drive fast in the city.
                Paying for a new car takes a lot of money.   It takes a lot of money to pay for a new car.

4. M1T T: Learning English takes time.   S: It takes time to learn English.
            It's hard to bargain for a car.   Bargaining for a car is hard.
            Learning to drive is easy.   It's easy to learn to drive.
            Speaking a foreign language is hard.   It's hard to speak a foreign language.
            It's fun to bargain for a car.   Bargaining for a car is fun.
            It's interesting to learn new customs.   Learning new customs is interesting.
            Buying a house is expensive.   It's expensive to buy a house.

5. M2   T: learning   S: Learning (a new language is boring).
            to learn   (It's interesting) to learn (new customs).
            bargaining
            to meet
            driving
            to buy
            meeting
            to drive
            to bargain
            planning
            to discuss
            traveling

6. C   T: Tell about an unusual experience you've had here and what you thought about it.

        S: (I bought a car last week. It was very hard to bargain for it.)
            (We met (famous person) last week. Talking to him was really interesting.)

SECTION THREE

MODALS — *MAY/MUST*

Part A.   *May*

Model: Mr. Jackson may use the dealer's finance plan.

```
NOTE: May has two meanings — possibility and permission.
```

1. M1   Possibility
           Listen: We don't know for certain what John will do.
        T: John might go to the movies tonight.   S: John may go to the movies tonight.
            John might be able to help you with your   John may be able to help you with your
              problem.   problem.
            John might not finish the homework.   John may not finish the homework.
            John might get a good deal on the car.   John may get a good deal on the car.
            John might bargain for a long time.   John may bargain for a long time.
            John might not pass the test.   John may not pass the test.
            John might not have to take the test.   John may not have to take the test.

2. M1   Permission
           Listen: John's mother said "yes" sometimes and "no" at other times.
           Rep: He may go to the movies.
           Sub: the baseball game   S: He may go to the baseball game.
                 his friend's house   He may go to his friend's house.
                 buy a car   He may buy a car.
                 get his driver's license   He may get his driver's license.
                 have long hair   He may have long hair.
                 not go to beer parties   He may not go to beer parties.
                 not drive the family car.   He may not drive the family car.

GENERALIZATION

Lesson Eleven: John might go to the movies.
Lesson Thirteen: John may go to the movies.

Depending on the context, *may* means possibility, the same as *might* does.

May is also used in formal, careful speech to indicate permission: "John has permission to go—he may go."

(In informal speech *can* is used to indicate permission: "Can I use your lighter?")

***You can tell from the context whether *may* means possibility or permission.

May + not is not usually contracted: "I don't know. I may not go to the party."

---

3. M1T   Listen to the situation. Tell whether the context indicates possibility or permission.
           T: John asked his mother about going to the movies. He may go.   S: Permission
               John doesn't know if he will go to the movies or not. He may go.   Possibility
               Mr. Jackson is going to bargain hard. He may get a good deal.   Possibility
               Jane's mother doesn't like beer parties. Jane may not go.   Permission
               Pete didn't study very hard. He may not pass the exam.   Possibility
               It's raining. Bill may not go to the baseball game.   Possibility
               Jill's parents are opposed to X-rated movies. Jill may not go.   Permission
               The snow storm is terrible. We may not make it home.   Possibility
               Jack's mother is very angry with him. He may not go to his friend's
                   house.   Permission

4. M1T   T: John may go to the movies.   Permission   S: John can go to the movies.
             John may go to the baseball game.   Possibility   John might go to the baseball game.
             Sally may not go to New York.   Possibility   Sally might not go to New York.
             Sally may not go to the party.   Permission   Sally can't go to the party.
             We may not finish.   Possibility   We might not finish.
             They may not drive the car.   Permission   They can't drive the car.
             We may come early.   Possibility   We might come early.
             Chen may not use the phone.   Permission   Chen can't use the phone.

5. M2   Ask permission
           T: use his pen   S1: May I use your pen?   S2: (Yes, of course.) (No, I'm sorry.
                                                                        I'm using it.)

               borrow a dollar   May I borrow a dollar?   (Sure. Here.) (Sorry. I'm broke.)
               see his book   May I see your book?
                              (exercise continued on next page)

281

	T:	look at his lighter	S1:	May I look at your lighter?
		have a light		May I have a light?
		look on with him		May I look on with you?
		sit here		May I sit here?
		come in		May I come in?
		be excused		May I be excused?
		ask a question		May I ask a question?
		borrow his pencil		May I borrow your pencil?
		use his book		May I use your book?

***6. M2   T: go to the party   S1: Are you going to the party?   S2: I don't know. I may not.
                                                                              (I have to study.)

              go to the museum   Are you going to the museum?   I don't know. I may not.
                                                                              (I was there last weekend.)

              buy the new car
              go to New York City
              take the psych. course
              go to the lecture
              buy a new TV
              sell your car
              go to the movies
              fly to Washington
              go to the baseball game

7. C   T: What are your plans for the weekend?   S: I (may go to Washington or I may stay
                                                                   home.)

               etc.

Part B.   *Must*

Model: The mechanic must be back by now.

1. M1   Necessity

	T:	Do you have to go?	S:	Must you go?
		Does he have to go to bed now?		Must he go to bed now?
		Does he have to take the test?		Must he take the test?
		Do you have to study tonight?		Must you study tonight?
		Does Jane have to work today?		Must Jane work today?
		Does he have to bargain for the car?		Must he bargain for the car?
		Do you have to write home every week?		Must you write home every week?
		Does he have to borrow from the finance company?		Must he borrow from the finance company?

2. M1   Deduction

Listen: It's 10:00. Someone always comes at 10:00. I hear footsteps.
Rep: It must be the teacher.

Sub: John		S:	It must be John.
the student			It must be the student.
the children			It must be the children.

(exercise continued on next page)

the professor	It must be the professor.
the girls	It must be the girls.
the janitor	It must be the janitor.
the cleaning woman	It must be the cleaning woman.

GENERALIZATION

Lesson Eleven: John has to do the work.   (Necessity)
Lesson Thirteen: John must do the work.

In formal speaking styles and in writing, *must* is often used to indicate necessity. *Have to* is more common in speech for this meaning.

A more common use of *must* in speech is in making deductions: "Charlie always calls at 8:00. It's 8:00 and the phone is ringing." Deduction: "It must be Charlie."

To indicate something *forbidden,* use *must + not*: "The boy mustn't go out in the rain.

---

3. M1T   T: John must finish the work.   S: John has to finish the work.
                We must go to class.   We have to go to class.
                They must pay the rent.   They have to pay the rent.
                You must speak slowly.   You have to speak slowly.
                Mary must be on time.   Mary has to be on time.
                I must go now.   I have to go now.
                We must arrive before the students.   We have to arrive before the students.

4. M1T   T: Bill isn't obligated to go to class. S: Bill doesn't have to go to class.
                John is forbidden to miss any more   John mustn't miss any more classes.
                    classes.
                Mary isn't obligated to wash the dishes.   Mary doesn't have to wash the dishes.
                Judy is forbidden to climb many steps.   Judy mustn't climb many steps.
                George is forbidden to smoke cigars.   George mustn't smoke cigars.
                Jane isn't obligated to sign the papers.   Jane doesn't have to sign the papers.
                Bob isn't obligated to be in the office.   Bob doesn't have to be in the office.
                Dick is forbidden to have girls in his room.   Dick mustn't have girls in his room.

5. M1T   T: Bill—do the work.   Necessary S: Bill has to do the work.
                The little boy—play in
                    the street   Forbidden   The little boy mustn't play in the street.
                The man—help his wife   A good idea   The man should help his wife.
                Chen—pay the bill   Not necessary   Chen doesn't have to pay the bill.
                The girls—sleep all day   Not a good idea   The girls shouldn't sleep all day.
                The children—write on
                    the walls   Forbidden   The children mustn't write on the walls.
                We—buy a new car   Necessary   We have to buy a new car.
                You—be late   Not a good idea   You shouldn't be late.
                Sally—come home early   Not necessary   Sally doesn't have to come home early.
                The man—carry the
                    heavy box   Not a good idea   The man shouldn't carry the heavy box.
                The woman—get some
                    coffee   Necessary   The woman has to get some coffee.

283

***6. M2   T: The rent is due on June 30. It's June 29.   S: (Necessity. We have to pay the
                                                                            rent tomorrow.)

                  Tom, Dick and Harry were invited. Tom   (Deduction. It must be Harry.)
                  and Dick are here. Someone is at the
                  door.
                  It's 10:00. The professor always comes at 10:00. Someone is coming.
                  We're out of milk. Lunch is in 10 minutes.
                  The gas gauge was very low this morning. Now the car is stopped.
                  The house is dirty. Mrs. Orlove is expecting company.
                  The tires are very old. The car is at the side of the road.
                  The exam is next week. Joe wants to pass, but he doesn't know the material.
                  It's noon. Karen always comes at noon. Someone is coming.
                  The party began at 8:00. The doorbell is ringing.
                  I'm late. My friend is waiting for me.
                  It's 11:00. The cat always comes in at 11:00. There is scratching at the door.
                  We don't have any more sugar. Guests are coming for coffee.
                  The bill is due tomorrow. I only have $10.
                  Ken, John, and Tom were here. There is a book on the table. It isn't Ken's or John's.
                  It's very windy. The windows are rattling. There is no one around.

7. M2   T: It is forbidden to smoke here.   S: (We) mustn't smoke here. (People) mustn't
                                                                smoke (in this room).
               It is forbidden for the little boy to go out in the rain.
               It is forbidden to drive faster than 25 m.p.h.
               It is forbidden to write on the tables.
               It is forbidden to smoke marijuana.
               It is forbidden to hurt wild birds.
               It is forbidden to walk on the grass.
               It is forbidden to cross the street in the middle of the block.
               It is forbidden to go through a red light.
               It is forbidden to drive when drunk.

8. C   T: What things are forbidden in your country? S: (People mustn't ——.)

9. C   T: What are your plans for the weekend? S: (I don't know. I may study.) (I might go
                                                           skiing.)
               Is there anything you have to do this   (Yes, my homework.) (No. I don't have
                  weekend?   to do anything.)
               Is there anything you usually do that you don't have to do today?
               What are your plans for vacation?
               Do you have permission to use the phone in the hotel?
               It's very cloudy. Are you going to take an umbrella?
               Is there anything you should do today? Are you going to?
               What are you going to do at the end of the term?
               Are you going to the movies this weekend?
               What advice would you give someone who is going to visit your country?
               When are you going to visit New York City?

SECTION FOUR

PAST TIME + *AGO*

Model: Mr. Jackson decided a week ago.

1. M1   T: I bought the car last week.   Rep: I bought the car a week ago.
              I heard the story last month.   I heard the story a month ago.
              I made the sale the day before yesterday.   I made the sale two days ago.
              I had a date two days before yesterday.   I had a date three days ago.
              I took the exam last year.   I took the exam a year ago.
              I sold the tape recorder in the last hour.   I sold the tape recorder an hour ago.
              I read the article last week.   I read the article a week ago.

GENERALIZATION

Ago is used with past tense verbs to relate past events to the present time.

Example: It's Tuesday. I bought a car last Saturday.
              I bought a car four days ago.

---

2. M1T   T: call him—last week   S: I called him a week ago.
              call him—next week   I'm going to call him next week.
              see her—last month   I saw her a month ago.
              trade in my car—every year   I trade in my car every year.
              write them—last month   I wrote them a month ago.
              close the deal—tomorrow   I'm going to close the deal tomorrow.
              balance the checkbook—last week   I balanced the checkbook a week ago.
              talk to the salesman—last month   I talked to the salesman a month ago.

3. M2   Situation: It's 10:00 a.m. on Tuesday, May 23.***
          T: ( ) came here in April.   S: He came here (a month ago) (last month).
              ( ) bought a car in January.   He bought a car (5 months ago) (a few months ago)
              ( ) registered for class last Friday.
              ( ) won the lottery in March.
              ( ) woke up at 9:45.
              ( ) bought a Rolls-Royce in February.
              ( ) sold his VW last Tuesday.
              ( ) bought a TV last Thursday.
              ( ) went to Paris in January.
              ( ) talked to his advisor last Wednesday.
              ( ) bought a stereo in February.
              ( ) went to New York in March.

4. M2   T: Hollywood produced the first   S1:   When did Hollywood produce the first X-rated
                 X-rated movie.   movie?
                                                 S2:   (A few years ago.)
          People began to worry about pollution.
          The astronauts walked on the moon.
          The reporters discovered a scandal.

                        (exercise continued on next page)

285

T: The U.S. government got out of Vietnam.
      The Mayor got reelected.
      The Governor proposed a foolish plan.
      The President of the U.S. refused to run again.
      The people of the U.S. voted for a clean atmosphere.
      The mail rates went up.
      The teachers went out on strike.
      The airport shut down.

4. C   T: When was there a change of government   S: (A year ago.)
                   in (country) (the U.S.)?
                When did you come to the U.S.?
                When did you send your application to ( ) University?
                When did you leave your country?
                When did you start studying English?
                When did you last call your friend?
                When did you last call home?
                When did you receive a letter from your country/family?
                When did you realize it's expensive to live in this country?
                When did you last sleep in?
                When did you last bargain for anything? What? Did you get a good deal?

SUMMARY DIALOGUE

Salesman: May I help you?

Chen: I'm looking for a good camera, not too expensive.

Salesman: Yes, sir. We have some very good ones under a hundred dollars.

Chen: I have an old one. Can I trade it in on a new one?

Salesman: I'm sorry. We don't take trade-ins.

Chen: O.K. Thanks. I'll look around for a store that does.

LESSON THIRTEEN — SUMMARY OF PATTERNS

How?	Manner Adverbs and Expressions
How can you ——?	Adjective + *-ly* (shrewdly)
	by + Noun *-ing* (by bargaining)
	with + Noun (with a key)

Modals: Summary

can	1. Ability	Chen can drive a car.
	2. Informal permission	John's mother says he can go.
will	Future intention	I'll do it tomorrow.
might	Possibility	I might go to the movies.
may	1. Possibility	I may go to the movies.
	2. Permission	John's mother says he may go.
should	A good idea	I should write home.
ought to	A good idea	Jane ought to study more.
must	1. Prohibition	People mustn't drive fast in a school zone.
	2. Deduction	Someone's coming. It must be John.
have to	Necessity	He has to get an A on the exam.
		He doesn't have to take chemistry.

NOTES

LESSON FOURTEEN

INTRODUCTION   Food poisoning

Carlos: Hi, Bill. *Have you heard about Chen?*

Bill: No, what happened?

Carlos: He's in the hospital. He's been there for three days—*since Saturday.*

Bill: What's the matter with him? Did he break his leg in the soccer game?

5   Carlos: No, it isn't that. Three days ago he ate some spoiled meat and got food poisoning.

Bill: He what?

Carlos: That's right. Nancy *has already seen* him. He told her all about it. He kept meat in the refrigerator for about a month and then he made himself a hamburger. In the middle of the night he had terrible pains in his stomach. His roommate called the police and they
10   rushed him to the hospital.

Bill: Of all the dumb things! Hasn't he learned about freezing meat?

Carlos: He's never had to cook. He just didn't know how quickly meat spoils.

Bill: I guess he knows now. Come on, let's go see him.

Later, Carlos is discussing the incident with Jill.

15   Carlos: I've been lucky, Jill. *I've been cooking* since January. I've kept a lot of meat in the refrigerator for quite a while and nothing has happened to me.

Jill: You *have* been lucky. You shouldn't keep meat in the refrigerator for more than a few days. Freezing is one thing; refrigerating is another.

Carlos: What things should I freeze?

20   Jill: Meat, mainly; but lots of things have to be refrigerated once you open the bottle or can—mayonnaise, mustard. It always says on the label "refrigerate after opening" or something like that.

Carlos: Can I keep cooked meat in the refrigerator?

Jill: Leftovers? Yes, but you should eat the leftover meat within a couple of days. Other-
25   wise, put it in the freezer.

OUTLINE OF PATTERNS   Example

Section One	Present Perfect	
Part A.	Presentation	
Part B.	Irregular Past Participles	Nancy has seen . . .
Part C.	Interrogative and Negative	Have you heard . . . ?
Part D.	Immediate Past Action	I've just talked to him.
Section Two	Present Perfect Continuous	I've been cooking . . .
Section Three	*Since* + Time Expression	. . . since Saturday.
Section Four	*Already/Yet*	I haven't seen Chen yet. Jill has already seen him.
Section Five	Tag Questions	
Part A.	Type I	They haven't left, have they?
Part B.	Type II	They've left, haven't they?

COMPREHENSION QUESTIONS

1. Where is Chen?

2. How long has he been there?

3. How did he get food poisoning?

4. How long did he keep the meat in the refrigerator?

*5. How did he get to the hospital?

*6. Why didn't he freeze the meat?

7. How long has Carlos been cooking?

*8. Why has Carlos been lucky?

*9. How long should you keep meat in the refrigerator?

10. When should you refrigerate mayonnaise and mustard?

11. What does the label say?

*12. What is the term for food remaining at the end of a meal?

13. How long should you keep leftovers in the refrigerator?

*14. Have you ever had food poisoning? What happened?

```
Vocabulary

            Nouns                    Verbs          Adjectives
     bell          mustard           correct        cooked
     best seller   pain              freeze         dumb
     coffee house  police            refrigerate    leftover
     food poisoning press conference rush           lucky
     leftover      refrigerator      spoil          spoiled
     market        soccer
     mayonnaise    stomach
```

SECTION ONE

PRESENT PERFECT

Model: Have you heard about Chen?
            I've been lucky.

***Part A.   *Presentation*[1]

Last Year	This Year	Jan.	Feb.	Mar.	Apr.	May	June
19——	19——	II	III	I	IIII	II	I
25		NY	SF	SF	Chi	NY	LA
							now

1. M1   Situation: It is now the middle of June, 19——. Mr. Hastings travels a lot.

         T: Listen: Mr. Hastings took 25 trips last year.
                       He took 2 trips in January.
                       He took 3 trips in February.
                       He took 1 trip in March.
                       He took 4 trips in April.
                       He took 2 trips in May.
         But: He's taken 1 trip this month.
                       He's taken 13 trips this year.

---

1. Adapted from Michael Ockenden, "The Unfinished Time Aspect of the Present Perfect Tense." <u>ELT</u>, Vol. XXI, No. 2, January 1967.

2. M1   Rep: He went to New York twice in January and twice in May.
                 He's gone to New York four times this year.

                 He went to San Francisco three times in February and once in March.
                 He's gone to San Francisco four times this year.

                 He went to Chicago four times in April.
                 He's gone to Chicago four times this year.

                 He's gone to Los Angeles once this month.
                 He's gone to Los Angeles once this year.

3. M1T   T: How many trips did Mr. Hastings take in 19——?   S: 25
                 How many trips has he taken in 19——?   13
                 How many times did he go to New York in January?   2
                 How many times has he gone to New York this year?   4
                 How many times did he go to San Francisco in February/
                     March?   3/1
                 How many times has he gone to San Francisco this year?   4
                 How many times has he gone to Chicago this year?   4
                 How many times did he go to Chicago in April?   4
                 How many trips has he taken in June?   1
                 How many times has he gone to Los Angeles this year?   1

GENERALIZATION

Use Simple Past when the time mentioned is completed; use Present Perfect when the time period extends to and includes the present.

   Example: Mr. Hastings took 25 trips last year.
               Mr. Hastings has taken 13 trips this year.

This year is not completed and there is the possibility that he can take more trips.

   Formation: *has* ⎫
                 have ⎭   + Past Participle (Lesson Eleven)

NOTE: Group Two Irregular Verbs (Lesson Eleven) are the only difficult ones; with the other verbs (including the regular verbs) the past participle is the same form as the past.

Reg: He walked downtown yesterday. He's walked downtown 3 times this week.
I: He made a trip to France last year. He's made a trip to France this year.
II: He *went* to Paris last month. He's *gone* to Paris once this year.
III: He bet $50 on the race last week. He's *bet* $50 on the races this year.

NOTE ALSO: He's giving it.   He *is* giving it.   (Present Continuous)
            He's given it.   He *has* given it.   (Present Perfect)

In some dialects there is no difference in pronunciation between forms like *giving* and *given.* Listen to the context of the sentence.

---

4. M1T   Listening comprehension: Raise one hand for Present Continuous, two hands for Present
               Perfect.
                 T: He's giving it.   S: (1)
                      He's given it.   (2)
                          (exercise continued on next page)

T:	He's eating it.	S:	(1)
	He's eating it.		(1)
	He's beaten it.		(2)
	He's beating it.		(1)
	He's given it.		(2)
	He's eating it.		(1)
	He's beaten it.		(2)

***Part B.   *Irregular Past Participles* (See Page 237 for list).

Model: Nancy has already seen him.

1. M1   T: given   S: He's given it.
                 eaten   He's eaten it.
                 done   He's done it.
                 driven   He's driven it.
                 sung   He's sung it.
                 drunk   He's drunk it.
                 written   He's written it.

2. M1T   T: He gave it.   S: He's given it.
                 He ate it.   He's eaten it.
                 He did it.   He's done it.
                 He drove it.   He's driven it.
                 He wrote it.   He's written it.
                 He drank it.   He's drunk it.
                 He sang it.   He's sung it.

3. M1   T: rung   S: We've rung it.
                 thrown   We've thrown it.
                 known   We've known it.
                 taken   We've taken it.
                 seen   We've seen it.
                 worn   We've worn it.
                 torn   We've torn it.

4. M1T   T: We rang it.   S: We've rung it.
                 We threw it.   We've thrown it.
                 We knew it.   We've known it.
                 We took it.   We've taken it.
                 We saw it.   We've seen it.
                 We wore it.   We've worn it.
                 We tore it.   We've torn it.

5. M1   T: chosen   S: I've chosen it.
                 spoken   I've spoken it.
                 broken   I've broken it.
                 gotten   I've gotten it.

6. M1T	T:	I chose it.	S:	I've chosen it.
		I spoke it.		I've spoken it.
		I broke it.		I've broken it.
		I got it.		I've gotten it.

7. M1	T:	come	S:	They've come a long way.
		gone		They've gone a long way.
		run		They've run a long way.
		swum		They've swum a long way.

8. M1T	T:	come	S:	They've come home.
		run		They've run home.
		go		They've gone home.
		swim		They've swum home.

Part C.   *Interrogative and Negative*

Model: Have you heard about Chen?

***1. M1	Rep:	Has he been to Paris?		
	Sub:	St. Louis	S:	Has he been to St. Louis?
		Bombay		Has he been to Bombay?
		Caracas		Has he been to Caracas?
		Managua		Has he been to Managua?
		Mexico City		Has he been to Mexico City?
		Teheran		Has he been to Teheran?
		Tripoli		Has he been to Tripoli?
		Bangkok		Has he been to Bangkok?
		Prague		Has he been to Prague?
		Istanbul		Has he been to Istanbul?
		Bogota		Has he been to Bogota?

2. M1	Rep:	I haven't seen him yet.		
	Sub:	done it	S:	I haven't done it yet.
		written a book		I haven't written a book yet.
		done the dishes		I haven't done the dishes yet.
		been to Mexico City		I haven't been to Mexico City yet.
		gone downtown		I haven't gone downtown yet.
		seen the new movie		I haven't seen the new movie yet.
		gotten a letter		I haven't gotten a letter yet.
		been to Canada		I haven't been to Canada yet.

3. M1T	Rep:	He hasn't gone to Paris.		
	Sub:	I	S:	I haven't gone to Paris.
		been		I haven't been to Paris.
		she		She hasn't been to Paris.
		London		She hasn't been to London.
		they		They haven't been to London.
		traveled		They haven't traveled to London.

(exercise continued on next page)

294

	T:	he	S:	He hasn't traveled to London.
		Madrid		He hasn't traveled to Madrid.
		we		We haven't traveled to Madrid.

4. M1T T: Has Mr. Hastings been to Paris this year?   S: No, he hasn't.
Has Mr. Hastings been to Chicago this year?   Yes, he has.
Did Mr. Hastings go to Chicago in May?   No, he didn't.
Has he gone to Los Angeles in June?   Yes, he has.
Did he go to Chicago in February?   No, he didn't.
Has he visited New York this year?   Yes, he has.
Has he gone to San Francisco in June?   No, he hasn't.
Has he visited Teheran this year?   No, he hasn't.
Did he go to Chicago in April?   Yes, he did.

***5. M1T Use the information on the chart.

T: go to the movies—March   S1: How many times did you go to the movies in March?
S2: I went to the movies once.

go to the movies—(current month)   S1: How many times have you gone to the movies in (June)?
S2: I've gone three times.

write home—(current month)
write home—January and February
drive a Rolls-Royce—19—
drive a Rolls-Royce—19—
do your friend a favor—(last month and current)
do your friend a favor—March
ride a bike to work—(last year)
take a taxi—March
take a bus—January and February
speak Thai—(last year)
speak Spanish—(this year)

6. M2 T: I've read two books this week.   S1: (Mrs. Bruder) has read two books this week,
What have you done?   (I've written home twice). What have you done?

S2: (Mrs. Bruder) has read two books this week.
You've written home twice; and I've (gotten two traffic tickets). What have you done?

etc.

7. C T: Ask ( ) about writing books this year.   S1: (How many books have you written this year?) (Have you written any books this year?)

S2: (I haven't written any books.) (No, I haven't.)

Ask ( ) about writing books in 1965.   S1: (How many) books did you write in 1965?
S2: (I wrote three books.)

Ask ( ) about driving a VW this year.
Ask ( ) about driving a Rolls-Royce last year.
Ask ( ) about doing the laundry this week.
Ask ( ) about mowing the lawn last year.

(exercise continued on next page)

T: Ask ( ) about going to Paris. (ever)
        Ask ( ) about seeing a movie downtown this month.
        Ask ( ) about living in (Oakland). (length of time)
        Ask ( ) about singing in the language lab last week.
        Ask ( ) about eating spoiled meat. (ever)
        Ask ( ) about swimming in the ocean in the U.S.
        Ask ( ) about taking pictures here. (in Niagara Falls)

8. C   T: How long have you been in the U.S.?   S: (I've been here for 3 months.)
                                                                    (For 3 months.)

        What has impressed you most?/least?
        Did you live in the capital of your country?
        (if no) How many times have you visited there?
        Have you made plans for the summer vacation?/the end of the term? What?
        How often have you gone downtown?
        How often have you discussed politics here?
        How many times have you been sick in the U.S. When? What happened?
        Have you ever eaten spoiled food? When? What happened?
        What cities have you visited in this country?
        Have you had any unpleasant experiences here? What?
        Did you know anyone here when you arrived? Who?
        Did you have any problems finding a room?
        How long was the trip from your country?

9.   (See Instructor's Manual)

Part D.   *Immediate Past Action*

NOTE: *just* with the Present Perfect indicates immediate past action.

He came in a minute ago.   He's just come in.
I talked to her a minute ago.   I've just talked to her.

NOTE: On style—informal style will use *just* with the simple past.

Formal: He's just come in.
Informal: He just came in.

---

1. M1   T: He came in.   S: He's just come in.
              He ate it.   He's just eaten it.
              She did it.   She's just done it.
              We finished it.   We've just finished it.
              We began it.   We've just begun it.
              They drank it.   They've just drunk it.
              She saw it.   She's just seen it.

2. M2   Tell what has just happened.
          T: Jill finished dinner a little while ago.   S: She's just (finished dinner) (eaten dinner)
                                                                  (had dinner).
               I finished the book yesterday.   (You've just read the book.)
               ( ) saw the movie last night.
               We moved to (Pittsburgh) last week.
               Carlos got out of the hospital this morning.
               ( ) came in a minute ago.
               The lecture began 5 minutes ago.
               We heard the news a little while ago.
               Mr. Hastings bought the car last week.
               He got a letter from home this morning.
               ( ) bought a new suit last weekend.

3. C   T: Tell something you've recently done.   S: I've just (seen a new movie).

SECTION TWO

PRESENT PERFECT CONTINUOUS

Model: I've been cooking since January.

1. M1   Rep: John's been studying all day.
          Sub: reading   S: John's been reading all day.
               working   John's been working all day.
               eating   John's been eating all day.
               watching TV   John's been watching TV all day.
               worrying   John's been worrying all day.
               skiing   John's been skiing all day.
               water skiing   John's been water skiing all day.
               flying   John's been flying all day.

2. M1   Rep: How long have you been living in that house?
          Sub: the Adams   S: How long have the Adams been living in that house?
               he   How long has he been living in that house?
               Mrs. Cameron   How long has Mrs. Cameron been living in that house?
               John and Christine   How long have John and Christine been living in that
                                            house?
               you   How long have you been living in that house?
               they   How long have they been living in that house?

GENERALIZATION

As with the continuous forms of the other tenses, the Present Perfect Continuous empha-
sizes the continuity of an action over a period of time.

Formation: *has*   John's been cooking.
                  have   + *been* + V *-ing*   We've been waiting.

297

***3. M1T   Situation: It's 6:00 in the evening.

T: The woman is cooking dinner. She began   S: She's been cooking dinner for three
        at 3:00.   hours.

      Bill is reading a book. He began at noon.   He's been reading for six hours.

      The men are riding in the car. They started   They've been riding in the car for
        at 6:00 a.m.   twelve hours.

      Bill is mowing the lawn. He started at 2:00.   He's been mowing the lawn for four hours.

      Jane is making a dress. She began at 5:00.   She's been making a dress for an hour.

      Bill and Jane are swimming. They went in the   They've been swimming for eight hours.
        water at 10:00.

      The Adams are playing Frisbee. They started   They've been playing Frisbee for five
        at 1:00.   hours.

      Jill is visiting Chen. She went to the hospital   She's been visiting for two hours.
        at 4:00.

      The instructor is correcting papers. He began   He's been correcting papers for two and
        at 3:30.   a half hours.

      Mrs. Jones is shopping. She went to the   She's been shopping for an hour and a
        market at 4:30.   half.

      Pablo is waiting for the doctor. He got to the   He's been waiting for four and a half
        office at 1:30.   hours.

      The girls are listening to records. They put   They've been listening to records for six
        the first record on at noon.   hours.

***4. M2   T: I've been ——.   S: I've been (living in Oakland for two months).
                  ( ) has been ——.   ( ) has been (studying English for ten years).
                  ( ) and ( ) have been——.   ( ) and ( ) have been (looking for an apartment for
                                                      two days).

                  The U.S. government——.
                  The political situation——.
                  etc.

5. C   T: Ask ( ) if he recently moved to   S1:   Have you just (moved) (come) here?
                (Pittsburgh).   S2:   Yes, (we moved (came) here last month).
                                                           No, (we've been living here for three years).

              Ask ( ) if he recently bought his car.

              Ask ( ) if he recently moved to a new apartment.

              Ask ( ) if he recently got a driver's license.

              Ask ( ) if he recently learned to swim.

              Ask ( ) if he recently learned to fly an airplane.

              Ask ( ) if he recently learned to use a typewriter.

              Ask ( ) if he recently learned to cook.

              Ask ( ) if he recently learned to play baseball.

              Ask ( ) if he recently learned to play bridge.

SECTION THREE

SINCE + TIME EXPRESSION

Model: Chen has been in the hospital since Saturday.

1. M1   Rep: Chen has been in the hospital since Saturday.

	Sub:		S:	
	Carlos			Carlos has been in the hospital since Saturday.
	in town			Carlos has been in town since Saturday.
	January			Carlos has been in town since January.
	Jill and Nancy			Jill and Nancy have been in town since January.
	in the class			Jill and Nancy have been in the class since January.
	last week			Jill and Nancy have been in the class since last week.
	The Latin American students			The Latin American students have been in the class since last week.
	in the city			The Latin American students have been in the city since last week.
	since Tuesday			The Latin American students have been in the city since Tuesday.

GENERALIZATION

Lesson Seven: How long were you in Paris?   For three days.
Lesson Fourteen: How long has he been here?   Since Saturday.

for + length of time is used with all tenses.
since + point of time is used mainly with the *perfect* tenses.

---

3. M1T   T: | | S: | |
|---|---|---|
| a week | | I've been here for a week. |
| Saturday | | I've been here since Saturday. |
| two years | | I've been here for two years. |
| last month | | I've been here since last month. |
| January | | I've been here since January. |
| three months | | I've been here for three months. |
| last weekend | | I've been here since last weekend. |
| two weeks | | I've been here for two weeks. |

NOTE: Lesson Thirteen: He went downtown a week *ago.*
        Lesson Fourteen: He hasn't gone downtown *since* last week.

Ago is used with Past Tense; *since* with Present Perfect.

---

4. M1T   T: | | S: | |
|---|---|---|
| He went there. | | He went there a week ago. |
| He's been there. | | He's been there since last week. |
| They bought a car. | | They bought a car a week ago. |
| She's had a cold. | | She's had a cold since last week. |
| I sold my books. | | I sold my books a week ago. |

(exercise continued on next page)

T: Someone stole our car.   S: Someone stole our car a week ago.
    He's been home from the hospital.   He's been home from the hospital since last week.
    We've been here.   We We've been here since last week.

5. M2   T: They had an election ——.   S: They had an election (a year) ago.
        They haven't had an election ——.   They haven't had an election (since 19—).
        Bill saw Chen in the hospital ——.
        Bill has seen Chen twice ——.
        She hasn't smoked a cigarette ——.
        We saw the new movie ——.
        Chen got out of the hospital ——.
        Nancy has read three books ——.
        Has Bill made any long distance phone calls ——?
        Did Mr. Hastings go to Chicago ——?
        Has Judy typed the paper ——?
        Did you get a letter from home ——?
        Have you seen your friend ——?

***6. M2   T: Have you called home lately?   S: I haven't called home (since yesterday) (for three
                                              days).
            Have you been downtown lately?
            Have you seen your friend lately?
            Have you done the laundry lately?
            Have you cut class lately?
            Have you received a letter lately?
            Have you eaten out lately?
            Have you read the New York Times lately?
            Have you been to the seashore lately?
            Have you eaten any spoiled food lately?

***7. C   T: see your friend   S1: (Have you seen your friend lately?) (When did you see
                                              your friend?)
                                         S2: (I saw him a week ago.) (I haven't seen him since last
                                              week.)

        read a good book
        see a good movie
        eat in a good restaurant
        cut classes
        have a good discussion about politics
        hear a good lecture
        see a good TV program
        go to a baseball game
        hear any good records
        get a bargain
        go on a trip
        find a good restaurant
        buy a new record

SECTION FOUR

ALREADY/YET

Model: I haven't seen Chen yet. Jill has already seen him.

1. M1   Rep: I haven't seen Chen yet.
                         We haven't read the book yet.
                         She hasn't come yet.
                         The rain hasn't stopped yet.
                         Have you seen Chen yet?
                         Has he moved yet?
                         Have you seen the new movie yet?

2. M1   Rep: Jill has already seen Chen.
                 Sub: read the book   S: Jill has already read the book.
                         seen the new movie   Jill has already seen the new movie.
                         moved to a new apartment   Jill has already moved to a new apartment.
                         finished the paper   Jill has already finished the paper.
                         gone home   Jill has already gone home.
                         called Bill   Jill has already called Bill.

GENERALIZATION

Already and *yet* are adverbs which mean by or at a certain time. As a rule, *already* is used in affirmative statements, and *yet* in questions and negative statements. *Yet* almost always comes at the end of a simple sentence:

> Is John at home yet?
> We haven't seen the new students yet.
> He isn't going to buy a new car yet.

Already has a more complicated placement:

    1. following BE as the main verb: John *is* already here.
                                                  The boys *were* already sick.
    2. preceding a simple verb: John already *has* a car.
                                                    The boys already *knew* the answer.
    3. following the auxiliary in a compound verb:
                                                We've already *called* the police.
                                                He's already *doing* the homework.
    4. at the end of the sentence: Jill has seen Chen already.

---

3. M1   T: Bill was tired at 10:00.   S: Bill was already tired at 10:00.
                         The students are here.   The students are already here.
                         Jane is sleepy.   Jane is already sleepy.
                         Chen was in the hospital.   Chen was already in the hospital.
                         The girls were late.   The girls were already late.
                         They are in the kitchen.   They are already in the kitchen.
                         I'm pretty busy.   I'm already pretty busy.

301

4. M1   T: The boys know the answer.   S: The boys already know the answer.
                Bill has a job.   Bill already has a job.
                He understands the problem.   He already understands the problem.
                They have a new car.   They already have a new car.
                John does a lot of work.   John already does a lot of work.
                I know the address.   I already know the address.

5. M1   T: Bill is doing the work.   S: Bill is already doing the work.
                Jane has seen Chen.   Jane has already seen Chen.
                The boys were flying to New York.   The boys were already flying to New York.
                I've been to California.   I've already been to California.
                The girls have left.   The girls have already left.
                He's bought the car.   He's already bought the car.
                You've seen the movie.   You've already seen the movie.

6. M1T   T: Jane was tired at noon.   S: Jane was already tired at noon.
                I know the number.   I already know the number.
                The girls are doing the dishes.   The girls are already doing the dishes.
                Chen has a new car.   Chen already has a new car.
                Jane has been to Mexico.   Jane has already been to Mexico.
                Charlie has quit his job.   Charlie has already quit his job.
                Carlos knew about cooking.   Carlos already knew about cooking.
                We're pretty busy.   We're already pretty busy.

7. M1T   T: The professor isn't here.   S: The professor isn't here yet.
                Has the professor come?   Has the professor come yet?
                The professor is here.   The professor is already here.
                The students have come.   The students have already come.
                Have the students come?   Have the students come yet?
                The bell has rung.   The bell has already rung.
                The bell hasn't rung.   The bell hasn't rung yet.
                The class has started.   The class has already started.
                The class hasn't started.   The class hasn't started yet.
                Is the instructor here?   Is the instructor here yet?
                Jane is talking.   Jane is already talking.
                Chen knows about cooking.   Chen already knows about cooking.

8. M2   T: Why don't you buy the book?   S: (I already have it.) (I don't have the money yet.)
                Why don't you get a new car?
                Why don't you say hello to John?
                Why doesn't the class begin?
                Why don't you introduce your friend?
                Why doesn't he type the paper?
                Why doesn't she do the laundry?
                Why don't you get an apartment?
                Why don't you take a vacation?
                Why don't you get some records?
                Why don't we say "hello" to the President?

***9. C   T: Ask ( ) about the new movie.   S1:   (Have you seen the new movie yet?) (Have you
                                                            been to the new movie yet?)
                                             S2:   (Yes, I've already seen it.) (No, I haven't seen
                                                            it yet.)

Ask ( ) about the best seller.
Ask ( ) about the new student.
Ask ( ) about the exciting news.
Ask ( ) about the morning newspaper.
Ask ( ) about the news about Chen.
Ask ( ) about the President's press conference.
Ask ( ) about the new coffee house.
Ask ( ) about the new professor.
Ask ( ) about the latest record by (popular recording star).
Ask ( ) about the new book about the war.
Ask ( ) about the latest actions by the Pentagon.
Ask ( ) about the Vice President's latest speech.

SECTION FIVE

TAG QUESTIONS

***Part A.   *Type I*

Model: They haven't left yet, have they?

1. M1   T: They haven't left yet.   S: They haven't left yet, have they?
                 I haven't paid the bill.   I haven't paid the bill, have I?
                 We haven't got the money.   We haven't got the money, have we?
                 They haven't been to the hospital.   They haven't been to the hospital, have they?
                 They haven't been cooking long.   They haven't been cooking long, have they?
                 You haven't eaten spoiled food.   You haven't eaten spoiled food, have you?
                 I haven't seen you before.   I haven't seen you before, have I?

2. M1   T: She hasn't cooked much.   S: She hasn't cooked much, has she?
                 He hasn't been here long.   He hasn't been here long, has he?
                 He hasn't written home.   He hasn't written home, has he?
                 John hasn't gone to the hospital.   John hasn't gone to the hospital, has he?
                 Dorothy hasn't served leftovers.   Dorothy hasn't served leftovers, has she?
                 Charlie hasn't left for Norfolk.   Charlie hasn't left for Norfolk, has he?

GENERALIZATION

The Type I tag questions are formed the same way as in Lessons Two, Four, Seven, and
Twelve.

Statement	Tag	Response
They haven't left yet,	have they?	No, they haven't.
She hasn't cooked much,	has she?	No, she hasn't.
—	+	—

---

3. M1T   T: Jane hasn't gone downtown.   G1:   Jane hasn't gone downtown, has she?
                                                    G2:   No, she hasn't.

               The students haven't been here   G1:   The students haven't been here long, have they?
                  long.   G2:   No, they haven't.

               We haven't paid the bill.   G1:   We haven't paid the bill, have we?
                                                    G2:   No, we haven't.

               Bill hasn't eaten spoiled food.   G1:   Bill hasn't eaten spoiled food, has he?
                                                    G2:   No, he hasn't.

               The students haven't studied   G1:   The students haven't studied the lesson, have they?
                  the lesson.   G2:   No, they haven't.

               Chen hasn't eaten pizza yet.   G1:   Chen hasn't eaten pizza yet, has he?
                                                    G2:   No, he hasn't.

               Mary hasn't finished the book   G1:   Mary hasn't finished the book yet, has she?
                  yet.   G2:   No, she hasn't.

Part B.   *Type II*

Model: They've left, haven't they?

1. M1   T: They've already left.   S: They've already left, haven't they?
               You've already eaten.   You've already eaten, haven't you?
               I've come late.   I've come late, haven't I?
               We've surprised you.   We've surprised you, haven't we?
               John and Judy have gone to the   John and Judy have gone to the hospital, haven't
                  hospital.   they?
               You and Bill have already eaten.   You and Bill have already eaten, haven't you?
               Carlos and Chen have already   Carlos and Chen have already passed the test,
                  passed the test.   haven't they?

2. M1   T: Bill has been to the hospital.   S: Bill has been to the hospital, hasn't he?
               Judy has cooked a lot.   Judy has cooked a lot, hasn't she?
               The woman has been to Paris.   The woman has been to Paris, hasn't she?
               The woman has finished the book.   The woman has finished the book, hasn't she?
               Judy has gone to New York.   Judy has gone to New York, hasn't she?
               Chen has already seen Carlos.   Chen has already seen Carlos, hasn't he?

GENERALIZATION

The Type II tag questions are the same as Lessons Two, Four, Seven and Twelve.

	Statement	Tag	Response
Type I:	They haven't left, —	have they? +	No, they haven't. —
Type II:	They've left, +	haven't they? —	Yes, they have. +

---

3. M1T   T: Bill has already left.   G1:   Bill has already left, hasn't he?
                                                  G2:   Yes, he has.

                The students have already gone. G1:   The students have already gone, haven't they?
                                                  G2:   Yes, they have.

                Bill and Jane have already   G1:   Bill and Jane have already seen Carlos, haven't they?
                  seen Carlos.   G2:   Yes, they have.

                Jane has been to Paris.   G1:   Jane has been to Paris, hasn't she?
                                                  G2:   Yes, she has.

                Mrs. Jackson has taught school.   G1:   Mrs. Jackson has taught school, hasn't she?
                                                  G2:   Yes, she has.

                Mrs. Newton has traveled a lot.   G1:   Mrs. Newton has traveled a lot, hasn't she?
                                                  G2:   Yes, she has.

                The girls have played bridge   G1:   The girls have played bridge every night, haven't
                  every night.   they?
                                                  G2:   Yes, they have.

4. M1T   T: Jane hasn't gone downtown.   S: Jane hasn't gone downtown, has she?
                Bill has already left.   Bill has already left, hasn't he?
                The boys have already eaten.   The boys have already eaten, haven't they?
                The students haven't studied.   The students haven't studied, have they?
                Jack hasn't been to Europe.   Jack hasn't been to Europe, has he?
                Joe and Jill have seen the President.   Joe and Jill have seen the President, haven't they?
                Mrs. Newton has gone to New York.   Mrs. Newton has gone to New York, hasn't she?
                Jill hasn't typed the paper.   Jill hasn't typed the paper, has she?
                Carlos and Chen have studied hard.   Carlos and Chen have studied hard, haven't they?
                The professors haven't left yet.   The professors haven't left yet, have they?

5. M2   T: go to Paris   S1:   (You've gone to Paris, haven't you?) (Joe hasn't
                                                          gone to Paris, has he?)
                                                  S2:   (Yes, I have.) (No, he hasn't.)

                eaten dinner
                been to the museum
                paid the bill
                cooked for a long time
                visited your friends recently
                seen the latest *Newsweek*
                read the morning paper
                written home
                balanced your checkbook
                been to Chicago
                had a party
                seen your friends

6. C   T: Situation: You meet a friend you haven't seen for a long time. Use this and other
                    tag questions to catch up on the news.

                S1:   Hi, how are you? What have you been doing?
                S2:   I've been in New York. Where have you been?
                S1:   Around here, all the time. You've seen ( ), haven't you?
                S2:   No, I haven't. What's he been doing?
                etc.

SUMMARY DIALOGUE

Nancy: Where have you been, Carlos? I haven't seen you for days.

Carlos: I went to New York last weekend, so I've been studying hard all week. There's a big exam next week and I haven't finished the reading yet.

Nancy: I saw Bill in the library yesterday. He must be studying hard, too.

Carlos: We have the same exam.

Nancy: Well, good luck.

Carlos: Thanks, see you later.

Nancy: So long.

SUMMARY OF PATTERNS

			Subject	*Have*	*Past Participle*	*Completer*	*Short Answer*
Statement			Mr. Hastings	has	gone	to Chicago this year.	
Question (Who)			Who	has	gone	to Chicago?	Mr. Hastings.
		Have					
Question (Yes/No)		Has	the student		seen	the new movie?	Yes, he has. No, he hasn't.
	QW						
Question (Wh)	How long	have	you		been	here?	Since January.
Continuous					*Been + V -ing*		
			They	have	been studying	since Tuesday.	
Question (Yes/No)		Have	they		been living	here for a long time?	Yes, they have. No, they haven't.
Tag Questions: 1.			She hasn't left, —		has she? +		No, she hasn't. —
2.			They've left, +		haven't they? −		Yes, they have. +

***LANGUAGE STYLE

In the following conversations, the same topic is discussed in three different situations. Your teacher will help you identify the differences in the situations as well as in the language used.

Variations on a Theme No. 3

A. Bill meets an old friend.

Bill: Hey, Jack! How are you?! Long time no see.

Jack: Bill! How're you? Yeah, it's been a long time. I'm working for an outfit downtown. How about you?

5   Bill: I'm about through the course work for an MBA.

Jack: Oh, yeah? How do you like it?

Bill: I'll be glad when it's over.

Jack: Yeah, know what you mean. You been at it a long time, no?

Bill: Too long. Won't be long now, though. I finish next term. How's the "real" world
10   treating you?

Jack: O.K. Just got a promotion, and the dough is great.

Bill: Glad to hear it. Look, I gotta go to class. When'll I see you?

Jack: You still at the same place?

Bill: Yeah.

15   Jack: O.K. Call you next week.

Bill: See you then. So long.

Jack: Glad I bumped into you. So long.

B. Bill meets a high school acquaintance whom he hasn't seen for quite a few years.

Bill: Hi, Jill. How are you?! I haven't seen you in years. What are you doing now?

Jill: Bill Jackson! How are *you*? Yes, it *has* been a long time. I'm working in an office downtown. How about you?

5   Bill: I'm almost finished with the course work for a Masters in Business Administration.

Jill: Really? How do you like it?

Bill: I'll be glad to get finished.

Jill: Yes, I know what you mean. You've been going to school for a long time, haven't you?

307

10 Bill: Too long. It won't be long now, though. I'll finish next term. How do you like the "real" world.

Jill: It's pretty good. I've just gotten a promotion, and the money is pretty good.

Bill: I'm glad to hear you like it. Look, I have to go to class. When can I call you? Are you still living at home?

Jill: Yes.

15 Bill: O.K. I'll call you sometime next week.

Jill: Fine, I'll talk to you then. It was really nice running into you. So long.

Bill: So long.

C. Bill goes to a lecture and meets an old friend of his father's whom he hasn't seen for quite a few years.

Bill: Hello, Mr. Cassetti. How *are* you? I haven't seen you for a long time.

Mr. Cassetti: Hello, Bill. How are *you*? It has been a long time. What are you doing these
5   days?

Bill: I'm studying Business Administration at Pitt—for a Masters.

Mr. Cassetti: Really? How do you like it?

Bill: It's going pretty well, but I'll be glad to get it finished.

Mr. Cassetti: Yes, I know what you mean. I remember what it was like. You've been going
10   to school for a long time, haven't you?

Bill: Five years. It won't be much longer, though. I hope to finish next term. Are you still working for (Gulf)?

Mr. Cassetti: Yes, I am.

Bill: How is "old Gulf" treating you these days?

15 Mr. Cassetti: Fine. I recently received a promotion, so I'm satisfied.

Bill: I'm very happy to hear that, Mr. Cassetti.

Mr. Cassetti: Say "hello" to your parents, will you?

Bill: I'll be glad to. It was nice talking to you, Mr. Cassetti. Hope to see you again.

LESSON FIFTEEN

INTRODUCTION   Thrift stores

Carlos meets Nancy and Bill on the street.

Bill: Hi, Carlos. We're going to the coffee shop. Come with us.

Carlos: I can't right now. I'm on my way to the Salvation Army Store.

Nancy: *Why are you going there?*

5   Carlos: *For a desk.* I need one *in order to organize* my room. Someone told me they have cheap things there.

Bill: Cheap, but second-hand.

Carlos: That's all right. I just want something inexpensive.

Nancy: There's a furniture store near my house. They have second-hand things. They're
10   usually cheap and fairly nice.

Bill: And there's the Goodwill Industries, or the Veterans' stores. There are lots of used furniture dealers.

Carlos: Yes, I know. Someone told me to look in the Yellow Pages of the phone book. It took me almost an hour to find the used furniture stores under "Furniture—Bought and Sold."

15   Nancy: The index to the Yellow Pages is confusing sometimes. How are you going to get the desk home?

Carlos: Don't they have a truck?

Nancy: A delivery truck? Some places do, but some don't. You should find out ahead of time. It depends on the store.

20   Carlos: Well, I'll look around . . . why are you going to the coffee shop in this weather?

Bill: I'm going for coffee. They only charge for the first cup.

Nancy: Not me. I hate coffee. I'm going because our friends will be there.

Carlos: O.K. Say hello to everyone. I'll see you later.

Bill: So long.

25   Nancy: See you.

NOTE:

Line 25: Parting expressions such as "so long" and "see you later" are standard informal expressions similar to the formal "It was nice talking to you." or "Goodbye." There is no specific future meeting implied or intended. Since it is informal, the people understand that the natural course of events (school, job, etc.) will bring them together again. The only time that such a parting should be considered specific is when a time and a place are stated, as "See you tomorrow after English class at the Student Union."

OUTLINE OF PATTERNS   Example

Section One	Why? + Reason Responses	
Part A.	*Why?*	Why are you gong there?
Part B.	*in order to/for*	For a desk. In order to organize my room.
Part C.	*Because* + clause	Because our friends will be there.
Section Two	Agent Nouns	Refrigerate/refrigerator
Section Three	Noun + Noun Modification	Salvation Army Store
Section Four	Conjunction (*and/or/but*)	. . . but some don't.

COMPREHENSION QUESTIONS

1. Where does Carlos meet Nancy and Bill?

2. Where are Nancy and Bill going?

*3. Why is Carlos going to the Salvation Army Store?

4. Why does he need a desk?

*5. What does Bill say about the furniture at the Salvation Army Store?

6. What second-hand furniture stores are there?

*7. Why did Carlos look in the Yellow Pages?

8. What is the difficulty with the Yellow Pages index?

*9. How will Carlos get the desk home?

10. Do all stores have a delivery truck?

11. Why is Bill going to the coffee shop? Nancy?

*12. Discuss the partings in terms of the note above.

*13. Discuss ways of finding used items in particular areas (stores, student newspapers, garage sales, house sales, etc.)

*14. Are there second-hand stores for futniture in ( )? What do students do for housing? furniture?

Vocabulary

Nouns		Verbs	Adjectives
author	index	advise	cracked
babysitter	living	collect	fresh (not stale)
bird	marker	counsel	humid
builder	mind	detect	icy
checkup	newsstand	divide	ripe
collector	player	dry	rotten
counselor	publisher	extinguish	second-hand
dancer	reporter	farm	smiling
delivery	sharpener	hang	sprained
desk	smoker	hold	
dime store	steak	inspect	
editor	textbook	join	
education	toaster	organize	
farmer	translator	publish	
grocery store	truck	wipe	
guitar	voice		
iced tea	writer		

SECTION ONE

WHY? AND REASON RESPONSES

Part A.   *Why?*

Model: Why are you going to the Salvation Army Store?

1. M1   Rep: Why are Nancy and Bill going to the coffee house?
          Sub: Nancy   S: Why is Nancy going to the coffee house?
               did   Why did Nancy go to the coffee house?
               drive   Why did Nancy drive to the coffee house?
               downtown   Why did Nancy drive downtown?
               you   Why did you drive downtown?
               walk   Why did you walk downtown?
               to the party   Why did you walk to the party?

2. M1   T: Are you going downtown for some reason?   S: Why are you going downtown?
               Were the boys absent for some reason?   Why were the boys absent?
               Did Chen buy a new desk for some reason?   Why did Chen buy a new desk?
               Are the girls taking the computer course for   Why are the girls taking the computer course?
                  some reason?
               Have you been absent this week for some   Why have you been absent this week?
                  reason?
               Has Chen been studying for some reason?   Why has Chen been studying?
               Should the boys get a desk for some reason?   Why should the boys get a desk?
               Does Charlie have to go to Puerto Rico for   Why does Charlie have to go to Puerto
                  some reason?   Rico?

GENERALIZATION

The question *why* asks about the reason for something. The subject and verb are inverted as with other *wh* questions:

Where are you going?   Downtown.

Why are you going downtown?
$$\begin{cases} \text{For a desk.} \\ \text{In order to find a desk.} \\ \text{Because I need a desk.} \end{cases}$$

There are three common answers to the question *Why* which will be discussed below.

NOTE: In speech *What . . . for?* = Why?
        What did he go downtown *for?*
        Why did he go downtown?

***3. M1T   T: Chen went to New York.   S: Why did he go there?
                   Chen wants a new desk.   Why does he want one?
                   Chen is buying the car.   Why is he buying it?
                   Chen has to go to the police station.   Why does he have to go there?
                   Chen should buy a car.   Why should he buy one?
                   Chen will sell his car.   Why will he sell it?
                   Chen has gone to the Thrift Store.   Why has he gone there?
                   Chen drove to Pittsburgh.   Why did he drive there?

4. M2   T: Ask ( ) a question about something he   S1:   (Why did you buy a new car last week?)
                  did last week.   S2:   (I didn't. I bought a new motorcycle.)
               Ask ( ) a question about something he's   S1:   (Why are you buying cigarettes?)
                  doing now.   S2:   (I'm not. I'm buying cigars.)
               Ask ( ) a question about something he's   S1:   (Why are you going to study Saturday?)
                  going to do next weekend.   S2:   (I'm not. I'm going to Bill's party.)
               Ask ( ) a question about something he has to do tomorrow.
               Ask ( ) a question about something he's been doing lately.
               Ask ( ) a question about something he did yesterday.
               Ask ( ) a question about something he'll do tomorrow.
               Ask ( ) a question about something he should do today.
               Ask ( ) a question about something he's going to do in the summer.
               Ask ( ) a question about something he's been doing this week.
               Ask ( ) a question about something he has to do next week.

(exercise continued on next page)

T: Ask ( ) a question about something he was doing last week.
       Ask ( ) a question about something he's doing now.

Part B.   *in order to/for*

Model: I went for a cup of coffee.
        I went in order to get a desk.

***1. M1   Rep: I went to the coffee house for a cup of coffee.

Sub:		S:	
restaurant—steak			I went to the restaurant for a steak.
drug store—medicine			I went to the drug store for some medicine.
grocery store—vegetables			I went to the grocery store for some vegetables.
car dealer—new car			I went to the car dealer for a new car.
furniture store—desk			I went to the furniture store for a desk.
newsstand—New York Times			I went to the newsstand for a New York Times.
post office—stamps			I went to the post office for some stamps.

2. M1   Rep: Bill is going to the store in order to buy a paper.

Sub:	S:	
downtown—get a suit		Bill is going downtown in order to get a suit.
drug store—buy cigarettes		Bill is going to the drug store in order to buy cigarettes.
grocery store—get some fresh vegetables		Bill is going to the grocery store in order to get some fresh vegetables.
university—get an education in business administration		Bill is going to the university in order to get an education in business administration.
barber shop—get a haircut		Bill is going to the barber shop in order to get a haircut.
home—get some sleep		Bill is going home in order to get some sleep.
post office—send a package		Bill is going to the post office in order to send a package.
coffee shop—have a cup of coffee		Bill is going to the coffee shop in order to have a cup of coffee.
second-hand furniture store—buy a desk		Bill is going to the second-hand furniture store in order to buy a desk.

GENERALIZATION

The question *Why?* can be answered by a phrase in the following manner:

		for + Noun Phrase
He went downtown		for a new suit.
or	*in order to* + Verb	+ Noun Phrase
He went downtown	in order to get	a new suit.

NOTE: *in order to* + Verb is often shortened to *to* + Verb:

    in order to get a desk.   —   to get a desk.

---

3. M1T   T:

	S:	
post office—some stamps		He's going to the post office for some stamps.
post office—mail a letter		He's going to the post office to mail a letter.
drug store—buy cigarettes		He's going to the drug store to buy cigarettes.
grocery store—some rice		He's going to the grocery store for some rice.

(exercise continued on next page)

T:	university—get a degree	S:	He's going to the university to get a degree.
	thrift store—buy a desk		He's going to the thrift store to buy a desk.
	drug store—his photographs		He's going to the drug store for his photographs.
	camera shop—some film		He's going to the camera shop for some film.

***4. M2   Ask about Carlos.

T:	downtown	S1:	Why (is he going) (did he go) (has he gone) downtown?
	buy a suit	S2:	He (same as question) downtown (in order) to buy a suit.
	downtown	S1:	Why ( ) ( ) ( ) downtown?
	suit	S2:	He ( ) for a suit.

    drug store—toothpaste
    department store—get a new shirt
    grocery store—buy fresh fruit
    barber shop—haircut
    university—course in economics
    ELI—learn English
    second-hand furniture store—desk
    bank—cash a check
    car dealer—buy a car
    hospital—checkup
    coffee house—meet his friends

Part C.   *Because + Clause*

Model: Because our friends will be there.

1. M1   Rep: Nancy is going because her friends will be there.

Sub:	I	S:	I'm going because my friends will be there.
	Bill		Bill is going because his friends will be there.
	the boys		The boys are going because their friends will be there.
	we		We are going because our friends will be there.
	you		You are going because your friends will be there.
	Jane		Jane is going because her friends will be there.
	Chen		Chen is going because his friends will be there

GENERALIZATION

Longer explanations to the question *why* are frequently introduced by *because* and consist of a clause instead of a phrase. (A clause has a subject and a verb, a phrase does not.)

Why are you going to the Thrift Store?	For a desk.	(phrase)
	To get a desk.	(phrase)
	Because I need a desk.	(clause)

---

2. M1T   T: get a desk   S: to get a desk
           a desk   for a desk
           I need a desk   because I need a desk
           cash a check   to cash a check

(exercise continued on next page)

314

	T:	S:
	Bill needs some money	because Bill needs some money
	a cup of coffee	for a cup of coffee
	we want a car	because we want a car
	have dinner	to have dinner
	lunch	for lunch
	Chen likes to drive	because Chen likes to drive

3. M2   T: I like (the United States) ——   S: I like the United States (because I can do what I like).

I don't like (the United States) ——   I don't like the United States (because the food is terrible).

I have to ——
I'm going to ——
I didn't ——
I don't want to ——
I didn't go ——
I don't like ——
I'm not going to ——
I don't have to ——
I should ——
I might not ——
I haven't ——

***4.   T: Ask ( ) about someplace he goes (add a time). Then ask "Why?"

S1: Where do you go (every day)?
S2: (To the Student Union.)
S1: Why do you go there?
S2: (To see my friends.) (For lunch.) (Because my friends have lunch there.)

Ask ( ) about someplace he went (add a time). Then ask "Why?"

S1: Where did you go (last week)?
S2: I went (to New York).
S1: Why did you go there?
S2: (To see Broadway.) (For a vacation.) (Because I wanted to see it.)

Ask ( ) where he's going (add a time).
Ask ( ) where he's going to go (add a time).
Ask ( ) what he's going to study (add a place).
Ask ( ) where he's going to study (add a time).
Ask ( ) what he studies (place).
Ask ( ) what he's been studying (time).
Ask ( ) where he went (time).
Ask ( ) what he did (time).
Ask ( ) where he's going (time).
Ask ( ) what he's been doing (time).
Ask ( ) where he's going to travel (time).

5. C   T: Does anyone want to go to the moon? Why?

S: I do.
(To be famous.) (For the excitement.) (Because I like adventure.)

Does anyone want to write a book? Why? About what?
Does anyone want to buy a Rolls-Royce? Why?
Does anyone want to invent something? What? Why?
Does anyone want to go to California? When? Why?

(exercise continued on next page)

315

T: Does anyone want to buy a new car? Why? What kind?
       Does anyone want to buy a house? Why? Where?
       Does anyone want to be in politics? What position? Why?
       Does anyone want to be in public service? What? Why?
       Does anyone want to be an engineer? What kind? Why?
       Does anyone want to go to New York? Why? When?

SECTION TWO

AGENT NOUNS

Model: My aunt is a publisher.
         Put leftovers in the refrigerator.

1. M1   Listen to the descriptions of the jobs.

	T:		S:	
		The man teaches English for a living.		He's a teacher.
		The man drives a truck for a living.		He's a driver.
		The girl dances in a chorus for a living.		She's a dancer.
		The woman sings on stage for a living.		She's a singer.
		The man farms for a living.		He's a farmer.
		The lady counsels students for a living.		She's a counselor.
		The man advises the President for a living.		He's an advisor.
		The man builds houses for a living.		He's a builder.

GENERALIZATION

Many verbs can be changed into agent nouns (one who/thing which) by adding *er/or* to the simple form of the verb.

Verb	Noun
teach	teacher
dance	dancer
counsel	counselor

---

2. M1T   T: To light cigarettes, ——   S: To light cigarettes, *you use a lighter.
                To refrigerate food, ——   To refrigerate food, you use a refrigerator.
                To wash the clothes, ——   To wash the clothes, you use a washer.
                To dry the clothes, ——   To dry the clothes, you use a dryer.
                To freeze leftovers, ——   To freeze leftovers, you use a freezer.
                To mark the clothes, ——   To mark the clothes, you use a marker.
                To sharpen the pencil, ——   To sharpen the pencil, you use a sharpener.
                To record your voice, ——   To record your voice, you use a recorder.
                To toast bread, ——   To toast bread, you use a toaster.

         *This is the general *you,* not the specific.

3. M2   T: He's a teacher.   S1:   Does he teach (English)?

                                                 S2:   No, he is a French teacher.

               She's a writer.   S1:   Does she write (textbooks)?

                                                 S2:   No, she's a cookbook writer.

               He's a translator.
               He's a reporter.
               He's a collector.
               She's a publisher.
               He's a builder.
               She's a singer.
               He's an editor.
               He's an advisor.
               He's a manager.
               They're writers.

4. C   T: toast   S1:   I'm (going to the Thrift Store to get) a toaster.

                                                 S2:   Why do you (need) a toaster?

                                                 S1:   To toast (the bread for breakfast).

               wash   S1:   I'm (going to Sears' to buy) a washer.

                                                 S2:   Why do you (want) a washer?

                                                 S1:   To wash (the clothes) (the dishes).

               refrigerate
               light
               dry
               record
               sharpen
               open
               freeze
               heat
               cool

SECTION THREE

NOUN + NOUN MODIFICATION

Model: I'm going to the Salvation Army Store.

1. M1   T: He teaches English.   S: He's an English teacher.
               It dries hair.   It's a hair dryer.
               It dries clothes.   It's a clothes dryer.
               It freezes ice cream.   It's an ice cream freezer.
               He collects clocks.   He's a clock collector.
               It opens cans.   It's a can opener.
               She publishes a newspaper.   She's a newspaper publisher.
               It lights cigarettes.   It's a cigarette lighter.

GENERALIZATION

| Previous Patterns: | The tall | girls are good | students. |

| Lesson Fifteen: | The *English* girls are *history* | students. |

When a noun *(English, history)* is in the same position as the adjective in the previous patterns, a compound noun results. Note that the stress pattern changes when there is a combination of two nouns. Listen carefully as your teacher pronounces the sentences.

2. M1T   T: He's a driver of trucks.   S: He's a truck driver.
                He's a teacher of English.   He's an English teacher.
                He's a driver of taxis.   He's a taxi driver.
                He's a dealer of cars.   He's a car dealer.
                He's a student of engineering.   He's an engineering student.
                He's a publisher of newspapers.   He's a newspaper publisher.
                He's a robber of banks.   He's a bank robber.
                He's an author of textbooks.   He's a textbook author.
                He's a counselor of students.   He's a student counselor.

***3. M2   T: I just saw the man who robbed the bank.   S: (You saw the bank robber!?)
                I can read your mind.   (You must be a mind reader.)
                I smoke a pipe occasionally.   (Are you a cigar smoker too?)
                My friend's father inspects food for the government.
                Some people make a lot of trouble for the Extablishment.
                I have some material from Thailand, but I don't know how to make a dress.
                We met some players on the baseball team.
                The police should stop those people from pushing dope.
                I drink a lot of coffee.
                Someone should clean the streets.
                We need someone to wash the windows.
                My aunt publishes a small newspaper in New York.
                Many people watch birds.

4. M2   T: sharpen—pencil   S1:   (How can I) sharpen this pencil?
                                        S2:   (Use the) pencil sharpener (over there).

                wash—dishes   S1:   (How did you) wash the dishes (so fast)?
                                        S2:   (I used) a dishwasher.

                sharpen—knife
                hang—coat
                detect—a lie
                wipe—the windshield
                extinguish—the fire
                clean—pipe
                cut—paper
                mow—lawn
                play—records
                cool—water
                open—letter
                divide—room
                hold—pot

5. M2   T: I'm going to the Salvation Army Store to get a toaster.

S1:   She's going to the Salvation Army Store to get a toaster. I'm going to the (drug store) (for some toothpaste).

S2:   She's going to the Salvation Army Store to get a toaster. ( ) is going to the (drug store) (for some toothpaste). I'm going ( ) to get ( ).
       etc.

6. C   T: How many people in your country own their own homes?

S: (About 50% of the people are home owners.)

How many people in your family earn wages?

(Two people in my family are wage earners.)

How many people in this class drink tea?
How many people in this class smoke cigarettes? pipes? cigars?
How many of the buildings in (capital) are skyscrapers?
Who in your family is the best teller of stories?
Does anyone in your family collect anything? What?
Are there any teachers in your family? What subjects?
How many of the farmers in your country are dairy farmers?
Are there small children in your family? Do you need a babysitter?

SECTION FOUR

CONJUNCTION *(AND/OR/BUT)*

Model: a desk and a chair
         ice cream or cake
         cold but not icy

1. M1   T: buy a desk/a chair   S: He's buying a desk and a chair.
               learn Spanish/English   He's learning Spanish and English.
               come tomorrow/the day after   He's coming tomorrow and the day after.
               invite Bill/Carlos   He's inviting Bill and Carlos.
               go home/go to bed   He's going home and going to bed.
               come/bring a friend   He's coming and bringing a friend.
               tell why/where   He's telling why and where.

2. M1   T: order a steak/a hamburger   S: Shall we order a steak or a hamburger?
               have milk/iced tea   Shall we have milk or iced tea?
               tell how/why   Shall we tell how or why?
               walk/take a taxi   Shall we walk or take a taxi?
               call Bill/Chen   Shall we call Bill or Chen?
               go tomorrow/the next day   Shall we go tomorrow or the next day?
               give him a call/drop him a line   Shall we give him a call or drop him a line?

3. M1   Rep: The teacher was smiling but not laughing.
               I take my coffee with cream but no sugar.
               Please come after noon but before 1:00.
               This fruit is ripe but not rotton.

(exercise continued on next page)

The weather is hot but not humid.
His arm was sprained but not broken.
The clothes are old but still good.

GENERALIZATION

The conjunctions *and, or* and *but* join sentences or parts of sentences (Lesson Seventeen). *And* indicates an addition of items, *or* a choice of items and *but* a contrary or unexpected item.

Subjects joined with *and* have a plural verb:

Bill and Nancy are going to the coffee shop.

Subjects joined with *or* or *but* have a singular verb:

Bill or Nancy is going to the coffee shop.
Bill but not Nancy is going to the coffee shop.

---

4. M1   Rep: Where can I find a good used car but a cheap one?
         Sub: apartment   S: Where can I find a good apartment but a cheap one?
              old records   Where can I find good old records but cheap ones?
              second hand desk   Where can I find a good second hand desk but a cheap one?
              old appliances   Where can I find good old appliances but cheap ones?
              second hand chair   Where can I find a good second hand chair but a cheap one?
              old books   Where can I find good old books but cheap ones?
              second hand TV   Where can I find a good second hand TV but a cheap one?
              second hand clothes   Where can I find good second hand clothes but cheap ones?

5. M1T   T: I called Jane. I called Jim.   S: I called Jane and Jim.
              I called Jane. I didn't call Jim.   I called Jane but not Jim.
              Maybe I'll call tonight. Maybe I'll   I'll call tonight or tomorrow.
                call tomorrow.
              We haven't seen Jane. We haven't seen   We haven't seen Jane or Judy.
                Judy.
              I'll write Bill. I won't write Jack.   I'll write Bill but not Jack.
              I'll talk to the students. I'll talk to   I'll talk to the students and the professor.
                the professor.
              We can go this week. We can go next week. We can go this week or next week.
              She wanted the new novel. She wanted   She wanted the new novel and the biography.
                the new biography.
              She can go to the GP movie. She can't   She can go to the GP movie but not the
                go to the X-rated movie.   X-rated movie.
              They might buy a VW. They might buy   They might buy a VW or a Rolls-Royce.
                a Rolls-Royce.

6. M2   T: She smiled but ——   S: She smiled but (said "No") (refused).
              She smiled and ——   She smiled and (agreed) (said "thank you").
              She will write a note or ——   She will write a note or (call).
              The President made a speech and ——
              The students studied hard but ——

(exercise continued on next page)

T: The house was old but not ——
        The boys will go to the movies or ——
        The man was handsome but ——
        The actress was beautiful and ——
        We can't buy a car or ——
        The furniture was cheap and ——
        The class is interesting ——
        The class is interesting but ——

7. C   T: What did you have for lunch yesterday?   S: I had (a hamburger and a cup of coffee).
        What are your plans for the weekend?   I (might go to Washington or New York).
        What is your opinion of (Pittsburgh)?   (It's an exciting city but not very clean.)
        What courses are you going to take next term?
        When are you going to call your friend?
        What was the weather like in ( ) last month?
        What countries are your friends from?
        What is (capital of country) like?
        Who are your favorite movie actors? actresses?
        What are your favorite songs?
        Have you seen the movies ( ) and ( )?
        How do you like your coffee/steak/hamburger?

SUMMARY DIALOGUE

Bill: Did you have a good time in Chicago last week?

Chen: It was interesting, but not exciting.

Bill: Why do you say that?

Chen: I bought lots of film and a new camera in order to have lots of pictures. But the weather was terrible. I didn't take one picture.

Bill: Too bad.

Chen: And I've always heard there's lots of excitement in Chicago. I didn't see one murder or robbery.

Bill: It's just as well you didn't. But anyway, you shouldn't believe all those stories about the 1920s. That was a long time ago.

NOTES

LESSON SIXTEEN

INTRODUCTION   Good Luck/Bad Luck

There is an exam today in biology class. Bill, who is waiting for Nancy and Carlos before class, is getting nervous.

Bill: Hurry up!

Carlos: What a terrible day!

5   Bill: What happened?

Nancy: We'll tell you after class. Did you bring the book *that we need for* the exam?

Bill: Yes, but I almost forgot it. I didn't think of it *until an hour ago.*

Nancy: That sounds like our luck today. Cross your fingers that the test isn't too hard.

(after the class)

10   Bill: Well, what did you think?

Nancy: I think it was easy enough—knock on wood—but the guy sitting in front of me was having a terrible time.

Carlos: What was he doing?

Nancy: Well, first he asked the date. I told him it was the 13th and he muttered something
15   about bad luck that I didn't hear. In the middle of the exam, his pen ran out of ink. He asked several people and finally found someone *who had an extra pencil.* About ten minutes later, the point broke. It was funny, but how can you laugh at someone who has such a hard time?

Carlos: There's a man *whose luck was bad,* but it can't beat our bad luck.

20   Bill: O.K., O.K. Who's going to tell me about it?

Carlos: Nancy is the one who isn't superstitious; she'll tell you.

Nancy: It has nothing to do with luck. People who believe in good luck charms and all that are silly.

Carlos: We were coming down Forbes Avenue in the car I just bought. A black cat ran across
25   in front of us and Nancy—who's just said she didn't believe in luck—screamed. I slammed on the brakes and the car that was behind us didn't stop soon enough. After all the forms and red tape, we had to drive very fast. I almost hit a man who was walking in the street to avoid going under a ladder.

30   Bill: (Laughing) You'll need a few four leaf clovers and a couple of horseshoes to help you
        now. Say, Nancy, I know a lady whose reputation as a fortune teller is very good. Shall I
        get you an appointment?

      Nancy: Oh, be quiet. That's enough.

OUTLINE OF PATTERNS   Example

Section One   Relative Clauses

    Part A.   Subject   ... someone who had an extra pencil. . .
    Part B.   Object   ... that we need for the exams . . .
    Part C.   Possessive   ... whose luck was bad . . .

Section Two   *Before/after/until* + Time phrase   ... after class

Section Three   *Too/enough*

    Part A.   *too*
        Adjective/adverb modification   The exam wasn't too hard.
        Noun modification   She has too many charms.
    Part B.   *enough*
        Adjective/adverb modification   The exam was easy enough.
        Noun modification   He didn't have enough time.

NOTE: Line 19:   *whose luck* = Possessive
         Line 20:   *Who's going to . . .* = *going to* future (Who is)
         Line 25:   *who's just said . . .* = Present Perfect (who has)

COMPREHENSION QUESTIONS

1. Which class is having an exam?

2. Who is Bill waiting for?

3. Why does Bill say "hurry up"?

4. When are they going to tell him what happened?

5. What did Bill almost forget?

6. When did Bill think of the book?

*7. What does Nancy hope about the exam?

8. What did the person in front of Nancy ask?

9. When did his pen run out of ink?

10. What happened ten minutes later?

*11. Why did Nancy want to laugh? Did she? Why not?

12. What does Nancy say about superstitious people?

13. Which street were Nancy and Carlos on?

14. Who screamed? Why?

15. What did Carlos do?

*16. What did the man behind them do?

*17. Why did they have to drive fast?

18. Whom did Carlos almost hit?

*19. What does Bill say they need? Why? Why does he offer to get Nancy an appointment with the fortune teller?

*20. According to the Introduction, what things are "bad" luck; "good"?

*21. Discussion of other items of luck in the U.S. and other countries:

Examples:	crossing one's fingers	four-leaf clovers
	stepping on a crack	horseshoes
	the number 7	lovers and daisies
	breaking a mirror	spilling salt
	Friday the 13th	knocking on wood
	black cats	a rabbit's foot
	walking under ladders	a wishbone

Vocabulary

Nouns		Verbs	Adjectives
appliance	middle	avoid	bitter
appointment	opponent	beat	extra
brakes	paperback	believe	funny
charm (lucky)	point (of a pencil)	boycott	nervous
coffee break	red tape	cry	silly
conscience	reputation	envy	spicy
energy	rip	fire	superstitious
evidence	speed trap	hire	
fortune teller	stereo	hitchhike	Adverbs
guy		run (manage)	legibly
hardware store		run into	clearly
insurance		run out of	
ladder		scream	
light pole		slam	
luck		suggest	

SECTION ONE

RELATIVE CLAUSES

Part A.   *Subject*

Model: The man who was sitting in front of me was having a terrible time.

1. M1   Rep: I know the man who ran into your car.
   Sub: she   S: She knows the man who ran into your car.
          found a hundred dollars   She knows the man who found a hundred dollars.
          we   We know the man who found a hundred dollars.

(exercise continued on next page)

runs the bank	We know the man who runs the bank.
they	They know the man who runs the bank.
directs the Institute	They know the man who directs the Institute.
he	He knows the man who directs the Institute.
is going to be President	He knows the man who is going to be President.

2. M1   Rep: I know a man who believes in superstitions.

Sub:		S:	
woman—talks to plants			I know a woman who talks to plants.
student—has a good luck charm			I know a student who has a good luck charm.
professor—never remembers anything			I know a professor who never remembers anything.
doctor—can write legibly			I know a doctor who can write legibly.
lawyer—writes understandably			I know a lawyer who writes understandably.
politician—tells the people the truth			I know a politician who tells the people the truth.
educator—speaks clearly			I know an educator who speaks clearly.
linguist—writes understandably			I know a linguist who writes understandably.

3. M1   Rep: I don't know anyone who has driven a Rolls-Royce.

Sub:		S:	
know—write a novel			I know someone who has written a novel.
don't believe—always tell lies			I don't believe anyone who has always told lies.
like—help others			I like someone who has helped others.
don't know—win a Nobel Prize			I don't know anyone who has won a Nobel Prize.
don't like—kill birds			I don't like anyone who has killed birds.
believe—follow his conscience			I believe someone who has followed his conscience.
don't know—buy a Rolls-Royce			I don't know anyone who has bought a Rolls-Royce.

4. M1   Rep: The boy who is coming is my brother.

Sub:		S:	
boys			The boys who are coming are my brothers.
girl			The girl who is coming is my sister.
girls			The girls who are coming are my sisters.
woman			The woman who is coming is my sister.
man			The man who is coming is my brother.
women			The women who are coming are my sisters.
men			The men who are coming are my brothers.

GENERALIZATION

Pattern — Lesson Six: The man *with the red shirt*   is John.
Pattern — Lesson Sixteen: The man *who has problems*   is John.

In earlier lessons, a noun was modified by a *phrase* following it. In this pattern there is a *clause* which modifies the noun. (A clause has a subject and a verb.) The *subject* of the clause refers to a word in the main sentence.

Example: *The boy* is in my class. The *boy* speaks slowly.
        The boy *who* speaks slowly is in my class.

        I spoke to *the boy*. *He* speaks slowly.
        I spoke to the boy *who* speaks slowly.

The examples above are "relative clauses." The words *who, which* and *that* are relative pronouns. *Who* (and sometimes *that*) refer to people; *which* and *that* refer to things.

---

5. M1T   T: What's a cigarette lighter? (gadget)   S: It's a gadget that lights cigarettes.

What's a dish washer? (machine)   It's a machine that washes dishes.

What's a pencil sharpener? (device)   It's a device that sharpens pencils.

What's a can opener? (machine)   It's a machine that opens cans.

What's a letter opener? (gadget)   It's a gadget that opens letters.

What's a hair dryer? (machine)   It's a machine that dries hair.

What's a clothes dryer? (machine)   It's a machine that dries clothes.

6. M1T   Give a definition.

T: What's a bank robber?   S: A bank robber is a person who robs banks.

What's a fortune teller?   A fortune teller is a person who tells fortunes.

What's a newspaper publisher?   A newspaper publisher is a person who publishes newspapers.

What's an English teacher?   An English teacher is a person who teaches English.

What's a student advisor?   A student advisor is a person who advises students.

What's a mind reader?   A mind reader is a person who reads minds.

What's a bank manager?   A bank manager is a person who manages banks.

What's a magazine publisher?   A magazine publisher is a person who publishes magazines.

7. M1T   T: Do you know any superstitious people?   S: Do you know any people who are superstitious?

Do you like exciting stories?   Do you like stories which are exciting?

Does the store have any cheap paperbacks?   Does the store have any paperbacks which are cheap?

Do you have any lucky charms?   Do you have any charms which are lucky?

Do you know any famous people?   Do you know any people who are famous?

Does your country have any women politicians?   Does your country have any politicians who are women?

Are there any nervous people in this class?   Are there any people in this class who are nervous?

Will you meet any important politicians?   Will you meet any politicians who are important?

8. M1T   T: Some people won't discuss politics. I don't understand them.   S: I don't understand people who won't discuss politics.

Some planes can carry a couple of hundred people. I've never flown in one.   I've never flown in a plane which can carry a couple of hundred people.

Some people won't listen to others. I don't understand them.   I don't understand people who won't listen to others.

Some people like computers. I don't understand those people.   I don't understand those people who like computers.

My friend is going to travel around the world. I envy him.   I envy my friend who is going to travel around the world.

Some leaders are wise and humorous. People usually prefer them.   People usually prefer leaders who are wise and humorous.

Some machines can make 2400 copies an hour. I've never seen one.   I've never seen a machine which can make 2400 copies an hour.

(exercise continued on next page)

	T:	Some secretaries can type 110 words a minute. I'm amazed at them.	S:	I'm amazed at secretaries who can type 110 words a minute.

T: Some secretaries can type 110 words a minute. I'm amazed at them.   S: I'm amazed at secretaries who can type 110 words a minute.

Some motorcycles can go 120 mph. I've never ridden one.   I've never ridden a motorcycle which can go 120 mph.

Some cars cost $10,000. I've never seen one.   I've never seen a car which costs $10,000.

9. M1T

T: The man broke his leg. He's in my class.   S: The man who broke his leg is in my class.

The women are studying computer science. They're waiting to see the professor.   The women who are studying computer science are waiting to see the professor.

The man came to dinner. He stayed for three weeks.   The man who came to dinner stayed for three weeks.

The vase was very valuable. It fell and broke into a million pieces.   The vase that/which was very valuable fell and broke into a million pieces.

The dog bit the little boy. The dog didn't have rabies.   The dog that bit the little boy didn't have rabies.

The cars were out of gas. They were VWs.   The cars that were out of gas were VWs.

The man was walking under a ladder. He hit his head.   The man who was walking under a ladder hit his head.

The lady tells fortunes. She lives down the street.   The lady who tells fortunes lives down the street.

The books have just come. They're on the table.   The books which have just come are on the table.

The architect built the cathedral. He began at the top.   The architect who built the cathedral began at the top.

10. M2

T: I don't understand people ——   S: I don't understand people (who hurt others).

Machines —— are strange.   Machines (which can go to the moon) are strange.

People —— are silly.

I've never seen a city ——.

Famous men —— are dangerous.

I went to a country ——.

Things —— are expensive.

I never knew a man ——.

Yesterday Carlos almost had an accident ——.

Nancy talked to the man ——.

The little car —— doesn't increase pollution.

The man —— ran out of ink.

Where's the new book ——?

The TV programs —— are stupid.

11. M2

T: strange people   S1: (Do you know any people who seem strange?)

S2: Strange people? (Yes, I know a man who is superstitious about everything.)

exciting stories   S1: (Have you heard any stories which are exciting?)

S2: Exciting stories? (Yes, I know one which is popular in my country.)

interesting news   S1: (Is there any news that sounds interesting?)

S2: Interesting news? (Yes. There's a story about a man who broke all the computers in his office.)

(exercise continued on next page)

T: fascinating women
       honest politicians
       frightening experience
       terrible dream
       horrible day
       silly thing
       reckless drivers
       shrewd politicians
       strange machines

12. C   T: What kind of classes do you like?   S: (I like classes which are lively and interesting.)
                What kind of people do you like?   (I like people who are friendly and helpful.)
                What kind of food do you like?
                What kind of records do you like?
                What kind of music does your friend (wife) (husband) like?
                What kind of novels do you think ( ) likes?
                What kind of movies are popular in your country?
                What kind of leaders do you prefer?
                What kind of cars are popular in your country?
                What kind of politicians do you prefer?
                What kind of food do you like to have at parties?
                What kind of actors are popular in your country?
                What styles of clothes are popular for girls?

Part B.   *Object*

Model: Did you bring the book that we need for the exam?

1. M1   Rep: Did you bring the book that we need for the exam?
           Sub: test   S: Did you bring the book that we need for the test?
                  pens   Did you bring the pens that we need for the test?
                  buy   Did you buy the pens that we need for the test?
                  quiz   Did you buy the pens that we need for the quiz?
                  pencils   Did you buy the pencils that we need for the quiz?
                  get   Did you get the pencils that we need for the quiz?

2. M1   Rep: He muttered something about luck which I didn't hear.
           Sub: said   S: He said something about luck which I didn't hear.
                  bad luck   He said something about bad luck which I didn't hear.
                  understand   He said something about bad luck which I didn't understand.
                  answered   He answered something about bad luck which I didn't understand.
                  superstitions   He answered something about superstitions which I didn't
                                            understand.
                  believe   He answered something about superstitions which I didn't believe.
                  discussed   He discussed something about superstitions which I didn't believe.
                  politics   He discussed something about politics which I didn't believe.
                  agree with   He discussed something about politics which I didn't agree with.

GENERALIZATION

In this pattern, the *object* of the clause refers to a word in the main sentence:

Did you bring *the book?* We need *it* for the exam.
Did you bring the book *which* we need for the exam?

Do you know *the man?* I called *him.*
Do you know the man *whom* I called?

In speech the relative pronouns of this pattern are frequently omitted:

Did you bring the book we need for the test?
Mr. Jones is the man we elected.

---

3. M1   Rep: Mr. Jones is the man we elected.
         Sub: called   S: Mr. Jones is the man we called.
              visited   Mr. Jones is the man we visited.
              fired   Mr. Jones is the man we fired.
              saw   Mr. Jones is the man we saw.
              hired   Mr. Jones is the man we hired.
              suggested   Mr. Jones is the man we suggested.
              invited   Mr. Jones is the man we invited.

4. M1   T: He's the man whom I met.   S: He's the man I met.
              It's the book that I need.   It's the book I need.
              He said something which I didn't believe.   He said something I didn't believe.
              They're the papers which I need.   They're the papers I need.
              He's the man whom she introduced.   He's the man she introduced.
              We're the people whom you sent for.   We're the people you sent for.
              Is this the paperback which you bought?   Is this the paperback you bought?
              Where are the cigarettes which I bought?   Where are the cigarettes I bought?

***5. M1T T: I've called the man. We invited him   S: I've called the man (that/whom) we invited
                 to dinner.   to dinner.
              Have you seen the new students? We   Have you seen the new students (that/whom)
                 met them at the party.   we met at the party?
              I can't find the charm bracelet. I need   I can't find the charm bracelet (that/which)
                 it for the trip.   I need for the trip.
              I bought the new car. Mr. Hastings   I bought the new car (that/which) Mr. Hastings
                 recommended it.   recommended.
              Carlos bought the new camera. He read   Carlos bought the new camera which he read
                 about it in the paper.   about in the paper.
              The student lives on Atwood Street.   The student (that/whom) I met last week lives
                 I met him last week.   on Atwood Street.
              We're invited to a party. It's next week.   The party (that/which) we're invited to is
                                                             next week.
              The pictures are very good. I took them   The pictures (that/which) I took in Washington,
                 in Washington, D.C.   D.C. are very good.
              Do you ever see the politician? We met   Do you ever see the politician (that/whom) we
                 him last year.   met last year?

(exercise continued on next page)

		T:	The lectures have been interesting.	S:	The lectures (that/which) you told me about
			You told me about them last month.		last month have been interesting.

6. M2   T: The politicians did a lot of things.   S: (Yes, I know the things (that) they did.)
(Yes, but I don't understand the things (that) they did.) (Yes, and I don't like the things (that) they did.)

Picasso painted a lot of pictures.
She invited some students to the party.
She introduced me to someone.
She bought a new book.
The President made a lot of speeches.
They brought someone to the party.
The teacher made a lot of mistakes.
The students invited someone to their party.
He met someone at the Student Union.
Hemingway wrote a lot of books.

7. M2   T: A man whom —— invited us to dinner. S: A man whom (I met yesterday) invited us
to dinner.

I once met a man whom ——.
The man whom —— gave us the information.
It's politics in the U.S. that ——.
Do you know the man whom ——?
What do you think about people that ——?
Have you read the book that ——?

8. C   T: Did you like the food when you came here?   S: (No. The food that I had then
was terrible.)

Do teenagers in ( ) like the same things you did?   (The things that we liked are very
different.) (I don't understand
the things they like.)

Do your parents like the same kind of movies as you do?
Is the popular music here the same as in your country?
What kind of music do you have at parties in ( )?
Do the students in ( ) wear clothes like the students here?
Are the games that students play in your country the same as here?
What is the difference between sports in the U.S. and in ( )?
What kind of industry are people developing in ( )?
What social issues are people most concerned about in ( )?
What economic issues are students discussing in the universities?

Part C.   *Possessive*

Model: There's a man whose luck was worse than ours.

1. M1   Rep: There's the man whose luck was bad.
         Sub: reputation is bad   S: There's the man whose reputation is bad.
              friend knows my brother   There's the man whose friend knows my brother.
              car was smashed in the   There's the man whose car was smashed in the accident.
                  accident

(exercise continued on next page)

	T:	S:
	brother is in my class	There's the man whose brother is in my class.
	leg was broken in the game	There's the man whose leg was broken in the game.
	father is the president of a large corporation	There's the man whose father is the president of a large corporation.
	house was robbed last week	There's the man whose house was robbed last week.

2. M1   Rep: The man whose car was in the accident lives on our street.

	Sub:	S:
	friend we're going to meet	The man whose friend we're going to meet lives on our street.
	sister became president	The man whose sister became president lives on our street.
	house was robbed	The man whose house was robbed lives on our street.
	book has recently been published	The man whose book has recently been published lives on our street.
	children hitchhiked around the world	The man whose children hitchhiked around the world lives on our street.
	wife is a leader in Women's Liberation	The man whose wife is a leader in Women's Liberation lives on our street.

GENERALIZATION

In this pattern an item in the relative clause is related to an item in the main clause by a possessive relationship. The item in the main clause may be the subject or the object.

I remember *the man. His son* won the game.
I remember the man *whose* son won the game.

The man is in my class. *His son* won the game.
The man *whose* son won the game is in my class.

The relative pronoun *whose* usually refers to people, but it can be used with nations, cities and some institutions. (The U.S. is the country whose astronauts were first on the moon.)

---

3. M1T   T:

	T:	S:
	I know the man. His father won the Nobel Prize.	I know the man whose father won the Nobel Prize.
	The man lives on our street. His car caused the accident.	The man whose car caused the accident lives on our street.
	The lady didn't come to class. Her car hit a bus.	The lady whose car hit a bus didn't come to class.
	Podunk is a city. Its population is very poor.	Podunk is a city whose population is very poor.
	I know the man. His daughter is a professor at ( ).	I know the man whose daughter is a professor at ( ).
	I can't remember the people. Their family came from Los Angeles.	I can't remember the people whose family came from Los Angeles.
	The actress' movies are lousy. She's very popular.	The actress whose movies are lousy is very popular.
	Some students called me. I can't pronounce their names.	Some students whose names I can't pronounce called me.

***4. M2   T: I know the men whose ——.   S: I know the men whose (daughters became movie
                                                      stars).

           The man whose —— came to   The man whose (son landed on the moon) came
             town yesterday.   to town yesterday.

           I can't remember the name of the man whose ——.
           The people whose —— had bad luck.
           The President announced the appointment of the man whose ——.
           The students whose —— went to the party.
           I don't understand people whose ——.
           Mr. Johnson whose —— is an opponent of Women's Liberation.
           ( ) is an actress whose ——.
           ( ) is an actor whose ——.
           The leader whose —— is Dixon.
           (Pablo Picasso) is the artist whose ——.
           (Stravinsky) is the composer whose ——.

***5. M2   T: I know the man ——.   S: I know the man (that/whom you introduced) (whose son
                                                      is in the Peace Corps) (who is the actor on TV).

           Where is the restaurant ——.   Where is the restaurant (that Mr. Hastings owns) (which
                                                     serves Japanese food)?

           I've never seen a city ——.
           Do you know the men ——?
           People —— are silly.
           Have you met the students ——?
           The ladies —— left yesterday.
           I want a new car ——.
           The man —— was foolish.
           Politics —— are interesting.
           I don't know anyone ——.
           Books —— are dull.

***6. C   T: Do you know anyone who has a strange occupation?   S: (I know a man (who is a
                                                                          clown) (whose job is
                                                                          telling fortunes).

           What is the strangest thing you can think of?   (A house that doesn't have
                                                                        a roof.) (A car which doesn't
                                                                        increase pollution.) (A man
                                                                        who understands his wife.)

           What kind of person do you admire?
           Have you ever been to a university which has a larger campus?
           Have you ever seen a city where the pollution is worse than here?
           What kind of movies do you enjoy?
           What kind of professors do you like?
           What kind of cars do you like?
           What kind of houses do you prefer?
           What kind of men are admired in your country?
           What kind of actors are popular in your country?

***7. C   T: You met someone last week   S1:   (Do you remember the man we met last week?)
                   whose name you can't remember.   S2:   (The man who was at the party?)
                                                       S1:   (Yes. What was his name?)
                                                       S2:   (I don't remember. He's the one who was signing
                                                              autographs.)
                                                       S1:   (Yes. The tall man who spoke with a New England
                                                              accent.)

SECTION TWO

BEFORE/AFTER/UNTIL + TIME PHRASE

Model: Bill is waiting for Nancy and Carlos before class.
         I forgot it until an hour ago.
         We'll tell you after class.

1. M1   Rep: Bill is waiting for Nancy and Carlos before class.
           Sub: Jane   S: Jane is waiting for Nancy and Carlos before class.
                talking to   Jane is talking to Nancy and Carlos before class.
                George and Alice   Jane is talking to George and Alice before class.
                the lecture   Jane is talking to George and Alice before the lecture.
                we   We are talking to George and Alice before the lecture.
                listening to   We are listening to George and Alice before the lecture.
                Frank and Jane   We are listening to Frank and Jane before the lecture.

2. M1   Rep: We'll tell you after class.
           Sub: school   S: We'll tell you after school.
                three o'clock   We'll tell you after three o'clock.
                the vacation   We'll tell you after the vacation.
                April 15th   We'll tell you after April 15th.
                the test   We'll tell you after the test.
                taking the test   We'll tell you after taking the test.

3. M1   Rep: I forgot the book until an hour ago.
           Sub: knew the answer—a minute ago   S: I knew the answer until a minute ago.
                had the paper—last week   I had the paper until last week.
                will be in Paris—May   I will be in Paris until May.
                will be here—2 months from now   I will be here until 2 months from now.
                was in London—1965   I was in London until 1965.
                will study—midnight   I will study until midnight.
                remembered the address—two seconds ago   I remembered the address until two seconds ago.

GENERALIZATION

When will you be in London?   *Before* June.
                                       After New Year's.

How long will you be in London?   *Until* March 12.

The difference in these prepositions is mainly in the questions they answer. The answers
will usually be *points* of time.

---

4. M1T   T: 3 months   S: for 3 months
                Monday   until Monday
                1978   until 1978
                2 hours   for two hours
                10 minutes   for ten minutes
                1865   until 1865
                an hour   for an hour
                the end of the term   until the end of the term

5. M2   T: before June   S1:   When (will he leave the city)?
                                        S2:   He'll leave before June.

                until January   S1:   How long (is he going to study)?
                                        S2:   He's going to study until January.

                after lunch
                until noon
                before the lecture
                after the exam
                until next term
                after dinner
                before midnight
                until the vacation
                after 1972
                before 1965
                until 2000

6. C   T: Ask ( ) how long he was in   S1:   How long were you in the U.S. before the beginning
                   the U.S. before the   of the term?
                   beginning of the term.   S2:   (For 2 days.)
                Ask ( ) if he came here during S1: Did you come here during the fall?
                   the fall.   S2:   (No, I came during the winter.) In the spring.)
                Ask ( ) what he thought of   S1:   What did you think of the weather?
                   the weather.   S2:   (I thought the weather was terrible.) (Until spring
                                                    the weather was terrible.)

                Ask ( ) how long he'll be studying here.
                Ask ( ) when he began his study here.
                Ask ( ) when he left home.
                Ask ( ) how long he was out of his country the first time.
                Ask ( ) how long he studied English before this term.
                Ask ( ) when he left his country.
                Ask ( ) how long he'll be without a car.
                Ask ( ) how long he was here without his family.

7. C   T: How long will you stay here?   S: (For 3 months.) (Until June.)
                Did you visit any other cities before coming here? Which ones? How long did you stay?
                Where will you go after this term?
                What will you study after the English class?
                Where did you go after you left your country?
                How long do you plan to stay in the U.S.?
                How long will you keep your apartment?
                Are you going to take a trip after this term?
                What are you going to do before the next exam?
                How long did you stay in ( )?
                              (exercise continued on next page)

335

T: Have you ever been to ( )? When? How long did you stay?
     What are your plans after your graduation?
     How long will you live in your (hotel)(apartment)?
     How long are you going to study English?

SECTION THREE

TOO/ENOUGH

Part A.   *Too*

☐ ADVERB/ADJECTIVE MODIFICATION

Model: The exam wasn't too hard.
         The man drove too fast.

GENERALIZATION

Too is an adverb—it modifies an adjective or an adverb—and indicates an excess. It precedes the adjective or adverb.

---

1. M1   T: I can't eat this food.
         Rep: It's too hot.
         Sub: salty   S: It's too salty.
              cold   It's too cold.
              sweet   It's too sweet.
              spicy   It's too spicy.
              bitter   It's too bitter.

2. M1   T: Nancy won't ride with Jack.
         Rep: He drives too fast.
         Sub: recklessly   S: He drives too recklessly.
              carelessly   He drives too carelessly.
              slowly   He drives too slowly.
              cautiously   He drives too cautiously.
              fast   He drives too fast.
              recklessly   He drives too recklessly.

3. M1   T: This apartment is just right.
         Rep: It isn't too big.
         Sub: small   S: It isn't too small.
              crowded   It isn't too crowded.
              far from the university   It isn't too far from the university.
              noisy   It isn't too noisy.
              expensive   It isn't too expensive.
              old   It isn't too old.

4. M1T   T: The box is heavy. We can't lift it.   S: The box is too heavy.
                The man is dangerous. He drives fast.   The man drives too fast.
                The book is difficult. They can't read it.   The book is too difficult.
                The train is late. It goes slow.   The train goes too slow.
                The students were busy. We didn't see   The students were too busy.
                   them.
                Mr. Jones was late. He missed the lecture.   Mr. Jones was too late.
                We've been tired. We haven't gone to   We've been too tired.
                   the movies.

5. M2   T: Mr. Jackson doesn't like VWs.   S1:   Why not?
                                                           S2:   (Maybe because they're too small.)
                Chen doesn't like American coffee.   S1:   Why not?
                                                           S2:   (Maybe because it's too strong.)
                Mrs. Hastings doesn't like to teach high school.
                Nancy doesn't like to ride on the bus.
                Bill doesn't like English class.
                Carlos doesn't like American meat.
                Jane doesn't like computers.
                Chen can't understand American politics.
                Mr. Hastings doesn't like cities.
                Nancy can't rent the big apartment.
                Bill didn't pass the exam.
                Carlos won't go to New York this weekend.

***6. M2   (Picture Cue)
            Mr. Jackson wears a size 40 jacket with 33 inch sleeves. He likes plain dark colors. What
               will he say when the salesman shows him these suits?
            S1:   (That one is too small.)
            S2:   (This one is the right size, but it's too light.)
                  etc.

7. C   T: Tell us something you don't like and why. S: (I don't like the coffee here. It's too
                                                                 strong.)

□ NOUN MODIFICATION

Model: She has too many good luck charms.
         They have too much work.

8. M1T   Rep: I have too many appointments.
          Sub: sugar   S: I have too much sugar.
                money   I have too much money.
                assignments   I have too many assignments.
                iced tea   I have too much iced tea.
                papers   I have too many papers.
                students   I have too many students.
                advice   I have too much advice.

GENERALIZATION

Too in these expressions means the same as above, an excess, and to modify nouns *too* precedes *much* or *many.*

Why do we use *much* and *many?*	((There are different kinds of nouns.))
What kind of nouns use *many?*	((Count.))
What kind of nouns use *much?*	((Non-count.))

***9. M2   T: The coffee tastes awful. (sugar)   S1:   What's the matter with it?
                                                            S2:   (It has too much sugar.)

            The air here is terrible. (pollution)   S1:   What's the matter with it?
                                                            S2:   (There's too much pollution.)

            The party wasn't much fun. (people) S1:   What was the matter with it?
                                                            S2:   (There were too many people.)

            The meat was terrible. (salt)
            The television program wasn't very good. (commercials)
            The computer course is bad. (assignments)
            The man didn't drive very well. (beer)
            The students didn't get good grades. (parties)
            The student failed the test. (mistakes)
            The lunch wasn't good. (people)
            The class wasn't interesting. (drills)
            The movie wasn't good. (murders)

Part B.   *Enough*

☐ AJECTIVE/ADVERB MODIFICATION

Model: The exam was easy enough.
          He drives carefully enough.

GENERALIZATION

Enough, like *too,* is an adverb, but it differs in meaning and position in the sentence. In an affirmative statement *too* indicates an excess, *enough* a sufficiency. *Enough* follows the adjective or adverb.

Example:	The suit is the right size.	It's big enough.
	John drives safely.	***He drives well enough.

---

1. M1   T: I'm going to rent this apartment because it's O.K.
          Rep: It's big enough.
          Sub: cheap   S: It's cheap enough.
               quiet   It's quiet enough.
               comfortable   It's comfortable enough.
               inexpensive   It's inexpensive enough.
               large   It's large enough.
               convenient   It's convenient enough.

2. M1   T: I like to ride with Charlie. He's a good driver.

          Rep: He drives carefully enough.

Sub:		S:	
	slowly		He drives slowly enough.
	safely		He drives safely enough.
	fast		He drives fast enough.
	cautiously		He drives cautiously enough.
	carefully		He drives carefully enough.
	slowly		He drives slowly enough.

3. M1T   T:

	S:	
The man is strong. He can lift the box.		The man is strong enough.
The man is tall. He can reach the ceiling.		The man is tall enough.
The town was small. We were able to visit everyone.		The town was small enough.
The assignments were short. I could finish them.		The assignments were short enough.
The car is small. I can drive it.		The car is small enough.
The clothes were dry. We wore them.		The clothes were dry enough.
Mr. Jones came early. He saw the whole game.		Mr. Jones came early enough.
Bill drove fast. He arrived on time.		He drove fast enough.
Chen spoke well. He won the debate.		Chen spoke well enough.

***4. M2   (Picture Cue)

    Mrs. Hastings wears a size 12 dress of knee length and she likes dresses with long sleeves and pleated or wide skirts. What will she say to the dresses the clerk shows her?

    S1:   (That one isn't large enough.)

    S2:   (That one is the right size. But it's not long enough.)

         etc.

☐ NOUN MODIFICATION

Model: He didn't have enough time.

         She won't have money enough.

1. M1   Rep: We have enough time to go to the movies.

Sub:		S:	
	money—concert		We have enough money to go to the concert.
	people—zoo		We have enough people to go to the zoo.
	time—Student Union		We have enough time to go to the Student Union.
	cash—night club		We have enough cash to go to the night club.
	people—game		We have enough people to go to the game.
	insurance—city		We have enough insurance to go to the city.
	energy—party		We have enough energy to go to the party.

2. M1   T:

	S:	
We don't have enough time.		We don't have time enough.
They haven't had enough exercise.		They haven't had exercise enough.
We don't get enough practice.		We don't get practice enough.
The lawyer has enough evidence.		The lawyer has evidence enough.
The boys will buy enough beer.		The boys will buy beer enough.
There will be enough food.		There will be food enough.
Does your apartment have enough room?		Does your apartment have room enough?

GENERALIZATION

Enough is used with nouns in the same sense as above. It may precede or follow the noun.

    Example: We have enough money.
                  We have   money enough.

---

3. M2   T: money for the ticket   S: (We don't have enough money for the ticket.) (Will
                                                you have money enough for the ticket?)

                time for the test
                food for the party
                coins for the telephone
                dimes for the dryer
                change for the bus
                gas for the trip
                people for the class
                good luck charms for the test
                clothes for the vacation
                decorations for the dance
                money for the taxi
                energy for the game

4. M2   Explain the statements.
        T: He can't finish the test.   S: (He's not fast enough.) (It's too long.) (He doesn't
                                                write fast enough.)
            He can buy the car.   (It isn't too expensive.) (It's cheap enough.)
            Mrs. Casetti was on time for the movie.
            Jack bought the stereo.
            All of the students passed the test.
            None of the students went to the class.
            Mrs. Jackson didn't like the best-seller.
            The students boycotted the lecture.
            The plane was late.
            The team lost the baseball game.
            Everyone walked out of the movie.
            No one wanted the used car.
            The car hit the light pole.
            The little boy was crying.

5. C   T: Why didn't you go to the concert?   S: (I didn't have enough time.) (I didn't have
                                                  money enough.) (I was too busy.) (It
                                                  cost too much money.)
           Why didn't you finish the exam?
           Why don't you take a vacation?
           Are you going to buy a new car? (When? Why not?)
           Did you go to New York City last weekend? (Why? Why not?)
           How do you like your apartment? (Why?)
           What do you think of the weather here? (Why?)
           Are you superstitious? (What about? Why? Why not?)
           Are you going to study here after the English course? (Why? Why not?)
           What do you find most difficult here? (Why?)
                      (exercise continued on next page)

T: Is traveling in the U.S. difficult? (Why? Why not?)
        Is traveling in your country easy for foreigners? (Why? Why not?)
        Is communicating with Americans difficult? (Why? Why not?)

SUMMARY DIALOGUE

Carlos: Say Bill. Do you really think Nancy is superstitious?

Bill: No, I was just teasing her. Why?*

Carlos: She was so upset.

Bill: She was too nervous about the test.

Carlos: I don't know why.** She's the one who studied for three days.

Bill: Some people never feel they've studied enough.

  * *Why?* in this context means "Why do you ask?"
 ** *Why?* at the end of the phrase "I don't know . . ." refers to the previous statement. "I don't
      know why she was nervous."

SUMMARY OF PATTERNS

	Main Sentence		*Relative Clause*		
		Object	*Subject*	*Verb*	*Object/Completer*
A. Subject Focus	He found a man		who	had	an extra pencil.
	He found a book		that	was	interesting.
B. Object Focus	He found a man	whom	he	punched	in the nose.
	He found a restaurant	where	he	had	dinner.
	He found a book	which	he	read	on the plane.
	He found a time	when	he	was	alone.
C. Possessive Focus	He found a man	whose	son	is	8 feet tall.

NOTES

LESSON SEVENTEEN

INTRODUCTION   ***Baseball

Chen *has wanted to see* a professional baseball game for a long time, *but the tickets are expensive,* and he doesn't understand the rules very well. Finally, he got a ticket and now he is asking Bill and Nancy about some of the rules.

Chen: I have a ticket for the game tomorrow and I need to know the rules.

5   Bill: *I'd like to help* you, but some of the rules are different from last year.

Nancy: We could tell him the basic rules . . .

Bill: O.K. Tell us the ones you know, and then I'll try to explain the others, and *Nancy will help too.*

Chen: I know about the teams and "innings" and "outs" and "strikes" and "balls". How does
10   the umpire know whether the pitcher throws a "ball" or a "strike"?

Bill: The pitcher has to throw the ball over "home plate" between the batter's chest and his knees for a strike. *When he throws it any other place,* it's a ball.

Chen: O.K. Four "balls" and he "walks"; three strikes and he's "out". A "foul" counts as a strike except on the third one. When the batter hits the ball, he runs *until he is in danger of*
15   *being out.* When a runner goes around all the bases and crosses home plate, he scores a "run". At the end of nine innings, the team which has the most runs wins.

Bill: O.K. What else do you want to know?

Chen: When I listen to the radio, I hear terms I don't know. For instance, the third base coach. Who is he and what does he do?

20   Nancy: A coach stands near third base where the batter can see him. *Before the pitcher throws,* the batter looks at the coach who signals to the batter. Usually, the coach has studied the pitcher during many games. Sometimes there is a new pitcher that the batter doesn't know *and the coach doesn't either.*

Chen: How about the "on deck circle"?

25   Bill: *While one man is batting,* another waits in a small area near home plate. He's the next to bat and the announcers say that he is "on deck".

Chen: How does the pitcher know which pitch to throw?

Bill: The pitcher waits for a signal from the catcher. Sometimes they don't agree at first, but eventually they decide on a pitch.

30   Chen: What about the "bull pen"?

Nancy: Often a team needs a number of pitchers in one game. The "bullpen" is the area where the extra pitchers practice until they begin to pitch in the game. This practice while they wait is called "warming up".

35

Chen: The vocabulary is very complicated. I've never heard of a game with so many special terms. I hope to enjoy it, but now I'm not sure that I will.

Bill: Sure you will. Take your transistor radio and listen to the commentary. The announcer will explain *after they make every play.*

Chen: That's a good idea. Thanks to you both.

Bill: Forget it.

Nancy: Have a good time.

OUTLINE OF PATTERNS

Example

Section One	Subordinate Clauses	
Part A.	*before/after/until*	Before the pitcher throws . . . . . . after they make every play. . . . until he is out of danger.
Part B.	*while*	While one man is batting . . .
Part C.	*when/where*	. . . when the batter hits. . . . where the batter can see him.
Section Two	Conjunctions	
Part A.	*and . . . too/and . . . either/but*	. . . and Nancy will help too. . . . and the coach doesn't either. . . . but eventually they do.
Part B.	Alternate Expressions	. . . so do I. . . . neither do I.
Section Three	Modals *could/would*	
Part A.	*could* Past Ability Polite Request Possibility	 I could swim . . . Could you help me. . . Could you do it later . . .
Part B.	*would* Polite Request/Invitation Preference/Desire	 would you . . . I'd like to sit down . . . I'd rather have tea . . .
Section Four	Verb + *to* + verb	. . . wanted to see . . .
Section Five	Two-word Verbs (non-separable)	. . . look at . . .

COMPREHENSION QUESTIONS

1. What has Chen wanted to do for a long time?

*2. Why did he hesitate to buy a ticket?

3. What did he finally do?

4. What is he asking Bill and Nancy?

*5. Why is Bill reluctant to explain the rules?

*6. What does Nancy suggest?

7. What things does Chen know about?

8. Where does the pitcher have to throw the ball for a "strike"?

9. How many "balls" make a "walk"?

10. How many "strikes" make an "out"?

11. What does the batter do when he hits the ball?

12. How does a batter score a run?

13. Which team wins the game?

14. What does the batter do before each pitch? *Why?

*15. Who is in the "on deck" circle?

*16. How does the pitcher know which pitch to throw?

*17. What is the "bull pen"?

*18. Why does Chen think he might not enjoy the game?

*19. What is Bill's advice?

20. When do the announcers explain the plays?

*21. Is baseball popular in your country? What is the "national sport" of your country?

Vocabulary

Nouns		Verbs	Adjectives
announcer	pair	crash	application
commentary	play (of a game)	last (be functional)	basic
fan (a baseball fan)	porch	signal	extra
flute	rule		forced
fuel	scandal		professional
landing	scholarship		reluctant
lightening	ticket		transistor
omelette	Western (movie)		

Baseball Terms

ball	catcher	on deck	strike
base	coach	out	third base coach
batter	home plate	pitch	umpire
bull pen	inning	pitcher	warm up

SECTION ONE

SUBORDINATE CLAUSES

Part A.   *before/after/until*

Model: Before the pitcher throws, the batter looks at the coach.
         The announcer will explain after they make every play.
         He runs until he is in danger of being out.

1. M1   Rep: We spoke to them before the game began.
        Sub: after the game was over   S: We spoke to them after the game was over.
               before the game started   We spoke to them before the game started.
               after the game started   We spoke to them after the game started.
               before we spoke to you   We spoke to them before we spoke to you.
               after we spoke to him   We spoke to them after we spoke to him.
               before you saw us   We spoke to them before you saw us.
               after you came   We spoke to them after you came.

2. M1   Rep: We saw them often until they moved to San Francisco.
        Sub: they left town   S: We saw them often until they left town.
              we left town   We saw them often until we left town.
              they moved   We saw them often until they moved.
              we moved   We saw them often until we moved.
              they had to move   We saw them often until they had to move.
              we went to South America   We saw them often until we went to South America.

GENERALIZATION

Lesson Sixteen: When were you in Paris?   Before the war. After 1960.
                      How long were you in Paris? Until 1968.

Lesson Seventeen: When does the coach give the signal?   Before the pitcher throws . . .
                                                                After the batter strikes . . .
                      How long does the man run?   Until he is in danger . . .

In Lesson Sixteen, these words introduced a phrase. The meaning is the same here, but they introduced a clause. (Remember—a clause has a subject and a verb.)

Note: Simple present tense is used following these words when talking about future time:

                                       ⎧ before he comes.
                      I'll be here   ⎨ after he comes.
                                       ⎩ until he comes.

---

3. M1T   Rep: I'll see them before they leave.
         Sub: her   S: I'll see her before she leaves.
               graduates   I'll see her before she graduates.
               after   I'll see her after she graduates.
               him   I'll see him after he graduates.
               finishes the exam   I'll see him after he finishes the exam.
               before   I'll see him before he finishes the exam.
               you   I'll see you before you finish the exam.

4. M1T　T: They're leaving next week. We'll see　　　　S: We'll see them before they leave.
them before then.

They'll return from vacation next week. We'll　　　We'll see them after they return
see them after that.　　　　　　　　　　　　　from vacation.

They'll come back next week. We won't see them　　We won't see them until they
until then.　　　　　　　　　　　　　　　　come back.

He'll finish the term next month. I'll call him　　　I'll call him after he finishes the
after that.　　　　　　　　　　　　　　　　term.

He's going to Europe next week. I'll call him　　　I'll call him before he goes to
before that.　　　　　　　　　　　　　　　　Europe.

He'll finish his exams next week. I won't call　　　I won't call him until he finishes
him until then.　　　　　　　　　　　　　　his exams.

She'll be home from the hospital in two days.　　　We'll call her after she is home
We'll call after that.　　　　　　　　　　　　from the hospital.

They're going to come home next month. We　　　We won't see them until they come
won't see them until then.　　　　　　　　　home.

He's coming here in June. I'll write him before then.　I'll write him before he comes here.

She's going to sell her car. She'll ride with me after　She'll ride with me after she sells
that.　　　　　　　　　　　　　　　　　　her car.

They're leaving next week. I'll see them every day　　I'll see them every day until they
until then.　　　　　　　　　　　　　　　　leave.

He's going to graduate next month. He has to　　　He has to finish the paper before
finish the paper before that.　　　　　　　　he graduates.

The new term will begin in a couple of weeks.　　　Can you see me after the new term
Can you see me after that?　　　　　　　　　begins?

The professor will send the grades next week. We　　We won't know about the course
won't know about the course until then.　　　　until the professor sends the grades.

5. M2　T: I saw him frequently before ——.　　　　S: I saw him frequently before (we had an
　　　　　　　　　　　　　　　　　　　　argument).

I thought he was a good man after ——.　　　　I thought he was a good man after (he
　　　　　　　　　　　　　　　　　　　　negotiated the peace).

I spoke to him frequently until ——.　　　　　I spoke to him frequently until (he was
　　　　　　　　　　　　　　　　　　　　arrested for burglary).

We never spoke to them again after ——.
I always thought he was wealthy until ——.
He never had an accident until ——.
I'm going to Europe before ——.
We were going downtown after ——.
I'll finish the research paper before ——.
I never understood modern novels until ——.
We should report the accident before ——.
I'll take a long vacation after ——.
I always wanted a Rolls-Royce until ——.
She can't wait until ——.
It will be three days before ——.

6. C　T: What will you do until your money comes from home?　S: (Borrow from my friends.)
Where will you go after you finish this term?
What did you do before you came here?
When will you see your friends?

(exercise continued on next page)

347

T: Can you stay in your apartment/room until the next term begins?
      Did you see your university before you came to the English Language Institute?
      Did you have to buy furniture after you moved into your apartment?
      When will you go to the west coast?
      When will you see your family?
      When did you have to pay the application fees?
      When will you have time to take a vacation?
      When are you going to leave (city)?

Part B.   *While*

Model: While one man is batting, another waits "on deck".
         The practice while they wait is called "warm up".

1. M1   Rep: While we were having lunch, the phone rang.
           Sub: doing the dishes   S: While we were doing the dishes, the phone rang.
                feeding the baby   While we were feeding the baby, the phone rang.
                watching TV   While we were watching TV, the phone rang.
                reading the newspaper   While we were reading the newspaper, the phone rang.
                listening to the radio   While we were listening to the radio, the phone rang.
                watching the game   While we were watching the game, the phone rang.
                waiting for the mail   While we were waiting for the mail, the phone rang.

2. M1   Rep: The guests arrived while we were setting the table for lunch.
           Sub: the accident happened   S: The accident happened while we were setting the table for
                                              lunch.
                lightening struck   Lightening struck while we were setting the table for lunch.
                the roof fell in   The roof fell in while we were setting the table for lunch.
                the doorbell rang   The doorbell rang while we were setting the table for lunch.
                the cake in the oven burned The cake in the oven burned while we were setting the
                                             table for lunch.
                a car stopped in front of   A car stopped in front of the house while we were setting
                   the house   the table for lunch.

GENERALIZATION

The clause following *while* indicates a continuousness or duration of simultaneous
actions. Often (but not always) the verb following *while* is the Continuous (V -ing)
form. Use Present or Present Continuous to indicate actions in the future time.
(Drill 3 below.)

I'm going to listen to the game while you { read / are reading } the paper.

---

3. M1   Rep: I'm going to listen to the game while you read the paper.
           Sub: doing the dishes   S: I'm going to listen to the game while you're doing the
                                              dishes.
                take a nap   I'm going to listen to the game while you take a nap.
                        (exercise continued on next page)

T: go shopping	S: I'm going to listen to the game while you go shopping.
reading your book	I'm going to listen to the game while you're reading your book.
set the table	I'm going to listen to the game while you set the table.
finishing the cross-word puzzle	I'm going to listen to the game while you're finishing the cross-word puzzle.
do the laundry	I'm going to listen to the game while you do the laundry.

4. M1T   T:

T:	S:
I talked to him while he was on his coffee break.	I talked to him during his coffee break.
While he was on his vacation, he went to Paris.	During his vacation, he went to Paris.
While they were staying at the lake, Ralph hurt his finger.	During their stay at the lake, Ralph hurt his finger.
They'll see the Capitol while they tour the city.	They'll see the Capitol during their tour of the city.
Will you buy souvenirs while you visit Mexico?	Will you buy souvenirs during your visit to Mexico?
She didn't see much of Europe while she was on her vacation.	She didn't see much of Europe during her vacation.
While the children took their nap, the women discussed Women's Lib.	During the children's nap, the women discussed Women's Lib.

5. M2   T:

T:	S:
She fell during the party.	She fell while (we were at the party) (they were having a party) (she was on her way to the party).
She fell during the trip.	She fell while (we were on a trip) (she was taking a trip).
She fell during our vacation.	
She fell during my visit.	
She fell during the storm.	
She fell during the game.	
She fell during work.	
She fell during the voyage to Europe.	
She fell during the trip to the west coast.	
She fell during the flight to Chicago.	
She fell during their vacation in the Rockies.	
She fell during our stay in Paris.	

6. M2   T:

T:	S:
She called ——.	She called (while I was taking a shower).
I'm going to go shopping ——.	I'm going to go shopping (while you listen to the game).
He'll write the paper ——.	
We're going to discuss politics ——.	
Sit down for a minute ——.	
I found the old book ——.	
He'll go swimming ——.	
Have a good time ——.	
We met the Hastings ——.	
She broke her leg ——.	
I was listening to the game ——.	
What shall we do ——?	
Can you sit down ——?	
The Newtons arrived ——.	

7. C   T: Did anything unusual happen while you were   S: (I saw the Mayor.) (There was a big
          in (New York)?   parade while we were there.)
          What do you want to do while you're in (city)?
          What were you doing while your roommate was studying for exams?
          Did you ever lose your wallet? What did you do while you were looking for it?
          Did you ever have an accident? What did you do while you were waiting for the police?
          What do you usually do while you're waiting for a plane?
          What do you usually do while you're waiting for the results of an exam?
          Do you sing while you're taking a shower? In what language?
          What do you think about while you're driving a car?
          What do you usually do while you're on vacation?
          When do you read the morning paper?
          What do you do while you're riding on a bus?
          What do you do while you're waiting for an appointment?

Part C.   *when/where*

Model: The runner has to run when the batter hits.
            The coach stands where the batter can see him.

1. M1   Rep: John saw the game when he was in Chicago.
         Sub: Bill   S: Bill saw the game when he was in Chicago.
            went to   Bill went to the game when he was in Chicago.
            the theater   Bill went to the theater when he was in Chicago.
            New York   Bill went to the theater when he was in New York.
            attended   Bill attended the theater when he was in New York.
            the concert   Bill attended the concert when he was in New York.
            Boston   Bill attended the concert when he was in Boston.

2. M1   Rep: I told him where he could find his friend.
         Sub: get a good meal   S: I told him where he could get a good meal.
            get a bus   I told him where he could get a bus.
            make a phone call   I told him where he could make a phone call.
            get a bus schedule   I told him where he could get a bus schedule.
            cash a check   I told him where he could cash a check.
            mail a letter   I told him where he could mail a letter.
            get tickets for the game I told him where he could get tickets for the game.

3. M1   Rep: Will he come when he has time?
         Sub: a vacation   S: Will he come when he has a vacation?
            the money   Will he come when he has the money?
            a new car   Will he come when he has a new car?
            a free weekend   Will he come when he has a free weekend?
            a long vacation   Will he come when he has a long vacation?
            a few extra dollars   Will he come when he has a few extra dollars?
            a little time   Will he come when he has a little time?

GENERALIZATION

When introduces clauses referring to a time; *where* introduces clauses referring to a place. Do not confuse these with question words—the word order is the same as in statements.

Wh Question:	Where *can he* get tickets?
Clause:	I don't know where *he can* get tickets.

Use Present or Present Perfect tense following *when* to express future time:

He'll come when he *has* time.
He'll come when he *has written* the paper.

In contrast to *while* (duration of action), *when* usually refers to an action at a point of time.

While I was watching TV, the earthquake struck.
I was watching TV *when* the earthquake struck.

---

4. M1T T: While I was driving downtown, the storm began. S: I was driving downtown when the storm began.

While he was talking on the phone, the doorbell rang. / He was talking on the phone when the doorbell rang.

While we were studying, the police came. / We were studying when the police came.

While they were at the game, the burglar robbed the house. / They were at the game when the burglar robbed the house.

While you were mowing the lawn the salesman called. / You were mowing the lawn when the salesman called.

While she was taking a bath, the phone rang. / She was taking a bath when the phone rang.

While they were working, the President declared peace. / They were working when the President declared peace.

5. M1T T: It happened while I was watching the game. S: I was watching the game when it happened.

She broke her leg while she was skiing. / She was skiing when she broke her leg.

I had an accident while I was driving home from school. / I was driving home from school when I had an accident.

The child ran in front of the car while John was coming down the street. / John was coming down the street when the child ran in front of the car.

The boat sank while we were sailing down the river. / We were sailing down the river when the boat sank.

Jane lost all her money while she was traveling in Mexico. / She was traveling in Mexico when she lost all her money.

The plane made a forced landing while I was flying to Paris. / I was flying to Paris when the plane made a forced landing.

The house burned while they were visiting friends. / They were visiting friends when the house burned.

He won the prize while he was on vacation. / He was on vacation when he won the prize.

They forgot about work while they were in Florida. / When they were in Florida they forgot about work.

351

***6. M1T   T: The storm came. We went home then.   S: (When the storm came, we went home.)

(We went home when the storm came.)

They met him in New York. We left him there.   They met him in New York where we left him.

I found the book on the shelf. You left it there.

They arrived at 10:00. We left then.

She lost her money. She went home then.

The plane ran out of fuel. It crashed then.

The store will send the bill. I'll pay it then.

The men will come to this city. We'll see them then.

I'll put the book on the table. You can find it easily there.

We aren't welcome. We shouldn't go there.

I can go shopping this weekend. I'll have money then.

He'll get a good job next year. He graduates from the university then.

I'll meet you at Bimbo's. We can have lunch there.

7. M2   T: Where were you when ——?   S1:   Where were you when (the men landed on the moon)?

S2:   When the men landed on the moon, (I was in the TV room at the Student Union).

What do you usually do while ——?   S1:   What do you usually do while (you're waiting for a plane)?

S2:   While I'm waiting for a plane (I usually read a book).

What's the weather like where ——?   S1:   What's the weather like where (you come from)?

S2:   Where I come from (the weather is always warm).

What did you think of the U.S. when ——?

What are you going to do while ——?

What do you usually do while ——?

What was ( ) doing when ——?

What is the city like where ——?

What are the people like where ——?

What did you do while ——?

What will your friends do when ——?

What will your parents do when ——?

Who is going to help you when ——?

What are you going to do while ——?

What is the food like where ——?

***8. C   T: Imagine your favorite { place / time.   What's it like?   S: (It's a place where there is no pollution.)

(It's a time when there are no tests or homework or English classes.)

What were you doing when { the typhoon hit? / the men landed on the moon?

What were you doing/thinking while { the men were walking on the moon? / you were waiting for news of ( )?

What did you think/do when (peace was declared)?

etc.

SECTION TWO

CONJUNCTIONS

Part A.   *and . . . too*/*and . . . either*/*but*

Model: I'll try to explain, and Nancy will help too.
          The batter doesn't know the pitcher and the coach doesn't either.
          Sometimes they don't agree at first, but eventually they do.

1. M1   Rep: Bill can tell Chen the rules of baseball and Nancy can too.
                   Bill could tell Chen the rules of baseball and Nancy could too.
                   Bill is able to tell Chen the rules of baseball and Nancy is too.
                   Bill was able to tell Chen the rules of baseball and Nancy was too.
                   Bill is going to tell Chen the rules of baseball and Nancy is too.
                   Bill told Chen the rules of baseball and Nancy did too.
                   Bill was telling Chen the rules of baseball and Nancy was too.
                   Bill has told Chen the rules of baseball and Nancy has too.

2. M1   Rep: Carlos doesn't like baseball and Jane doesn't either.
                   Carlos didn't like baseball and Jane didn't either.
                   Carlos can't go to the game and Jane can't either.
                   Carlos shouldn't go to the game and Jane shouldn't either.

3. M1   Rep: They're going to the game, but Jack isn't.
                   They can't go to the game, but Jack can.
                   They'll go to the game, but Jack won't.
                   They didn't go to the game, but Jack did.
                   They've gone to the game, but Jack hasn't.
                   They might not go to the game, but Jack might.

GENERALIZATION

In these patterns there are two sentences:

Both sentences are Affirmative	John likes baseball. I like baseball.
	John likes baseball *and* I do *too.*
Both sentences are Negative	John doesn't like baseball. I don't like baseball.
	John doesn't like baseball *and* I don't *either.*
One is Affirmative, and One is Negative	John likes baseball. I don't like baseball.
	John likes baseball, *but* I don't.
	John doesn't like baseball. I like baseball.
	John doesn't like baseball, *but* I do.

Note that the short answer substitute verb (do, did, can't, etc.) is used in the second part of the sentence when both verbs are the same.

***4. M1T   Rep: Chen went to the games and Bill did too.
       Sub: is going   S: Chen is going to the games and Bill is too.
            can go   Chen can go to the games and Bill can too.
            will go   Chen will go to the games and Bill will too.
            could go   Chen could go to the games and Bill could too.
            goes   Chen goes to the games and Bill does too.
            has gone   Chen has gone to the games and Bill has too.

5. M1   Rep: Carlos doesn't like baseball and Jane doesn't either.
          Sub: didn't   S: Carlos didn't like baseball and Jane didn't either.
               won't   Carlos won't like baseball and Jane won't either.
               isn't going to   Carlos isn't going to like baseball and Jane isn't going to either.
               might not   Carlos might not like baseball and Jane might not either.
               may not   Carlos may not like baseball and Jane may not either.
               doesn't   Carlos doesn't like baseball and Jane doesn't either.

6. M1T   Rep: We don't understand baseball, but Jack does.
          Sub: we didn't see the game   S: We didn't see the game, but Jack did.
               we saw the game   We saw the game, but Jack didn't.
               we aren't having a picnic   We aren't having a picnic, but Jack is.
               we can understand the rules We can understand the rules, but Jack can't.
               we won't have time   We won't have time, but Jack will.
               we shouldn't eat any more   We shouldn't eat any more, but Jack should.
               we were on time   We were on time, but Jack wasn't.

7. M1T   T: John didn't do the homework. Bill   S: John didn't do the homework and Bill didn't
              didn't do the homework.   either.
              The boys can't go to the game. The   The boys can't go to the game and the girls
              girls can't go to the game.   can't either.
              Carlos wasn't on time. Bill and Jane   Carlos wasn't on time and Bill and Jane
              weren't on time.   weren't either.
              The girls shouldn't eat a lot of candy. The girls shouldn't eat a lot of candy and
              Jack shouldn't eat a lot of candy.   Jack shouldn't either.
              Mr. and Mrs. Newton didn't go to   Mr. and Mrs. Newton didn't go to Paris and
              Paris. Mary Jackson didn't go to   Mary Jackson didn't either.
              Paris.
              Bill hasn't played baseball. The foreign Bill hasn't played baseball and the foreign
              students haven't played baseball.   students haven't either.
              I'm not going to do the homework. My   I'm not going to do the homework and my
              brother isn't going to do the homework. brother isn't either.

8. M1T   T: I should go to bed early. You should S: I should go to bed early and you should too.
              go to bed early.
              I need to learn the rules. He needs   I need to learn the rules and he does too.
              to learn the rules.
              Jane finished the paper. Bill finished   Jane finished the paper and Bill did too.
              the paper.
              The boys will go home next week. Nancy   The boys will go home next week and Nancy
              will go home next week.   will too.
              The baseball players were late for the   The baseball players were late for the game and
              game. The fans were late for the   the fans were too.
              game.

(exercise continued on next page)

T: The batter saw the ball. The catcher   S: The batter saw the ball and the catcher
     saw the ball.   did too.
     The pitcher hit the umpire. The catcher   The pitcher hit the umpire and the
     hit the umpire.   catcher did too.

9. M1T   T: Our team lost the game. The other teams   S: Our team lost the game, but the other
              didn't lose.   teams didn't.
              Our friends aren't looking for an apartment.   Our friends aren't looking for an apartment,
              Some other people are looking for an   but some other people are.
              apartment.
              Their son has gotten a scholarship. The other   Their son has gotten a scholarship, but
              boy hasn't gotten a scholarship.   the other boy hasn't.
              This car won't last another year. That car   This car won't last another year, but
              will last another year.   that car will.
              This lake is polluted. The other lakes   This lake is polluted, but the other lakes
              aren't polluted.   aren't.
              My coat is large enough. The other coat   My coat is large enough, but the other
              isn't large enough.   coat isn't.
              George might not have enough money. Jane   George might not have enough money,
              might have enough money.   but Jane might.

***10. M2   T: I want a cheap car. I'm going to get a   S: (A Cadillac isn't a cheap car, and a Rolls-
                 Cadillac or a Rolls-Royce.   Royce isn't either.)
                 I need some film. Please get me some   (Kodak makes film, but Zippo doesn't.)
                 Kodak or Zippo.
                 Get me some ice cream at the museum or   (The museum doesn't have ice cream and
                 the tobacco shop.   the tobacco shop doesn't either.)

         I'm going to take a vacation on one of the Great Lakes—the Atlantic or the Pacific.
         Ask Carlos or Mohammed. They're both from the Middle East.
         I don't want cigarettes, get me Winstons or Salems.
         We want to start our trip on a lucky day; maybe Friday, the 13th, or Tuesday, the 7th.
         I'm going to bet on one of the professional baseball teams—the Steelers or the Packers.
         We aren't going to Southeast Asia—maybe we'll go to Thailand or Malaysia.
         My friends are going to South America this year—Mexico and Brazil.
         The Newtons are visiting cities on the east coast this year—Pittsburgh and Chicago.
         Get me a novel by Faulkner, please—*Light in August* or *The Sun Also Rises*.
         He doesn't like imported cars; he's going to buy a Volkswagen or a Datsun.
         I'm going to live in a small town—New York City or Los Angeles.
         He's going to subscribe to a weekly news magazine—the *New York Times* or *Newsweek*.

Part B.   *Alternate Expressions*

Model: John likes baseball and so do I.
         John doesn't like English and neither do I.

1. M1   Listen: John likes baseball and I do too.   Rep: John likes baseball and so do I.
                      John can play baseball and I can too.   John can play baseball and so can I.
                      John went to the baseball game and   John went to the baseball game and so did I.
                      I did too.

355

2. M1T   T: John should be on time and I should too.   S: John should be on time and so should I.
              John will finish the lesson and I will too.   John will finish the lesson and so will I.
              John's been to the game and I have too.   John's been to the game and so have I.
              John's going to the game and I am too.   John's going to the game and so am I.
              John said "goodbye" and I did too.   John said "goodbye" and so did I.
              John can play baseball and I can too.   John can play baseball and so can I.

3. M1   Listen: John doesn't like boxing and I don't either.   Rep: John doesn't like boxing and neither do I.
              John can't swim and I can't either.   John can't swim and neither can I.
              John didn't go and I didn't either.   John didn't go and neither did I.
              John shouldn't go and I shouldn't either.   John shouldn't go and neither should I.

GENERALIZATION

These alternate forms are very common in spoken American English, and are used to express agreement with the speaker:

        A: "I hate baseball."
        B: "So do I."
    or
        A: "I didn't do the homework."
        B: "Neither did I."

Note that the negative element in the second is *neither,* and the verb is then affirmative.

To express disagreement with the speaker, use the *but* expressions.

    A: "I hate baseball."   A: "I didn't do the homework."
    B: "But I don't."   or   B: "But I did."

Note: In very *informal* styles, you may hear "Me, too." or "Me, neither."

---

4. M1T   T: John doesn't like boxing and I don't either. S: John doesn't like boxing and neither do I.
              John can't swim and I can't either.   John can't swim and neither can I.
              The boys didn't go and I didn't either.   The boys didn't go and neither did I.
              Jane shouldn't go and I shouldn't either.   Jane shouldn't go and neither should I.
              Chen won't go and I won't either.   Chen won't go and neither will I.
              Bill hasn't gone and I haven't either.   Bill hasn't gone and neither have I.
              Nancy and Bill aren't going and I'm not either.   Nancy and Bill aren't going and neither am I.

5. M1T   T: I can't go to the game.   S: Neither can I.
              I've finished the homework.   So have I.
              I have to work tonight.   So do I.
              I'm going to study tonight.   So am I.
              I wasn't sick last week.   Neither was I.
              I haven't been to the movies in   Neither have I.
                 weeks.
              I can swim.   So can I.
              I won't be able to go.   Neither will I.
              I don't want a Rolls-Royce.   Neither do I.

6. M2   T: Make a statement of personal opinion: S1:   (I like the weather here.)
             about the weather.   S2:   (So do I—it's great.) (But I don't—
                                                                   it's too humid.)
             about the weather   S1:   (I don't like the weather here.)
                                                             S2:   (Neither do I—it's too cold.) (But I do—
                                                                   it's very pleasant now.)

             about American food
             about people
             about this city
             about this university
             about baseball
             about politics
             about the air
             about the water
             about the cost of living
             about popular music
             about sports in this country

7. C   (See Instructor's Manual)

SECTION THREE

MODALS — *COULD/WOULD*

Model: I'd like to help you, but some of the rules are different.
         We could tell him some of the rules.

Part A.   *Could*

☐ PAST ABILITY

1. M1   Rep: I could swim yesterday and I can swim today.
              I could play the piano yesterday and I can play the piano now.
              I couldn't fly the plane last year, but I can this year.

2. M1   T: I can swim now.   S: I could swim last year.
             He can play the piano now.   He could play the piano last year.
             She can't go to Paris now.   She couldn't go to Paris last year.
             We can't fly a plane now.   We couldn't fly a plane last year.
             They can play baseball now.   They could play baseball last year.
             I can't play the flute now.   I couldn't play the flute last year.
             She can't sail a boat now.   She couldn't sail a boat last year.
             He can't cook an omelette now.   He couldn't cook an omelette last year.

☐ POLITE REQUEST

3. M1   Listen: Can I have a glass, please?   Rep: Could I have a glass, please?
                Can I use your phone?   Could I use your phone?
                Can you help me?   Could you help me?

4. M1   T: You need some information.   S: Could you give me some information, please?
               You need some advice.   Could you give me some advice, please?
               You need a glass.   Could you give me a glass, please?
               You need some help.   Could you give me some help, please?
               You need a schedule.   Could you give me a schedule, please?
               You need some checks.   Could you give me some checks, please?
               You need a receipt.   Could you give me a receipt, please?
               You need a menu.   Could you give me a menu, please?

***□ PRESENT OR FUTURE POSSIBILITY

5. M1 Listen: We can go tomorrow.   Rep: We could go tomorrow.
                 We can wait a while.   We could wait a while.
                 We can tell him some of the rules.   We could tell him some of the rules.

6. M1   T: It's possible to go now.   S: We could go now.
               It's possible to wait for him.   We could wait for him.
               It's possible to buy it now.   We could buy it now.
               It's possible to see her tomorrow.   We could see her tomorrow.
               It's possible to leave next week.   We could leave next week.
               It's possible to send it airmail.   We could send it airmail.
               It's possible to go swimming.   We could go swimming.
               It's possible to make an appointment.   We could make an appointment.

GENERALIZATION

Could is a modal verb which is used in several different ways with different meanings.

Past Ability (can)

I can't do the work now.   I couldn't do the work yesterday.

Polite Request (can/may)

May I have a light, please?   Could I have a light, please?

Future Possibility (can)

I can go tomorrow.   I could go tomorrow.

The context will indicate the meaning.

---

7. M1T   T: Could you tell me the time?   S: Request
                Could you speak English before you came?   Ability
                Could you go tomorrow?   Possibility
                Could he come later?   Possibility
                Could she cook before she was married?   Ability
                Could you get me some cigarettes?   Request
                Could Chen understand baseball after the discussion?   Ability
                Could you lend me a dime?   Request

8. M2   T: have a light   S1:   Could I have a light, please?
                                         S2:   (Yes, certainly.) (Sorry, I don't smoke.)

               use the phone   S1:   Could I use the phone, please?
                                         S2:   (Yes—it's right over here.) (Sorry, no one is allowed
                                                   to use it for personal calls.)

               give me some advice   S: Could you give me some advice, please?
               tell me the name of the   Could you tell me the name of the director, please?
                   director

               give me some information   Could you give me some information, please?
               help me with these forms   Could you help me with these forms, please?
               show me the police station   Could you show me the police station, please?
               help me look for a doctor   Could you help me look for a doctor, please?
               tell me the name of a   Could you tell me the name of a good dentist, please?
                   good dentist

               tell me where the bus stop is   Could you tell me where the bus stop is, please?
               tell me how to cash a check   Could you tell me how to cash a check, please?
               cash this check for me   Could you cash this check for me, please?

9. M2   T: go with you now   S1:   I can't go with you now.
                                         S2:   (Could/can you go tomorrow?)
                                         S1:   (I guess I could.) (Probably.) (Maybe—I'll see.)

               do the work last night   S1:   I couldn't do the work last night.
                                         S2:   (Can/could you do it (tonight)?)
                                         S1:   (I might be able to.)

               see you tomorrow   S: I can't see you tomorrow.
               help you this week   I can't help you this week.
               go to the movie tonight   I can't go to the movie tonight.
               write the letter now   I can't write the letter now.
               go to the beach this weekend   I can't go to the beach this weekend.
               call your friend yesterday   I couldn't call your friend yesterday.
               meet your friends tonight   I can't meet your friends tonight.
               call your office last week   I couldn't call your office last week.
               make an appointment today   I can't make an appointment today.
               write the paper last week   I couldn't write the paper last week.

10. C   T: Tell something you could do last year, but   S1:   (I could speak French last year, but
                   can't do now.   I can't now.)
               Make a polite request of your neighbor.   (Could you tell me the time, please?)
               Tell me something you weren't able to do   (I couldn't speak English last year, but
                   last year, but can now.   I can now.)
               etc.

Part B.   *would*

□ POLITE REQUEST/INVITATION

1. M1 Listen: Will you sit down?   Rep: Would you sit down?
                  Will you have a cup of coffee?   Would you have a cup of coffee?
                  Will you help me?   Would you help me?
                  Will you wait a minute?   Would you wait a minute?

☐ EXPRESSIONS OF DESIRE OR PREFERENCE

2. M1   Rep: I'd like to sit down.
                   I'd like to go to Paris.
                   I'd like a cup of coffee.
                   I'd rather have a cup of coffee.
                   I'd rather sit down.

GENERALIZATION

Would is used like *could* as a polite request:

      Would you help me, please?

It is also used as an invitation:

      Would you like a cup of coffee?

and in the fixed expressions *would like* (desire) and *would rather* (preference):

Desire: I'd like something to eat.
Preference: I'd rather have something to drink.

Note the contraction for *would* is *'d.* There is no similar contraction for *could.*

---

3. M1T   T: coffee or tea   S1:   Would you like coffee or tea?
                                        S2:   I'd rather (have tea), thanks.
                sit down or stand   S1:   Would you like to sit down or stand?
                                          S2:   I'd rather (sit down), thanks.

                go to a movie or a concert
                pie or ice cream
                a steak or a hamburger
                walk or drive
                take the bus or a taxi
                hot tea or iced tea
                chocolate or vanilla ice cream
                a novel or a biography
                a detective story or a western
                sit in the living room or in the yard
                use a pen or a typewriter
                pie or cake

4. M2   T: Ask ( ) to help you with (something).   S1:   Would you help me with (the homework), please?
                                                              S2:   (Sure.) (Not right now, but I could help you in an hour.)

                Ask ( ) what he wants for dessert.   S1:   Would you like (ice cream or cake) for dessert?
                  Give him a choice.   S2:   (I'd rather have ice cream.)

                Ask ( ) to tell you the rules for (baseball).
                Ask ( ) if he'd like to sit down.

                        (exercise continued on next page)

T: Ask ( ) to tell you the time.
      Ask ( ) to lend you something.
      Ask ( ) what he wants for dinner. Give him a choice.
      Ask ( ) to do you a favor.
      Ask ( ) to explain about registration.
      Ask ( ) what he wants to drink. Give him a choice.
      Ask ( ) to help you bargain for a car.
      Ask ( ) what flavor ice cream he wants. Give him a choice.

5. C   (See Instructor's Manual)

SECTION FOUR

VERB + *TO* + VERB

Model: Chen has wanted to see a professional baseball game for a long time.
        I'd like to help you.

1. M1   Rep: Chen wanted to see a baseball game last month.
         Sub: try   S: Chen tried to see a baseball game last month.
              plan   Chen planned to see a baseball game last month.
              hope   Chen hoped to see a baseball game last month.
              decide   Chen decided to see a baseball game last month.
              promise   Chen promised to see a baseball game last month.
              want   Chen wanted to see a baseball game last month.

2. M1   Rep: We didn't learn to do the work.
         Sub: start   S: We didn't start to do the work.
              forget   We didn't forget to do the work.
              continue   We didn't continue to do the work.
              like   We didn't like to do the work.
              need   We didn't need to do the work.
              know how   We didn't know how to do the work.

3. M1   Rep: We tried not to be late.
         Sub: plan   S: We planned not to be late.
              hope   We hoped not to be late.
              decide   We decided not to be late.
              promise   We promised not to be late.
              want   We wanted not to be late.
              like   We liked not to be late.

4. M1   Rep: He didn't understand baseball, but he tried to.
         Sub: plan   S: He didn't understand baseball, but he planned to.
              hope   He didn't understand baseball, but he hoped to.
              decide   He didn't understand baseball, but he decided to.
              promise   He didn't understand baseball, but he promised to.
              want   He didn't understand baseball, but he wanted to.
              need   He didn't understand baseball, but he needed to.

GENERALIZATION

Many verbs require *to* before a verb which follows. The ones in drills 1-4 are only a few of the common ones.

Note that either verb may be negative, and the meaning is different:

He promised to be on time.
He *didn't* promise to be on time.   (No promise was made.)
He promised *not* to be on time.   (He promised to be late.)

Negation of both verbs in the same sentence is rate because the meaning is obscure.

Note also that short answers have Verb + *to*:

Did he go downtown?   No, but he wanted to.

---

5. M2   T: People should try ——.   S: People should try (to understand others).
               People should try not ——.   People should try not (to hurt others).
               This year I want ——.
               Last year I didn't want ——.
               Before I came here I promised ——.
               Before I came here I promised not ——.
               When I came here I didn't know how ——.
               In the next few years I hope ——.
               In recent weeks I've decided ——.
               Yesterday I forgot ——.
               Recently I've decided not ——.
               Right now I'm trying not ——.
               Two months ago I needed ——.
               Every day I continue ——.
               I like ——.

6. C   T: Do you like the weather here?   S: (No, and I hope to leave very soon.)
               Do you understand American   (No, but I'm trying to.) (No, and I'm trying
                  politics?   not to.)
               Do you like your apartment/room?
               Have you gone to New York City?
               Did you remember to do the homework?
               Were you late?
               Could you do the work?
               Did you see the baseball game?
               Do you like TV?
               Do you like the coffee here?
               Do you like the weather here?
               Have you met many people here?
               Do you understand American politics?
               Do you like to ski/swim?
               Have you learned how to do anything new here?

SECTION FIVE

TWO-WORD VERBS (NON-SEPARABLE)

Model: The batter looks at the coach.
The pitcher waits for the signal.
. . . they decide on a pitch.
I've never heard of a game with so many rules.
. . . listen to the commentary.

1. M1   Rep: I don't want to depend on it.
Sub: look at   S: I don't want to look at it.
wait for   I don't want to wait for it.
decide on   I don't want to decide on it.
listen to   I don't want to listen to it.
think of   I don't want to think of it.
think about   I don't want to think about it.
hear about   I don't want to hear about it.
learn about   I don't want to learn about it.
run out of   I don't want to run out of it.
laugh at   I don't want to laugh at it.
insist on   I don't want to insist on it.
catch up on   I don't want to catch up on it.

2. M1   Rep: He'd really like to call on her.
Sub: run into   S: He'd really like to run into her.
talk with   He'd really like to talk with her.
learn about   He'd really like to learn about her.
hear about   He'd really like to hear about her.
talk to   He'd really like to talk to her.

GENERALIZATION

Most of these two-word verbs appeared in previous lessons as vocabulary items. Note
that more than one preposition may occur with the same verb. (*run into; run out of*)
The preposition is never separated from the verb, so you should learn the verbs and the
prepositions as units in various contexts.

---

3. M1   Rep: He told me his plan, but I didn't listen to it.
Sub: a joke—laugh at   S: He told me a joke, but I didn't laugh at it.
his problem—think about   He told me his problem, but I didn't think about it.
his opinion—listen to   He told me his opinion, but I didn't listen to it.
the choice—decide on   He told me the choice, but I didn't decide on it.
the time of the lecture—   He told me the time of the lecture, but I didn't wait
  wait for   for it.
the answer to the question—   He told me the answer to the question, but I didn't
  depend on   depend on it.

4. M1T   Rep: We shouldn't decide on it.
          Sub: wait   S: We shouldn't wait for it.
               listen   We shouldn't listen to it.
               depend   We shouldn't depend on it.
               insist   We shouldn't insist on it.
               laugh   We shouldn't laugh at it.
               look   We shouldn't look at it.
               run out   We shouldn't run out of it.

5. M1T   Rep: When did they hear about the problem?
          Sub: what—think—the speech   S: What did they think about the speech?
               why—insist—discussing   Why did they insist on discussing politics?
                 politics
               how—decide—the VW   How did they decide on the VW?
               when—learn—the scandal   When did they learn about the scandal?
               where—wait—the election   Where did they wait for the election results?
                 results
               why—laugh—the lonely man   Why did they laugh at the lonely man?

6. M2   T: I don't have any more sugar. (run)   S: (You ran out of sugar.)
               I don't know anything about the   (You should learn about it.)
                 Middle-East situation. (learn)
               The new professor seems very
                 interesting. (talk)
               The boys are late. (wait)
               I can't make up my mind. I might go to the university or take a trip. (decide)
               The car seems very expensive. (think)
               We must pay the bill on time. (insist)
               I might not go to the game. (depend)
               He has some new slides. (look)
               That's a great record. (listen)
               He made the funniest sound. (laugh)
               We've just returned from a trip around the world. (hear)
               The new student is very lonely. (call)
               I owed 13 letters, but I wrote them all last weekend. (catch)

7. C   T: What do you think of people who insist on   S: (I try not to talk to them.)
                 discussing politics?
               Do you know anyone who is always running out of things? What? What does he do then?
               Is there someone who depends on you? For what?
               How do you catch up on the news from home?
               Do you often have to wait for your friends? Why?
               How do you hear about politics in your country?
               Have you ever run into a friend when you were far from home?
               Is there anything you often run out of? What do you do?
               What kind of music do you like to listen to?
               How did you decide on your apartment/this university?
               What kind of TV programs do you look at?

SUMMARY DIALOGUE

Chen: Miss, could you help me, please?

Saleslady: Certainly, sir. What would you like?

Chen: I've run out of socks. I need to get some new ones.

Saleslady: Yes, sir. What color would you like?

Chen: These blue ones are nice, but I'd rather have dark gray or bla

Saleslady: These wool ones are very nice. They'll last forever.

Chen: Yes, those look fine. I'd like four pairs.

SUMMARY OF PATTERNS

I. Subordinate Clauses

Main Clause	Subordinator	Subordinate Clause
I'll see him	before	he leaves.
I'll see him	after	he returns.
I'll see him	when	he returns.
I'll see him	while	you're shopping.
I'll see him	until	he has to leave.

Note: The order of these clauses may be reversed: After he returns, I'll see him.

II.   Conjunction

| He can | go | and | { | I can too. |
| | | | | so can I. |

| He can't | go | and | { | I can't either. |
| | | | | neither can I. |

| He can | go | but | { | I can't. |
| He can't | go | but | | I can. |

NOTES

LESSON EIGHTEEN

INTRODUCTION   Climates

Bill and Chen are discussing Chen's impressions about the weather in the United States.

Bill: Now that you've been here for a while, what do you think of this country and
           about this city in particular?

Chen: Your area probably *has more variety of climate* than any other place in the world;
5   at least the weather changes faster than any other place I've been.

Bill: *Isn't it* the same as your country?

Chen: I'll say it's not! It's completely different from my country. For instance, you have
           the most unpredictable weather I've ever seen.

Bill: Maybe it's the worst you've seen, but it's worse in New England. They have a saying
10   there, "If you don't like the weather, wait a minute."

Chen: Just like here.

Bill: Oh, no! We don't have the same weather as New England. Our winter is not nearly
           as long as theirs. It's much shorter.

Chen: Just kidding, Bill. Seriously, do you have as much snow as New England?

15   Bill: We have much less snow than New England. In fact, last winter, the worst in the past
           few years, we had less than five feet of snow all winter. In some parts of New England there
           was snow as deep as twenty feet.

Chen: All I can say is, I'm glad I don't live there. I'm going to visit there when it's summer.
           They *do* have summer, don't they?

20   Bill: Of course. But I like to go there in the fall when the trees are changing color. That's
           the best time in New England.

Chen: Don't the trees change color here?

Bill: Yes, they do. But up north there are many more trees that turn red and orange.

Chen: It sounds beautiful, but I'll trade the beautiful scenery for your "mild weather."
25   *I don't know when I'll go* to New England, but it won't be in the winter.

OUTLINE OF PATTERNS   Example

Section One		Comparison II	
	Part A.	Nouns	. . . the same length as . . . . . . as much snow as . . .
	Part B.	Adjectives/Adverbs	. . . as long as . . . . . . change as rapidly as . . .
Section Two		X + *Wh* + Statement	I don't know when I'll go . . .
Section Three		Comparison III	Our winter is shorter than New England's.
		(-er than/more X . . . than)	You have more variety . . . than . . .
Section Four		Comparison IV	. . . the worst winter . . .
		(the . . . -est/the most . . . X)	. . . the most unpredictable weather . . .
Section Five		Negative Questions	Isn't it the same . . .

COMPREHENSION QUESTIONS

1. What are Chen and Bill discussing?

2. What does Chen say about the weather in this area?

3. Is the weather the same as Chen's country?

4. Is the weather always the same according to Chen?

5. Where is it worse?

6. What is the saying about the weather in New England?

7. How does the length of winter compare to New England's.?

8. Do they have as much snow in Bill's area as New England?

9. How many feet of snow were there in Bill's city last year?

10. How many feet of snow were there in parts of New England?

*11. When does Bill say that Chen should go to New England? Why?

12. Do the trees change color in Bill's city?

*13. What is the difference in the trees in New England?

*14. What is Chen's decision? When is he going to New England?

*15. Discussion of the weather in students' countries.

NOTE: The word *like* is used in two different ways:

It's just like here.   (Preposition — similarity)
I like to go there in the fall.   (Verb — preference)

Vocabulary

Nouns	Verbs	Adjectives	Adverbs
board	flunk	delicious	fluently
brick	register	less	seriously
industry	socialize	mild	
scenery		rock and roll	
season		severe	
service		worse/worst	
shape			
silk			
skin			
straw			
variety			
width			

SECTION ONE

COMPARISON II

Part A.   *Nouns*

Model: My room is the same size as yours.
         Do you have as much snow as New England?

1. M1   Rep: My room is the same size as yours.
        Sub: city—size   S: My city is the same size as yours.
               book—price   My book is the same price as yours.
               lecture—length   My lecture is the same length as yours.
               living room—width   My living room is the same width as yours.
               hat—shape   My hat is the same shape as yours.
               car—color   My car is the same color as yours.

2. M1   Rep: We have as much snow as New England.
        Sub: rain   S: We have as much rain as New England.
              California   We have as much rain as California.
              pollution   We have as much pollution as California.
              Chicago   We have as much pollution as Chicago.
              wind   We have as much wind as Chicago.
              New York   We have as much wind as New York.
              fog   We have as much fog as New York.
              San Francisco   We have as much fog as San Francisco.

3. M1   Rep: Chen gets as many phone calls as Carlos.
        Sub: letters   S: Chen gets as many letters as Carlos.
              bills   Chen gets as many bills as Carlos.
              packages   Chen gets as many packages as Carlos.
              dinner invitations   Chen gets as many dinner invitations as Carlos.
              (exercise continued on next page)

T:	good grades	S:	Chen gets as many good grades as Carlos.
	bad grades		Chen gets as many bad grades as Carlos.

GENERALIZATION

In the exercises above, there are two sentences combined and they compare nouns which are equal in some way. If the comparison is one of quantity, use ——

$$as \begin{Bmatrix} much \\ many \end{Bmatrix} as:$$ We have as much snow as New England (does).
We have as many seasons as New England (does).

When do you use *as much as?*   ((With non-count nouns.))
When do you use *as many as?*   ((With count nouns.))

Examples:

We have a lot of snow. New England has a lot of snow.
We have as much snow as New England (does).

Chen has a lot of books. Carlos has a lot of books.
Chen has as many books as Carlos (does).

When the nouns are compared on other attributes, the pattern is

the same . . . as: My coat is the same length as yours.

In speech, the auxiliary in the subordinate clause is often omitted when its subject is a noun   (I have as many books as Carlos.) When its subject is a personal pronoun, omission of the auxiliary makes the pattern very formal (Carlos has as many books as I (do).)

---

4. M1T   T: VW—Volvo (size)   S: My VW is the same size as her Volvo.
              hat—coat (color)   My hat is the same color as her coat.
              novel—short story (length)   My novel is the same length as her short story.
              Ford—Oldsmobile (width)   My Ford is the same width as her Oldsmobile.
              magazine—newspaper (price)   My magazine is the same price as her newspaper.
              Cadillac—Rolls-Royce (size)   My Cadillac is the same size as her Rolls-Royce.
              brother—sister (height)   My brother is the same height as her sister.
              car—truck (weight)   My car is the same weight as her truck.

5. M1T   T: Carlos has a lot of books. So does Chen.   S: Chen has as many books as Carlos.
              Bill drinks a lot of coffee. So do Nancy   Nancy and Chen drink as much coffee
                and Chen.   as Bill.
              Nancy goes to a lot of parties. So does Carlos.   Carlos goes to as many parties as Nancy.
              Jane has a lot of homework. So do Chen and   Chen and Carlos have as much homework
                Carlos.   as Jane.
              Mr. Jackson does a lot of work. So does   Mrs. Jackson does as much work as
                Mrs. Jackson.   Mr. Jackson.
              Jane reads a lot of books. So do Bill and Chen.   Bill and Chen read as many books as Jane.
              The students take a lot of trips. So does   The teacher takes as many trips as the
                the teacher.   students.

6. M2   T: books   S1: (How many books do you read every week?)

                                  S2: (I read as many books as (Carlos), but not as many as (Mrs. Bruder).)

                  coffee   S1: (Do you drink a lot of coffee?)

                                    S2: (I drink as much coffee as (Maria), but not as much as (Luis Carlos).)

                  magazines
                  movies
                  tea
                  milk
                  clothes
                  mail
                  trips
                  friends
                  phone calls
                  ice cream
                  pizza

Part B.   *Adjectives and Adverbs*

Model: Our winter is not as long as theirs.
           Our weather doesn't change as rapidly as theirs.

1. M1   Rep: Karen is as tall as you are.

Sub:		S:	
old			Karen is as old as you are.
thin			Karen is as thin as you are.
young			Karen is as young as you are.
intelligent			Karen is as intelligent as you are.
happy			Karen is as happy as you are.
sad			Karen is as sad as you are.

2. M1   Rep: Robert sings as well as we do.

Sub:		S:	
swims			Robert swims as well as we do.
fast			Robert swims as fast as we do.
reads			Robert reads as fast as we do.
rapidly			Robert reads as rapidly as we do.
bargains			Robert bargains as rapidly as we do.
shrewdly			Robert bargains as shrewdly as we do.
thinks			Robert thinks as shrewdly as we do.
slowly			Robert thinks as slowly as we do.

GENERALIZATION

Adjectives and adverbs in comparisons have the *as . . . as* pattern.

Noun: We have as { much snow / many seasons } as New England.

Adjective: Karen is   as pretty as Joan.

Adverb: Karen types as fast as   Joan.

---

3. M1   Rep: Our winter is as long as theirs.
         Sub: summer—warm   S: Our summer is as warm as theirs.
              city—polluted   Our city is as polluted as theirs.
              lake—cold   Our lake is as cold as theirs.
              work—difficult   Our work is as difficult as theirs.
              apartment—big   Our apartment is as big as theirs.
              books—expensive   Our books are as expensive as theirs.
              friends—intelligent   Our friends are as intelligent as theirs.

4. M1   Rep: Carlos speaks English as well as Chen.
         Sub: reads   S: Carlos reads English as well as Chen.
              French   Carlos reads French as well as Chen.
              fast   Carlos reads French as fast as Chen.
              writes   Carlos writes French as fast as Chen.
              quickly   Carlos writes French as quickly as Chen.
              speaks   Carlos speaks French as quickly as Chen.
              English   Carlos speaks English as quickly as Chen.
              fluently   Carlos speaks English as fluently as Chen.

***5. M1T T: John is handsome. George is handsome.   S: John is as handsome as George.
                My hat is size 8. Yours is size 6.   (My hat is not the same size as yours.)
                                                                (My hat is not as small as yours.)
                George sings well. Harry sings very well.   (George doesn't sing as well as Harry.)
                We have a short winter. Baltimore has a short winter.
                There are four seasons here. There is one season in Central America.
                Peter's grades were high. Jack's grades were very high.
                We have a 1973 car. Our neighbor's car is a 1973.
                Jane has a few friends. Nancy has many friends.
                Our winter lasts for three months. New England's lasts for five months.
                Bill speaks Spanish pretty well. Marie speaks Spanish fluently.
                They have a VW. She has a Ford.
                We go out to dinner once a week. He goes out twice a week.
                George swims well. So does Jane.
                The Empire State Building has 148 stories. The World Trade Center has about 160.

6. M2   T: VWs in my country ——.   S: VWs in my country (are not the same price as here).
              The winter in ( ) ——.
              Women's styles in ( ) ——.
              The seasons in ( ) ——.
              People in ( ) speak ——.
              Lakes in ( ) ——.
              Cars in ( ) ——.
              Men's work in ( ) ——.
              The capital of ( ) ——.
              Books in ( ) cost ——.
              Houses in ( ) are ——.
              Beef in ( ) is ——.
              Customs in ( ) ——.

7. C   Compare with your country.
        T: pollution   S: (There is as much pollution here as in my country.) (There is
                                                          not as much pollution in my country as here.)

                traffic
                Washington, D.C. (with capital)
                drivers
                tourists
                prices
                cars
                food—cost/kind
                TV
                newspapers
                cost of living
                seasons
                weather

SECTION TWO

X + *WH* + STATEMENT

Model: I don't know when I'll go to New England.

1. M1   Rep: He doesn't know when he's going to do the work.
          Sub: why   S: He doesn't know why he's going to do the work.
               where   He doesn't know where he's going to do the work.
               how   He doesn't know how he's going to do the work.
               how often   He doesn't know how often he's going to do the work.
               how long   He doesn't know how long he's going to do the work.
               when   He doesn't know when he's going to do the work.

2. M1   Rep: Do you know when you'll see the President?
          Sub: he   S: Does he know when he'll see the President?
               how   Does he know how he'll see the President?
               secret papers   Does he know how he'll see the secret papers?
               they   Do they know how they'll see the secret papers?
               where   Do they know where they'll see the secret papers?
               the new movie   Do they know where they'll see the new movie?
               she   Does she know where she'll see the new movie?
               when   Does she know when she'll see the new movie?

GENERALIZATION

This pattern combines two statements using a *wh* word:

I don't know | the time. | I'll see my friend | sometime. |

I don't know | the time | | when | I'll see my friend.

I don't know | when | I'll see my friend.

Although this pattern is often a response to a question, and may be part of a question (2, above), the clause beginning with the *wh* word is a statement and has statement word order.

3. M1T   T: I'll see them sometime. I don't know when.   S: I don't know when I'll see them.
                I'll do it somehow. I don't know how.   I don't know how I'll do it.
                I'll finish it sometime. I don't know when.   I don't know when I'll finish it.
                I'll go there for some reason. I don't know why.   I don't know why I'll go there.
                I'll meet him somewhere. I don't know where.   I don't know where I'll meet him.
                It'll take some time. I don't know how long.   I don't know how long it'll take.
                It'll cost some money. I don't know how much.   I don't know how much money
                                                                        it'll cost.

                It'll be a few days. I don't know how many.   I don't know how many days it'll be.

4. M1T   T: It was a few days.   S: Do you know how many days it was?
                There were exams sometime.   Do you know when there were exams?
                It was someplace in N.Y.   Do you know where it was in N.Y.?
                It was dark for some reason.   Do you know why it was dark?
                There were a few people.   Do you know how many people there were?
                It was sometime last week.   Do you know when it was last week?
                There was a little rain.   Do you know how much rain there was?
                There was a snow storm   Do you know when there was a snow storm?
                    sometime.

5. M1T   T: Where did Carlos go on his vacation?   S: I don't know where he went.
                When did Bill go to New England?   I don't know when he went.
                Why is Suzie going to Mexico?   I don't know why she's going.
                Where have the students been?   I don't know where they've been.
                How much snow was there?   I don't know how much there was.
                When will the students leave?   I don't know when they'll leave.
                How many people are coming?   I don't know how many are coming.
                How often has Carlos seen Nancy?   I don't know how often he's seen her.
                How long did Chen stay in New England?   I don't know how long he stayed there.

6. M1T   T: Chen went somewhere.   G1:   Where did Chen go?
                                                      G2:   I don't know where he went.
                The students are studying for some   G1:   Why are the students studying?
                    reason.   G2:   I don't know why they're studying.
                Charlie went to Virginia sometime.   G1:   When did Charlie go to Virginia?
                                                      G2:   I don't know when he went.
                Carlos has been here for some time.   G1:   How long has Carlos been here?
                                                      G2:   I don't know how long he's been here.
                A new car will cost some money.   G1:   How much will a new car cost?
                                                      G2:   I don't know how much one will cost.
                It rains often.   G1:   How often does it rain?
                                                      G2:   I don't know how often it rains.
                The students will travel somehow.   G1:   How will the students travel?
                                                      G2:   I don't know how they'll travel.
                Mary has left for some reason.   G1:   Why has Mary left?
                                                      G2:   I don't know why she's left.
                John said something.   G1:   What did John say?
                                                      G2:   I don't know what he said.
                The men can go sometime.   G1:   When can the men go?
                                                      G2:   I don't know when they can go.
                Suzie can stay somewhere.   G1:   Where can Suzie stay?
                                                      G2:   I don't know where she can stay.

***7. M2   T: Do you know where ——?   S1:   Do you know where (I can get a good meal)?

                                                           S2:   No, I don't, but I think my friend does. Do you know where he can get a good meal?

                                                           S3:   (Sure, there's a good restaurant down the street. It's called ——.)

                                                           S1:   (Thanks a lot.)

             Can you tell me how much ——?   S1:   Can you tell me how much (I'll need for a trip to New England)?

                                                            S2:   No, I can't, but I think my friend can. Can you tell him how much he'll need for a trip to New England?

                                                            S3:   (Oh, you'll probably need about $——.)

                                                            S1:   (Thanks.)

Do you know why ——?
Can you tell me how long ——?
I'd like to know when ——.
Do you know how often ——?
Can you tell me how many ——?
Do you know how ——?
Please tell me where ——.
Can you help me find out how ——?
Do you know why ——?
Can you tell me what ——?
Do you know where ——?
Can you tell me how much ——?

***8. M2   T: Chen went to New England.   S1:   (Why did he go there?)

                                                            S2:   I don't know why he went. (Maybe he wanted to see the trees change color.)

             The students didn't study.   S1:   (What did they do?)

                                                            S2:   I don't know what they did. (Maybe they went to the movies.)

             The girls don't have any more money.   S1:   (What have they spent it on?)

                                                            S2:   I don't know what they've spent it on. (Maybe they needed some new clothes.)

Carlos doesn't like it here.
Bill won't take a trip this year.
The professor went to New York.
The man stopped smoking.
The Newtons were away from a long time.
Charlie was going to a new place.
The girls spent a lot of money.
Chen goes to the Student Union very often.
Suzie was able to see the President.
The children have been very naughty.
Our friends just moved to a new apartment.
The students learned English very fast.

***9. C   T: Ask a question about something in the news recently.

        S1:   (Why did X lose the election?)

        S2:   I don't know (why he lost. Maybe the people didn't understand his proposals.)

SECTION THREE

COMPARISON III — -ER . . . THAN/MORE . . . THAN

Model: Our winter is shorter than New England's.
        Their weather changes much faster than ours.
        You have more variety of climate than any other place.

1. M1   Rep: Suzie's vacation was longer than ours.
         Sub: more expensive   S: Suzie's vacation was more expensive than ours.
              shorter   Suzie's vacation was shorter than ours.
              less expensive   Suzie's vacation was less expensive than ours.
              better   Suzie's vacation was better than ours.
              more exciting   Suzie's vacation was more exciting than ours.
              less economical   Suzie's vacation was less economical than ours.
              earlier   Suzie's vacation was earlier than ours.
              more interesting   Suzie's vacation was more interesting than ours.
              worse   Suzie's vacation was worse than ours.

2. M1   Rep: People here drive faster than in Boston.
         Sub: more carefully   S: People here drive more carefully than in Boston.
              better   People here drive better than in Boston.
              more dangerously   People here drive more dangerously than in Boston.
              slower   People here drive slower than in Boston.
              less carefully   People here drive less carefully than in Boston.
              more recklessly   People here drive more recklessly than in Boston.
              worse   People here drive worse than in Boston.

3. M1   Rep: We have more good luck charms than we need.
         Sub: more skyscrapers   S: We have more skyscrapers than we need.
              more three-day   We have more three-day weekends than we need.
                weekends
              more super-highways   We have more super-highways than we need.
              fewer sunny days   We have fewer sunny days than we need.
              fewer pollution-free cars We have fewer pollution-free cars than we need.
              fewer accident-free   We have fewer accident-free drivers than we need.
                drivers

4. M1   Rep: Did he have more old furniture than he needed?
         Sub: more money   S: Did he have more money than he needed?
              more beer   Did he have more beer than he needed?
              more homework   Did he have more homework than he needed?
              less energy   Did he have less energy than he needed?
              less gas   Did he have less gas than he needed?
              less money   Did he have less money than he needed?
              less time   Did he have less time than he needed?

GENERALIZATION

Adjectives, adverbs and nouns can also be compared to specify the difference between items:

Nouns: Count   I have $\begin{Bmatrix} more \\ fewer \end{Bmatrix}$ books than Bill.

            Non-Count   I have $\begin{Bmatrix} more \\ less \end{Bmatrix}$ money than Bill.

Adverbs/Adjectives: I drive   faster   than Bill.
                             I am   taller   than Bill.

                             I drive $\begin{Bmatrix} more \\ less \end{Bmatrix}$ carefully than Bill.

                             I am $\begin{Bmatrix} more \\ less \end{Bmatrix}$ industrious than Bill.

Add -er to one-syllable adjectives and adverbs (and some common two-syllable ones).

big	bigger
long	longer
early	earlier
pretty	prettier

***Note that *good* and *bad* are irregular:

good	better
bad	worse

Much (*many* before count nouns) is frequently used preceding the comparison forms for emphasis:

We have *many* more books than we need.
He drives *much* faster than I do.

5. M1T   T: Skiing is harder than it looks.   S: Skiing is much harder than it looks.
             She has more boyfriends than she   She has many more boyfriends than she
                knows what to do with.   knows what to do with.
             That boy is more intelligent than   That boy is much more intelligent than
                he looks.   he looks.
             Joe swam more miles than Bill.   Joe swam many more miles than Bill.
             That job takes more experience than   That job takes much more experience than
                he has.   he has.
             I have less work than last week.   I have much less work than last week.
             Her pies are better than her cakes.   Her pies are much better than her cakes.

6. M2   T: Is skiing harder than skating?   S: (Oh, yes. It's much harder than skating.)
                                                             (Oh, no. Skating is much harder than skiing.)

             Is New York City larger than Pittsburgh?
             Does New York City have more skyscrapers than (capital)?
             Do you have more money at the beginning of the month than at the end?
             Do cars cause more pollution than bicycles?
             Do women drive more carefully than men?
             Is ( ) a better place to live than here?
             Is speaking English more fun than reading English?
             Do you have less freedom here than in ( )?
                          (exercise continued on next page)

T: Do women work harder than men?
Does a VW cost more than a Mercedes?
Is English easier to learn than (   )?

7. M2   T: The Rockefellers have a lot of money.   S: (The Gettys have more money than the
The Gettys have more.   Rockefellers.)
Nancy is 19; Bill is 21.   (Nancy is younger than Bill.) (Bill is
older than Nancy.)

English is easy. Spanish is very easy.
New York is a large city. Chicago is a pretty big city.
Chen has a hard time with English. Carlos has a terrible time.
Last winter was bad. The winter before was really bad.
Hamburger is expensive. Steak is very expensive.
Women are bad drivers. Men are very bad drivers.
Women bargain shrewdly. Men bargain very shrewdly.
Bill speaks Spanish well. Nancy speaks Spanish very well.
The Finger Lakes are deep. The Great Lakes are very deep.
We have a hard time in school. They have a very hard time.
Jane has a bad headache. Bill has a terrible headache.
Jane needs some help. Jack needs a lot of help.

8. C   T: your apartment   S1: (What is your apartment like?) (How big is your apartment?)
S2: (It's bigger than ( )'s, but not as big as ( )'s.)
English   S1: (How well do you speak English?) (Do you speak English well?)
S2: (I speak better than some people, but not as well as the teacher.)

drive
capital
cost of living in ( )
political situation in ( )
pollution in ( )
car
eat
skyscrapers in ( )
haircut
short skirts
ski
sing
swim

SECTION FOUR

COMPARISON IV — SUPERLATIVE (*THE . . . -EST/THE MOST . . . X)*

Model: You have the most unpredictable weather I've ever seen.
Last winter was the worst in many years.

1. M1   Rep: John is the tallest student.
         Sub: shortest   S: John is the shortest student.
              smartest   John is the smartest student.
              youngest   John is the youngest student.
              oldest   John is the oldest student.
              best   John is the best student.
              tallest   John is the tallest student.

2. M1   Rep: Chen studies the most carefully.
         Sub: enthusiastically   S: Chen studies the most enthusiastically.
              diligently   Chen studies the most diligently.
              patiently   Chen studies the most patiently.
              eagerly   Chen studies the most eagerly.
              intelligently   Chen studies the most intelligently.
              quietly   Chen studies the most quietly.
              carefully   Chen studies the most carefully.

GENERALIZATION

Items may be designated as higher (or lower) than all others in quality or quantity by using the superlative construction.

Comparison III — Comparative		Comparison IV — Superlative	
Nouns: Count	$\begin{Bmatrix} more \\ fewer \end{Bmatrix}$ books *than*	the $\begin{Bmatrix} most \\ fewest \end{Bmatrix}$ books	
Non-Count	$\begin{Bmatrix} more \\ less \end{Bmatrix}$ money *than*	the $\begin{Bmatrix} most \\ least \end{Bmatrix}$ money	
Adverbs/ Adjectives:	faster *than*	the fas*test*	
	taller *than*	the tall*est*	
	$\begin{Bmatrix} more \\ less \end{Bmatrix}$ carefully *than*	the most the least $\}$ careful	
	$\begin{Bmatrix} more \\ less \end{Bmatrix}$ industrious *than*	the most the least $\}$ industrious	

The adjectives and adverbs which add *-er* in Comparison III, add *-est* in Comparison IV.

Note the irregular forms:

	good/well	better than	the best
	bad	worse than	the worst
	little	less than	the least
	few	fewer than	the fewest

---

3. M1   Rep: It's the most interesting movie I've seen since I came here.
         Sub: expensive   S: It's the most expensive movie I've seen since I came here.
              beautiful   It's the most beautiful movie I've seen since I came here.
              difficult   It's the most difficult movie I've seen since I came here.
              important   It's the most important movie I've seen since I came here.
              understandable   It's the most understandable movie I've seen since I came here.
              inexpensive   It's the most inexpensive movie I've seen since I came here.

4. M1T   T: The tall one is a lazy girl.   S: She's the laziest girl I've ever met.
               The tall one is a good student.   She's the best student I've ever met.
               The tall one is a heavy girl.   She's the heaviest girl I've ever met.
               The tall one is a bad helper.   She's the worst helper I've ever met.
               The tall one is a thin girl.   She's the thinnest girl I've ever met.
               The tall one is a pretty girl.   She's the prettiest girl I've ever met.
               The tall one is a bad worker.   She's the worst worker I've ever met.

5. M1T   T: John works hard.   S: He works the hardest of all the students.
               John listens well.   He listens the best of all the students.
               John seems happy.   He seems the happiest of all the students.
               John learns fast.   He learns the fastest of all the students.
               John studies hard.   He studies the hardest of all the students.
               John works slowly.   He works the slowest of all the students.

6. M1T   Rep: Jane worked the most diligently of all the girls.
          Sub: spoke—intelligently   S: Jane spoke the most intelligently of all the girls.
               listened—patiently   Jane listened the most patiently of all the girls.
               played—eagerly   Jane played the most eagerly of all the girls.
               told the story—interestingly   Jane told the story the most interestingly of all the girls.
               wrote—enthusiastically   Jane wrote the most enthusiastically of all the girls.

7. M1T   T: You and I had more difficulties than   S: We had the most difficulties.
                  anyone else.
               You and I had fewer problems than   We had the fewest problems.
                  anyone else.
               You and I had more papers than anyone else.   We had the most papers.
               You and I had fewer drinks than anyone else. We had the fewest drinks.
               You and I had more accidents than anyone else. We had the most accidents.
               You and I had fewer letters than anyone else. We had the fewest letters.
               You and I had more telephone calls than   We had the most telephone calls.
                  anyone else.
               You and I had fewer wrong answers than   We had the fewest wrong answers.
                  anyone else.

8. M1T   T: He and I used more paper than anyone   S: You used the most paper.
                  else.
               He and I spent less money than anyone else.   You spent the least money.
               He and I ate more pizza than anyone else.   You ate the most pizza.
               He and I had more milk than anyone else.   You had the most milk.
               He and I drank less beer than anyone else.   You drank the least beer.
               He and I used less energy than anyone else.   You used the least energy.
               He and I did less work than anyone else.   You did the least work.
               He and I had less money than anyone else.   You had the least money.

9. M2   T: These are good novels.   S1:   Which is the best one?
                                              S2:   (On Her Majesty's Secret Service) is the best one.

               Those men worked enthusias-   S1:   (Who) (Which man) worked the most enthusiastically.
                  tically.   S2:   (Mr. Hastings) worked the most enthusiastically.

               Those students got a lot of   S1:   (Who) (Which one) got the most mail?
                  mail.   S2:   (Chen) got the most.

(exercise continued on next page)

T: Those girls eat a lot.
Those students drink a lot of beer.
Those girls listened patiently.
Those women played bridge well.
Those men had little energy.
Those people are important.
Those boys drove fast.
Those girls drove recklessly.
Those women need a lot of help.
Those boys have little money.
Those students read well.

10. M2   T: Pittsburgh   S: (Pittsburgh is the loneliest place in the world.)
U.S. politics   (U.S. politics are the most confusing I've ever studied.)
Women's Liberation
mini-skirts
New York City
San Francisco
the World Trade Center Building
world peace
Vietnam
TV
the *New York Times*
exploration of the moon
American food
English

11. C   T: Ask about the best restaurant in town.   S1:   (Where can I find the best restaurant
in town?)
S2:   (( ) is the one I like the best.)

Ask about the biggest hamburger in town.
Ask about the cheapest ice cream cone.
Ask about the most delicious pizza.
Ask about the biggest pizza.
Ask about the restaurant with the most atmosphere.
Ask about the restaurant with the best service.
Ask about the best department store in town.
Ask about the worst department store in town.
Ask about the latest date when you can pay the credit card bill.
Ask about the time when it's easiest to go downtown.
Ask about the best season in this area.
Ask about the worst season in this area.

SECTION FIVE

NEGATIVE QUESTIONS

Model: Isn't it the same in your country? No, it's very different.
Don't the trees change color here? Yes, but not as much as in New England.

1. M1   Rep: Did he go? Didn't he go?
                 Is he sick? Isn't he sick?
                 Are they here? Aren't they here?
                 Was he absent? Wasn't he absent?
                 Can you go? Can't you go?
                 Have you seen him? Haven't you seen him?
                 Have you studied English before? Haven't you studied English before?
                 Should we go? Shouldn't we go?

GENERALIZATION***

Often the negative is added to the Auxiliary or Modal. Sometimes the speaker intends surprise, but not always.

Didn't Humphrey win in 1968? Answer:	No, he didn't.
Didn't Nixon win in 1968?	Yes, he did.

The negative question is very common with *why?*

Chen couldn't come.	
Why couldn't he come? Answer:	Because he was sick.

***2. M1T   T: Did men reach the moon in 1965?   S1: Didn't men reach the moon in 1965?
                                                          S2: No, they didn't.

                   Is there going to be a Presidential   S1: Isn't there going to be a Presidential election
                      election in 1988?   in 1988?
                                                          S2: Yes, there is.

                   Was there a strike in 1971?   S1: Wasn't there a strike in 1971?
                                                          S2: Yes, there was.

                   Have the astronauts reached the   S1: Haven't the astronauts reached the moon
                      moon four times?   four times?
                                                          S2: Yes, they have.

                   Is there an ocean in the middle   S1: Isn't there an ocean in the middle of
                      of Michigan?   Michigan?
                                                          S2: No, there isn't.

                   Have we almost finished 19 lessons?   S1: Haven't we almost finished 19 lessons?
                                                          S2: No, we haven't.

                   Did we begin this term on ( )?   S1: Didn't we begin this term on ( )?
                                                          S2: Yes, we did.

                   Does this term end on ( )?   S1: Doesn't this term end on ( )?
                                                          S2: Yes, it does.

                   Does this state have a sales tax?   S1: Doesn't this state have a sales tax?
                                                          S2: Yes, it does.

                   Does the bus cost more than   S1: Doesn't the bus cost more than twenty
                      twenty cents?   cents?
                                                          S2: Yes, it does.

                   Do the trees turn color here?   S1: Don't the trees turn color here?
                                                          S2: Yes, they do.

                   Have you learned the word   S1: Haven't you learned the word "supercali-
                      "supercalifragilisticexpialidocious"?   fragilisticexpialidocious"?
                                                          S2: No, we haven't.

3. M2   T: Chen doesn't like the weather here.   S1:   Why doesn't Chen like the weather?
                                                       S2:   (Because it changes so often.)

               Nancy can't go to the baseball game.   S1:   Why can't Nancy go to the baseball game?
                                                        S2:   (Because she doesn't have enough money.)

               Bill didn't go to work last week.   S1:   Why didn't Bill go to work last week?
               Carlos shouldn't buy a new car.   Why shouldn't Carlos buy a new car?
               Nancy hasn't done the homework for   Why hasn't Nancy done the homework for
                 a week.   a week?
               Charlie doesn't want to go to the movies.   Why doesn't Charlie want to go to the movies?
               Mrs. Bruder doesn't like computers.   Why doesn't Mrs. Bruder like computers?
               The Camerons don't like baseball.   Why don't the Camerons like baseball?
               The students can't do the homework.   Why can't the students do the homework?
               Chen hasn't taken any pictures.   Why hasn't Chen taken any pictures?
               Bill and Nancy haven't been to New York.   Why haven't Bill and Nancy been to New York?
               Chen doesn't understand American   Why doesn't Chen understand American
                 politics.   politics?

4. M2   T: go to the game—can   S1:   Can't you go to the game?
                                      S2:   (Yes, I can.) (No, I can't. I have to work.)

               see the game—next week   S1:   Aren't you going to see the game next week?
                                          S2:   (Yes, I am.) (No, I'm not. I'm going to New York.)

               go home now—should
               write the paper—have to
               drive to New York—last weekend
               finish the lesson—today
               see the game—last week
               type the paper—can
               want to see the movie—tonight
               speak English fluently—now
               write the application—should
               pay the invoice—have to
               drive more slowly—should
               leave early—have to

***5 C   Make a statement about something you don't like or don't understand in this country.
              Other students will discuss it.

           S1:   (I'll never understand this country.)
           S2:   (Why not?)
           S1:   (Don't people ever send written invitations for parties?)
                  etc.

6. C   (See Instructor's Manual)

SUMMARY DIALOGUE

Chen: This is the worst day I've ever had.

Bill: What happened?

Chen: The more I study, the less I remember. I studied harder than anyone else in the math class and got the worst grade on the exam.

Bill: Maybe you should socialize more and study less.

Chen: How can socializing help me get better grades?

Bill: It can't, but at least you'll have a good time before you flunk the next test.

Chen: Thanks a lot.

SUMMARY OF PATTERNS

Comparison II	The weather here is	the same temperature as	in my country.
	The weather here is	as cold as	in my country.
Comparison III	The weather here is	colder than	in my country.
	The weather here is	more severe than	in my country.
Comparison IV	The weather here is	the coldest.	
	The weather here is	the most severe.	
X + *Wh* + Statement	I don't know	where	the students went.
	Do you remember	why	John wants a new car?
Negative Questions	Isn't it like your country?		
	Didn't John go to New England?		

LESSON NINETEEN

INTRODUCTION   A Legend

Last week Carlos *asked Bill and Nancy to tell him an American legend,* but they couldn't think of any. Now they have thought it over and Carlos asks again.

Carlos: O.K., Bill, you've had time to think. Now, tell us one of your legends.

Bill: I've been thinking it over, and I've decided that Nancy is the one who should tell it.
5   She's had experience explaining things to her younger brothers and sisters.

Nancy: Now, wait a minute, Bill. *You can tell it yourself* . . .   Oh, all right. Which one do you want to hear?

Bill: Rip Van Winkle . . . Once upon a time, Rip Van Winkle lived . . .

Nancy: Bill! If you want me to tell it, I'm going to tell it by myself.

10   Bill: Sorry, Nancy . . . go ahead.

Nancy: Rip Van Winkle lived a long time ago with his wife and his dog in the hills of eastern New York. Rip wasn't basically a lazy man, but he preferred to hunt and fish rather than to work steadily. His wife wanted him to have a regular job, so she nagged and nagged him, and he worked sometimes. It was fall and Rip *had been thinking about a hunting trip* for a
15   couple of months. *He had thought and planned a way to get away by himself.* His wife knew this and had nagged and scolded more and more. One day Rip had had enough. "That does it," he said, "I'm going hunting." And off he went with his dog and his gun. Deep in the woods he came upon a group of little men playing nine pins. They seemed happy and carefree and asked him to join them. At first Rip was frightened, but finally
20   he joined in and had a very good time. At the end of the game, they asked Rip to have a drink of their special refreshment. When Rip had drunk it, he felt very sleepy, so he lay down under a big tree to take a nap. When he woke up, he felt refreshed, picked up his gun and headed for town.

He was surprised to see that the town had changed a great deal. There were new stores and
25   the people looked so different. He looked around and scratched his head. The children, who had run away from him at first, now came very near and laughed and shouted at him. He turned and ran to his house where his wife was sitting on the porch. "Wife! What is the matter? I went for an afternoon hunt and now everything is different."

"An afternoon hunt! Indeed!? Look at yourself, you lazy scoundrel!" She handed a mirror
30   to him. Rip looked and didn't recognize himself. He saw a long gray beard and long gray hair. He looked again at his wife who began in an all too familiar tone. "You've been away for 20 years! Where have you been? What have you been doing? I certainly hope you've had a good time! For 20 years I've had to work my fingers to the bone just to stay alive, while you've been wandering around the country.

35   Rip had taken a "nap" of twenty years and everything had changed except his wife.

Bill: It just goes to show you that women are always the same.

Nancy: Let's have no remarks like that. I was only telling the story.

OUTLINE OF PATTERNS   Example

    Section One   Past Perfect Tense

        Part A.   Simple Past Perfect   He had thought . . .
        Part B.   Continuous   Rip had been thinking . . .

    Section Two   Verb + Direct Object + *to* + Indirect Object

        Part A.   Statement   She handed a mirror to him . . .
        Part B.   *Who?*   Who did she give the mirror to?

    Section Three   Reflexives

        Part A.   With *by*   . . . get away by himself.
        Part B.   Emphatic   You can tell it yourself.

COMPREHENSION QUESTIONS

  1. When did Carlos ask Bill and Nancy to tell him a legend?

*2. What did Carlos ask Bill and Nancy to do?

  3. Why didn't they tell one last week?

*4. Why does Carlos ask again?

*5. What has Bill decided? Why?

  6. Which one do they want?

  7. Where did Rip Van Winkle live?

*8. Did he have a pet?

*9. Was Rip a lazy man?

10. What did he like to do?

11. Why did his wife nag him? *What was the result?

12. What season was it?

13. What was Rip thinking about? *How long had he been thinking about it?

*14. Why did his wife scold more and more?

*15. What did Rip do one day?

16. Whom did he meet in the woods?

17. What were they doing?

*18. Why did Rip hesitate to join them?

19. What did they offer him at the end of the game?

20. What did he do after he had drunk the refreshment?

21. Where did he go when he woke up?

*22. Why was he surprised when he saw the town?

23. What did the children do?

*24. What did he ask his wife?

25. What did his wife give him?

*26. Why didn't he recognize himself?

27. How long had he been gone?

*28. What was his wife like?

*29. Discuss legends. Tell a legend from your country.

Vocabulary

Nouns		Verbs		Adjectives
ability	postcard	fish	recognize	alive
beard	review	head	relax	carefree
flood	route	hunt	run away from	familiar
gun	scoundrel	join	scold	frightened
job	storytelling	lift	scratch	refreshed
legend	tone	mention	shout	regular
mirror	woods	nag	tie	special
nine pins		pick up	think over	steady
		prefer	wander	

SECTION ONE

PAST PERFECT TENSE

Part A.   *Simple Past Perfect*

Model: Rip had thought about hunting for a long time.
His wife had nagged more and more.

☐ PRESENTATION

1775 July	Aug.	Sept.	Oct.	Nov.
/	//	///	// /	↓
Boston	New York	Phila.	N.Y. Boston	15th

Situation: It was November 15, 1775, when Rip went to sleep in the forest and began his nap of 20 years. Before that, in order to escape his wife's nagging, he traveled to various cities. We only know his activities from July to November. Let's assume that life was bearable (he probably had a job) until that time.

Listen: In 1775 in July, August, September and October, Rip took 9 trips. He went to New York twice in August and twice in October. He went to Philadelphia three times in September. He went to Boston once in October and once in July. For two weeks in November he planned his hunting trip.

In 1775, he had taken 9 trips before he went to sleep for twenty years. He had gone to New York 4 times before he went to sleep for twenty years. He had gone to Philadelphia 3 times before he went to sleep for twenty years. He had gone to Boston twice before he went to sleep for twenty years.

☐ PRACTICE

1. M1   Rep: In 1775 he went to New York twice in August and twice in October.
In 1775 he had gone to New York four times before he went to sleep.

In 1775 he went to Philadelphia three times in September.
In 1775 he had gone to Philadelphia three times before he went to sleep.

In 1775 he went to Boston once in October and once in July.
In 1775 he had gone to Boston twice before he went to sleep.

In 1775 he took nine trips in July, August, September, and October.
In 1775 he had taken six trips before he went to sleep.

2. M1T   T: How many times did he go to New York in 1775?   S: Four.
How many times had he gone to New York before he went   Four.
  to sleep?
How many trips did he take in October?   Three.
How many trips had he taken before he fell asleep?   Nine.
How many times did he go to New York in August?   Two.
How many times had he gone to New York before he went   Four.
  to sleep?
How many times did he go to Boston in October?   One.
How many times had he gone to Boston before he went to sleep?   Two.
How many times had he gone to Philadelphia before he went   Three.
  to sleep?
How many times did he go to Philadelphia in 1775?   Three.
How many trips did he take in August and September?   Five.
How long did he plan his hunting trip?   Two weeks.
How long had he planned the trip before he left home?   Two weeks.

388

GENERALIZATION

Just as the Present Perfect extends to the present time, the Past Perfect functions the same way in the past; i.e., one action happens *before* another action:

John read the paper at 8:00. He ate breakfast at 9:00.
John had read the paper before he ate breakfast.

Formation: *had* + past participle   Short Answers: Yes, he had. No, he hadn't.

Note: The contraction *'d* is very common in spoken English. There can be no confusion with the contraction for *would* — *'d* which is followed by the simple verb:

I'd go.   *(would)*
I'd gone.   *(had)*

Note: The Past Perfect tense is not common in informal speaking styles; the Past tense plus time words combined with context usually is enough. In formal speaking styles and in writing, the Past Perfect is used more frequently.

---

3. M1   Rep: I'd gone to Paris before I came here.
           Sub: he   S: He'd gone to Paris before he came here.
                she   She'd gone to Paris before she came here.
                we   We'd gone to Paris before we came here.
                they   They'd gone to Paris before they came here.
                you   You'd gone to Paris before you came here.
                it   It'd gone to Paris before it came here.

4. M1T   Rep: Mr. Jackson had spoken to Mrs. Jackson before he bought the new car.
           Sub: Chen—talk to—Bill—rent an apartment   S: Chen had talked to Bill before he
                                                                rented an apartment.

                Carlos—ask—Nancy's advice—get a credit   Carlos had asked Nancy's advice
                card   before he got a credit card.

                Bob—speak to—Judy—pay for the tape   Bob had spoken to Judy before he
                recorder   paid for the tape recorder.

                Charlie—ask—Mary's opinion—buy the airplane   Charlie had asked Mary's opinion
                                                                 before he bought the airplane.

                Mr. Newton—talk to—Mrs. Newton—buy the   Mr. Newton had talked to Mrs. Newton
                boat   before he bought the boat.

5. M1   Situation: Carlos studied many languages at home, but he never spoke them until he began
           to travel.

           Rep: Before Carlos came to the U.S., he hadn't spoken English.
           Sub: went to France—French   S: Before Carlos went to France, he hadn't spoken French.
                traveled in Germany—German   Before Carlos traveled in Germany, he hadn't spoken
                                                   German.

                studied in Italy—Italian   Before Carlos studied in Italy, he hadn't spoken Italian.
                moved to Canada—English   Before Carlos moved to Canada, he hadn't spoken
                                                   English.

                visited Lebanon—Arabic   Before Carlos visited Lebanon, he hadn't spoken Arabic.
                went to Sweden—Swedish   Before Carlos went to Sweden, he hadn't spoken
                                                   Swedish.

                visited Thailand—Thai   Before Carlos visited Thailand, he hadn't spoken Thai.

---

6. M1   Rep: Had you studied English before you came to the university?

Sub: been in the U.S.   S: Had you been in the U.S. before you came to the university?

seen this country   Had you seen this country before you came to the university?

eaten American food   Had you eaten American food before you came to the university?

read American newspapers   Had you read American newspapers before you came to the university?

written papers in English   Had you written papers in English before you came to the university?

driven an American car   Had you driven an American car before you came to the university?

sung American songs   Had you sung American songs before you came to the university?

***7. M1T T:

Had Rip gone to Paris before he took his nap?	S: No, he hadn't.
Had Rip gone to New York before he took his nap?	Yes, he had.
Had Rip gone to Paris?	No, he hadn't.
Did Rip go to New York in August?	Yes, he did.
Had Rip traveled to New York?	Yes, he had.
Did Rip travel to London?	No, he didn't.
Had Rip been in Pittsburgh before his nap?	No, he hadn't.
Was he in Boston?	Yes, he was.
Did he go to Boston in October?	Yes, he did.
Had he and his dog visited Paris?	No, they hadn't.
Was he in Philadelphia in November?	No, he wasn't.
Were he and his dog in Pittsburgh in November?	No, they weren't.
Had he been to Europe in 1775?	No, he hadn't.
Did he go to New York in August?	Yes, he did.
Was he in Pittsburgh in November?	No, he wasn't.
Had he seen London?	No, he hadn't.

8. M2 T: speak English—study English S1: (Had you spoken English before you studied it?)

(Had you studied English before you spoke it?)

S2: (Yes, I had.) (No, I hadn't.)

meet any people from the U.S.—come here

hear about U.S. taxes—pay them

find an apartment—arrive here

read current novels in English—begin this course

learn popular songs in English—study English

see a baseball game—come here

be able to understand people in the stores—study English

travel in the U.S.—begin the English classes

eat marshmallows—come here

see terrible pollution—arrive here

discuss U.S. politics—come here

know anything about bargaining in the U.S.—begin this class

9. C   T: Ask about writing books this year.   S1:   (How many books) have you written this year?

                                                         S2:   (I haven't written any books.) (I've written three.)

                 Ask about writing books last year.   S1:   (How many books) did you write last year?

                                                          S2:   (I wrote two.) (I didn't write any.)

                 Ask about writing books before coming here.   S1:   (How many books had you written before you came here?)

                                                          S2:   (I'd written two books.) (I hadn't written any.)

Ask about visiting New York before coming here.
Ask about speaking English last year.
Ask about going to Europe this year.
Ask about studying English before beginning this course.
Ask about writing home before calling last weekend.
Ask about being in (capital) last year.
Ask about reading American newspapers before coming here.
Ask about singing American songs this term.
Ask about eating out this month.
Ask about understanding American students before coming here.
Ask about understanding American politics this year.
Ask about understanding American movies before studying English.

10. C   T: Tell something you had thought to be true of the U.S. before you came here and whether or not you still have the same belief.

         S: (I had expected all Americans to be very friendly. Now I can see that some people are friendly, and others aren't.)

              (I had thought that all the cars are made in the U.S. Most people do have American cars, but there are a lot of foreign cars, too.)

              (I had thought that most people speak only English, and they do. I've met only a few people who speak (Spanish).)

Part B.   *Past Perfect Continuous*

Model: Rip had been thinking about a hunting trip for a long time.

1. M1   Rep: I'd been traveling for three years when I met him.

Sub:		S:	
working			I'd been working for three years when I met him.
two months			I'd been working for two months when I met him.
saw			I'd been working for two months when I saw him.
her			I'd been working for two months when I saw her.
we			We'd been working for two months when we saw her.
studying			We'd been studying for two months when we saw her.
two days			We'd been studying for two days when we saw her.
them			We'd been studying for two days when we saw them.

GENERALIZATION

The Past Perfect Continuous tense functions in the same manner as the other Continuous tenses—to emphasize the length of time of an action, in this case *before* another action in the past:

I'd been studying Engish for three years before I came to the United States.

Formation: *had + been* + verb *-ing*

---

2. M1   T: I'd been studying English for two months   S: How long had you been studying
                before I understood the newscasts.   English before you understood the
                                                                  newscasts?

        He had been reading the novel for three   How long had he been reading the
            hours when she called him.   novel when she called him?
        They had been swimming for an hour when   How long had they been swimming
            the storm came.   when the storm came?
        She had been living here for two weeks when   How long had she been living here
            he met her.   when he met her?
        They had been waiting for four hours when   How long had they been waiting when
            the beer came.   the beer came?
        It had been raining for three days when the   How long had it been raining when the
            flood came.   flood came?
        She had been thinking about getting married   How long had she been thinking about
            for two years before she decided.   getting married before she decided?
        He had been looking for a gift for a week   How long had he been looking for a gift
            when he finally found one.   when he finally found one?

***3. M1T   Situation: Last night at midnight the telephone rang.
            T: Bill sat down to study at 10:00.   S: Bill had been studying for two hours when the
                                                                  telephone rang.
                Bill started reading the detective story   He had been reading the detective story for
                    at 8:00.   four hours when the telephone rang.
                Bill turned on the TV at 9:00.   He had been watching TV for 3 hours when
                                                                     the telephone rang.
                Bill went to sleep at 11:00.   He had been sleeping for an hour when the
                                                                     telephone rang.
                Bill picked up the pizza at 11:30.   He had been eating pizza for half an hour when
                                                                     the telephone rang.
                Bill started the letter at 10:30.   He had been writing the letter for an hour and a
                                                                     half when the telephone rang.
                Bill turned on the "late show" at 11:30.   He had been watching the "late show" for half
                                                                     an hour when the telephone rang.
                Bill turned on the radio at 9:30.   He had been listening to the radio for two and
                                                                     a half hours when the telephone rang.
                Bill turned on the record player at 8:30.   He had been listening to records for three and
                                                                     a half hours when the telephone rang.
                Bill picked up the *New York Times* at 9:30. He had been reading the *New York Times* for two
                                                                     and a half hours when the telephone rang.
                Bill began his homework at 11:00.   He had been doing his homework for an hour
                                                                     when the telephone rang.
                Bill opened the beer at 11:30.   He had been drinking beer for half an hour when
                                                                     the telephone rang.

***4. M2   T: Last night at 6:00 I had been   S1:   Last night at 6:00 (Mr/s. ( )) had been studying
                   studying for two hours.   for two hours and I (had been eating for
                                                                  fifteen minutes.)
                                                   S2:   Last night at 6:00 ( ) had been studying for two
                                                          hours, ( ) had been eating for 15 minutes and I
                                                          had been ( ).
          etc.

5. C   T: How long have you been in the U.S.?
                 Had you studied English before you came here?
                 What had you heard about this country that is true/false?
                 When did you decide on this university/your major?
                 Had you decided on your major before you finished undergraduate school?
                 How many times had you visited the U.S. before you came in (month)?
                 What had you heard about U.S. politics?
                 Have you changed any of your ideas about this country? Which ones? Why?

SECTION TWO

***VERB + DIRECT OBJECT + *TO* + INDIRECT OBJECT

Part A.   *Statement*

Model: She handed a mirror to him.

1. M1   Rep: She's handed a mirror to him.
           Sub: send a letter   S: She's sent a letter to him.
                 teach the song   She's taught the song to him.
                 take a book   She's taken a book to him.
                 tell a legend   She's told a legend to him.
                 throw the frisbee   She's thrown the frisbee to him.
                 pay the money   She's paid the money to him.
                 pass the salt   She's passed the salt to him.
                 give the keys   She's given the keys to him.
                 read the letter   She's read the letter to him.

2. M1   Rep: I'd said "hello" to them before I came.
           Sub: speak French   S: I'd spoken French to them before I came.
                 describe the city   I'd described the city to them before I came.
                 explain the route   I'd explained the route to them before I came.
                 repeat the directions   I'd repeated the directions to them before I came.
                 introduce my brother   I'd introduced my brother to them before I came.
                 mention the university   I'd mentioned the university to them before I came.
                 report the accident   I'd reported the accident to them before I came.

GENERALIZATION

In Lesson Twelve there were verbs followed by two objects:

Lesson Twelve:	Verb	Indirect Object	Direct Object
	The doctor sends	me	a bill.
	We asked	Bill	a question.

In this lesson, there is a different pattern for these verbs and some others:

Lesson Nineteen:	Verb	Direct Object	_to_	Indirect Object
	The doctor sends	the bill	to	me.
	I spoke	French	to	them.

The verbs in Lesson Twelve may follow either pattern (except for _ask_ which has only the Lesson Twelve pattern). Some verbs have only the pattern in Lesson Nineteen (the verbs in Drill 5). The best way to learn these verbs with their patterns is to practice repeatedly the Drills 1-5.

---

3. M1   T:

T:	S:
I threw her the frisbee.	I threw the frisbee to her.
I showed them the slides.	I showed the slides to them.
I read him the letter.	I read the letter to him.
He taught us the song.	He taught the song to us.
He handed me the mirror.	He handed the mirror to me.
He gave her a dollar.	He gave a dollar to her.
We sold them the car.	We sold the car to them.
I paid him the rent.	I paid the rent to him.
We sent you a package.	We sent a package to you.
I passed her the meat.	I passed the meat to her.
We took them the mail.	We took the mail to them.

4. M1   T:

T:	S:
Who took them the mail?	Who took the mail to them?
Who wrote you a letter?	Who wrote a letter to you?
Who passed her the meat?	Who passed the meat to her?
Who sent you a package?	Who sent a package to you?
Who paid him the rent?	Who paid the rent to him?
Who sold them the car?	Who sold the car to them?
Who gave her a dollar?	Who gave a dollar to her?
Who handed me the mirror?	Who handed the mirror to me?
Who taught us the song?	Who taught the song to us?
Who read him the letter?	Who read the letter to him?
Who showed them the slides?	Who showed the slides to them?
Who threw her the frisbee?	Who threw the frisbee to her?

***5. M1   T:

T:	S:
I've already said "goodbye".	I've already said "goodbye" to them.
We've already mentioned the novel.	We've already mentioned the novel to them.
He's already introduced his girl.	He's already introduced his girl to them.
She's already described the house.	She's already described the house to them.
He's already reported the accident.	He's already reported the accident to them.
You've already spoken Spanish.	You've already spoken Spanish to them.
They've already explained the slides.	They've already explained the slides to them.
You've already repeated the question.	You've already repeated the question to them.

***6. C   T: say "goodbye"   S1:   (Have you said) "goodbye" to (the hostess)?

                                          S2:   (Yes, I have, but I haven't said "goodbye" to (the host).)
(No, I haven't. I'm going to say "goodbye" to her now.)

               introduce a friend   S1:   (Did you) introduce your friend to ( )?

                                            S2:   (Yes, I did, but I didn't introduce him/her to ( ).) (No, I didn't. I'm going to introduce her to ( ) now.)

               describe the party
               mention the movie
               speak Arabic
               explain the homework
               repeat the request
               explain the story
               introduce your friends
               say "hello"
               explain the plot
               describe your country
               say "thanks"
               explain the directions

Part B.   *Who?*

Model: Who did Mrs. Van Winkle give the mirror to?

1. M1   T: I'll mention the novel to someone.   S: Who will you mention the novel to?

                   I sent the book to someone.   Who did you send the book to?

                   I'm going to write a letter to someone.   Who are you going to write a letter to?

                   I was showing my slides to someone.   Who were you showing your slides to?

                   I have to report the accident to someone.   Who do you have to report the accident to?

                   I can explain the problem to someone.   Who can you explain the problem to?

                   I might describe the exam to someone.   Who might you describe the exam to?

                   I've reported the accident to someone.   Who have you reported the accident to?

                   I've taken the mail to someone.   Who have you taken the mail to?

                   I'll send the letter to someone.   Who will you send the letter to?

                   I'm going to show the slides to someone.   Who are you going to show the slides to?

2. M1   T: She's taken someone the mail.   S: Who has she taken the mail to?

                   They wrote someone a letter.   Who did they write a letter to?

                   He's going to send someone a package.   Who is he going to send a package to?

                   They're showing someone the slides.   Who are they showing the slides to?

                   They'd read someone the letter.   Who had they read the letter to?

                   He's given someone the book.   Who has he given the book to?

                   They threw someone the frisbee.   Who did they throw the frisbee to?

Note: The *Who* question pattern is the same for Lesson Twelve and Lesson Nineteen:

    Lesson Twelve: I passed someone the book.   } Who did you pass the book to?
    Lesson Nineteen: I passed the book to someone.

This pattern is used in spoken styles. Very formal spoken and written styles will have: *To whom* did you teach the song?

---

3. M2   T: ( ) gave someone a dollar.   S1:   Who did you give a dollar to?
                                                 S2:   (I gave a dollar to ( ).) (I gave ( ) a dollar.)

         ( ) has explained the problem   S1:   Who have you explained the problem to?
         to someone.   S2:   (I've explained the problem to ( ).)
         ( ) is going to write someone a letter.
         ( ) was repeating the question to someone.
         ( ) will show someone his slides.
         ( ) can describe the movie to someone.
         ( ) has told someone the legend.
         ( ) is telling someone a story.
         ( ) has introduced his friends to someone.
         ( ) was speaking (native language) to someone.
         ( ) has to report the accident to someone.
         ( ) is going to say "hello" to someone.
         ( ) might teach someone the new song.

4. M2   T: ( ) gave Bill something.   S1:   What did you give (to) Bill?
                                           S2:   (I gave him a dollar.) (I gave a dollar to him.)
         ( ) gave someone a dollar.   S1:   Who did you give a dollar to?
                                      S2:   (I gave the boy a dollar.) (I gave a dollar to the boy.)
         ( ) described something to his friend.
         ( ) sent someone a package.
         ( ) said something to the teacher.
         ( ) sent Bill something.
         ( ) said "hello" to someone.
         ( ) described his country to someone.
         ( ) reported something to the police.
         ( ) told someone a legend.
         ( ) sent someone a gift.
         ( ) told his friend something.
         ( ) wrote someone a postcard.
         ( ) explained something to the child.

5. C   T: describe   S1:   (What did you describe to your friend?) (Who will you describe
                                      your country to?)
                               S2:   (I described my country to him.) (I'll describe my country to
                                      the class.)

         give
         say
         read
         explain
         sell
         report
         bring
         send
         mention
         repeat
         write
         describe

***6. C   T: ( ) doesn't understand the math problem.   S1:   (Who can explain it to him?)

                                                            S2:   (( ) can. He's explained math to me many times.)

                ( ) has had an accident with his car.   S1:   (Who should he report it to?)

                                                            S2:   (The police. We have to report all accidents to the police)

                ( ) didn't hear the question.   S1:   (Someone should repeat it to him.)

                                                            S2:   (I can't. I didn't hear it either.)

( ) hasn't had a letter from home for a long time.
The children want to hear a story.
The class would like to see some slides.
( ) has never been to your country.
( ) is new here and doesn't have many friends.
The student bought a gift for his parents.
The professor would like some coffee from the cafeteria.
The boys don't know how to play frisbee.
( ) didn't understand the movie.
( ) saw a fire yesterday.
( ) got some slides from his country yesterday.
The batter fell down.

SECTION THREE

REFLEXIVES

Part A.   *With <u>by</u>*

Model: I'm going to tell it by myself.

1. M1   Rep: I'd rather do it by myself.

           Sub: she   S: She'd rather do it by herself.

                 he   He'd rather do it by himself.

                 we   We'd rather do it by ourselves.

                 you   You'd rather do it by yourself.

                 you and Joe   You and Joe would rather do it by yourselves.

                 they   They'd rather do it by themselves.

                 I   I'd rather do it by myself.

GENERALIZATION

Lesson Twelve: The *self* words were Indirect Objects: He bought himself a coat.

Lesson Nineteen: *by + -self* means *alone, without help.* He doesn't need help; he can do it by himself.

---

2. M1T   Rep: No one can learn a language for you. You have to do it by yourself.
          Sub: him   S: No one can learn a language for him. He has to do it by himself.
               her   No one can learn a language for her. She has to do it by herself.
               us   No one can learn a language for us. We have to do it by ourselves.
               them   No one can learn a language for them. They have to do it by themselves.
               me   No one can learn a language for me. I have to do it by myself.
               you and your   No one can learn a language for you and your friend. You have to do
                  friend   it by yourselves.

3. M2   T: Shall we help Bill with his homework? (can)   S: No, he can (do it by himself).
                Shall we help the boys report their accident? (have to)   No, they (have to do it by themselves).
                Shall I help you find the book? (going to)
                Shall we ask the boys to help us mow the lawn? (can)
                Shall we help Jane set the table? (will)
                Shall I do the boys' laundry? (should)
                Shall we help the girls buy the groceries? (ought to)
                Shall we help Nancy with the dishes? (want to)
                Shall we help the men wash the car? (should)
                Shall I help you with the homework? (ought to)
                Shall I help Jack with the painting? (will)
                Shall we finish my work? (should)
                Shall I help Jane and Bill with the plans for the picnic? (can)

***Part B.   *Emphatic*

Model: You can tell it yourself.

1. M1   T: They asked me to report the accident.   S: They should report it themselves.
                She asked him to report the accident.   She should report it herself.
                He asked her to report the accident.   He should report it himself.
                We asked them to report the accident.   You should report it yourselves.
                I asked her to report the accident   You should report it yourself.
                They asked me to report the accident.   They should report it themselves.
                She asked me to report the accident.   She should report it herself.

GENERALIZATION

In this pattern, the pronouns emphasize a noun (usually the subject of a sentence). It is used in place of stress.

He told the story.
He told the story himself.

---

2. M2   T: He's a pretty good story teller.   S: (You're a pretty good one yourself.)
                He admired their new car.   (He has a new one himself.)
                The girls asked me to do the work.   (They ought to do some work themselves.)
                We asked them to be on time.   (You should be on time yourselves.)
                Nancy admired Bill's storytelling.
                They laughed at my old car.

(exercise continued on next page)

T: The boys should learn to swim.
      Bill criticized Nancy's review.
      They got a good grade on the exam.
      The boys shouldn't work so hard.
      We admired their language learning ability.
      Jane laughed at Bill's swimming.
      Jane and Jack laughed at Bill's answer.
      We told them to relax.

3. M2   T: Can I help you with the work?   S: (No, thanks. I can do it by myself.)
               John asked me to report the accident.   (He should do it himself.)
               Is John going to the theater with us?   (Yes, he doesn't like to go by himself.)
               He needs help with the research paper.   (He should do it by himself.)   (I need help
                                                              myself.)

         We're going to get John some good records.
         Do you want me to help with the dishes?
         George wants you to do the laundry.
         The girls advised us to be on time.
         Mary and John want you to go out to dinner with them.
         Someone should watch the children when they're swimming.
         Jane wants you to make the decision.
         Will you help John? He wants to lift the heavy chair.
         Can I help you do the shopping?
         Jane is a very good cook.

4. C   T: What kinds of things do you like to do   S: (I like to study alone.) (I like to go
                by yourself?   to the movies by myself.)
              Do you always type your own papers?
              Do you live alone or do you have a roommate?
              Did someone help you with your last application?
              Does someone help you cook?
              Did you come here by yourself?
              Who helped you buy your car?
              Do you like to travel with friends?
              Who helps you shop for groceries/clothes?
              Who will help you fill out the forms for (registration)?

SUMMARY DIALOGUE

Bill: Listen, I'll tell you this very funny story.

Nancy: I don't want to hear a story now. I'm busy.

Bill: You should go out more, Nancy. You're always by yourself.

Nancy: Look who's talking! You should take that advice yourself!

Bill: O.K., O.K. I'm just kidding. Now listen to this . . .

Nancy: O.K., I'm listening.

LESSON NINETEEN – SUMMARY OF PATTERNS

I. PAST PERFECT

	Subject	Had	Past Participle	Completer	Short Answer
Statement	Rip	had	gone	for a walk.	
Question (Yes/No)	*Had* Rip	had	gone	for a walk?	Yes, he had. No, he hadn't.

II. PAST PERFECT CONTINUOUS

	Subject	Had	*been V -ing*	Completer	Short Answer
Statement	Rip	had	been planning	a hunting trip.	
Question (Yes/No)	Had Rip		been planning	a hunting trip?	Yes, he had. No, he hadn't.

III. SENTENCES WITH TWO OBJECTS

	Subject	Verb	Indirect Object	Direct Object		Indirect Object
A.	He	sent	me	a bill.		
	He	asked	me	a question.		
B.	He	sent		a bill	to	me.
	He	described		the movie	to	me.

LESSON TWENTY

INTRODUCTION   Abbreviations and Acronyms

Chen and Carlos have learned to get along very well in English, but acronyms give Chen trouble and abbreviations confuse Carlos.

Carlos: *If you have time, Bill, I'd like some help.*

Bill: Sure, Carlos. What's the trouble?

5   Carlos: I have friends in many parts of the United States and when they put only the abbreviations of the place in the address, it's hard to know where they are. For instance, here's Mo., Me., Miss., Mich., Minn., Mass., and Mont.

Bill: (laughing) That's not how we pronounce them.

Carlos: O.K. *Pronounce them for me* then.

10   Bill: Missouri, Maine, Mississippi, Michigan, Minnesota, Massachusetts, and Montana. It's easy to see that they could be confusing. The state abbreviations are only used in writing. If you're talking about the state, you usually say the whole name. If you're writing a formal or business letter, you usually spell out the name completely.

Carlos: How do they decide on the abbreviations?

15   Bill: A long word often uses the first syllable as an abbreviation; a short one sometimes uses the first and last letters. There are some exceptions, though. States of two words use the first letter of each word, such as New York—N.Y.

Carlos: I see.

Chen: *You could have looked them up in the dictionary.* There's usually a list at the back.

20   Carlos: Yes, and I suppose I should have, but I might have chosen the wrong one. Then my letter never would have gotten to my friend.

Bill: Haven't you written to any of your friends yet?

Carlos: Yes. If I can't read the abbreviation, I usually try to copy it exactly and *ask the clerk at the post office to check it.* If he can read it, I know my friend is going to get the letter.
25   Sometimes the clerk corrects it for me.

Chen: Abbreviations like that aren't too hard to figure out. But I think it's impossible when people here talk in letters.

Bill: "Talk in letters"?

Chen: Yes, you know—FBI, CIA, SEC, HEW, FDA, FCC.

30   Bill: I see what you mean. Those are usually government agencies. It takes less time to
say FBI than Federal Bureau of Investigation. Usually, we say each letter, but sometimes
the abbreviations are so common that they've become words—NASA and NATO for example.
I guess the journalists and commentators always look for ways to save reporting time and space.

    Carlos: If you've learned the abbreviations and acronyms of this language, you've really
35   mastered it.

    Chen: No . . . Once we've learned these, they'll *make up some new ones* and we'll have to
start over.

OUTLINE OF PATTERNS

Example

Section One	*If* clauses		
Part A.	Request		If you have time, I'd like some help.
Part B.	Habit		If I can't read the abbreviations, I try . . .
Part C.	Conclusion/Generalization		If you've learned . . . you've learned the language.
Section Two	Modals		
Part A.	Perfect Modals		you could have looked up . . .
Part B.	Perfect Continuous Modals		They should have been studying.
Part C.	Negative and Short Answers		
Section Three	Verb + Direct Object + *for* + Indirect Object		
Part A.	Statement, Negatives, Questions		Pronounce them for me . . .
Part B.	*Who* as Indirect Object		
Section Four	Verb + NP + *to* verb		I ask the clerk to check it.
Section Five	Separable Two-Word verbs		. . . looked them up . . .

NOTE: Appendix I is a list of state abbreviations and some common government agencies.

COMPREHENSION QUESTIONS

1. How do Carlos and Chen do in English?

2. What gives Chen trouble?

3. What confuses Carlos?

*4. Why does Carlos have trouble knowing where his friends are?

5. Are the state abbreviations used in speech?

6. Do you use abbreviations in formal letters?

*7. How do they decide on the abbreviations?

*8. Are there any exceptions? Which ones?

 9. How could Carlos have found the abbreviations?

*10. What might have happened?

11. Has he written to any of his friends?

*12. How does he make sure his friends will get the letter?

13. What agencies usually talk in letters?

*14. Which acronyms have become words?

15. Why do journalists and commentators use acronyms?

*16. If you've learned the abbreviations and acronyms of a language, have you learned the language?

*17. Does your language use abbreviations and acronyms? What are some common ones?

*18. Discuss post office regulations and special problems such as: a forwarding address, returned mail, registered letters, insurance, tracing a lost letter, zip code, etc.

Vocabulary

Nouns	Verbs		Adjectives
abbreviation	allow	miss	influential
acronym	babysit	oblige	lonely
beach	cool off	oversleep	whole
commentator	encourage	persuade	
failure	expect	remind	**Adverb**
handwriting	fill out	request	
journalist	force	start over	exactly
recital	get out of	trace (a letter)	
	hand in	turn off	
	hang up	turn on	
	instruct	urge	
	look up	warn	
	make up (invent)	write down	

SECTION ONE

IF CLAUSES — I

Part A.   *Request*

Model: If you have time, I'd like some help.

1. M1 Rep: If you have time, I'd like some help.
       Sub: a minute—advice   S: If you have a minute, I'd like some advice.
                a while—company   If you have a while, I'd like some company.
                an hour—suggestions   If you have an hour, I'd like some suggestions.
                          (exercise continued on next page)

T: a few minutes—information   S: If you have a few minutes, I'd like some information.
     a second—addresses   If you have a second, I'd like some addresses.
     a minute—help   If you have a minute, I'd like some help.

GENERALIZATION

If clauses often precede a polite request for assistance of some kind. It acknowledges that you're asking the person to take time (often a valuable thing to people from the United States—as you may have noticed). Notice that the *tense* of the verb in the *if* clause is present; the other clause most often contains a polite expression such as "I'd like ——" or "please ——."

---

2. M2   T: If you have time,——.   S: If you have time (please give me some advice).
             If they have a minute,——.   If they have a minute, (please ask them to look at this book).
             If she has an hour or two,——.
             If you have a few minutes, ——.
             If they have a few hours, ——.
             If you have a second, ——.
             If you have a free week, ——.
             If they have a free hour, ——.
             If they have a free day, ——.
             If she has a free minute, ——.
             If he has a free hour, ——.
             If she has a minute, ——.
             If he has a couple of minutes, ——.
             If they have an hour or so, ——.

Part B.   *Habit*

Model: If I can't read the abbreviation, I try to copy it exactly.

1. M1   Rep: If I can't read the abbreviation, I try to copy it exactly.
        Sub: have the money—try to go on   S: If I have the money, I try to go on a vacation
               a vacation every year   every year.
             have the time—go downtown   If I have the time, I go downtown once a week.
               once a week
             need the exercise—walk around   If I need the exercise, I walk around the campus.
               the campus
             am lonely—write long letters   If I am lonely, I write long letters to my friends.
               to my friends
             don't need to lose weight—   If I don't need to lose weight, I don't go on a
               don't go on a diet   diet.
             am angry—cool off before I   If I am angry, I cool off before I see anyone.
               see anyone

GENERALIZATION

If clauses are also used to relate habitual actions. *If* in these clauses means about the same as *when.* The present tense of the verb is usually used in both clauses.

When I have time I go downtown.   If I have time I go downtown.

---

2. M2   T: If my roommate sleeps too late, ——.   S: If my roommate sleeps too late, (I try
                                                              to wake him gently).

         If I have a test, ——.
         If I fail a test, ——.
         If I get up too late for class, ——.
         If my friend is late for an appointment, ——.
         If my friend gets into trouble, ——.
         If my friend passes a big exam, ——.
         If I pass a test, ——.
         If my friends are rude to the professor, ——.
         If my brother is late, ——.
         If my sister gets in trouble with the police, ——.

Part C.   *Conclusion/Generalization*

Model: If you've learned the acronyms of this language, you've really mastered it.

1. M1   Rep: If you've learned the acronyms, you've mastered the language.
         Sub: have been to New York—   S: If you've been to New York, you've seen pollution.
               have seen pollution
               can drive a VW—can drive anything   If you can drive a VW, you can drive anything.
               need a vacation—should take   If you need a vacation, you should take some
               some time off   time off.
               can afford a Rolls-Royce—can   If you can afford a Rolls-Royce, you can buy an
               buy an airplane   airplane.
               have seen one city—have seen   If you have seen one city, you have seen them all.
               them all
               have done the work—should pass   If you have done the work, you should pass the
               the test   test.

GENERALIZATION

If clauses are also used to make generalizations or draw conclusions. *If* here usually means the same as *when* in Part B. and *you* (often) has the impersonal meaning, particularly in informal speech. The *time* indicated is generally present (or no specification), the *tense* is usually present or persent perfect.

---

2. M1T   T: If you have time, I'd like some suggestions.   S: Request
               If he has a test, he studies for three days.   Habit
               If you've learned the acronyms, you've learned the   Generalization
               language.
               If my friend is late, I try to cover up for him.   Habit
               If you've read one English book, you've read them all.   Generalization
               If you go to the store, I'd like some cigarettes.   Request
               If they have time, they do the homework every day.   Habit
               If John is going to the party, ask him to give my regrets. Request
               If Mary gains weight, she goes on a diet.   Habit

3. M2   T: If you have a car, ——.   S: If you have a car, (you can go downtown).
                If you don't have time, ——.   If you don't have time, (you can't finish your test).
                If you don't know the address, ——.
                If you don't have money, ——.
                If you have a degree in (country), ——.
                If you have money, ——.
                If you have influential friends, ——.
                If you don't have influential friends, ——.
                If you don't get good grades, ——.
                If you don't learn English, ——.
                If you learn English, ——.
                If you get good grades, ——.

4. M2   T: Make a request or invitation.
                If you're in town, ——.   S: If you're in town, (please call me).
                If you're going to the drugstore, ——.
                If you're going to be in London, ——.
                If you have time, ——.
                If you have a minute, ——.
                If you have a free weekend, ——.
                If you have a few minutes, ——.
                If you're going to the grocery store, ——.
                If you're going to the news stand, ——.
                If you see Bill, ——.
                If you call the theater, ——.
                If you find my coat, ——.
                If you have any difficulty, ——.

5. M2   T: Ask ( ) his habits on a free   S1:   (What do you do if you have a free weekend?)
                weekend.   S2:   If I have a free weekend, (I visit my friends).
                Ask ( ) his habits if he runs out of money.
                Ask ( ) his habits if he gets very tired.
                Ask ( ) his habits if he gets angry.
                Ask ( ) his habits if he can't get a newspaper.
                Ask ( ) his habits if he can't cash a check.
                Ask ( ) his habits if he can't read someone's handwriting.
                Ask ( ) his habits if he doesn't understand the assignment.
                Ask ( ) his habits if he doesn't like the food.
                Ask ( ) his habits if he has difficulty with the police.
                Ask ( ) his habits if he has a headache.
                Ask ( ) his habits if he is in an embarrassing situation.

6. M2   T: Make a generalization.
                You succeed ——.   S: You succeed (if you know the right people).
                You know about cities ——.
                You know about the world ——.
                You know about people ——.
                You've learned a great lesson ——.
                You've succeeded in learning a language ——.
                You've succeeded in life ——.
                A person is happy ——.
                Men fail ——.

(exercise continued on next page)

T: Life is easy ——.
      Life is difficult ——.
      People are unhappy ——.
      People are fat ——.

7. C   T: You think that your friend is going to the grocery store. Ask him to get some cigarettes.

        S: (If you're going to the grocery store, please get me some cigarettes.)

        T: How do you know if someone has succeeded?
              What do you do if you get angry?
              What do you do if you run out of gas in the middle of the night?
              Can you tell if someone is lying? How?
              Where can you go if you want to be by yourself?
              Where can you get help if you need advice?
              If your friend asks to borrow money, what do you do?
              You think your friend is going to the bank. Ask him to cash a check for you.
              How can you tell if someone has a successful life?
              You think your friend is going to the store. Ask him to get you some tomato juice.

SECTION TWO

MODALS

Part A.   *Perfect Modals*

Model: You could have looked up the abbreviations.
          I might have gotten the wrong one.

1. M1   Rep: He could have looked up the words.
         Sub: should   S: He should have looked up the words.
              found   He should have found the words.
              the restaurant   He should have found the restaurant.
              might   He might have found the restaurant.
              missed   He might have missed the restaurant.
              the turn   He might have missed the turn.
              must   He must have missed the turn.

GENERALIZATION

In Lessons Nine, Eleven, Thirteen and Seventeen, the modals indicated Present or Future actions or intentions. In this lesson, the modals indicate Past actions or intentions. The formation of the perfect modals is always:

Modal + *have* + Past Participle

Previous Patterns	New Patterns
I can go (now) (tomorrow).	I could have gone yesterday.
I'll go tomorrow.	I would have gone yesterday.
I should go (now) (tomorrow).	I should have gone yesterday.
It must be the mailman at the door.	It must have been the mailman at the door.
He might be late.	He might have been late.
It may be a good movie.	It may have been a good movie.

Note:

may have
might have   + Past Participle = "possibility"

Example: They didn't start very early. They ⎰ may ⎱ have been late.
⎱ might ⎰

Note: In speech, *have* is usually pronounced [əv]. Listen carefully as your teacher pronounces the sentences under "new patterns" above.

2. M1T   Rep: I could have looked up the words yesterday.

Sub:		S:	
today			I could look up the words today.
my friends			I could look up my friends today.
call			I could call my friends today.
should			I should call my friends today.
yesterday			I should have called my friends yesterday.
my family			I should have called my family yesterday.
written			I should have written my family yesterday.
today			I should write my family today.

□ *MUST HAVE* + PAST PARTICIPLE

NOTE: This pattern has only the deduction meaning, never the obligation meaning which is possible with *must* + Verb.

	must + Verb	*must have* + PP
Obligation	We must pay the bill.	
	The boy mustn't go out in the rain.	————————
Deduction	Someone is here. It must be Bill.	Someone was here. It must have been Bill.

408

3. M1T   T: Someone is coming.   S: It must be John.
                Someone called you.   It must have been John.
                Someone is waiting.   It must be John.
                Someone planned the party.   It must have been John.
                Someone bought a Rolls-Royce.   It must have been John.
                Someone is hungry.   It must be John.

4. M2   T: There was a message for John to go to   S: He must not have (gotten it. He wasn't
                   the office.   at the office.)
                There was a notice for the students about   They must not have (seen it. No one
                   the meeting.   came to the meeting).
                There was an article in the paper about the   He must not have (read it. He didn't
                   musical group Bill likes.   say anything about it).
                There was a message for Nancy to call you.
                There was a notice about the lecture on Jose's country.
                There was an article about the political scandals that Bob is interested in.
                There was a note on the door for Bill to get the beer.
                There was a message at the office for Charlie to bring glasses.
                There was a sign on the door for the students to come to the party.
                There was a message at the office for Nancy to bring records.

5. M2   T: John slept in until 10:00 this morning.   S: (He must have stayed out late last night.)
                                                                 (He must have been tired.)
                Bill and Jim had to break a window to get   (They must have lost their key.)
                   into their apartment.
                When the professor returned the exams, Jane looked sad.
                Nancy's mother was angry with her.
                Our instructor was very disappointed with me.
                When Jack came in after the storm, his clothes were all wet.
                Karen was very happy when the instructor returned the paper.
                The students missed the plane.
                The boys had to wash dishes at the restaurant after they ate dinner that night.
                Bill's gas gauge read empty this morning. Now he's walking along the country road.
                Last summer Jane didn't know how to swim. Now she's in the swimming competition.
                Last year Bill couldn't drive a car. Now he races every weekend.
                The salesman was going to call back at 5:00. The phone rang while I was in the shower.

☐ *COULD HAVE* + PAST PARTICIPLE***

NOTE: The perfect modal with *could* has two meanings. Look at the examples below.

Probability

    A.   Someone called me at midnight. It was probably John.

    B.   It couldn't have been John; we were playing bridge at midnight.

    or   Yes, it could have been John. He mentioned calling you.

Ability

    A.   We needed someone to go to the meeting. No one could go.

    B.   I could have gone; I wasn't busy.

    or   I couldn't have gone either. I had a doctor's appointment.

In this sense, both the affirmative and negative statements indicate that the action did not occur.

      Example: I could have gone, but I didn't.

                      I couldn't have gone, and I didn't.

Listen carefully to the context of the sentences, and you will be able to tell which meaning is used.

---

6. M1T   T: It wasn't possible for me to go with you.   S: I couldn't have gone with you.

                It was possible for me to go to the lab.   I could have gone to the lab.

                It was possible for Bill to go to the meeting.   Bill could have gone to the meeting.

                It wasn't possible for Nancy to finish the work.   Nancy couldn't have finished the work.

                It wasn't possible for Joe to leave.   Joe couldn't have left.

                It was possible for us to fly to Toronto.   We could have flown to Toronto.

                It was possible for them to come with us.   They could have come with us.

                It wasn't possible for us to take a vacation.   We couldn't have taken a vacation.

7. M2   T: We had enough room for you on the trip   S: I couldn't have (gone anyway. I had to to Niagara Falls.   study).

                There were enough books at the bookstore.   I couldn't have (gotten one anyway. I didn't have any money).

                We needed a fourth for bridge.   I couldn't have (played. I had a dentist's appointment).

                We wanted someone to buy the beer.

                There was enough food at the party.

                We needed someone to write the letter.

                There weren't enough people to play soccer.

                We needed someone to pick up the refreshments.

                We didn't have enough people to play bridge.

                We wanted someone to bring records.

                There weren't enough people to help with the party.

                We needed someone to do the work.

☐ *SHOULD HAVE* + PAST PARTICIPLE

NOTE: In Lesson Nine, *should* + Verb meant "good idea"; or "not a good idea."

    Example: I should go home now.

                    He shouldn't stay out late.

In this lesson, the meaning of the modal is the same, but the meaning of the sentence is different.

    Example: I should have gone home.   (I didn't go home.)

                    He shouldn't have stayed out late.   (He stayed out late.)

Note the comparison of the sentence meanings with *could:*

I could have gone. (I didn't go.)	I should have gone. (I didn't go.)
I couldn't have gone. (I didn't go.)	I shouldn't have gone. (I went.)

---

8. M1T

T:	S:
Chen couldn't have attended the meeting.	Chen didn't attend the meeting.
Bill shouldn't have gone to the movie.	Bill went to the movie.
Jane could have bought the beer.	Jane didn't buy the beer.
Carlos should have written home.	Carlos didn't write home.
Nancy shouldn't have failed the test.	Nancy failed the test.
Judy could have played bridge.	Judy didn't play bridge.
Karen should have come early.	Karen didn't come early.

9. M1T

T:	S:
Bill didn't go to the game because he was busy.	He couldn't have gone to the game.
Bill went to the game and then he failed an exam.	He shouldn't have gone to the game.
Bill didn't go to the game because he didn't know about it.	He could have gone to the game.
Bill forgot there was a game; the team lost because he wasn't there.	He should have gone to the game.
Nancy didn't write home; her parents were worried.	She should have written home.
Nancy didn't write home because she broke her hand.	She couldn't have written home.
Carlos wasn't busy, but he didn't go to the meeting.	He could have gone to the meeting.
Carlos forgot to go to the meeting and his friends were angry.	He should have gone to the meeting.

10. M2

T:		
go to the meeting	S1:	(I should have gone to the meeting.)
	S2:	Why didn't you?
	S1:	(I forgot about it.)
not buy the car	S1:	( ) shouldn't have bought the (new) car.
	S2:	Why not?
	S1:	(Now he doesn't have enough money to pay his invoice.)

leave the party early

not stay downtown so long

(exercise continued on next page)

T: not spend so much money
      sell my books from last term
      not sleep so long in the morning
      drive to school
      not take a long vacation
      not write that angry letter
      go shopping with my friend
      not eat so much pizza

11. M2   Listen to the situation; then make a comment.

T: John, who didn't study, failed the exam.   S: (He should have studied.)
      Nancy, who studied very hard, failed the   (Maybe she shouldn't have studied
          exam.   so hard.)
      No one answered the phone when I called   (She must have been out.) (She might
          Nancy's house.   have gone to the library.)
      The drive to New York City takes six hours.   (He could have been there by 6:00.)
          He left at noon.
      Carlos didn't write to his friends because he didn't know their post office code.
      Chen didn't go to the game because he didn't know the rules.
      Susan didn't go to the beach because she didn't know how to swim.
      I had an appointment with the professor at 4:00, but he didn't come.
      We couldn't find the street you life on.
      I haven't seen Joe since last term.
      He wanted to go to New York for the weekend, but he didn't know how to get there.
      They wanted a second-hand desk, but they didn't know where to find one.
      He ran out of money last weekend when the banks were closed.
      I didn't do the homework because I didn't understand it.
      She wanted to go to France, but she didn't speak French.
      I called and called Jane yesterday, but no one answered.

☐ *WOULD HAVE* + PAST PARTICIPLE

NOTE: The difference between the perfect modals with *could* and *would* is very much the
same as that between *can* (ability, possibility) and *will* (intention).

Example: I can go and I will.   I could have gone and I would have.

The results of the sentences with the perfect modals is the same, i.e., the action didn't occur.

Example: I would have gone.   (I didn't go.)
              I wouldn't have gone.   (I didn't go.)

Sentences with the perfect modal with *would* reveal opinions or beliefs of the speaker.

Example: There was a free beer party in honor of the president.
              A.   I could have gone, I didn't have anything to do.
              B.   I would have gone, but I was busy.
              C.   I wouldn't have gone for free champagne.

---

12. M1   Situation: There was a meeting to support the President's policies. I was busy so I couldn't go to the meeting.

Rep: But I wouldn't have gone anyway because I don't like his policies.

Sub:	S:
think his policies are dangerous	But I wouldn't have gone anyway because I think his policies are dangerous.
don't like his ideas about military spending	But I wouldn't have gone anyway because I don't like his ideas about military spending.
think his ideas about civil rights are foolish	But I wouldn't have gone anyway because I think his ideas about civil rights are foolish.
think his policies on education are old-fashioned	But I wouldn't have gone anyway because I think his policies on education are old-fashioned.
don't approve of his attitude toward minority groups	But I wouldn't have gone anyway because I don't approve of his attitude toward minority groups.
think his policies on the environment are ridiculous	But I wouldn't have gone anyway because I think his policies on the environment are ridiculous.

***13. M2   Situation: There was a party to raise money for ( ).

T:	S:
I would ——	I would (have attended, but I was busy.)
I could ——	I could (have gone, but I forgot about it.)
I wouldn't ——	I wouldn't have (given them any money. They spend it on foolish things.)
I couldn't ——	I couldn't have (gone. I didn't have a ticket.)

□ *WH* QUESTIONS AND SHORT ANSWERS

14. M1

T:	S:
Chen should have gone somewhere.	Where should he have gone?
Bill could have phoned sometime.	When could he have phoned?
Jane would have said something.	What would she have said?
Charlie might have gone somewhere.	Where might he have gone?
Bill should have bought something.	What should he have bought?
Mary would have seen someone.	Who would she have seen?
The Camerons should have gone somewhere.	Where should they have gone?
The Bruders could have said something.	What could they have said?

GENERALIZATION

The formation of the WH questions is the same as with the other patterns.

Someone   should have gone.

Who   should have gone?   Chen.

Chen   should have gone   somewhere.

Where   should he have gone?   To the party.

The short answers are as follows:

Should Chen have looked up the number?   *Yes, he should have.
                                  No, he shouldn't have.

*NOTE: *have* is not usually reduced here. Listen to your teacher.

---

15. M1 T: Could Chen have phoned?   S: No, but Bill could have.
            Should Chen have been at the meeting?   No, but Bill should have.
            Would Chen have written a letter?   No, but Bill would have.
            Might Chen have gone home?   No, but Bill might have.
            Should Chen have called Jane?   No, but Bill should have.
            Could Chen have bought a Rolls-Royce?   No, but Bill could have.
            Would Chen have lent me a hundred   No, but Bill would have.
              dollars?

***16 C T: Joe made a mistake. He dialed the   S1: (What should he have done?) (How could
             wrong number and had to pay for   he have gotten out of paying for it?)
             the call.   S2: (He could have called the operator.) (He
                                                      should have made sure of the number.)

            It was very embarrassing. The guests S1: (What could have happened?) (What should
            were two hours late.   they have done?)
                                                  S2: (They must have gotten lost.) (They should
                                                      have called.)

            I called the police four times before S1: (Where could they have been?) (What might
            someone answered.   have been wrong?)
                                                  S2: (They might have been very busy.) (The
                                                      phones might have been out.)

            The student made a mistake. He called the police to report a fire.
            Joe doesn't know what happened. He wrote his family two weeks ago, but he hasn't
              heard from them.
            The girls are embarrassed. The party they planned was a failure.
            The professor was furious. All of the students were an hour late for his lecture.
            Carlos was unhappy. His letter to his friend came back marked "no such address."
            Jill studied for two weeks. She failed the exam.
            Chen was very disappointed. He went to the baseball game, but he didn't understand
              anything.
            The boys were three hours late for their date.
            Bill sent a gift to his parents. It was broken when it arrived.
            Charlie sent a very important letter. He fotgot to register it.

17. C   T: Tell something you could/should/might have done in the past, but didn't.

        S: (I should have learned English before I came to the U.S.)
            (I could have visited the U.S. last year, but I went to Europe instead.)
            (I might have gone to Georgetown, but I came here instead.)

Part B.   *Perfect Continuous Modals*

1. M1   Rep: I should have been studying, but I went to the movies.
        Sub: he   S: He should have been studying, but he went to the movies.
              could   He could have been studying, but he went to the movies.
              working   He could have been working, but he went to the movies.
              they   They could have been working, but they went to the movies.
              should   They should have been working, but they went to the movies.
              practicing   They should have been practicing, but they went to the movies.

GENERALIZATION

The continuous forms of the Perfect Modals have a form and function similar to the other continuous patterns. They emphasize the duration of the action.

Formation:
could
should
would
may
might
must
} + *have* + *been* + V *-ing*

NOTE: *may/might* = possibility
        must   = deduction

Example: He didn't answer when I called.
           He may/might have been working outside.
           He must have been away.

NOTE: Short Answers: Yes, he might have been.
                         No, he couldn't have been.

2. M2   T: Mr. Hastings takes his car out every   S: (It must have been raining yesterday.)
             day when it doesn't rain. He didn't
             take his car out yesterday.
             I knocked on John's door because he said   (He might have been sleeping.)
             he would be home. No one answered.
             Jane has a test tomorrow. I saw her at the dance last night.
             Susan usually goes for a walk in the afternoon. When I called at 3:00 yesterday, no one
                 answered.
             The boys said they were going to the library yesterday, but I didn't see them.
             Nancy usually listens to the game in her room. When I called, no one answered.
             John said he would come when his friend arrived. He never came.
             The girls like to sew on weekends. They didn't come to the party last weekend.
             I don't understand why John didn't come to the party.
             I don't understand why the boys didn't keep their appointment with the professor.
             Mrs. Hastings' mother is in the hospital. Mrs. Hastings didn't come to the club meeting.
             George hasn't written home in weeks. He had time yesterday but he was listening to
                 the baseball game.
             He is giving a piano recital tomorrow. He went to the movies last night.
             The baseball team lost yesterday's game. This morning they all slept late.

3. C   T: What were you doing last weekend? What could you have been doing? What should
                 you have been doing? What might you have been doing?
             Did you ever call a friend when he didn't answer? What did you think he might/must
                 have been doing?
             Have you ever wasted a lot of time? What could/should you have been doing?
             Have you ever misunderstood what someone said? What happened? What must he have
                 said?
             Have you ever been insulted by someone? What happened? What should you have done?
                 What should he have said/done?

Part C.   *Negative Statements and Short Answers*

1. M1   T: Did David do the homework?   S: Yes, and he should have.
               Did David see a lawyer?   Yes, and he should have.
               Did David get the money?   Yes, and he should have.
               Did David find a job?   Yes, and he should have.
               Did David get a haircut?   Yes, and he should have.

               Did David go to the movies?   Yes, but he shouldn't have.
               Did David eat the whole cake?   Yes, but he shouldn't have.
               Did David lose the game?   Yes, but he shouldn't have.
               Did David drive too fast?   Yes, but he shouldn't have.
               Did David spend all the money?   Yes, but he shouldn't have.

               Was David doing the work?   Yes, and he should have been.
               Was David watching TV?   Yes, and he should have been.
               Was David working hard?   Yes, and he should have been.
               Was David buying a car?   Yes, and he should have been.
               Was David writing home?   Yes, and he should have been.

               Was David singing in the shower?   Yes, but he shouldn't have been.
               Was David walking downtown?   Yes, but he shouldn't have been.
               Was David watching TV?   Yes, but he shouldn't have been.
               Was David buying a Rolls-Royce?   Yes, but he shouldn't have been.

2. M1   T: John was going to New York last   S: He must not have; I saw him at the picnic.
                  weekend. (saw him at the picnic)
               John had to hand in the paper   He must not have; I saw him in the library
                  yesterday. (saw him in the library   last night.
                  last night)
               John was going to get a new car last   He must not have; I saw him in the old
                  week. (saw him in the old one)   one.
               John was going to get a new apartment.   He must not have; I saw him in front of
                  (saw him in front of his old building)   his old building.
               John was going to sell his car. (saw him He must not have; I saw him in it this
                  in it this morning)   morning.
               John was going to the party Saturday.   He must not have; I didn't see him there.
                  (didn't see him there)
               John was going to go to the baseball   He must not have; I saw him at the picnic.
                  game Saturday. (saw him at the picnic)

3. M1   Listen: I didn't see Judy at the party.   Rep: She might not have been there—she had to
                                                              finish a paper.

                  John wasn't in class when it began.   He might not have been on time—he overslept
                                                              this morning.

                  I got up late, so I didn't go to the   They might not have had any during the
                    store for a *New York Times.*   strike.
                  There was an ad in the paper for a   John might not have seen it—he doesn't
                    good used car.   get the paper.

GENERALIZATION

Would, could and *should* contract with *not* in the Perfect tenses in the same manner as the other tenses; *may, must* and *might* do not usually contract with the negative.

Example: He wouldn't have gone.
                  He couldn't have gone.
                  He shouldn't have gone.
                  He may not have gone.
                  He must not have gone.
                  He might not have gone.

---

4. M1   T: Was John working?   S: No, but he should've been.
               Was Mary sewing?   No, but she should've been.
               Were the boys studying?   No, but they should've been.
               Were the girls doing their homework?   No, but they should've been.
               Was Bill washing the car?   No, but he should've been.
               Were Carlos and Chen finishing the paper?   No, but they should've been.
               Was Jane writing to her friends?   No, but she should've been.

5. M1   T: Was John working yesterday?   S: He couldn't have been; I saw him at the party.
               Was Mary studying last night?   She couldn't have been; I saw her at the party.
               Was Carlos visiting his friend in   He couldn't have been; I saw him at the party.
                  New York?
               Were the girls babysitting last   They couldn't have been; I saw them at the party.
                  Saturday?
               Were the Hastings visiting their   They couldn't have been; I saw them at the party.
                  friends in Philadelphia?
               Was Chen catching up on his   He couldn't have been; I saw him at the party.
                  correspondence last Saturday
                  night?
               Was Jane studying last Saturday?   She couldn't have been; I saw her at the party.

6. M1T   T: Did Charlie finish the paper?   S: No, but he should have.
               Was Charlie working on the test?   No, but he should have been.
               Were the students studying?   No, but they should have been.
               Did Jane write home?   No, but she should have.
               Was Mary writing the research paper?   No, but she should have been.
               Did the Newtons go fishing?   No, but they should have.
               Were the neighbors swimming?   No, but they should have been.
               Was Charlie at home?   No, but he should have been.
               Did Charlie get to work on time?   No, but he should have.

7. M2   T: study last weekend   S1:   Did you study last weekend?
                                               S2:   (Yes, I did.) (No, I didn't, but I should have;
                                                        I have a test next week.)

               studying last weekend   S1:   Were you studying last weekend?
                                               S2:   (Yes, I was.) (No, I wasn't; but I could have
                                                        been; I just wasted my time.)

               write home yesterday
               calling someone at 3:00 yesterday
                        (exercise continued on next page)

417

T: go for a drive last weekend
    studying when I called
    watching TV last night
    eat dinner out yesterday
    eating dinner when I called
    taking a nap when ( ) came
    persuade ( ) to go to a movie
    make up a story for the children
    ask the post office clerk about the abbreviation
    writing a letter when I called
    learn the acronyms before you went to Washington, D.C.

8. C   See Instructor's Manual

SECTION THREE

***VERB + DIRECT OBJECT + *FOR* + INDIRECT OBJECT

Part A.   *Statement, Negatives, Questions*

Model: Pronounce them for me.
        Sometimes he corrects it for me.

1. M1   Rep: Could you have bought him a ticket?
           Sub: do a favor   S: Could you have done him a favor?
                teach a new song   Could you have taught him a new song?
                make a cake   Could you have made him a cake?
                find an apartment   Could you have found him an apartment?
                leave the money   Could you have left him the money?
                save some time   Could you have saved him some time?
                order a taxi   Could you have ordered him a taxi?

2. M1   Rep: I shouldn't have closed the account for him.
           Sub: answer the letter   S: I shouldn't have answered the letter for him.
                prepare the paper   I shouldn't have prepared the paper for him.
                fix the ticket   I shouldn't have fixed the ticket for him.
                keep the appointment   I shouldn't have kept the appointment for him.
                correct the answers   I shouldn't have corrected the answers for him.
                cash the check   I shouldn't have cashed the check for him.
                pronounce the words   I shouldn't have pronounced the words for him.
                open the account   I shouldn't have opened the account for him.

GENERALIZATION

In Lesson Twelve, there were verbs with two objects:

V	+	Indirect Object	+	Direct Object
Order		me		a cup of coffee.
I found		John		an apartment.

In this lesson there is a different pattern for these verbs and some others:

V	+	Direct Object	+	*for*	+	Indirect Object
Order		a cup of coffee		for		me.
I found		an apartment		for		John.

The verbs in Lesson Twelve may have either pattern. The verbs in Drill 5 have only the new pattern. It might be advisable to memorize the sentences in Drills 2 and 5.

3. M1   (Verbs with both patterns)

T: Who should have bought them a book?   S: Who should have bought a book for them?
    Who should have done him a favor?   Who should have done a favor for him?
    Who should have ordered her a coke?   Who should have ordered a coke for her?
    Who should have made us some sandwiches?   Who should have made some sandwiches for us?

    Who should have found them an apartment?   Who should have found an apartment for them?

    Who should have left us the car?   Who should have left the car for us?
    Who should have saved you some money?   Who should have saved some money for you?
    Who should have gotten me the appointment?   Who should have gotten the appointment for me?

4. M1   (Verbs with both patterns)

T: Could he have gotten me the appointment? S: Could he have gotten the appointment for me?

    Could he have saved you some money?   Could he have saved some money for you?
    Could he have left us the car?   Could he have left the car for us?
    Could he have found them an apartment?   Could he have found an apartment for them?
    Could he have made us some sandwiches?   Could he have made some sandwiches for us?
    Could he have ordered her a coke?   Could he have ordered a coke for her?
    Could he have bought them a book?   Could he have bought a book for them?
    Could he have done us a favor?   Could he have done a favor for us?

5. M1   (Verbs + *for* + Indirect Object)

T: He might not have corrected the paper.   S: He might not have corrected the paper for her.
    He might not have kept the children.   He might not have kept the children for her.
    He might not have fixed the light.   He might not have fixed the light for her.
    He might not have prepared the dinner.   He might not have prepared the dinner for her.
    He might not have closed the account.   He might not have closed the account for her.
    He might not have cashed the check.   He might not have cashed the check for her.
    He might not have answered the door.   He might not have answered the door for her.
    He might not have opened the account.   He might not have opened the account for her.
    He might not have pronounced the   He might not have pronounced the acronyms
      acronyms.   for her.

***6. M1T   T: I bought a book.   S: I bought him a book.
                     I cashed a check.   I cashed a check for him.
                     I opened an account.   I opened an account for him.
                     I did a favor.   I did him a favor.
                     I pronounced the words.   I pronounced the words for him.
                     I answered the letter.   I answered the letter for him.
                     I ordered a cup of coffee.   I ordered him a cup of coffee.
                     I fixed the typewriter.   I fixed the typewriter for him.

7. M2   T: pronounce the words   S1:   (Did you) pronounce the words for ( )?
                                                 S2:   (Yes, but I shouldn't have. I should have
                                                            pronounced them for ( ).)

                   open an account   S1:   (Have you opened a savings account for your
                                                            wife?)
                                                 S2:   (Yes, and I opened one for myself too.)

                   close the window
                   answer the question
                   fix the ticket
                   keep the money
                   correct the lesson
                   prepare the dinner
                   cash the check
                   open the window
                   close the account
                   keep the money
                   correct the abbreviations
                   pronounce the words
                   open an account

Part B.   _Who? as Indirect Object_

1. M1   T: She bought a _New York Times_ for   S: Who did she buy a _New York Times_ for?
                      someone.
                   She fixed an omelette for someone.   Who did she fix an omelette for?
                   She got a present for someone.   Who did she get a present for?
                   She opened the door for someone.   Who did she open the door for?
                   She left sandwiches for someone.   Who did she leave sandwiches for?
                   She did a favor for someone.   Who did she do a favor for?
                   She typed the paper for someone.   Who did she type the paper for?
                   She cashed a check for someone.   Who did she cash a check for?
                   She answered a question for someone.   Who did she answer a question for?

NOTE: Just as with the verbs which take _to_ (Lesson Nineteen), the question pattern for both kinds of verbs is the same.

Lesson Twelve: I ordered John a cup of coffee.   ⎫   Who did you order a
Lesson Twenty: I ordered a cup of coffee for John. ⎬   cup of coffee for?
                   I kept the book for her.   ⎭   Who did you keep the book for?

This question pattern is used in most spoken styles. In very formal styles and in writing, it will be: _For whom_ . . .

420

2. M2   T: ( ) should have cashed the check for   S1:   Who should he have cashed the check for?
               someone.   S2:   He should have cashed the check for ( ).
              Why?   S2:   (Because he needed money.)
              ( ) could have bought cigarettes for   S1:   Who could he have bought cigarettes for?
               someone.   S2:   He could have bought me cigarettes.
              How?   S2:   (By stopping at the drug store.)

( ) must have found an apartment for someone. How do you know?
( ) should have saved a seat for someone. Why?
( ) might have prepared dinner for someone. Why do you think so?
( ) must have cashed a check for someone. How do you know?
( ) could have done a favor for someone. How?
( ) should have kept the car for someone. Why?
( ) might have answered the letter for someone. What makes you think so?
( ) must have found a date for someone. How do you know?
( ) could have fixed the door for someone. How?
( ) should have ordered a cup of coffee for someone. Why?
( ) must have opened an account for someone. How do you know?
( ) could have saved money for someone. How?

3. C   T: open   S1:   (Who did you open the door for?)
                                  S2:   (I opened the door for my girlfriend.)
              order   S1:   (Who are you ordering a cup of coffee for?)
                                  S2:   (I'm ordering myself a cup of coffee.)

              close
              save
              correct
              find
              keep
              order
              fix
              answer
              do a favor
              prepare
              pronounce
              make
              cash a check
              get
              buy
              open

***4. C   T: Yesterday after the banks had closed ( )   S1:   (Someone must have cashed a check for him.)
               had no cash. Last night I saw him at   S2:   (Who would have cashed a check for him?)
               an expensive restaurant.   S1:   (His roommate might have. I couldn't have;
                                                             I didn't have any money either.)

              Last night ( ) went home without her key.   S1:   (She might have climbed in the window.)
               The door was locked. This morning I   S2:   (She couldn't have; they are all locked.
               saw her coming out of her apartment.   Someone must have opened the door for
                                                               her.)
                                                S1:   (Oh, yes. Probably her roommate.)

( ) doesn't like to order food in a restaurant because he doesn't know the names of the
       foods. I saw him by himself with a 3-course dinner.

(exercise continued on next page)

T: Yesterday ( ) couldn't pronounce "Tschaikovsky." Today he can do it perfectly.
( ) wanted to leave for California but didn't know how to get his money out of
his savings account. Later I saw him at the airport.
( ) wanted to go to the dance but he didn't have a date. Later I saw him at the
girl's dorm with a bunch of flowers.
( ) had a stomach ache and was sick in bed. That evening he was in the Student
Union. (buy medicine)
( ) handed in a paper with many mistakes. When he handed it in again, the
professor praised him.
When ( ) got home last night the refrigerator had stopped. This morning he had
cold orange juice for breakfast.
( ) got a parking ticket. He told me this morning that he did not have to pay it.
( ) does not know how to cook. Yesterday he brought a homemade cake to class.
( ) had a broken hand and could not write. Today his parents got a letter from him.
The old woman couldn't hear well enough to talk on the phone. I just saw a taxi in
front of her house.
Yesterday the children only knew one song. Today they can sing two.

SECTION FOUR

VERB + NP + *TO* + VERB

Model: I ask the clerk to check it.

1. M1   Rep: I always ask the clerk to check it.
   Sub: remind   S: I always remind the clerk to check it.
        want   I always want the clerk to check it.
        instruct   I always instruct the clerk to check it.
        allow   I always allow the clerk to check it.
        request   I always request the clerk to check it.
        urge   I always urge the clerk to check it.
        encourage   I always encourage the clerk to check it.
        expect   I always expect the clerk to check it.
        tell   I always tell the clerk to check it.
        advise   I always advise the clerk to check it.

2. M1   Rep: They warned us not to be late.
   Sub: persuaded   S: They persuaded us not to be late.
        advised   They advised us not to be late.
        asked   They asked us not to be late.
        told   They told us not to be late.
        reminded   They reminded us not to be late.
        requested   They requested us not to be late.

GENERALIZATION

Lesson Seventeen had many verbs which required *to* before a following verb:

Chen wanted to see a baseball game.

Lesson Twenty has a small number of verbs which permit a noun or pronoun before the *to* verb:

We asked *the boys* to do the work.
Chen wanted *us* to see the game.

Note that the *to* verb may be made negative:

They warned us not to be late.

---

3. M2   T: ( ) warned someone not to be late.   S1:   Who did you warn not to be late?
                                                      S2:   I warned (the students) not to be late.
          ( ) asked ( ) to do something.   S1:   What did you ask ( ) to do?
                                                      S2:   I asked (him) to (get me some cigarettes).
          ( ) reminded someone not to forget the homework.
          ( ) persuaded ( ) to do something.
          ( ) expected someone to meet him at 3:00.
          ( ) reminded ( ) to do something.
          ( ) asked someone not to forget his books.
          ( ) told someone not to forget the party.
          ( ) wanted ( ) to do something.
          ( ) requested ( ) not to do something.
          ( ) persuaded someone not to buy a car.
          ( ) asked ( ) to do something.
          ( ) requested someone to turn down the radio.
          ( ) told ( ) to do something.

4. C   T: What does your friend remind you to do?
                Who persuades you to do things? What?
                Does anyone force you to do anything? What? How?
                What do you remind your friend to do?
                What does your family ask/want/expect you to do?
                Does your friend ever request you to do anything? What?
                What did your family instruct you to do before you came here?
                Who advises you? To do what?
                Has anyone asked you to do him a favor lately? What?

SECTION FIVE

SEPARABLE TWO-WORD VERBS

Model: You could have looked them up.

1. M1   T: Please look the words up.   S: Please look them up.
               Please call John up.   Please call him up.
               Please turn the light off.   Please turn it off.
               Please turn the radio on.   Please turn it on.
               Please turn the TV up.   Please turn it up.
               Please turn the lights down.   Please turn them down.
               Please wake the children up.   Please wake them up.
               Please hand the paper in.   Please hand it in.

2. M1   T: He wrote down the names.   S: He wrote the names down.
               They took off their coats.   They took their coats off.
               Don't wake up the children.   Don't wake the children up.
               We turned off the TV at midnight.   We turned the TV off at midnight.
               He's going to trade in the car.   He's going to trade the car in.
               He wants to think over the deal.   He wants to think the deal over.
               We should have looked up the address.   We should have looked the address up.
               He has to fill out a million forms.   He has to fill a million forms out.
               The professor asked us to hand in   .The professor asked us to hand the
                 the papers.   papers in.
               The people upstairs want us to turn   The people upstairs want us to turn the
                 down the record player.   record player down.
               She'll never teach that child to hang   She'll never teach that child to hang his
                 up his clothes.   clothes up.

GENERALIZATION

The parts of the two-word verbs in Lesson Seventeen are never separated:

I'm *waiting for* my friends.

The two-word verbs in this lesson may be separated by a noun (Drill 2) and are *always* separated when the object is a pronoun (see Drill 1):

You could have *looked* the words *up.*
You could have *looked up* the words.
But: You could have *looked* them *up.*

---

3. M1T   T: He's waiting for his friends.   S: He's waiting for them.
               He's looking up his friends.   He's looking them up.
               He's calling on his friends.   He's calling on them.
               He's calling up his friends.   He's calling them up.
               He's running into his friends.   He's running into them.
               He's waking up his friends.   He's waking them up.
               He's looking for his friends.   He's looking for them.
               He's listening to his friends.   He's listening to them.

4. M2   T: Here are seven forms. (fill)   S: (Do I have to fill them all out?)
               Bill's radio is too loud. (turn)   (I'll ask him to turn it down.)
               The children always leave their clothes on the floor. (hang)
               Mr. Hastings is going to buy a new car. (trade)
               I need to know John's address. (look)
               It's very dark in here. (turn)
                    (exercise continued on next page)

424

T: The children have just gone to sleep. (wake)
    When are the research papers due? (hand)
    We can't decide about the new house right away. (think)
    The light is shining in my eyes. (turn)
    It's too warm in here to wear your jacket. (take)
    I can't find the address anywhere. (write)
    I don't know if the car is good or not. (check)
    I don't know if John can come. (call)

5. C   T: What do you say in the following situations?
                Use two-word verbs.
            You don't want to decide right away.   S: (I'll have to think it over. (I want
                                                            to look around.) (I need some time
                                                            to think about it.)

            Someone's cigarette smoke is blowing in   (Would you please put out your
                your face.   cigarette?)
            You don't understand what the clerk in the store said.
            You're at a hotel and you want to get up at 7:00. Call the desk.
            Your guest looks very uncomfortable because it's hot. He has on a jacket and tie at
                an informal party.
            You want to get an allowance for an old car on a new one.
            The children have just gone to sleep. The guests are making a lot of noise.

6. C   T: What do you have to do to get a scholarship?   S: (You have to fill out a million
                                                                application forms.)
            What should you do before you buy a car?
            How do you contact your friends?
            When you're in a new city, how do you find someone's phone number?
            If it's cold outside, what should you do?
            At 11:00 in the dormitory, what should you do to the radio?
            When you have a jacket on and the room is warm, what do you do?
            What should you do with your coat when you take it off?
            How can you remember someone's address?
            Do you buy an expensive item right away?
            What do you do if your neighbor's radio is too loud?

SUMMARY DIALOGUE

Carlos: Yesterday was a great day!

Nancy: What happened?

Carlos: I'd been wanting my friend to call me and he finally did. I'd been waiting for months.

Nancy: Maybe you should have called him.

Carlos: Yes, but I didn't know his address.

Nancy: Did you know the city?

Carlos: Sure.

Nancy: Then you should have called the Directory Assistance Operator. She would have given
    you his number.

Carlos: I never thought of that.

LESSON TWENTY – SUMMARY OF PATTERNS

I. PERFECT MODALS

	Subject	Modal	(not)	have	Past Participle	Completer	Short Answer
Statement	She	should		have	studied	last night.	
	They	might	not	have	left	too early.	

		Modal					
Question (Yes/No)		Would	she	have	gone	home?	Yes, she would have.
							No, she wouldn't have.

II. PERFECT MODALS – CONTINUOUS

	Subject	Modal	(not)	have	been + V -ing	Completer
Statement	He	must		have	been studying	last night.
	We	could	not	have	been sleeping	at 5:00.

		Modal					Short Answer
Question (Yes/No)		Should	you	have	been driving?		Yes, I should have been.
							No, I shouldn't have been.

III. VERBS WITH TWO OBJECTS

	Subject	Verb	Indirect Object	for	Direct Object
A.	I	got	him		a cup of coffee.
B.	I	cashed	the check	for	him.

LESSON TWENTY-ONE

INTRODUCTION   Finding an Apartment

Chen wants to move to an apartment near the university. He calls Nancy.

Chen: Nancy, I'd like to find a different apartment—one nearer the university.

Nancy: What's the matter with the one you have?

Chen: *It's too far for me to come every day.* And there are too many children in the building.
5   It's very hard to concentrate on my studies.

Nancy: O.K. *If I finish my work this morning, I'll help you this afternoon.* Meantime, try to
         get a copy of the student newspaper. There are usually lots of apartment ads in it.

Chen: Thanks. I'll talk to you later. Bye.

At the Student Union:

10   Nancy: Apartments are usually easy to find in the summer; much easier than the fall or winter.
         Do you want it furnished?

Chen: Oh, yes! If I get an unfurnished one, I'll have to buy a lot of furniture. I don't want
         to do that.

Nancy: O.K. Here's one you can sublet for the summer.

15   Chen: Sublet?

Nancy: That means you rent it from the people who are living there now, not from the owner.
         That arrangement is used when people want to go away from a while—usually the summer—and
         then return to the apartment. They keep the apartment and don't lose the rent money.

Chen: If I do that, I'll have to move again in September, won't I?

20   Nancy: Yes, you will. I guess that's not so good. Here's another one. Furnished, one bedroom,
         all utilities included, $100 a month. A year's lease is required.

Chen: The price is right. Is it air-conditioned?

Nancy: The ad doesn't say. It's easy for you to find out—just call this number.

Chen: I will. Is there anything else I should ask?

25   Nancy: You should find out what floor it's on, and what kind of building it is. Also ask about
         the other tenants. It'll be just as hard for you to study if there are a lot of small children.

Chen: What about a deposit?

Nancy: Usually the landlords ask for a month's rent as a security deposit. They'll give it back when you move out if nothing is damaged.

30   Chen: I'll go call now. If it sounds good, will you come with me to look at it?

Nancy: Sure.

OUTLINE OF PATTERNS   Example

Section One   *if* Clauses — Condition I   If I finish . . . , I'll help you . . .

Section Two   Adjective Phrases   It's too far for me to come.

Section Three   Passive Voice — I (Present)   That arrangement is used . . .

COMPREHENSION QUESTIONS

1. Where does Chen want to move?

2. Who does he call?

3. Why does he want to move?

4. What does Chen want Nancy to do?

5. When will she help him? Under what condition?

*6. Why is it easier to find an apartment in the summer?

7. Does Chen want an unfurnished apartment? Why not?

*8. If you want an apartment for only a short time, what kind of arrangement should you look for?

9. Why do people sublet their apartments?

10. Why doesn't Chen want to sublet an apartment?

11. What is the description of the apartment?

*12. What does the phrase "all utilities included" mean?

13. Is the apartment air-conditioned? How can Chen find out?

14. What else should Chen ask?

15. What is a "security deposit"? Do you get it back?

*16. Discuss the problems in renting apartments in the local area, including rent, lease, number of rooms, etc.

NOTE: If you must sign a lease when renting an apartment, ask a friend who is familiar with such things to help you. The language in legal forms is archaic and difficult to understand (even for native speakers of English).

Look for the terms of the security deposit and find out if there is a penalty for paying the rent after a certain day of each month.

If you rent near a university, ask other students for advice. Landlords who have a "bad reputation" (i.e., for being difficult about refunding the deposit, etc.) should be avoided.

You should also find out who is responsible for making repairs and how soon repairs are made.

Vocabulary

Nouns	Verbs	Adjectives
arrangement	afford	air-conditioned
contract	concentrate	challenging
currency	dislike	damaged
deposit	go off	domestic
heat	mistrust	furnished
lease	rent	sublet
plumbing	sublet	unfurnished
product		
security deposit		
"status quo"		
tenant		
utilities		

SECTION ONE

IF CLAUSES — CONDITION I

Model: If I finish my work this morning, I'll help you look this afternoon.

1. M1   Rep: If I finish my work, I'll help you this afternoon.

Sub: I'll go with you   S: If I finish my work, I'll go with you this afternoon.

I'll call you   If I finish my work, I'll call you this afternoon.

I'll call Chen and Carlos   If I finish my work, I'll call Chen and Carlos this afternoon.

I'll go shopping with you   If I finish my work, I'll go shopping with you this afternoon.

I'll watch the baseball   If I finish my work, I'll watch the baseball game on game on TV   TV this afternoon.

I'll go to the Student Union   If I finish my work, I'll go to the Student Union this afternoon.

I'll take a nap   If I finish my work, I'll take a nap this afternoon.

2. M1   Situation: Carlos and I are going on a trip. We asked Chen to come with us, but he hasn't decided yet.

Rep: He'll come with us if he has the money.

Sub: he can get away   S: He'll come with us if he can get away

the weather is good   He'll come with us if the weather is good.

it isn't too expensive   He'll come with us if it isn't too expensive.

we don't leave too soon   He'll come with us if we don't leave too soon.

(exercise continued on next page)

T: he doesn't have to work   S: He'll come with us if he doesn't have to work.
       we promise to drive carefully   He'll come with us if we promise to drive carefully.
       he finishes his research paper   He'll come with us if he finishes his research paper in
       in time   time.

GENERALIZATION

The *if* clauses in Lesson Twenty expressed Requests, Habits, Generalizations.

> Example: If you've seen one city, you've seen them all. (Generalization)
>   If you have time, get me some apples.   (Request)
>   If I have the money, I go to the movies on Saturday. (Habit)

The tense of the verb is usually in the same tense in both clauses.

The clauses in this lesson express conditions which must be filled in order for the action to be completed.

> Example: If I finish my work, I'll help you.

What tense of the verb is used in the *if* clause? ((Present))   In the main clause? ((Future))
What *time* is being discussed? ((Future))

Notice that the *order* of the clauses may be reversed:

> I'll help you if I finish my work.

---

3. M1   T: If he goes, I'll go.   S: If he doesn't go, I won't go.
               If it rains, we'll stay home.   If it doesn't rain, we won't stay home.
               If she comes, we'll leave.   If she doesn't come, we won't leave.
               If they have a dollar, we'll buy a gift.   If they don't have a dollar, we won't buy a gift.
               If it's a good day, we'll have a picnic.   If it isn't a good day, we won't have a picnic.
               If I find a good apartment, I'll rent.   If I don't find a good apartment, I won't rent.
               If I can find my friends, I'll call you.   If I can't find my friends, I won't call you.
               If the car starts, we'll come.   If the car doesn't start, we won't come.

4. M1   T: We'll go if we have enough money.   S: We won't go if we don't have enough money.
               I'll rent the apartment if it's   I won't rent the apartment if it isn't
               air-conditioned.   air-conditioned.
               She'll do the work if she has time   She won't do the work if she doesn't have
               enough.   time enough.
               We'll have a picnic if it's warm enough.   We won't have a picnic if it isn't warm enough.
               He'll help us if he can leave early.   He won't help us if he can't leave early.
               They'll go to France if there is time.   They won't go to France if there isn't time.
               We'll go to the lake if the weather is   We won't go to the lake if the weather isn't
               good.   good.
               I'll buy the car if it's cheap enough.   I won't buy the car if it isn't cheap enough.

5. M1   T: We'll go if it doesn't rain.   S: We won't go if it rains.
               I'll rent the apartment if I don't   I won't rent the apartment if I have to sign
               have to sign a lease.   a lease.
               She'll buy the VW if it isn't too   She won't buy the VW if it's too expensive.
               expensive.

(exercise continued on next page)

T: They'll have a picnic if the weather isn't cold.   S: They won't have a picnic if the weather is cold.

I'll call the lawyer if the landlord doesn't return the deposit.

I won't call the lawyer if the landlord returns the deposit.

She'll go to the movies if it isn't too expensive.

She won't go to the movies if it's too expensive.

They'll be here on time if it doesn't rain.

They won't be here on time if it rains.

Carlos will help us if he isn't busy.

Carlos won't help us if he's busy.

Chen will rent the apartment if there aren't too many children.

Chen won't rent the apartment if there are too many children.

6. M1T   T: The apartment may be too expensive. Then we won't rent it.   S: If the apartment is too expensive, we won't rent it.

The apartment may not be air-conditioned. Then I won't rent it.

If the apartment isn't air-conditioned, I won't rent it.

There may be too many children in the building. Then we won't rent the apartment.

If there are too many children in the building, we won't rent the apartment.

The weather may be nice. Then we'll go on a picnic.

If the weather is nice, we'll go on a picnic.

The girls may be busy. Then they won't go to New York for the weekend.

If the girls are busy, they won't go to New York for the weekend.

The teacher may announce an exam. Then we'll have to study.

If the teacher announces an exam, we'll have to study.

7. M2   T: I'll go downtown this weekend ——.   S: I'll go downtown this weekend (if I have enough money) (if my friends can go too).

I won't rent the apartment ——.

I won't rent the apartment (if I have to sign a lease) (if it's too expensive).

They'll have a picnic Sunday ——.
Carlos will move to a new apartment ——.
She won't study for the exam ——.
The students will call the lawyer ——.
Judy will help Chen ——.
The teachers won't be angry ——.
The Director of the Institute will ask to see you ——.
The students won't go to the movies ——.
Miss Wilson will drive to Ohio ——.
Suzie won't go to Mexico ——.
The Libyan students will be happy ——.
The Latin American students won't be happy ——.

8. M2   T: If I have enough time tomorrow ——.   S: If I have enough time tomorrow, (I'll look for an apartment).

If we have good weather this weekend ——.

If we have good weather this weekend, (we won't stay at home).

If the students like the movie ——.
If the landlord doesn't return the deposit ——.

(exercise continued on next page)

T: If the Kuwaiti students don't come to class ——.
      If the Thai students want to move ——.
      If Carlos can't study in his apartment ——.
      If the weather isn't warm ——.
      If it doesn't rain ——.
      If we can finish the work early ——.
      If she can't understand the lease ——.
      If the students need help with the contract ——.
      If I can't be on time for dinner ——.
      If Judy can finish her work ——.

9. M2   T: If it rains on Saturday ——.   S: If it rains on Saturday, (I won't go to the game)
                                                        (I'll stay at home).
               We'll call you next week ——.   We'll call you next week (if we can come to the
                                                        party) (if we can't make it to the party).
               If I see John ——.
               We won't have to study ——.
               The students will have to call the lawyer ——.
               If I can't finish on time ——.
               If I don't receive money from home next week ——.
               If Carlos can find an air-conditioned apartment ——.
               Chen will go to New York this weekend ——.
               The students won't be happy ——.
               If the children are too noisy ——.
               The instructor will be pleased ——.
               If the students have enough time ——.

10. M2   T: If I have enough time tomorrow, I'll   S1:   If ( ) has enough time tomorrow, ( )'ll
               finish my research paper.   finish his research paper. (If I have
                                                              enough money next week, I'll buy a car.)
                                                       S2:   If ( ) has enough time tomorrow, ( )'ll
                                                              finish his research paper; if ( ) has enough
                                                              money next week ( )'ll buy a car; (if I have
                                                              enough time next weekend, I'll help my
                                                              friends from Libya.)
                                                       S3:   etc.

11. C   T: Ask ( ) what he'll do if his check   S1:   What will you do if your check doesn't
               doesn't come on time.   come on time?
                                                       S2:   If it doesn't come (I'll ask the landlord to
                                                              wait for the rent) (I'll try to borrow some
                                                              money from a friend).
         Ask ( ) what he'll do next weekend if he can't go to ( ).
         Ask ( ) what he'll do if the landlord doesn't return his security deposit.
         Ask ( ) what he'll do if he can't finish the research paper on time.
         Ask ( ) who he'll call if the electricity in his apartment goes off during the party.
         Ask ( ) who he'll call if someone breaks into his apartment when he's in New York.
         Ask ( ) what he'll say if his neighbor's children make too much noise during the
            dinner party.

(exercise continued on next page)

T: Ask ( ) what he'll do if he finds a cheap car next week.

Ask ( ) what he'll do if the TV stops working during the championship.

Ask ( ) what he'll do if he has to leave before the lease is up.

Ask ( ) what he'll do if the plumbing doesn't work during the party.

Ask ( ) what he'll do if he wants to find a new apartment for the summer.

Ask ( ) what he'll do if he has extra money next month.

12. C   T: Try to propose a very difficult situation. The next student will think of a sensible solution.

S1: (You're on a trip in the desert. Your car runs out of gas.)

S2: If I'm in the desert and my car runs out of gas, I'll (wait for another car to come. Then I'll ask the driver to give me some gas).

S3: (Your landlord refuses to return the security deposit.)

S4: If he won't return it, (I'll call the university lawyer and ask him to help me).

SECTION TWO

ADJECTIVE PHRASES

Model: It's too far for me to travel.

1. M1   Situation: In this country some things are very hard for foreign students. Other things are easy.

T:	S:
difficult—meet North Americans	It's difficult for us to meet North Americans.
easy—rent furnished apartments	It's easy for us to rent furnished apartments.
difficult—talk on the telephone in English	It's difficult for us to talk on the telephone in English.
difficult—understand U.S. politics	It's difficult for us to understand U.S. politics.
easy—spend a lot of money	It's easy for us to spend a lot of money.
easy—learn English grammar	It's easy for us to learn English grammar.
difficult—get jobs in the U.S.	It's difficult for us to get jobs in the U.S.

GENERALIZATION

This pattern combines two statements:

1. A VW is easy to drive.

2. I can drive a VW easily.

3. A VW is easy for me to drive.

---

2. M1   Situation: I can afford some things; other things are too expensive.

T:	S:
A VW is cheap.	A VW is cheap enough for me to buy.
A Rolls-Royce is expensive.	A Rolls-Royce is too expensive for me to buy.
Hamburger is cheap.	Hamburger is cheap enough for me to buy.

(exercise continued on next page)

T: Steak is expensive.   S: Steak is too expensive for me to buy.
     A $10,000 house is cheap.   A $10,000 house is cheap enough for me to buy.
     A $100,000 house is   A $100,000 house is too expensive for me to buy.
     expensive.
     A $5 book is cheap.   A $5 book is cheap enough for me to buy.
     A $50 book is expensive.   A $50 book is too expensive for me to buy.

3. M1T T: This apartment is cheap. She can rent it.   S: This apartment is cheap enough for her to rent.

     This car is big. ( ) can't drive it.   This car is too big for ( ) to drive.
     These chairs are heavy. We can't lift them. These chairs are too heavy for us to lift.
     A VW is small. ( ) can afford one.   A VW is small enough for ( ) to afford.
     New York is far. We can't drive there on   New York is too far for us to drive there
       a weekend.   on a weekend.
     This city is dirty. I can't enjoy it.   This city is too dirty for me to enjoy.
     This house isn't expensive. We'll buy it.   This house isn't too expensive for us to
                                                    buy.
     This apartment is big. I can't clean it.   This apartment is too big for me to clean.

NOTE: This pattern occurs often with *it* in subject position. (Lesson Thirteen.)

Example: A VW   is easy for me to drive.
             It's   easy for me to drive a VW.

---

4. M1T T: Eating American food is hard for me. S: It's hard for me to eat American food.
     Learning about politics was useful for us.   It was useful for us to learn about politics.
     Talking on the phone is going to be   It's going to be impossible for her to talk
       impossible for her.   on the phone.
     Writing research papers will be very   It will be very hard for him to write
       hard for him.   research papers.
     Meeting Americans was easy for us   It was easy for us to meet Americans in
       in Pittsburgh.   Pittsburgh.
     Renting a furnished apartment was   It was expensive for them to rent a
       expensive for them in the U.S.   furnished apartment in the U.S.
     Using the telephone in the U.S. used   It used to be very hard for him to use the
       to be very hard for him.   telephone in the U.S.

5. M2   T: buy a VW   S1: (Are you going to) (Do you want to) buy a VW?
                          S2: (No. It's too difficult for me to drive VWs.) (Yes. VWs are
                                  cheap enough for me to buy one.)
     buy a Rolls-Royce
     drive to San Francisco
     study computer science
     take a vacation in Acapulco
     fly to Paris
     rent an air-conditioned apartment
     eat in a restaurant every day
               (exercise continued on next page)

T: buy a color TV
      learn Arabic
      study Thai
      take a vacation in Athens
      get up early on Saturday and Sunday

6. C   T: Do you prefer an apartment or the   S: (An apartment. It's too noisy for me to study
             dorms?   in the dorm.) (The dorms. Apartments are
                                                               hard for foreign students to find.)
         How did you find your apartment? Did anyone help you? Who? Why did you ask him/her?
         Have you ever bought a car? At home? In the U.S.? Was it easy? Did anyone help you?
         Are apartments easy or hard to find in your country? Do people have to sign a lease? Are
             the arrangements easy to make? Who makes them?
         At the universities in your country, where do most of the students live? Do they make
             their own arrangements? Do they have to give a deposit?
         What are the difficulties in finding a place to live in your country? In the U.S.?

SECTION THREE

PASSIVE VOICE — I

Model: That arrangement is used . . .
         The apartments are furnished . . .

1. M1   Listen: People use credit cards to buy many   Rep: Credit cards are used to buy many things.
                 things.
                 People study English for many reasons.   English is studied for many reasons.
                 People buy big cars for their comfort.   Big cars are bought for their comfort.
                 People use a sublet arrangement for   A sublet arrangement is used for renting
                 renting in the summer.   in the summer.
                 People buy little cars for their economy.   Little cars are bought for their economy.
                 People tell lies when the truth is difficult.   Lies are told when the truth is difficult.

GENERALIZATION

This construction is used in making generalizations when the subject is unknown or
unimportant.

    Someone buys a new car every day.
            A new car is bought (by someone) every day.
            A new car is bought every day.

    Someone constructs new buildings every year.
            New buildings are constructed (by someone) every year.
            New buildings are constructed every year.

    Formation: S   +   BE   +   Past Participle

NOTE: This pattern is used in speech and is very common in advertising. It is *not* good
practice to use it often in formal writing. (Why not, do you think?) ((Good formal
writing should be specific.))

435

2. M1T   T: The tobacco companies sell millions of   S: Millions of cigarettes are sold every
                cigarettes every year.   year.
                The government builds many new roads   Many new roads are built every year.
                every year.

                The automobile companies manufacture   Millions of new cars are manufactured
                millions of new cars every year.   every year.
                The government spends billions of dollars   Billions of dollars are spent on defense
                on defense every year.   every year.
                The auto companies spend millions of   Millions of dollars are spent on
                dollars on advertising every year.   advertising every year.
                The government builds many new office   Many new office buildings are built
                buildings every year.   every year.
                The government collects billions of dollars   Billions of dollars are collected in taxes
                in taxes every year.   every year.

3. M1T   T: They don't speak Spanish in Brazil.   S: Spanish isn't spoken in Brazil.
                They don't speak English in Mexico.   English isn't spoken in Mexico.
                They don't sell beer in the grocery store.   Beer isn't sold in the grocery store.
                They don't serve lunch on Sunday.   Lunch isn't served on Sunday.
                They don't criticize the President.   The President isn't criticized.
                They don't sell wine in the drug store.   Wine isn't sold in the drug store.

4. M1T   T: They don't sell cigarettes in some hospitals. S: Cigarettes are not sold in some hospitals.
                They speak French in Canada.   French is spoken in Canada.
                They close the doors at midnight.   The doors are closed at midnight.
                They require a security deposit.   A security deposit is required.
                They don't furnish the apartments.   The apartments aren't furnished.
                They air-condition the building.   The building is air-conditioned.
                They give the exam every month.   The exam is given every month.
                They don't finish the term until August.   The term isn't finished until August.

5. M2   T: speak Thai—Libya   S1:   Do they speak Thai in Libya?
                                                             S2:   No. (Arabic is spoken in Libya. Thai is spoken in
                                                                   Thailand.)

          drink milk with meals—( )
          eat ice cream for dessert—( )
          criticize the government in the newspapers—( )
          prefer foreign cars—( )
          use dollars as domestic currency—( )
          sell beer in grocery stores—( )
          require an entrance exam at universities—( )
          furnish apartments—( )
          provide air-conditioning in apartments—( )
          teach many foreign languages—( )
          close the schools for summer vacation—( )
          begin the school day at 8:00—( )

6. C   T: How often do they hold elections in your   S: (Elections are held every four years.)
                        country?
                    How many languages do people speak in ( )? Which ones?
                    Do people always eat dessert after lunch? What kind?
                    Do people use buses frequently? In the city? In the country?
                    How often are apartments furnished? air-conditioned?
                    Is the government criticized? When? By whom?
                    Which cars are preferred in ( )? Why?
                    Which sports are most liked?
                    Do they inspect all luggage arriving in your country?
                    Do they allow beer in the dormitories?
                    Do they permit smoking in the classrooms?

SUMMARY DIALOGUE

Landlord: Hello.

Carlos: I'm calling about the ad in the newspaper for the apartment.

Landlord: Yes.

Carlos: How much is it?

Landlord: $200 a month.

Carlos: Are the utilities included?

Landlord: Yes, everything except the telephone.

Carlos: Yes, of course. Is it air-conditioned?

Landlord: Yes, it is. And there is wall-to-wall carpeting.

Carlos: That's good. It'll be quieter. Are there small children?

Landlord: The people on the first floor have a small baby.

Carlos: If it's noisy, it'll be hard for me to study.

Landlord: The baby goes to bed early. I'm sure it's very quiet in the evening.

Carlos: O.K. If I come over right now, will I be able to see it?

Landlord: Yes, certainly. What's your name, please?

Carlos: Carlos Rivera.

Landlord: I'll be waiting.

LESSON TWENTY-ONE – SUMMARY OF PATTERNS

I. ADJECTIVE PHRASES

Subject	+	BE	+	Adjective	(for + Person)	(to Verb)
Volkswagons		are		easy		to drive.
Exercise		is		good	for me.	
A Rolls-Royce		is		too expensive	for him	to buy.

II. PASSIVE VOICE – PRESENT

Subject	BE (Present)	Past Participle	(by + "X")
Buildings	are (not)	constructed.	
VWs	are	driven	by many people.

438

LESSON TWENTY-TWO

INTRODUCTION   Orientation

Nancy and Bill haven't seen Carlos and Chen for quite a while. The new term is to begin next week and *Carlos and Chen have been asked* to help with the orientation program for the new foreign students.

5

Nancy: That's great. The Foreign Student Advisor's office must think you've really learned your way around.

Bill: Right. If I had a job like that, I wouldn't know where to begin.

Carlos: Sure you would. Don't forget that you and Nancy helped us get used to the university when we first got here.

Bill: I'd forgotten about that. What do you have to do?

10

Chen: We'll be assigned to a small group of students. They'll ask us questions and we'll try to help them with any of their problems.

Nancy: The "big brother" approach. Will they all be from your country?

Carlos: If the students don't speak much English, they'll be given a "big brother" who speaks their native language. Otherwise, they'll be all mixed up.

15

Bill: It should be interesting. Do you think you'll be able to answer all their questions?

Chen: It shouldn't be too hard. If they ask something difficult, I'll call you or Nancy.

Bill: I see. I'd call Nancy if I were you. She's *used to* all kinds of questions.

Nancy: You'll probably be asked simple questions like "where can I *have my clothes cleaned?*" and "where is the cheapest place to have my hair cut?"

20

Chen: Yes, but I wouldn't be surprised if they had a lot of questions about registration, invoices, I.D. cards and things like that.

Carlos: And having papers typed, and checks cashed.

Bill: Things like that are no problem. But what about driver's licenses and leases?

Chen: That's no problem, either. We've been well taught that anything "legal" should be answered by you or Nancy.

25

Bill: O.K., I just hope they won't be too hard.

OUTLINE OF PATTERNS   Example

    Section One   *If* Clauses — Condition II   If I had a job . . . , I wouldn't know . . .

    Section Two   *Have* (Causative)   . . . have my hair cut.

    Section Three   Passive Voice II

        Part A.   Present Perfect   . . . Carlos and Chen have been asked . . .
        Part B.   Future   . . . they'll be given . . .

    Section Four $\left.\begin{array}{l} be \\ get \end{array}\right\}$ + *used to* + NP   Nancy is used to a lot of questions.

COMPREHENSION QUESTIONS

  1. When does the new term begin?

  2. What have Carlos and Chen been asked to do?

*3. What does the Foreign Student Advisor's office think about Carlos and Chen?

*4. Would Bill like a job like Carlos and Chen's?

  5. What will they have to do?

  6. Who will assign the students to them?

  7. What will happen if the new students don't speak English?

  8. What will they do if the new students ask difficult questions?

  9. What kinds of easy questions will they probably be asked?

*10. Why does Bill suggest they call Nancy?

 11. What kind of difficult questions will there be?

*12. What kinds of things were difficult when you first came?

*13. How do you pay your tuition here?

*14. How do you get a driver's license here?

*15. When is registration for the next term?

*16. How do you register?

*17. How do you get an I.D. card? What can it be used for?

NOTES: Line 20, 21:   The registration, invoicing and I.D. card procedures are different at each
                               university. Make sure you know exactly what they are to avoid paying
                               extra fees for being late.

           Line 1:   Note: *is to* + verb to indicate a future event.

Vocabulary

Nouns	Verbs	Adjectives
court	accuse	wrinkled
driver's license	announce	
flat tire	arrest	
heel (of a shoe)	assign	
hole	cheat	
junk yard	hike	Expressions
late fee	hire	
orientation	notify	"big brother"
recommendation	polish	get caught in
red light	put in (install)	out of order
registration	recall (as with a car)	
spending	repair	
storm	request	
tear	testify	
thief	tow away	
turnpike	wrinkle	

SECTION ONE

IF CLAUSES — CONDITION II

Model: If I had a job like that, I wouldn't know what to do.

1. M1   Rep: If I had a job like that, I wouldn't know what to do.

Sub:		S:	
friend			If I had a friend like that, I wouldn't know what to do.
what to say			If I had a friend like that, I wouldn't know what to say.
test			If I had a test like that, I wouldn't know what to say.
how to study			If I had a test like that, I wouldn't know how to study.
course			If I had a course like that, I wouldn't know how to study.
where to turn			If I had a course like that, I wouldn't know where to turn.
choice			If I had a choice like that, I wouldn't know where to turn.
where to go			If I had a choice like that, I wouldn't know where to go.
car			If I had a car like that, I wouldn't know where to go.

2. M1   Rep: John would help the students, if he knew the answers to their questions.

Sub:		S:	
if he could			John would help the students if he could.
if he had the time			John would help the students if he had the time.
if he didn't have so much to do			John would help the students if he didn't have so much to do.
if someone asked him to			John would help the students if someone asked him to.
if his friend told him to			John would help the students if his friend told him to.
if he knew how to			John would help the students if he knew how to.
if he could understand their English			John would help the students if he could understand their English.

GENERALIZATION

Compare:
Lesson Twenty-one: If I have time, I'll help you this afternoon.
Lesson Twenty-two: If I had time, I'd help you this afternoon.

In Lesson Twenty-two: What tense is used in the *if* clause? ((Simple Past)) in the
                        result clause? ((Conditional — Modal + Simple Verb))

                        What does *'d* stand for? ((*would*))

Note that the Lesson Twenty-one pattern is a promise if the condition is realized; the
Lesson Twenty-two is an apology in some cases (as above), or a "day dream" in others:
"If I had a million dollars, I'd travel around the world." because the speaker thinks that
the condition will not be fulfilled.

Note: The time is about the same in both patterns; the difference lies in the matter of
         whether the condition is to be fulfilled (in the opinion of the speaker).

Note: In formal style, the verb BE is *were* in all cases:

         If I *were* you, I would go downtown at once.
         If he *were* in Chicago, he wouldn't buy that car.

         In very informal styles you will hear: "I was"; "he was"; "she was"; "it was".
But you should practice the other forms.

---

3. M1T   Rep: If I were rich, I'd travel around the world.
          Sub: he   S: If he were rich, he'd travel around the world.
               famous   If he were famous, he'd travel around the world.
               buy a plane   If he were famous, he'd buy a plane.
               she   If she were famous, she'd buy a plane.
               a millionaire   If she were a millionaire, she'd buy a plane.
               get a Rolls-Royce   If she were a millionaire, she'd get a Rolls-Royce.
               they   If they were millionaires, they'd get a Rolls-Royce.
               in England   If they were in England, they'd get a Rolls-Royce.
               visit the British museum   If they were in England, they'd visit the British museum.

***4. M1T   T: I might have time. I'll go downtown if   S: (I'll go downtown if I have time.
                I do.   (If I have time, I'll go downtown.)
                I don't have time. I'd go downtown if I did. (I'd go downtown if I had time.) (If I
                                                              had time, I'd go downtown.)
                John might have the money. He'll go out   (John will go out to dinner if he has
                to dinner if he does.   the money.)
                John doesn't have the money; he'd go out   (John would go out to dinner if he had
                to dinner if he did.   the money.)
                The students don't have the time. They'd   (If the students had the time, they'd
                study if they did.   study.)
                We might have the money next month.   (We'll buy a car next month if we have
                We'll buy a car if we do.   the money.)
                Carlos might be able to answer the questions. (Carlos will be able to answer the
                If they're easy, he will.   questions if they're easy.)

                        (lesson continued on next page)

442

T: We don't have the cash. We'd buy the house if we did.	S: (If we had the cash, we'd buy the house.)

T: We don't have the cash. We'd buy the house if we did.
The students don't know about registration. They wouldn't have to pay a late fee if they did.
Chen might help the foreign students. If someone asks him to, he will.
Suzie doesn't want to go to Canada. If she did, she'd go by plane.
Faye might take a vacation in August. If her husband wants to, she will.
Lois might go hiking. She will if the weather is good.

S: (If we had the cash, we'd buy the house.)
(The students wouldn't have to pay a late fee if they knew about registration.)
(If someone asks him to, Chen will help the foreign students.)
(If Suzie wanted to go to Canada, she'd go by plane.)
(If her husband wants to, Faye will take a vacation in August.)
(Lois will go hiking if the weather is good.)

5. M2 T: If it's nice next weekend ——. S: If it's nice next weekend (I'll go for a long walk).
If it were sunny ——. If it were sunny (we could have a picnic).
The letter will be late ——. The letter will be late (if I don't mail it today).
The letter would arrive on time ——. The letter would arrive on time (if I mailed it now).
We can't have a picnic ——.
If it doesn't rain ——.
If I studied ——.
The professor would be angry ——.
We could go out for dinner ——.
There will be a late fee ——.
If we're late ——.
We can finish the work ——.
John won't buy a car ——.
If the apartment were too noisy ——.
I'd travel to Paris ——.
If we all failed the test ——.

6. M2 T: weather is bad S1: What would you do if the weather were bad (for the picnic)?
S2: (We'd cancel it.)
fail the test S1: What would you do if you failed the (grammar) test?
S2: (I'd have to study harder for the next one.)

lose your money
someone steals your credit cards
find a wallet with a hundred dollars
get caught in a storm
apartment is too noisy
roommate gets sick
teacher gets angry
dial the wrong number three times at 1:00 a.m.
your check from home is lost
your car runs out of gas on the turnpike
your (girlfriend) (boyfriend) (wife) (husband) is angry
your invoice is late

7. C   Situation: ( ) is driving to ( ) next week. He should be prepared in case of any emergency.
          Think of things which might happen and give him problems to solve.

          S1:   (What would you do if your car ran out of gas on the turnpike?)
          X: I'd ( ).
          S2:   (What would you do if ——?)
          X: I'd ( )
                etc.

NOTE: In informal conversation style, "What (will, would) you do if . . ." is frequently
shortened to *what if . . . "*

          Example: What if you're late?
                          What if you lost your money?

---

8. C   T: ( ) is moving to a new apartment next week. He has to think ahead and plan what
                to do if any problems should come up. (Same as 7.)
                ( ) is going to take a very important exam next week.
                ( ) is going to take the test for his driver's license.
                ( ) is going to take a new girlfriend out to dinner.
                ( ) is going to give a big party.
                etc.

***NOTE: Although you will not practice past conditions in this lesson, you should be
able to form the sentences easily.

          I.   If I go downtown, I'll stop for a beer.
          II.   If I went downtown, I'd stop for a beer.
          III.   If I had gone downtown, I'd have stopped for a beer.

What tense is used in the *if* clause? ((Past Perfect)) In the result clause? ((Past Conditional-
Perfect Modal)) The time? ((Past))

SECTION TWO

HAVE — CAUSATIVE

Model: Where can I have my hair cut?

1. M1   Rep: John wants to have his hair cut.
          Sub: car fixed   S: John wants to have his car fixed.
               paper typed   John wants to have his paper typed.
               coat cleaned   John wants to have his coat cleaned.
               check cashed   John wants to have his check cashed.
               shoes polished   John wants to have his shoes polished.
               laundry done   John wants to have his laundry done.
               car washed   John wants to have his car washed.

2. M1   Rep: She had her hair cut last week.
           Sub: house painted   S: She had her house painted last week.
                rugs cleaned   She had her rugs cleaned last week.
                hair done   She had her hair done last week.
                watch fixed   She had her watch fixed last week.
                car repaired   She had her car repaired last week.
                lawn mowed   She had her lawn mowed last week.
                winter clothes cleaned   She had her winter clothes cleaned last week.

GENERALIZATION

The barber is cutting Chen's hair.

Chen is having his hair cut (by the barber).

The pattern *have* + noun phrase + past participle expresses causation. The person *performing* the action is not usually mentioned, or if he is, it is in a *by* expression. Note that the causative pattern can follow another verb (Drill 1, above) or be the main verb in the sentence (Drill 2, above).

Note: *get* is frequently heard in this pattern:

I *got* my check cashed yesterday.

She wants to *get* her hair cut.

---

3. M1T   If the sentence expresses *necessity,* say "necessity"; if *cause,* say "cause".
           T: John had to cut the grass.   S: Necessity
               John had the grass cut.   Cause
               Bill will have the paper typed.   Cause
               Jane will have to type the paper.   Necessity
               Charlie is going to have the building painted.   Cause
               Mary is going to have to write the book.   Necessity
               The Newtons had to fly to San Francisco.   Necessity
               Christina had the rug repaired.   Cause
               The teachers have had the lessons recorded.   Cause
               The girl should have had the car fixed.   Cause

4. M1T   T: The barber cut my hair.   S: You had your hair cut.
               The garage man fixed my car.   You had your car fixed.
               Mrs. Smith did my laundry.   You had your laundry done.
               The boys mowed my lawn.   You had your lawn mowed.
               The telephone company put in a phone. You had a phone put in.
               The man at the bank cashed my check.   You had your check cashed.
               Karen typed my book.   You had your book typed.
               The shoe man fixed my heel.   You had your heel fixed.

5. M2   T: The outside of the house looks   S: (You should have it painted.) (Why
                  terrible.   don't you have it painted?)
               That boy's hair looks terrible.
               I have a flat tire.
               My shoe has a hole in it.
                       (exercise continued on next page)

445

T: The windows are very dirty.
       The grass is tall.
       Someone ran into my car.
       The telephone is out of order.
       The winter clothes are very dirty.
       This shirt has a hole in it.
       That shirt is wrinkled.
       This book is falling apart.

6. C   T: Find out if ( ) has to do something   S1:   (What do you have to do today?)
              today.   S2:   (I have to write my research paper.)
                                                               (Nothing. I'm free all day.)

              Find out if ( ) has something done   S1:   (Do you have your laundry done every week?)
              every week.   S2:   (No, I do it myself at the laundromat.)

              Find out if ( ) and ( ) had to do something last week.
              Find out if ( ) and ( ) will have something done this afternoon.
              Find out if ( ) had to go somewhere last weekend.

7. C   T: Do you wash and iron your clothes   S: (Yes, I do.) (No, I don't I have them done
              yourself?   at ( ).)
              Where do you have your clothes cleaned?
              Does your roommate cut your hair?
              If your shoe has a hole, who fixes it?
              Do you polish your shoes yourself?
              Does your landlord mow the lawn himself?
              If your car is damaged, do you fix it yourself?
              If you tear your shirt, do you fix it yourself?
              Does your landlord paint the apartments himself?
              Do professors usually type their own books?
              Do people usually wash their rugs themselves?
              In your country, what is the custom about these things?

8. C   Situation: You've just moved to a new city. ( ) has lived there for a long time. Ask him
       about the best sources of the services discussed above. Get the price, location, etc.
       Compare with your former city.

SECTION THREE

PASSIVE VOICE

Part A.   *Present Perfect*

Model: Carlos and Chen have been asked to help the new foreign students.

1. M1   Rep: The car has been stolen four times.
          Sub: taken once by the police   S: The car has been taken once by the police.
               driven a hundred miles   The car has been driven a hundred miles.
               sent back to the factory twice   The car has been sent back to the factory twice.
               repaired three times by the   The car has been repaired three times by the
                 garageman   garageman.

(exercise continued on next page)

T:	fixed ten times	S:	The car has been fixed ten times.
	towed away four times		The car has been towed away four times.

GENERALIZATION

Lesson Twenty-one:	The car is washed once a week. (Present)
Lesson Twenty-two:	The car has been washed once a week. (Present Perfect)

Formation: S + $\begin{Bmatrix} has \\ have \end{Bmatrix}$ + *been* + Past Participle

The Present Perfect Passive functions in the same way as Present Perfect in Lesson Fourteen; the only difference is that the actor is unknown or unimportant.

Lesson Fourteen:	Someone has stolen my car four times.
Lesson Twenty-two:	My car has been stolen (by someone) four times.
	My car has been stolen four times.

---

2. M1   Rep: I've been asked to help the foreign students.

Sub:	we	S:	We've been asked to help the foreign students.
	told		We've been told to help the foreign students.
	to look for		We've been told to look for the foreign students.
	the lost papers		We've been told to look for the lost papers.
	she		She's been told to look for the lost papers.
	requested		She's been requested to look for the lost papers.
	to find		She's been requested to find the lost papers.
	the stolen car		She's been requested to find the stolen car.

3. M1T

T:	No one has asked me to help.	S:	You haven't been asked to help.
	No one has given him the answer.		He hasn't been given the answer.
	No one has told her the date.		She hasn't been told the date.
	No one has given us the information.		We haven't been given the information.
	No one has requested me to call.		You haven't been requested to call.
	No one has sent her a letter.		She hasn't been sent a letter.
	No one has asked him to finish the paper.		He hasn't been asked to finish the paper.

4. M1T

T:	Has anyone finished the work?	S:	Has the work been finished?
	Has anyone stolen your car?		Has your car been stolen?
	Has anyone invited them to the party?		Have they been invited to the party?
	Has anyone made the coffee?		Has the coffee been made?
	Has anyone picked up the refreshments?		Have the refreshments been picked up?

***5. M2

T:	car stolen	S1:	(Has your car ever been stolen?)
		S2:	(Yes, once.) (No, it hasn't. I don't have a car.)
	friends arrested	S1:	(Have your friends ever been arrested?)
		S2:	(Yes, they have—for speeding.) (I don't know, but I hope not.)

car—towed away
credit cards—stolen
you—requested to help new students

(exercise continued on next page)

T: teachers—asked to make recommendations
      you—invited to meet the leader of your country
      you—taken to jail
      friends—asked to testify in court
      car—recalled by the factory
      you—hired for a strange job
      friends—stopped for speeding

Part B.   *Future*

Model: They'll be given a "big brother" . . .

1. M1   Rep: They'll be given a "big brother".
           Sub: he   S: He'll be given a "big brother".
                a promotion   He'll be given a promotion.
                she   She'll be given a promotion.
                an award   She'll be given an award.
                I   I'll be given an award.
                a new job   I'll be given a new job.
                we   We'll be given a new job.

GENERALIZATION

Pattern A: They've been given a new job.   (Present Perfect)
Pattern B: They'll be given a new job.   (Future)

Formation: S   +   *will be*   +   Past Participle

Note: Be careful to distinguish:

      They'll be driving home at 6:00.   (Active)
      They'll be driven home at 6:00.   (Passive)

In rapid speech (and in some regional dialects) there may be no difference in pronunciation. The context surrounding the sentence will usually make the meaning clear.

---

2. M1T   Listen: If you know the actor, say "Active"; if not, say "Passive".
          T: The Newtons always eat early. They'll be eating at 6:00.   S: (A)
                These vegetables are ready. They'll be eaten for supper.   (P)
                The students did very well. They'll be given a good grade.   (P)
                The teacher doesn't think the students are working. He'll be   (A)
                  giving a test soon.
                The children are tired. They'll be taking a nap soon.   (A)
                These cars are no good. They'll be taken away to the junk yard.   (P)

3. M1T   T: No one will ask him to do it.   S: He won't be asked to do it.
                No one will give her a prize.   She won't be given a prize.
                No one will tell us to do it.   We won't be told to do it.
                No one will remind them to come.   They won't be reminded to come.
                No one will give us a test.   We won't be given a test.
                No one will help him with the test.   He won't be helped with the test.
                No one will hire her for the job.   She won't be hired for the job.

448

$\dfrac{\text{be}}{\text{get}}\Big\}+$ **used** to + NP

4. M1T T: Will they ask us to help? S: Will we be asked to help?
Will they clean the streets tomorrow? Will the streets be cleaned tomorrow?
Will they install my phone next week? Will my phone be installed next week?
Will they arrest the thief? Will the thief be arrested?
Will they tow my car away? Will my car be towed away?
Will they clean the windows today? Will the windows be cleaned today?
Will they finish the cake on time? Will the cake be finished on time?

5. M2 T: cake—order S1: Has the cake (for the party) been ordered (yet)?
S2: No, it hasn't, but (I think it'll be ordered tomorrow).
thief—caught S1: Has the thief been caught (yet) (by the police)?
S2: No, he hasn't, but (I'm sure) he'll be caught (soon).

windows—cleaned
house—finished
grass—cut
beer—ordered
records—picked up
schedule—announced
food—prepared
flowers—ordered
invitations—sent
the Wilsons—invited

***6. C T: park illegally S1: What ('ll happen) if I park (my car) illegally?
S2: (You'll be given a ticket.) (It'll be towed away.) (You'll be
arrested.)
students don't S1: What (will you do) if (the new students) don't speak English?
speak English S2: (They'll be given a "big brother" who speaks their language.)
stopped for speeding
don't pay the invoce on time
don't pay the rent
disturb the other people in the apartment building
have an automobile accident
accused of cheating on a test
go through a red light
can't get the paper finished
register late
miss too many classes

SECTION FOUR

$\dfrac{BE}{GET}\Big\}+$ *USED TO* + NP

Model: Nancy is used to all kinds of questions.

1. M1 Rep: We're used to all kinds of questions.
Sub: weather S: We're used to all kinds of weather.
work We're used to all kinds of work.

(exercise continued on next page)

$\dfrac{\text{be}}{\text{get}}$ + <u>used to</u> + NP

food	We're used to all kinds of food.
people	We're used to all kinds of people.
customs	We're used to all kinds of customs.
classes	We're used to all kinds of classes.
professors	We're used to all kinds of professors.

2. M1   Rep: How did you get used to the weather here?

Sub:
food	S:	How did you get used to the food here?
customs		How did you get used to the customs here?
people		How did you get used to the people here?
work		How did you get used to the work here?
professors		How did you get used to the professors here?
schedule		How did you get used to the schedule here?
life		How did you get used to the life here?

GENERALIZATION

Lesson Eleven: I used to have credit cards.   (*used to* + Verb)

Lesson Twenty-Two: I'm used to the food here.   (BE + *used to* + Noun)
                           He got used to the food here.   (*get*)

What follows the Lesson Eleven pattern? ((Verb)) What does it mean? ((formerly))

The present pattern means *be* (or become) *accustomed to* something. What part of speech follows this pattern? ((Noun or Pronoun))

---

3. M1T   Listen: If you hear the Lesson Eleven pattern, say "Formerly"; if the Lesson Twenty-two pattern, say "Accustomed to".

T:		S:	
I used to live in Boston.			(F)
I'm used to life here.			(A)
He used to like the food.			(F)
He's used to the food.			(A)
She's used to the strange professors.			(A)
We used to have a strange professor.			(F)
They used to go swimming every day.			(F)
He's used to dinner at noon.			(A)
I used to have a dog.			(F)
She's used to a dog.			(A)

***4. M2   Situation: You are (1) a new student, or (2) a student who's been here for a while giving advice.

T: food   S1:   How (can I) (did you get) used to the food in the dorms?

                              S2:   (By eating it every day.) (You can't. I got an apartment and now I cook the things I used to eat at home.)

     people
     short lunch hour
     fast life
     traffic
     customs
     high prices

(exercise continued on next page)

T: coffee
       crazy professors
       politics
       red tape
       weather

5. C   T: What customs are very different here? Have you gotten used to them? How?
                Did you like the food here right away? Do you now? How did you get used to it?
                Is there anything you haven't gotten used to? What? Do you think you ever will?
                  (Why not?)

SUMMARY DIALOGUE

Chen and Carlos are trying to help a new student.

Ricardo: I'm glad you're going to help me. I have about a million questions.

Carlos: Ask anything you want. We're used to all kinds of things.

Ricardo: Where's the cheapest place to get a haircut?

Chen: If I were you, I'd go to the place on the corner of Main and Forbes. He's not too
          expensive and he's good.

Carlos: I used to have my hair cut twice a month, but now only once a month.

Ricardo: Well, long hair is the style anyway.

Chen: Good thing it is. But I'll have mine cut soon. My parents are coming and long hair
          is not as popular in my country. They wouldn't be pleased if they saw me like this.

LESSON TWENTY-TWO — SUMMARY OF PATTERNS

I. HAVE — CAUSATIVE

Subject	(V)	have	+	Object	+	Past Participle
He's	going to	have		his hair		cut.
She		had		her house		redone.

II. PASSIVE VOICE

A. Present Perfect

Subject	+	have / has	been	+	Past Participle	(by X)
They		have been			arrested.	
We		have been			reported	by the police.

B. Future

Subject	+	will be	+	Past Participle	(by X)
Dorothy		will be		invited.	
Carlos & Chen		will be		questioned	by the new foreign students.

III. BE / GET USED TO

Subject	+	be used to	+	Noun
Nancy		is used to		questions.
Chen		got used to		the food.

452

Appendix I
Common Abbreviations

STATES

Alabama (Ala.)
Alaska (Alas.)
Arkansas (Ark.)
Arizona (Ariz.)
California (Calif.)
Colorado (Colo.)
Connecticut (Conn.)
Delaware (Del.)
Florida (Fla.)
Georgia (Ga.)
Hawaii (Hi.)
Idaho (Id.)

Illinois (Ill.)
Indiana (Ind.)
Iowa (Ia.)
Kansas (Kan.)
Kentucky (Ken.)
Louisiana (La.)
Maine (Me.)
Maryland (Md.)
Massachusetts (Mass.)
Michigan (Mich.)
Minnesota (Minn.)
Mississippi (Miss.)

Missouri (Mo.)
Montana (Mont.)
Nebraska (Neb.)
Nevada (Nev.)
New Hampshire (N.H.)
New Jersey (N.J.)
New Mexico (N.M.)
New York (N.Y.)
North Dakota (N.D.)
North Carolina (N.C.)
Ohio (O.)
Oklahoma (Okla.)

Oregon (Ore.)
Pennsylvania (Pa.)
Rhode Island (R.I.)
South Dakota (S.D.)
South Carolina (S.C.)
Texas (Tex.)
Utah (Ut.)
Vermont (Vt.)
Virginia (Va.)
Washington (Wash.)
West Virginia (W.Va.)
Wisconsin (Wisc.)
Wyoming (Wyo.)

CITIES

Boston (Bos.)
Chicago (Chi.)

Los Angeles (L.A.)
New York (N.Y.C.)

Philadelphia (Phila.)
Pittsburgh (Pgh.)

San Francisco (S.F.)
Washington (D.C.)

GOVERNMENT AGENCIES

CIA	Central Intelligence Agency
DOD	Department of Defense
FBI	Federal Bureau of Investigation
FCC	Federal Communications Commission
USDA	U.S. Department of Agriculture

FDA	Food and Drug Administration
HEW	Department of Health, Education and Welfare
NASA	National Aeronautics and Space Administration
NATO	North Atlantic Treaty Organization
SEATO	South-east Asia Treaty Organization
SEC	Securities and Exchange Commission

Appendix II
Common Given Names and Nicknames

Male Formal Name	Nickname	Female Formal Name	Nickname
Allan	Al	Alice	Ali
Albert	Al	Ann(e)	Annie
Alfred	Al	Barbara	Barb
Brian		Betty	
Bruce		Carol, Carolyn	
Charles	Charley(ie), Chuck	Catherine	Cathy
Christopher	Chris	Christine	Chris
David	Dave	Cheryl	Sherry
Daniel, Dan	Dan(ny)	Deborah	Debby(ie)
Douglas	Doug	Dorothy	Dot, Dotty
Edward	Ed(die)	Edith	Edie
Francis	Fran	Ellen	Ellie
Franklin	Frank(ie)	Elizabeth	Beth, Betty
Gary		Frances	Fran
Gregory	Greg	Grace	
Harry		Helen	
James	Jim(my)	Jane	
John	Jack, John(ny)	Jenifer	Jenny (ie)
Joseph	Joe	Judith	Judy
Kenneth	Ken	Julie	
Lawrence	Larry	Karen	
Louis, Lewis	Lou, Lew	Kathryn, Kathleen	Kate, Katie, Kathy
Michael	Mike	Linda	Lynn
Patrick	Pat	Lois	
Philip	Phil	Louise	
Peter	Pete	Lucy	
Ralph		Marian	
Raymond	Ray	Marilyn	
Richard	Dick	Mary	
Robert	Bob(by), Rob(by)	Nancy	Nan
Stephen/Steven	Steve	Patricia	Pat, Patty, Patsy
Terrence	Terry	Phyllis	Phyl
Theodore	Ted(dy)	Rebecca	Becky
Thomas	Tom(my)	Roberta	Bobbie
Victor	Vic	Ruth	
		Sarah	
		Sharon	
		Susan	Suzy(ie)
		Veronica	Ronnie
		Victoria	Vicky (ie)

NOTE: This list is in no way complete. Where there are blanks under the nicknames, there is no wide-spread common nickname. Often people have nicknames peculiar to their family history which no outsider could possibly know. Often the (-y) endings of male nicknames are discarded by teenagers as "childish."

Appendix III
Phonetic Symbols

CONSONANTS

Symbol	Example	Symbol	Example
[p]	pit	[b]	bit
[t]	tin	[d]	din
[k]	cat	[g]	gun
[č]	church	[ǰ]	judge
[f]	fun	[v]	van
[θ]	thin	[ð]	then
[s]	sun	[z]	zoo
[š]	shirt	[ž]	azure
[m]	man	[n]	no
[ŋ]	sing	[r]	run
[l]	leg	[w]	win
[y]	yes	[h]	his

VOWELS

Symbol	Example
[i]	eat
[I]	it
[e]	ate
[ɛ]	let
[æ]	at
[ə]	but
[a]	lot
[u]	loot
[U]	hook
[ɔ]	bought
[aI]	right
[aU]	out
[ɔI]	boy

INDEX OF PATTERNS

The grammatical patterns have been indexed alphabetically according to the traditional terminology found in most handbooks of English grammar. The first number following each entry refers to the lesson in which the item first appears as a teaching point; the second number refers to the page.

Index

Index

Index

Index

Index

Index